Clive Oxenden

Paul Sel...

Christina Latham-Koenig

English File

teacher's book

2

OXFORD UNIVERSITY PRESS

OXFORD
UNIVERSITY PRESS

Great Clarendon Street, Oxford OX2 6DP

Oxford University Press is a department of the University of Oxford. It furthers the University's objective of excellence in research, scholarship, and education by publishing worldwide in

Oxford New York

Athens Auckland Bangkok Bogotá Buenos Aires Calcutta Cape Town Chennai Dar es Salaam Delhi Florence Hong Kong Istanbul Karachi Kuala Lumpur Madrid Melbourne Mexico City Mumbai Nairobi Paris São Paulo Singapore Taipei Tokyo Toronto Warsaw

with associated companies in Berlin Ibadan

Oxford and Oxford English are registered trade marks of Oxford University Press in the UK and in certain other countries

© Oxford University Press 1997

ISBN 0 19 435523 3

Printed in Hong Kong

Acknowledgements

The Publisher and Authors would like to thank the following teachers whose feedback helped shape this course:
Sarah Bampton, David Barnes, Cristina Brieba, David Dunn, Bernie Hayden, Tim Herdon, Sue Inkster, Amanda Jeffries, Catherine Kendall, Pam Murphy, Cristina Nogueira, Roy Pearse, Cristina Rajagopalan, Jacqui Robinson, Lynda Ryalls, Jacek Rysiewicz, Agota Tongori.

The Authors' thanks to:
Staff and students at the British Council, Valencia, the Friends Centre, Brighton, Portslade Community College, Kingsway College, London, and Eurocentre, Brighton for all their help in piloting the course and making valuable suggestions; Svetlana Bogdanova, Charles Bornat, Jan Latham-Koenig, Natalia Morskova, Sinead O' Connor, and Julie Willis for agreeing to be interviewed; Joseph Brennan (for the Sinead interview), Michael O'Brien (for *Love me tender*), Robert Knibbs (for information about Mexico City), Carmen Dolz (for input on the pronunciation charts), Angela O'Leary (for help with quotes), Sarah Chrisp (for the American photos), John Heslop (for information about New York), Gill Hamilton (for several photocopiable activities), and Bernie Hayden for help with the Workbook.

Special thanks to Cristina Mayo, Ma Angeles Rodriguez, and Carmen Dolz for all their support, and to Joaquin, Marco, and Krysia who were always in mind.

The Publisher and Authors would like to thanks the following for their kind permission to use articles, extracts, or adaptations from copyright material:
Every breath you take written and composed by Gordon M Sumner © 1983, used by permission Magnetic Publishing Limited. *You don't have to say you love me* music by Pino Donaggio and words by Vito Pallavicini, sub-authors Simon Napier-Bell and Vicki Wickham © 1965, Edizioni Musicali Accordo, USA, reproduced by permission of B Feldman and Co Ltd / EMI United Partnership Ltd, London WC2H 0EA. *Love me tender* words and music by Elvis Presley and Vera Matson © Elvis Presley Music, USA Carlin Music Corporation, Iron Bridge House, 3 Bridge Approach, London NW1, used by permission of Music Sales Limited, all rights reserved, international copyright secured. *Don't you want me* (EMI - 66.6% ownership) words and music by Philip Oakley, Adrian Wright and Jo Callis © 1981, reproduced by permission of EMI Virgin Music Ltd, London WC2H 0EA; (IMP – 33.34% ownership) © 1981 Warner / Chappell Music Ltd, London W1Y 3FA, reproduced by permission of International Music Publications Ltd. *Another day in Paradise* © 1989 Philip Collins Ltd/Hit & Run Music (Publishing) Ltd, international copyright secured, all rights reserved, used by permission. *I want to break free* words and music by John Deacon © 1984, reproduced by permission of Queen Music Ltd / EMI Music Publishing Ltd, London WC2H 0EA. *Message in a bottle* written and composed by Gordon M Sumner © 1979, used by permission Magnetic Publishing Ltd. *Imagine* words and music by John Lennon copyright 1971 Lenono Music Ltd, all rights administered by BMG Music Publishing Ltd, used by permission, all rights reserved. *Nothing compares to you* © 1986 Controversy Music, Warner / Chappell Music Ltd, London W1Y 3FA, reproduced by permission of International Music Publications Ltd. Extracts adapted from *Drama techniques in language learning* by A. Maley and A. Duff (1983), and *Grammar games* by M. Rinvolucri (1985), reproduced by permission of Cambridge University Press; extract adapted from *One year ago today* by Becky Coleman in Literary Cavalcade (May 1964) © 1964 by Scholastic Inc., reprinted by permission.

The Publishers would like to thank the following for permission to reproduce photographs:
All-Action – Jean Cummings, Bruce Peters, Doug Peters, Duncan Raban Corbis (UK); Famous – Rob Howard; Hulton Deutsch Collection; James Davis Travel Photography; Tony Stone Images – Roy Giles; Trip Photographic Library

Illustrations by:
Rupert Besley, Roger Fereday, Ros Fowler, Neil Gower, Nick Hardcastle, John Haslam, Tim Kahane, Belle Mellor, Ellis Nadler, Pantelis Palios, Harry Venning, Margaret Welbank

Contents

Level 1 Grammar review

Verbs and tenses

1 Verb *be* (present)	4 Present simple	7 Future: (*be*) *going to*	10 *have* (*got*) and *have*
2 Verb *be* (past)	5 Imperatives	8 Time expressions (past and future)	11 *There is* / *are* and *There was* / *were*
3 Present continuous	6 Past simple	9 *can* / *can't* (ability, requests, and permission)	12 *like* / *love* / *hate* + verb + *-ing*

	New grammar	*New vocabulary*
File 1 Tenses: present, past, and future, present perfect		
Introduction		Classroom language
A **Summer in Siberia**	*What's the weather like? It's …*	The weather, compass points
B **A typical Hollywood star?**	—	Activities: daily routine
C **An unforgettable holiday**	*What was (the food) like?*	Activities: free time
D **What a bore!**	Present perfect, past participles	*Me too. / Me neither.*
📖 **Getting there**	FUNCTION Checking in, arriving, losing your luggage, 📖 **1** Airport	
◁▷ **Past, present, and future**	—	—
🔍 **Focus on pronunciation**	English sounds, word stress, sentence stress, intonation	—
File 2 Present perfect or past simple, *have to*, *can* / *can't*, relative pronouns		
A **Classical experiences**	Present perfect v. past simple	*ever* / *never*, irregular past participle, classical music
B **What's your job really like?**	*have to* / *don't have to* (obligation)	Jobs: adjectives, verbs, nouns
C **Going back to the past**	*can* / *can't* (permission), impersonal *you*	Appearance: *short hair*, etc., clothes
D **What's the word?**	Relative pronouns: *who* / *which* / *where*	Shapes: *round*, etc., materials: *wood*, etc.
📖 **From the airport to the hotel**	FUNCTION Changing money, getting a train / taxi, 📖 **2** High numbers, money	
◁▷ **The verb *have***	—	—
🔍 **Focus on listening**	Listening for the general idea / focus on key words, listening for specific information	
File 3 Possessives, continuous forms: present / future / past, prepositions of movement		
A **Love me tender**	Possessive pronouns	*Whose …?* or *Who's …?*
B **Old friends**	Present continuous (future), invitations: *Would you like to …?*	Verbs: *arrive in* / *at*, etc.
C **The slowest journey in history?**	*How long does it take? It takes …*, prepositions of movement (*along*, etc.)	Time: *half an hour*, etc., the country: *forest*, etc.
D **It was a cold, dark night …**	Past continuous, contrast with past simple	—
📖 **At the hotel**	FUNCTION Checking into a hotel, calling Reception, 📖 **3** Hotel: *room service*, etc.	
◁▷ **There's always a first time**	—	—
🔍 **Focus on Easy Readers**	Recognizing different kinds of texts, skimming, guessing meaning from context, using pronoun reference	
File 4 Comparatives and superlatives, first conditional, *some* / *any* / *nothing*		
A **Same language, different people**	*as … as*, *much* / *a bit* + comparatives	Towns / cities: adjectives, nouns
B **If …**	First conditional (*if* + *will* / *won't* + infinitive)	Confusing verbs: *lend* / *borrow*, etc.
C **Somebody told me**	*something* / *anything* / *nothing*, etc.	*else*
D **The best and the worst**	Superlative adjectives, article *the*	Adjectives, places
📖 **At the restaurant**	FUNCTION Ordering a meal (*I'll have* / *I'd like …*), complaining, 📖 **4** Condiments, cutlery, ways of cooking	
🔍 **Focus on speaking**	Paraphrasing, fluency	—
◁▷ **Another day in Paradise**	—	—

Adjectives, adverbs etc.

Pronunciation	*Revision*	*End-of-File*
Introduction Word and sentence stress, alphabet	Tenses, question formation, alphabet	**V**1
A /w/	Present tenses, past simple, adverbs of frequency, months, seasons, clothes	Activities B
B Present simple endings /z/, /s/, /ɪz/	Present simple (routines), expressions of frequency, daily routine, connectors, the time	Prepositions A Study tips: learn words in groups, how to record new words / phrases
C /d/, /t/, /ɪd/ endings of past simple regular verbs	Past simple: regular and irregular verbs, adjectives of opinion	
D /h/, /v/, weak forms /bɪn/ and /tə/	*What's it like?*, adjectives of opinion, countries	**Workbook** Read and write 1: A letter to a penfriend
Intonation (dialogue)	Question auxiliaries, *Would you like ...?*, *Could I / you ...?*, colours	
—	All tenses, routines, study habits, family, weather, places	
—	—	
A /əʊ/, /e/, /ʌ/, /ɪ/	Past simple	**V**2
B /f/, /ə/, /hæftə/	Jobs, present simple	The body B Study tips: learn verbs with their prepositions, using a bi-lingual dictionary
C *can / can't*: weak / strong forms, sentence stress	*have to*, colours, clothes	
D Word and sentence stress	Article: *a / an*, small objects	
Intonation (dialogue)	*What time ...?*, *this / that / these / those*	**Workbook** Read and write 2: A formal letter
—	Four uses of *have*: present perfect, *have to*, *have / have got*, *can* (permission), job vocabulary	
—	—	
A /s/ or /z/, *whose ...* (linking / sentence stress)	Possessive *'s*, possessive adjectives, clothes, possessions	**V**3
B Intonation in invitations	Dates	Food A Study tips: remember words with their opposites, how to remember words
C —	Daily routines: *get up*, etc., transport	
D /ə/, /ɒ/, /ɜː/ weak / strong forms of *was / were*	Prepositions of place / movement, the time	
Intonation (dialogue)	Ordinal numbers: *1st* to *7th*, polite requests: *Could you / I ...?*	**Workbook** Read and write 3: A story
—	Present continuous (future), past continuous or past simple?	—
—	Past tenses	—
A /ə/: *er* endings, weak forms of *as* and *than*, sentence stress	Comparative adjectives, adverbs	**V**4
B /l/	Adjectives and their opposites	**R** Verbs A
C /ʌ/, /əʊ/, /ɒ/, /ɔː/	*some / any*, present perfect	**R** Adjectives A Study tips: record and learn synonyms together, British or American words
D /ð/, /d/, /ðə/ or /ðiː/	Comparative adjectives	
Intonation (dialogue)	Food, *I'd like ...*	
—	Giving definitions, *There is / are ...*, furniture, prepositions of place	**Workbook** Read and write 4: A description of a town / city
—	First conditional, comparative and superlative adjectives, *some / any / nobody / where*, etc.	

▶ **Workbook** Grammar checks 1–4, Listen and speaks 1–4, Read and writes 1–4, Quicktests 1 and 2

SYLLABUS CHECKLIST	*New grammar*	*New vocabulary*

File 5   *for / since*, verb + *to*, *so / because*, questions with / without auxiliaries

A	Born in the USSR	Present perfect + *for / since*	Sport: *team*, etc., *buy* (*for*), *give* (*to*)
B	As old as you feel?	Verb + *to* + infinitive, *would like to* + verb or *like* + -*ing*	Age-groups: *middle-aged*, etc., verbs + *to*: *want*, etc.
C	Love stories	*so / because*, *had to / didn't have to*	Connectors: *then*, etc.
D	Famous in the 20th century	Questions with / without auxiliaries	Verbs: *invent*, etc.
🖽	Asking the way	FUNCTION Giving directions, asking the way, 🖽 5 Buildings / places in a town	
◁▷	Double lives		Events in your life: *be born*, etc.

File 6   Gerund or infinitive, *like / look like*, quantities, *too / enough*

A	A pain or a pleasure?	Verb + -*ing* (= gerund), gerund or infinitive?	Housework: *ironing*, etc., shopping: *bargain*, etc.
B	First impressions	*look* or *look like*?	Adjectives of personality: *shy*, etc., zodiac signs: *Aries*, etc.
C	What's in your rubbish?	*a lot of / much / many / a little / a few*	Food, containers / packaging: *packet*, *plastic*, etc., *agree / disagree*, the environment: *recycle*, etc.
D	The day the birds died	*too much / many*, (*not*) *enough*	Town facilities and problems: *car park*, *traffic*, etc., *n. / v. / adj.* families: *pollute*, etc.
🖽	Shopping	FUNCTION Buying food / clothes, taking things back, 🖽 6 *one / ones*	
◁▷	Going, doing, playing, watching	—	*go / do / play* + sports

File 7   *yet / already / just*, *to / for*, *should / shouldn't*, phrasal verbs

A	A business trip	Present perfect + *yet / already / just*	More irregular verbs, travel verbs: *book* (*a hotel*), etc.
B	Heart of gold	*Why …? To* + verb / *For* + noun	Aid organizations: *The Red Cross*, etc., verbs: *feed*, etc.
C	Problems	*should / shouldn't* (advice / opinion)	Feelings, -*ed* or -*ing* adjectives: *bored / boring*
D	True stories	Phrasal verbs + object	Phrasal verbs: *turn off*, etc.
🖽	Talking on the phone	FUNCTION Using the phone, leaving a message on an answerphone, 🖽 7 Phone verbs: *put through*, etc., hotel services: *laundry*, etc.	
◁▷	Message in a bottle	—	Verb *get*

File 8   Echo questions, *so / neither*, *will / won't*, passives

A	What types of film do you like?	Echo questions, *So / Neither do I*.	Types of film
B	We all make mistakes	Uses of *will / won't* (offers, promises, unplanned decisions, predictions), future forms: *will be able to*, etc.	*Possibly. / Maybe. / Perhaps.*
C	A passion for chocolate!	Present passive	Verbs: *produce*, etc., products: *uranium*, etc.
D	The Tower of London	Past passive + *by*	Verbs: *build*, etc.
🖽	Going to the doctor's	FUNCTION Describing illness, going to the doctor's, giving strong advice: *must / mustn't*, 🖽 8 Advice about illnesses	
◁▷	Coincidences?	—	Verbs: *execute*, etc.

File 9   Revision, preview: second conditional

A	George and Mabel	—	
B	A musician all her life	—	
🖽	Going home	—	
C	Are you a good citizen?	Second conditional	

Key to symbols in the Teacher's Book

Lessons	In lesson plans			
🖽 = Travel with English	⸬ = Listening	**V** = Vocabulary	**R** = Revision	♫ = Song
◁▷ = Revision and extension	▶◀ = Communication	⚠ = Possible problem	🎲 = Games bank	
🔍 = Focus on (skills)	✎ = Word bank	🖽 = Travel phrasebook	P = Photocopiable activities	

Introduction

Course aims

By the end of *English File 2*, students will be able to express themselves simply but correctly in the main tenses of English, know approximately 2,200 high frequency words and phrases, and be able to 'survive' in a variety of practical situations. *English File* responds to what we believe both teachers and students really want from a course.

For students (SS)

– enjoyable lessons with clear objectives and a real sense of progress.
– easy-to-use grammar reference plus check exercises.
– a highly-organized approach to vocabulary learning.
– systematic help with pronunciation.
– practical language for communication in key situations.
– clear, useful home-study activities.
– regular revision and testing.

For teachers (TT)

– well-planned lessons that work.
– an easily-accessible resource of supplementary materials.
– a realistic syllabus which can be completed.
– real help developing students' skills (including study skills).
– graded, motivating listening material.
– built-in flexibility to tailor the course simply to individual needs.

Components

Student's Book 2

Student's Book 2 is divided into nine units, called Files. Files 1 to 8 present and practise new language. File 9 is optional. (It revises Book 2 and gives teachers the option of teaching the second conditional.)

The lessons are divided into essential 'core' lessons and optional 'non-core' lessons which can be omitted on shorter courses.

Core lessons There are forty 'core' lessons (lessons A, B, C and D, plus the Travel with English lessons).

Non-core lessons There are twelve revision lessons (the **Revision and Extension** lessons and File 9), four skills-specific lessons (**Focus on pronunciation**, **listening**, **reading** and **speaking**).

Vocabulary file and **Grammar file** Each File ends with two revision pages. The **Vocabulary file** revises and extends lexical fields from the File and includes tips to train students to organize their vocabulary learning. The **Grammar file** is an active reference page. It summarizes the new grammar of the File using student-friendly explanations and tick-off rules.

The front of Student's Book 2

Level 1 Grammar review *p. 2* Six pages of active grammar revision summarizing the grammatical syllabus of *English File 1*. This is a useful checklist for SS (and TT) of what was covered in Level 1. Use before or while doing File 1. Set manageable blocks for homework, and refer to it as necessary throughout the course.

Progress chart *p. 8* This is a tick-off chart at the beginning of the book. SS can

– check what they've done in each lesson.
– check what they need to know before tests.
– check what they're going to study during the course.

A typical file

Core lessons

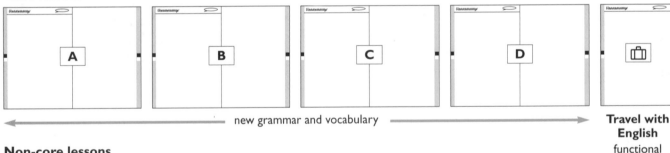

new grammar and vocabulary

Travel with English
functional language

Non-core lessons

Revision and extension
consolidates the core lessons

Focus on (skills)
an extra lesson of skills-specific practice

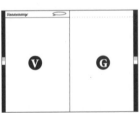

Vocabulary file and **Grammar file**
active reference pages

The back of the Student's Book

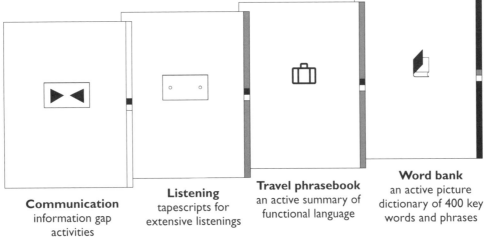

Communication
information gap
activities

Listening
tapescripts for
extensive listenings

Travel phrasebook
an active summary of
functional language

Word bank
an active picture
dictionary of 400 key
words and phrases

Colour-coding and symbols

blue = grammar
pink = pronunciation
grey = key dialogues to learn
yellow = vocabulary
⎕ = Travel with English / Travel phrasebook
◁▷ = Revision and extension
🔍 = Focus on (skills)
🎲 = Game
G = Grammar
V = Vocabulary
R = Revision
📕 = Word bank
►◄ = Communication
⌐ = Listening
G◄◄ = Level 1 Grammar review

Class cassettes

The three class cassettes contain all the listening materials for
the Student's Book, including dialogues, drills, songs, and
pronunciation activities.

Workbook

This provides thorough support for home-study.

Level 1 Grammar check *p. 3* Three pages of grammar
exercises to do alongside the **SB Level 1 Grammar review**.

Level 1 Vocabulary review *p. 6* Three pages listing the key
vocabulary SS should know before beginning *English File 2.*

Language practice A page of practice exercises and 'Words
to learn' for each core lesson.

Grammar check A page of grammar practice exercises to do
alongside each **SB Grammar file**.

Read and write *p. 61* Guided writing activities. At the end of
each File SS read and study a model text before writing
their own.

Listen and speak *p. 69* Lesson-by-lesson listening,
pronunciation, and speaking practice based around the
'Listen and Speak' cassette. **Sound bank** – a chart to help
SS recognize and practise sound / spelling relationships.

Quicktests *p. 83* Four self-check grammar and vocabulary
tests, after Files 2, 4, 6, and 8. These test grammar and
vocabulary.

Grammar words *p. 87* A reference page of grammar words
to learn, plus an active **Contractions file**.

Pull-out key Answers to all Workbook exercises.

The file system

To encourage SS to organize their learning, we suggest
they put their Workbooks into a ring file along with sections
for their lesson notes, photocopies, and vocabulary lists
(see **WB** *p. 2*). Ideally, after class SS should transfer all new
vocabulary and phrases from their lesson notes into the
appropriate sections of their vocabulary lists.

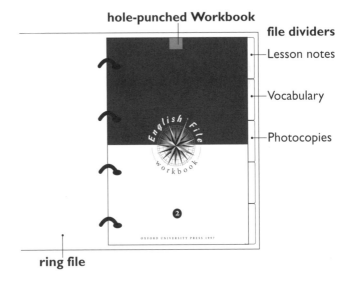

hole-punched Workbook

file dividers

Lesson notes

Vocabulary

Photocopies

ring file

Student's 'Listen and speak' cassette

A cassette specifically designed for home-study by busy
adults, at home, in a car, or on a personal stereo, with or
without the Workbook. SS can listen before or after class to
practise new language from each 'core' lesson (A, B, C, D,
and Travel with English). The **Listen and speak** section
(**WB** *p. 69*) has tapescripts plus suggestions for further tasks
to do with the cassette. We recommend you take SS through
the instructions, and explain how to use it.

Teacher's Book

Step-by-step lesson plans, books-closed presentations, extra ideas for each lesson, and over 60 pages of ready-prepared photocopiable materials to support the course.

A typical lesson plan

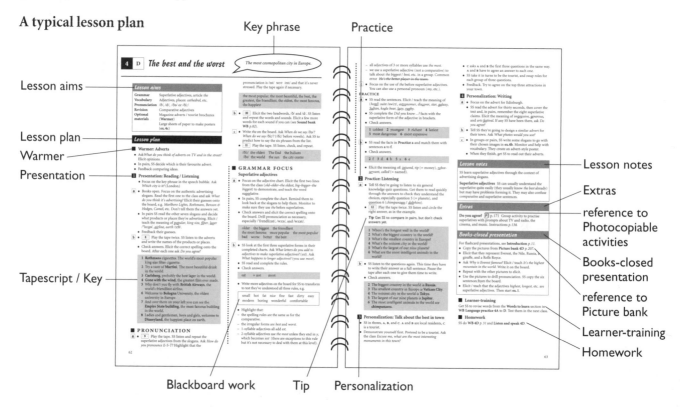

Labels (clockwise):
Key phrase — Practice — Lesson notes — Extras — reference to Photocopiable activities — Books-closed presentation — reference to Picture bank — Learner-training — Homework — Personalization — Tip — Blackboard work — Tapescript / Key — Presentation — Warmer — Lesson plan — Lesson aims

---

Course structure

Length / Fast-track route

English File 2 is flexible. It provides over 120 hours of classroom material if you use all the extra ideas and photocopiable activities in the Teacher's Book. However, the course length can be easily adapted to suit different teaching situations. For shorter courses of 45 to 60 classroom hours, you can cover the Level 2 syllabus by following the fast-track route.

- Do 'core' lessons **A, B, C, D** and **Travel with English** for Files 1 to 8. Set the **Vocabulary files** and **Grammar files** for homework.

- Omit the **Revision and extension** and **Focus on** (**skills**) lessons. Omit File 9 and the warmers, extra ideas, and photocopiable material in the Teacher's Book.

If you do the fast-track route, explain clearly to your SS what you are doing.

Encourage SS to use the **Word bank** (**SB**), the **Workbook**, and the **Student's 'Listen and speak' cassette** for extra practice.

Teacher's Book extra resources

Photocopiable activities Over 60 pages of extra activities plus instructions.

Picture bank Three photocopiable pages of flashcard or blackboard drawings to copy.

Games bank Games and emergency ideas for fillers or revision.

Tests and **Keys** Three photocopiable tests, plus instructions / keys, after Files 3, 6, and 8 (or 9) (see p.211).

Word list An alphabetical File-by-File reference of active vocabulary.

The 'six-strand' syllabus

There are six complete syllabuses in *English File 2* which interlink to form our 'six strand' syllabus (as in the diagram below). Since we believe the key to successful language-learning is constant recycling and revision, this is the central and key strand in our syllabus.

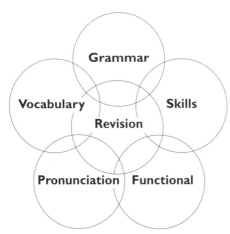

Grammar
Grammar focus and Practice
Grammar file
Level 1 Grammar review (**WB**)
Grammar check (**WB**)

Vocabulary
Vocabulary files
Vocabulary boxes
Word bank
Level 1 Vocabulary review (**WB**)
Words to learn (per lesson)
  (**WB**)

Pronunciation
Focus on … pronunciation
English Sounds chart
English Sounds poster
Exercises on sounds, stress,
  and intonation
Listen and Speak cassette (**WB**)
Sound and spelling bank (**WB**)

Functional
Travel with English lessons
Travel with English
  phrasebook
Classroom phrasebook

Skills
Integrated skills work (**SB**)
Focus on …
pronunciation, listening,
reading, speaking
Read and write (**WB**)
Listen and speak cassette

Revision
Revision and extension
  lessons
Vocabulary files
Grammar files
File 9
Grammar check (**WB**)
Tests (**WB** and **TB**)

Special features

Word bank (SB p. 134)

An active picture dictionary illustrating key vocabulary fields. Use the **Word bank**:
– to present and revise vocabulary in small, coherent sets.
– to drill and revise structures.
– as a model for organizing vocabulary into 'families'.
– for easy reference, revision, and self-testing in and out of class.

English sounds chart

The 44 sounds of English are taught through illustrated key words which incorporate the phonetic symbols. SS visualize and remember the word and sound together, e.g.

bird

The word is then used as a reference point when learning the pronunciation of other words, e.g. *nurse* is like *bird*. SS will become familiar with the symbols, but you can use the chart <u>without</u> teaching the phonetic symbols to correct pronunciation by comparing a new word with a 'sound word' from the chart. The pictures are summarized in the **English sounds** chart *p. 142*. The system motivates SS, showing them that the number of sounds in English isn't limitless, and that they can practise them on their own. The chart is available as a free classroom poster from Oxford University Press.

Using the chart and poster
– Present the sounds in groups. Elicit and drill the picture words.
– Drill the sounds within each picture.
– SS test each other in pairs.
– The chart is introduced in an optional **Focus on pronunciation** lesson in File 1.

Songs (SB)

There are nine 'classic' songs in *English File*, either incorporated into lessons or as options.

Photocopiable activities (TB p. 126)

Over 60 pages of optional materials to extend or adapt a lesson, or use later to revise. An end-of-File revision activity is provided for each File. Be selective – use the activities most appropriate for your SS.

Books-closed presentations (TB)

The presentation of new grammar can be more effective when the whole class is listening to you / looking at the board. There is an alternative 'books-closed' presentation for each new main language structure.

Picture bank (TB p. 205)

A resource of blackboard or flashcard pictures for you to use for books-closed presentations. The drawings are easy to copy, even for teachers who can't draw. To use the **Picture bank**:
– Copy the six drawings for the structure you're presenting onto large pieces of card, or draw them on the board.
– Show / point to the pictures one at a time, and elicit / teach / drill each sentence.
– After each new sentence, revise all the previous ones, then show the next picture.
– Use the pictures as prompts for SS to practise in pairs.
– Elicit and write the sentences on the board for SS to copy.

Games bank (TB p. 208)

Nine language games to practise and revise. Many can be re-played to practise more than one language point.

Ten ideas to use in an emergency (TB p. 210)

In class you often need a quick activity to fill a few minutes, e.g. when you don't want to start a new lesson or when the cassette player goes wrong! You can use these instant fillers and revision ideas to help you in these situations.

1 Introduction

> *Why are you learning English?*
> *I need it for my job.*

Lesson aims

Vocabulary	classroom language
Pronunciation	Word and sentence stress, alphabet
Revision	Tenses, question formation, alphabet

Lesson plan

■ Warmer: Learning names

- Introduce yourself to the class (*Hello. I'm …*) and then to individual SS. Elicit *Nice to meet you*. Get SS to mingle and introduce themselves to each other. Feedback to see how many names you can all remember.

1 Revision: Question formation

a • Books open. Focus on the **Student profile** form. Be prepared to explain / translate *profile* (*personal information*) *birth* (= n. from *born*), *previous* (= *before*). In pairs, SS complete questions 1 to 10 beside the form. Elicit the first two or three questions as examples.

b • ∘1∘ SS in pairs. Play the tape once. Pause after each question. SS check questions 1 to 10.
- Focus on **V** **Stress**. Explain that, in the book, stress is marked by pink + underlining. Remind SS that there are two types of stress:
  word stress – in individual words, one <u>syllable</u> is pronounced more strongly, e.g. natio<u>nal</u>ity.
  sentence stress – in a sentence, some <u>words</u> are pronounced more strongly, e.g. <u>Where</u> are you <u>from</u>?
- Play the tape again. Pause after each question. SS underline the stressed words, as in the example.

> 1 What's your <u>first</u> <u>name</u>? What's **your** <u>surname</u>?
> 2 <u>Where</u> do you <u>live</u>?
> 3 <u>Where</u> **are** you <u>from</u>?
> 4 <u>What</u> **do** you <u>do</u>?
> 5 <u>Where</u> **were** you <u>born</u>?
> 6 <u>What</u> <u>languages</u> **do** you <u>speak</u>?
> 7 **Why** **are** you <u>learning</u> <u>English</u>?
> 8 **Did** you <u>study</u> <u>English</u> last <u>year</u>? Where?
> 9 **Are** you <u>going</u> **to** <u>travel</u> <u>abroad</u> <u>next</u> <u>summer</u>? /
>   <u>Where</u> **are you** **going** to <u>go</u>?
> 10 <u>What</u> **do** you <u>like</u> **doing** in your <u>free</u> <u>time</u>?

- Ask *Which words do we stress in English sentences?* (the words that give important information).

2 Revision: Personal information

- Drill questions 1 to 10 with the class. SS repeat after you or the tape. Encourage SS to stress the underlined words and to copy the intonation.
- SS cover the questions and look only at the **Student profile** form. They try to remember the question for each heading. Get SS to ask <u>you</u> the questions (except questions 7 and 8).
- Revise **V** **Classroom language** as it comes up. Encourage SS to say *Sorry?* / *Pardon?* and *How do you spell it?*

- Focus on question 4: *What do you do?* Ask if SS know how to say their jobs in English. If not, refer to **V** **Classroom language**: *How do you say … in English?*
- Focus on question 7 *Why are you learning English?* Tell SS to look at the key phrase at the top of the page. Elicit other possible answers. (*Because I need it for travelling.*, etc.)
- In pairs, **A** and **B**. SS roleplay an interview. SS sit opposite each other, and **A** completes the form with **B**'s answers. Encourage short, natural answers.
- SS swap roles. When the interviews are finished, ask individual SS to tell the class one interesting thing about their partner.
  Carlo was born in Sicily. He only came to Rome last year.

■ PRONUNCIATION
The alphabet

a • Remind SS that it's important to be able to spell aloud in English, for example, on the phone.
- Elicit the seven headwords. Explain that these are picture words to help SS to remember English sounds and their phonetic symbols. Tell SS there are 44 sounds altogether, and show them the **English sounds** chart (**SB** *p. 142*).
- ∘2∘ Play the tape. Drill the words and the sounds.

> 1 train /eɪ/   2 tree /iː/   3 egg /e/   4 bike /aɪ/
> 5 phone /əʊ/   6 boot /uː/   7 car /ɑː/

b • Show SS how letters A to F are written in the chart according to their pronunciation. In pairs, SS complete the chart for letters G to Z. Encourage SS to say the letters aloud before writing them in.
- ∘3∘ Quickly write the headwords on the board. Play the tape for SS to check. Elicit the alphabet onto the board:

train	tree	egg	bike	phone	boot	car
A	B	F	I	O	Q	R
H	C	L	Y		U	
J	D	M			W	
K	E	N				
	G	S				
	P	X				
	T	Z				
	V					

- Get SS to repeat the letters in their columns, with the tape or after you. Ask *Which letters are difficult for you?* Give more practice with these letters and other letters usually confused, e.g. *a / e / i, g / j, p / b / v,* etc. by writing them on the board and pointing.
- Focus on **V** **Spelling**. Ask SS to spell some words or names, e.g. *television, jogging, coffee, Michael Jordan.* Try to include the letters they find difficult.

c • ⏺ 4 ⏺ Tell SS they're going to hear people spelling names. Play the tape twice. In pairs, SS listen and write the three names.

> **Tip** Pause the tape after each conversation to give SS time to write.

• Ask SS to tell you what each name is. SS quickly read the tapescript and check answers.

> 1 MAJESTIC   It's a hotel.
> 2 GREYFIELD It's a road.
> 3 BURFORD   It's a small town.
> Tapescript **SB Listening** *p.126*

• Spell your name to the class.
• In pairs, SS spell their names. They help/correct each other.

3 Revision: Error correction

a • Focus on the text about Ania. In pairs, SS read, circle, and correct ten more mistakes.
• Elicit the mistakes and corrections from the class. Ask *Is it a mistake of grammar, spelling, or capital letters?*

> My <u>name's</u> Ania Grabowska, and I'm from Poland.
> I <u>was</u> <u>born</u> in Cracow but I live in Warsaw. I'm <u>a</u>
> nurse and I work in a hospital near the centre.
> I speak <u>Polish</u>, Russian, and a little French.
> <u>I'm learning</u> English because I need it. I want to
> <u>travel</u> and perhaps work abroad in the future so
> English is very important.
> ~~The~~ last year I <u>studied</u> English at home because
> I <u>didn't</u> <u>have</u> time to go to classes. Next <u>July I'm</u>
> <u>going</u> to study English in Bristol for a month.

• Elicit when we use capital letters in English. Refer SS to the **Level 1 Grammar review** (= 🌐◄◄ 16 **SB** *p.6*).

b • In pairs, **A** covers the text and tells **B** everything he / she remembers about Ania. **B** listens and checks.
⚠️Remind SS not to forget the third person *s*. Write a large 'S' on the board and refer SS to it as you monitor.

4 Personalization: Writing

a • SS write a similar paragraph about themselves. Get them to use the **Student profile** *p.10* as a guide.

b • Give SS a few minutes to check their paragraph and correct any mistakes. They then give it to you to correct. This activity could also be homework.

5 Learner-training: Classroom language

• SS complete 📋 **Classroom language A** *p.143*. Check understanding with examples or L1.

> Could do 's Can 's does don't or is
> see Have Could are 'm to on Have too

• Get SS to test each other on the phrases, using L1.

> **Tip** Make SS use these expressions. Don't allow them to say anything from the list in their L1.

Lesson notes

The aim of this lesson is for you to get to know your class and to find out why they are learning English. SS revise auxiliaries and the basic tenses. SS also meet a number of course features, e.g. English sounds and stress, the **Word bank**.

Level 1 Grammar review (**SB**) This can be used with the accompanying **Level 1 Grammar check** and **Vocabulary review** (**WB**):
– in class and / or for homework before you start File 1.
– in sections while SS are doing File 1.
– for reference during the course.

You can check answers to the **WB** exercises in class, or get SS to use the self-check key.

The alphabet SS will probably have problems remembering all the letters.

Word and sentence stress It's important to make SS aware of these two essential aspects of pronunciation and to continue to work on them regularly.

Extras

Vocabulary revision Put some categories on the board:

> family   clothes   in the classroom   drinks

In pairs, SS brainstorm and list words, about one minute for each group. Feedback all their suggestions onto the board. Elicit and mark the word stress. Get SS to choose ten useful words and record them on a sheet of paper.

Why are you learning English? 📄 *p.143* A form for SS to analyze their own learning needs. Instructions *p.127*.

No article 📄 *p.144* A pairwork activity for SS to revise and practise the omission of the article. Instructions *p.127*.

A first lesson for classes without books

On the first day, SS often don't have the **SB**. If so:
– Do the **Warmer**.
– Copy the **Student profile** form onto the board. Elicit and get SS to write the questions, and then interview you and each other in pairs.
– Copy the alphabet columns on the board for SS to complete and practise spelling.
– Do **Vocabulary revision** from **Extras**.

■ Learner-training
Recommend SS buy:
– the **Workbook** and 'Listen and speak' **Student's cassette** if they don't already have them.
– a ring file to keep their **Workbook**, photocopiable activities, lesson notes, and vocabulary lists together.
– a highlighter pen.
– a good bi-lingual dictionary.

■ Homework
SS do **WB 1 Introduction** *p.9*. and **Listen and speak 1 Introduction** and revise 📋 **Classroom language A**. **SB** *p.143*
Writing: ex.4 SS write a paragraph about themselves.

13

1 A Summer in Siberia

> *What's the weather like in Moscow?*
> *Lovely! It's 22° and sunny.*

Lesson aims

Grammar	*What's the weather like? It's …*
Vocabulary	The weather, compass points
Pronunciation	/w/
Revision	Present tenses, past simple, adverbs of frequency, months, seasons, clothes

Lesson plan

■ Warmer: Months / alphabet

- Get SS to say the months round the class.
- Get SS to spell them to you, and write them on the board. Drill pronunciation and underline the stress

1 Revision: Seasons

- In pairs, SS match the seasons and photos A to D, and name the cities. Check answers. Ask *Why do you think it's (winter)?* Elicit *Because it's (cold / snowing).*, etc. Drill pronunciation, especially autumn /ˈɔːtəm/.

> A Washington – autumn B Berlin – winter
> C Rome – summer D Paris – spring

2 Presentation: The weather

a
- Books closed. Point to the window and ask *What's the weather like today?* to elicit some weather words.
- Focus on the question *What's the weather like?* and symbols 1 to 6. Get SS to complete the first part of the chart with the **Weather** words from the list.
- Check answers. Drill pronunciation.

> 1 It's cloudy. 2 It's foggy. 3 It's sunny.
> 4 It's windy. 5 It's raining. 6 It's snowing.

- Ask *Which words are verbs?* (*raining, snowing*).
- Focus on the question *What's the temperature?*. Explain/mime that *boiling* = very hot and *freezing* = very cold. They are often used colloquially. Get SS to complete the rest of the chart with the **Temperature** words from the list. Check answers. Drill pronunciation.

> 8 It's hot. 9 It's warm. 10 It's cool.
> 11 It's cold.

- ⚠ Describing the temperature as *warm* or *cool* will depend on local climate.
- Focus on ⓥ **Temperature**. Drill pronunciation. Highlight that:
- – we say *zero* not *oh* for temperatures.
- – we don't usually say *degrees* after *minus*.

b
- In pairs, SS cover the words and test each other with the chart by pointing at the weather symbols.
  > A *What's the weather like?*
  > B *It's cloudy.*
- Then SS cover the words and test each other by pointing at the temperatures, e.g.

> A *What's the temperature?*
> B *It's forty degrees. It's boiling.*

c
- ● ⸱5⸱ Tell SS they're going to hear two extracts from Vivaldi's *Four Seasons*. Pause after each one. Ask *What season is it? What kind of weather do you imagine when you listen to it?*

> 1 spring 2 winter

■ PRONUNCIATION

- SS circle the word with a different pronunciation of *w*. In pairs, get them to compare answers. Don't confirm.
- ⸱6⸱ Play the tape for SS to check.

> 1 wrong 2 who 3 always

- Elicit that:
- – *wh* is usually pronounced /w/ (*who, whose* are exceptions).
- – *wr* is always pronounced /r/.
- – *w* at the end of the word is not pronounced.
- Elicit more words with these spellings, e.g. *which, write, now*, (see **Sound bank WB** *p. 82*).

■ GRAMMAR FOCUS 1
What's the weather like? It's …

a
- Focus on the examples in the box. Ask *What does 'it' mean here?* (the weather).
- Highlight the use of *like*.

b
- Highlight the pronoun *it* in the answer, meaning *weather* and *temperature*.

PRACTICE 1

a
- Drill the question form *What's the weather like in (Rome)?* In pairs, SS go back to the photos in **ex. 1** and ask about the weather.

b
- SS ask and answer about the weather and temperature in their town at different times.

> **Tip** Write was = /wəz/ on the board. Remind SS to use it in past questions and answers.

3 Practice: Listening

- Ask *Do you watch the weather report on TV, or listen to it on the radio?*
- ⸱7⸱ Tell SS they're going to listen to a European TV weather report. SS listen and complete the chart, as in the example. Play the tape at least twice.

> Tapescript **SB Listening** *p. 126*

- Check answers. Ask *What month / season do you think it is?* (probably spring).

> Moscow: freezing, snowing, −2°
> Budapest: cold and cloudy, 10°
> Milan: very foggy, 13°
> Athens: quite warm, very windy, 17°

14

- SS check the tapescript if necessary.

4 Practice: Reading

a • SS cover the text and look at the photo of Siberia. Ask *Where's Siberia? What are the people wearing? What's the weather like?*

Tip Before reading the text, get SS to predict some of the answers to ex. 4b.

b • ◦ 8 ◦ SS listen and read. Encourage SS to guess vocabulary from the context. Be prepared to explain / translate *disappear, still, fur, central heating, changeable*.

• In pairs, SS answer questions 1 to 6. Check answers.

> **1** About seven months (from November to May).
> **2** Children can't go to school, but adults still go to work.
> **3** They wear warm clothes, and have central heating.
> **4** The windows. **5** No. **6** It was colder.

• Ask *Would you like to live there? Why (not?)*

■ GRAMMAR FOCUS 2

Revision of adverbs of frequency

a • Focus on the two highlighted examples. SS highlight other adverbs of frequency. Check answers.

> usually sometimes never hardly ever often

• Check that SS remember the meaning of the adverbs.
• SS complete the rules. Check answers.

> **1** after **2** before

• Focus on the rules. Write on the board:

> The snow doesn't normally disappear until May.

Elicit that adverbs of frequency:
– go after the auxiliary verb in negatives.
– are normally used with the present simple tense.

b • Remind SS of the difference between the two present tenses. SS complete the examples with *usually* or *now*.

> Oh look! It's raining. = **now**
> It doesn't rain much. / Does it often snow?
> = **usually**

PRACTICE 2

• SS put the adverbs in the right place in the sentences. Check answers.

> **2** Summer evenings are **usually** warm.
> **3** It **hardly ever** snows in Buenos Aires.
> **4** It doesn't **normally** rain in the summer.
> **5** The temperature **never** goes below 0°.
> **6** December is **usually** very hot.

5 Personalization: Talk about the weather

(See **Lesson notes**.)

• Focus on the compass. Drill the pronunciation of *north, south, east,* and *west*. Elicit *south east, north west,* etc.

• In groups of four, SS talk about the weather in their country. Encourage SS to use adverbs of frequency. Common error ~~It's raining a lot in the winter.~~

Tip If your SS are from the same country where the climate is similar everywhere, get them to talk about the weather in other countries.

• Feedback, comparing opinions.

Lesson notes

In this lesson SS learn to talk about the weather, revise adverbs of frequency, and contrast the present tenses.

Present simple and continuous Some languages don't have a present continuous and SS may confuse the two tenses. Common error ~~It's usually raining in the winter. Look! It rains.~~

Refer SS to the **Level 1 Grammar review** (= **G◄◄** 3, 4 SB *p. 2*), and to the **Level 1 Grammar check** (**WB** *p. 3*).

Talk about … A regular feature to encourage real conversation. Explain to SS that the focus is on fluency rather than accuracy. Avoid over-correcting SS while they're speaking, but make a note of any frequent errors and correct them with the whole class at the end.

Extras

Question words [P] *p. 145* Prompts to revise all the questions SS should know from Level 1 and get to know each other better. Instructions *p. 127*.

Find your way round *English File* [P] *p. 146* A reading activity to help SS get to know their course books. Instructions *p. 128*.

Books-closed presentation

The weather For flashcard presentations, see **Introduction** *p. 11*.

• Do before **ex. 1**. Copy the pictures from **Picture bank 1A** *p. 205* onto cards.
• Ask *What's the weather like?*, show each flashcard in turn and elicit / teach, and drill the six answers.
• Elicit and drill the question *What's the weather like?* Then stick the pictures on the board and number them 1 to 6. In pairs, SS practise the question *What's the weather like in picture (1)?* and answers.
• Write up the question and answers for SS to copy. Then start **ex. 1**.

■ Learner-training

'Weather' is the first new vocabulary group in the book. Encourage SS to write the words down on a page in their ring file. Remind them to test themselves / each other. Remember to test them.

■ Homework

SS do **WB 1A** *p. 10* and **Listen and speak 1A**. Make sure they know about the self-check key.

Writing: Our weather SS write a paragraph about the weather in their country using the Siberia text as a model.

15

A typical Hollywood star?

> *What does he usually do before breakfast?*
> *He goes jogging.*

Lesson aims

Vocabulary	daily routine
Pronunciation	Present simple endings /s/, /z/, and /ɪz/
Revision	Present simple (routines), expressions of frequency, daily routine, connectors, the time

Lesson plan

■ Warmer: The weather, the time

- Ask *What's the weather like today? What was it like yesterday?*
- Write these times on the board:

  > 6.30 8.45 3.15 4.20 5.35 11.10 12.55 9.18

- Point to different times and ask *What's the time?* If SS answer using digital time, e.g. *six thirty*, elicit also the alternative form, e.g. *half past six*.
- SS practise asking and answering in pairs.

  Tip If necessary, refer SS to Ⓖ◄◄ 21 (**SB** *p. 7*).

1 Revision: Daily routine

a
- SS turn to 📖 **Activities A** *p. 134*, and match the verbs and pictures. Check they understand the difference between *wake up / get up* and *go to / get to*.

  > **2** get up **3** have a shower / bath **4** get dressed
  > **5** have breakfast / lunch / dinner
  > **6** go to work / school / university
  > **7** get to work / school / university
  > **8** start / finish work / school / university
  > **9** go home **10** get home **11** go to bed

b
- Elicit some connectors onto the board, e.g. *Then / After that / Finally*. To elicit *Then / After that* NOT *After …*, write on the board:

  > I get up and _____ I have a shower.

- From the pictures, tell SS about your typical day, using connectors.
- In pairs, SS tell each other about their typical day. Encourage them to connect sentences, reminding them with the connectors on the board.
  I wake up at half past seven. Then I get up and get dressed.
- Feedback. Find out who gets up the earliest / goes to bed the latest.

2 Revision: Anthony Hopkins's day

a
- Focus on the photo of Anthony Hopkins and get SS to cover the text.
  Ask *What does he do? Where's he from? When was he born? How old do you think he is?*, etc.
- SS quickly read the introduction to the article to check.

b
- SS in pairs, A and B. Set a time limit of about two

minutes. A reads **Part 1**, B reads **Part 2**. Make sure they cover the other part of the text. Tell SS to highlight new words but not to ask you for the meaning yet.

⚠ a mile = about 1500m, 5 miles = 8 km
- SS tell each other five things about his day.
- Feedback, eliciting from individual SS all the things he does.

⚠ Remind them to use the third person *s*.

3 Reading: Vocabulary and comprehension

a
- Tell A to read **Part 2** and B **Part 1** quickly.
- In pairs, SS skim-read the whole text and find words to match the definitions. They should highlight any more new words they find.
- Check answers and drill pronunciation. Get SS to underline the word stress.

  > **1** tracksuit /ˈtræksuːt/ **2** grapefruit **3** script
  > **4** highlighter pen **5** restless **6** suit /suːt/
  > **7** answerphone

- Explain / translate other words or phrases that SS have highlighted, e.g. *couple* (= two), *public transport*, *during*, *especially*, *light* (= not heavy), *cook* (*n.*), *noise*.

b
- In pairs, SS mark ten sentences about Anthony Hopkins true or false, and correct the false sentences.
- Check answers.

  > **2** F He's married and doesn't have any children.
  > **3** T
  > **4** F He learns film scripts.
  > **5** F He never reads a newspaper or listens to the radio.
  > **6** T
  > **7** F He likes buying clothes by Armani or Cerruti.
  > **8** T
  > **9** F He only goes out once or twice a week.
  > **10** F He often wakes up at 4.00 in the morning.

c
- Ask *How do typical Hollywood stars live? Where do they live? How do they spend the day? How do they usually travel? What do they do in their free time?* etc.
- Ask *Is Anthony Hopkins a typical Hollywood star?* (no) *Why* (*not*)*?* (he walks everywhere / doesn't go out much / goes to bed early).
- Tell SS that Anthony Hopkins gave this interview a few years ago. Ask *Do you think his life is still the same?* Refer SS to the footnote at the bottom of *p. 15*.

■ GRAMMAR FOCUS
Revision of the present simple

a
- In pairs, SS look at the examples in the chart and complete the rules. Check answers.

  > | | |
  > |---|---|
  > | **+** | Add *s* for *he / she / it*. |
  > | **−** | Use *don't* or *doesn't* + infinitive. |
  > | **?** | Use *do* or *does* + infinitive. |

b • Remind SS of the word order in questions and the memory aid **ASI** (= **A**uxiliary **S**ubject **I**nfinitive) and **QASI** (= **Q**uestion **A**uxiliary **S**ubject **I**nfinitive). Remind them too that auxiliary verbs 'help' you to form a question or negative.

• Write these two examples on the board:

> I always have coffee for breakfast.
> How often do you go out? About twice a week.

• Ask *What tense is it?* Elicit / remind SS that we use the present simple to talk about:
– what you do every day / week / month, etc.
– how often you do things.
• Highlight that longer expressions of frequency go at the beginning or end of a sentence:
We go out twice a week. Twice a week we go out.
• Focus on expressions of frequency,
e.g. *every week / month, three times a year,* etc.

Tip Refer SS to 🌀◀◀ 14 (**SB** *p.6*) if necessary.

PRACTICE

a • In pairs, SS make the sentences negative, as in the example. Common errors ~~He hasn't lunch in a restaurant. He doesn't uses public transport.~~

> 2 He **doesn't use** public transport.
> 3 They **don't go** out a lot.
> 4 His wife **doesn't cook** at lunchtime.
> 5 They **don't have** a big car. OR
>   They **haven't got** a big car.

b • In pairs, SS complete questions and answers about the text.
• Check answers.

> 2 What time **does he get** up?
>   He **gets up** at about 6.30.
> 3 What **does he do** before breakfast?
>   He **goes** jogging.
> 4 What **does he have** for breakfast?
>   He **has** a grapefruit and an orange.
> 5 How often **does he use** public transport?
>   Never. He **walks** everywhere.
> 6 What **does he do in the** mornings?
>   He **learns** film scripts.
> 7 Why **doesn't he** read the paper?
>   Because **it's** all bad news.

■ PRONUNCIATION

a • Books closed. Write the nine verbs on the board in the three groups. Ask SS to say the *he / she* form out loud. Ask *Which group is pronounced* /ɪz/?
• ∘9∘ SS listen and repeat nine sentences illustrating present simple verb endings.

b • Focus on the verbs in the list. Ask *Which of these verbs are pronounced* /ɪz/ *in the third person?* (wash, use). Drill pronunciation of the other verbs (*runs, reads, buys, goes* = /z/, the most common form, *cooks* = /s/). Remind SS that verbs ending in *es* or *ies* are pronounced /ɪz/ (exceptions *goes, does*). If SS want the full rule, tell them:

1 unvoiced endings (e.g. /p/, /k/, /f/, /t/) + *s* are pronounced /s/.
2 voiced endings (e.g. /n/, /m/, /v/, /b/) + *s* are pronounced /z/.
3 verbs ending in /sh/, /x/, /s/, /ch/, /z/ + *es* and verbs ending in *ies* are pronounced /ɪz/ (see 🌀◀◀ 4 **SB** *p.3*).

⚠ Emphasize that the difference between /s/ and /z/ is very small. Concentrate on getting the /ɪz/ pronunciation right.

4 Personalization: Asking about each other

• This is the first ▶◀ **Communication** activity. Make sure SS know exactly what to do before they start. SS in pairs, A and B. If you have an odd number, put two As with a B. SS face each other and turn to ▶◀ **Lifestyles** A *p.120*, B *p.123*.
• Give them a minute to read their instructions and question prompts. Get SS to ask you some of the questions first. Remind them to use *do you?*
• A and B take turns to ask each other questions.

Tip Encourage SS to ask *What about you?* and other follow-up questions. Elicit some examples onto the board and remind SS to use them.

• Feedback. Ask individual SS to tell you something interesting about their partner.

Lesson notes

The context is a day in the life of the actor Anthony Hopkins. SS revise the present simple to talk about daily routines. Special emphasis is given to the third person singular endings and word order in questions.

Extras

How often do you …? P *p.147* A picture-based activity to revise / practise expressions / adverbs of frequency. Instructions *p.128*.

■ Learner-training

Remind SS to record new vocabulary that has come up in the lesson, e.g. the words in **ex.3a.**, and to mark the stress. Show SS how to test themselves with the **Word bank** by covering the words and remembering from the pictures. Tell them to test themselves at home after each section.

■ Homework

SS do **WB 1B** *p.11* and **Listen and speak 1B**.

Writing: My typical day SS write a paragraph about a typical day in their lives. Suggest they use 🖉 **Activities A** *p.134* to help them. You could collect them in and read one or two aloud for the class to guess who it is, or build on the error correction activity in **1 Introduction** and get SS to correct each others' work for Grammar / Spelling / capital letters.

> *Did you enjoy it?*
> *No, it was awful.*

Lesson aims

Grammar	*What was the food like?*
Vocabulary	Activities: free time
Pronunciation	/d/, /t/, and /ɪd/ endings of past simple
Revision	Past simple: regular and irregular verbs, adjectives of opinion
Optional materials	A personal holiday anecdote (**ex. 4**)

Lesson plan

■ Warmer: Holiday vocabulary

- Write on the board:

Going on Holiday	
Transport	**Accommodation**
plane	hotel

- In threes, give SS a minute to write at least three words in each category.
- Feedback all their suggestions onto the board.

Possible answers:	
Transport	**Accommodation**
train	rented house / flat / apartment
coach / bus	bed and breakfast
car etc.	campsite / tent etc.

1 Presentation: Free-time activities

a
- SS turn to 🔖 **Activities B** *p. 134* and match the verbs and pictures. Check answers. Drill pronunciation.

B go cycling **C** go dancing **D** go for a walk
E go jogging **F** go on holiday **G** go out
H go shopping **I** go sightseeing **J** go swimming
K go to the cinema / theatre

b
- Ask SS a few questions with different past time expressions, e.g. *Did you go (cycling) yesterday / last weekend?* etc. Then get SS to ask you.
- In pairs, SS use the 🔖 pictures to revise *Did you …? Yes, I did. / No, I didn't.*
- SS continue in pairs, covering the expressions, and using only the pictures. Encourage them to give more information after *Yes, I did.*, as in the example.

2 Listening: ® Past simple

a
- Focus on the magazine article. Ask *What does 'unforgettable' mean?* (= you can't forget it). Ask *Why can a holiday be unforgettable?* (because it was very good or very bad).
- Tell SS to look at the holiday pictures. Ask *Where did Bruce and Maureen go?* (the Caribbean, New York) *Have you been there?*
- Tell SS they're going to hear an interview with Bruce about his holiday. In pairs, SS look at the chart and

write the ten questions the interviewer asked him. Remind SS of the word order for questions with a question word (**Q**uestion **A**uxiliary **S**ubject **V**erb).
- ⚠ Be careful with question 2: *Did you have a good time?* (= Did you enjoy the holiday?) – some nationalities may confuse *time* with *weather*.

b
- ⏺ **10** ⏺ Play the tape once. SS check the questions, and underline the sentence stress. Drill for intonation.

2 Did you <u>have</u> a good <u>time</u>? **3** <u>When</u> did you <u>go</u> there? **4** <u>Who</u> did you <u>go</u> with? **5** <u>How</u> did you get <u>there</u>? **6** <u>Where</u> did you <u>stay</u>? **7** <u>What</u> was the <u>weather</u> like? **8** <u>What</u> was the <u>food</u> like? **9** <u>What</u> did you <u>do</u>? **10** <u>How</u> <u>long</u> did you <u>stay</u>?
Tapescript **SB Listening** *p. 126*

c
- Tell SS to focus on Bruce's answers. Play the tape again. SS listen and complete column 1 of the chart. Check answers.

2 No.   **3** (About) two years ago. **4** Nobody. (He was) alone.   **5** By plane and boat. **6** In a small hotel on the beach.   **7** 45° every day. **8** Awful.   **9** Nothing – he stayed in the hotel all the time.   **10** Three days.

- Ask more comprehension questions, e.g. *Why was it a terrible holiday? Why was the food awful?*
- SS check the tapescript on *p. 126*.

3 Practice: Reading and speaking

a
- Focus on the photo of Maureen. Tell SS she's a British TV actress. Ask *How old do you think she is?* (born 15.5.1946). SS read about her holiday and complete column 2 of the chart.
- Focus on vocabulary. Elicit the meaning of (*not*) *mind*, *show* (*n.*), *over 40*, and *teenagers*. Highlight the strong adjective *delicious* (= very nice – used only for food).
- Check answers to questions 1 to 10.

1 New York. **2** Yes. **3** Last Easter. **4** A friend, Julia. **5** By plane **6** In a hotel near Broadway. **7** Freezing. **8** Delicious. **9** Went shopping / to the theatre / restaurants. **10** Ten days.

b
- SS in pairs, A and B. A is Bruce, B the interviewer. They use the chart to roleplay the interview. Monitor to make sure SS are using the past simple and encourage A to use full sentences.
- SS swap roles. A is the interviewer, B is Maureen.

■ GRAMMAR FOCUS
Revision of the past simple

a
- Focus on Maureen's text again.

1
- Tell SS to highlight three ⊞ regular past simple verbs in Maureen's text and to write the infinitives. Ask *Which one doubles the final consonant?*

stayed – stay   sto**pp**ed – stop   lived – live

- Write *stay*, *live*, and *stop* on the board. Elicit / give the rules for *stay* and *live* (+ *ed*, or + *d* if the verb ends in *e*) and for *stop* (double the final consonant when the verb ends in consonant / vowel / consonant, + *ed*).
- Write *study* on the board. Ask *What happens when the verb ends in consonant + y?* (~~y~~, + *ied*).
- Check they understand with a few more examples: *try, need, play, wait, visit, cook, love, travel,* etc.

2
- Tell SS to find six + irregular verbs from the text and tell you their infinitives.

> flew – fly   was – be   went – go   saw – see
> had – have   forgot – forget

b
- SS complete the − and ? forms.

> **He didn't go** to Cairo.   **Did he go** to Cairo?

- Elicit the rules.

> − Use *didn't* + infinitive.
> ? Use *did* + person + infinitive.

Elicit that the form is the same for all persons (except with the verb *be*). Emphasize that we use the past simple for any completed action, even if it was a very short time ago, e.g. *I wrote this two minutes ago.*

PRACTICE

a
- Tell SS to read quickly through Inès's holiday story. Ask *Did she enjoy it?* (no) *Why not?*

  Tip Encourage SS to do this for all gap fill exercises, as it helps them get the gist of a text first.

b
- SS read and complete the story with the verbs in past simple, as in the example. Check answers.

> **2** stayed **3** was **4** had **5** was **6** hated
> **7** was **8** didn't know **9** couldn't **10** spoke
> **11** was **12** cried **13** wrote **14** missed
> **15** spent **16** wanted

- Ask SS to guess the meaning of <u>boarding school</u>, <u>pool</u>, <u>court</u>, <u>afraid</u>, <u>homesick</u>, <u>so much</u>.

c
- SS write five more − past simple sentences. Check answers, and drill pronunciation of the sentences.

> **2** She didn't stay in a hotel. **3** She didn't write to her boyfriend. **4** She couldn't speak Spanish.
> **5** She wasn't happy. **6** She didn't have a good time.

■ PRONUNCIATION
Regular verbs

a
- ·11· SS listen and repeat the regular verbs in isolation. Elicit which sound they hear at the end of the verbs in each group. Establish that they are the three possible ways of pronouncing -*ed* (/ɪd/ after voiced endings and /ɪd/ after *t* or *d*).

b
- ·12· SS listen and repeat the regular verbs in the sentences. Ask *What does ‿ mean?* (linker) *When do you link with the next word?* (when the next word starts with a vowel, e.g. stayed in = /steɪdɪn/).

  Tip Tell SS never to pronounce the *e* of *ed* except after *t* or *d*.

4 **Personalization: Talk about holidays**
- Focus on **V** Adjectives of opinion. Drill pronunciation. As these are expressive adjectives, get SS to exaggerate the stress. Remind SS that we don't use *very* with these strong adjectives NOT *very lovely*.
- Give SS a minute or two to think of one of their own unforgettable holidays (good or bad). Do the same yourself. If they can't think of one, tell them to talk about their last holiday, or imagine one.
- Focus on the chart. Get SS to interview you. Elicit the questions starting with *Where did you go?*. Make sure they realise that for each '/' sign they have to add in a missing word or words.
- In pairs, SS interview each other. Monitor and help.
- Feedback. Ask *Where did your partner go? Was it a good or a bad holiday? Why?*, etc.

Lesson notes

SS revise the past simple (all forms) in the context of memorable holidays. They also revise / learn typical free-time activities and adjectives of opinion.

Past simple Some SS may still have problems forming questions and negatives, and not remember irregular forms. If they haven't already done them, refer SS to G◄◄6 (SB *p.3*) and the accompanying practice exercises in the **Workbook** *p.3* for full rules and further practice. Refer them also to Irregular verbs (SB *p.141*).

Pronunciation SS will probably still have difficulties with the pronunciation of the *ed* ending.

Extras

Are you stressed? P *p.148* A past simple questionnaire to discover SS' stress level. Instructions *p.128*.

Books-closed presentation

What was it like?
- Do before **ex.2**. Tell SS you're going to tell them about your last holiday. Copy the pictures from **Picture bank 1C** *p.205* onto the board or onto flashcards which you can pin up on the board.
- Tell SS *I went to (Mexico) last summer.* Point to the picture of the hotel. Draw a big question mark above each picture to elicit the question *What was the hotel like?*, etc. Invent an answer, e.g. *It was fantastic.*
- Repeat with the other pictures to elicit and drill *What was the food like? What was the weather like? What were the people like?* and invent your answers, e.g. *delicious.* Then start **ex.2**.

■ Learner-training

Tell SS to make a note of the irregular verbs from this lesson, and of new irregular verbs as they come up.

■ Homework

SS do **WB 1C** p.*12* and **Listen and speak 1C**.

Writing: An unforgettable holiday SS write a paragraph about a memorable holiday they've had.

What a bore!

> *Have you been to China?*
> *Yes, I have. It's incredible.*

Lesson aims

Grammar	Present perfect, past participles
Vocabulary	*Me too.* / *Me neither.*
Pronunciation	/h/, /v/, weak forms /bɪn/ and /tə/
Revision	*What's it like?*, adjectives of opinion
Optional materials	Magazine photos / postcards of places (**Grammar Focus ex.1a**)

Lesson plan

■ Warmer: ℝ Adjectives of opinion

- Copy this chart onto the board:

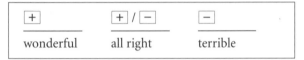

+ ____	+ / − ____	− ____
wonderful	all right	terrible

- In pairs or groups give SS two minutes to write more adjectives in each category.
- Feedback onto the board. Drill pronunciation.

> **Possible answers:**
> + good, fantastic, incredible, delicious, marvellous, lovely, great, nice, brilliant
> + / − OK, nothing special
> − bad, awful, horrible, boring

1 Presentation: Listening

a
- Tell SS to cover the text and look at the picture. Ask *What can you see? What's he like? What's he thinking? Are they having a good time?*.
- Focus on the chart. Check the meaning of *CD*.
- `·13·` Play the tape once. SS listen and complete the chart with the adjectives the man uses.
- Check answers, especially the spelling of *marvellous* and pronunciation of *interesting* /ˈɪntrəstɪŋ/. Play the tape again if necessary.

> 2 brilliant   3 nice   4 marvellous   5 interesting
> 6 delicious   7 incredible

b
- Ask *What happens at the end of the conversation?* (he wants to show the woman his photos, but she leaves) *Why does she leave?* (because the man's very boring).
- Focus on the lesson title. Explain that *a bore* = a boring person. Ask *Do you know any bores?*

2 Presentation: Present perfect, past participles

a
- Write the first three past participles on the board. Ask *What form of the verb are they?* Some SS may know that they are *past participles*.

1
- Focus on the verbs in the chart. Ask *What are their infinitives?* Check SS know their meaning.

> | | | |
> |---|---|---|
> | travel – travelled | hear – heard | be – been |
> | try – tried | have – had | go – gone |
> | work – worked | meet – met | see – seen |
> | look – looked | read /riːd/ – read /red/ | |

2
- In pairs, SS read and complete the dialogue.

b
- Play the tape again for SS to listen and check their answers. Be prepared to explain / translate *personally*, *try* (= taste / eat), *in fact*, *look at* (v. *see*).

> 2 met   3 seen   4 read   5 met   6 worked
> 7 travelled   8 been   9 tried   10 been   11 had
> 12 been   13 gone   14 looked

> ⚠ If SS ask why 8, 10, and 12 are *been* and not *gone*, tell them to look now at the section in the **Grammar focus** and explain the difference.

c
- In pairs, SS answer the two comprehension questions to lead into the use of the present perfect.

> 1 Egypt, Brazil, Japan, China, and 19 more. We don't know when.
> 2 Whitney Houston. We don't know when.

■ GRAMMAR FOCUS

The present perfect

a
- Tell SS to look at the chart and complete the rule and contractions. Check answers.

> Form the present perfect with the auxiliary verb **have** + past participle. **Contractions** 's = **has**, haven't = **have not**, hasn't = **has not**

> ⚠ Point out that *'s = is* or *has*, and that they need to check from the context.

- Drill + , − , and ? from the chart, focusing especially on the contractions.

> *Tip* Use magazine pictures / postcards to illustrate and drill *I've been to* (+ picture), *I haven't been to* (+ picture), *Have you been to* (+ picture)?.

b
- Ask *What has the man in the dialogue done?* to elicit *He's been to 23 countries, heard the new Whitney Houston CD.*, etc. Then ask *When?* (we don't know – at some time before now but we don't know exactly when).
- Focus on the rule of use. Emphasize that we don't use the present perfect with a past time expression, or when it's clear from the context when an action happened. NOT *I've been to Egypt three years ago.*

Past participles

a
- SS turn to ✎ **Irregular verbs A** *p.141* and put the past participles in the chart. Tell them they will complete the chart during the course and that they should try to learn it a little at a time.

b • Tell SS to look again at **ex. 2a**. Ask *Why are the past participles in three groups?* (the verbs in the first column are regular, the others are irregular. Of the irregular verbs, the past participle is the same as the past simple (column 2) and the past simple and past participle have different forms (column 3).

been or *gone*?

• Explain that *been to* = gone and come back, and *gone to* = gone and still there. Highlight the use of *to* after *been*. Ask *Which sentence matches the picture?* (He's been to the bank.)

PRACTICE

a • SS write sentences in the present perfect, as in the example. Check answers.

> 2 He hasn't been to Indonesia.
> 3 Have you heard any Arab music?
> 4 Has she met his girlfriend?
> 5 They've worked in ten countries.
> 6 I haven't studied this before.

3 Personalization: Local places

a • Tell SS to make a list of five well-known or interesting local places (e.g. a new restaurant / shop / disco, etc.) that they've been to. You make a list too, and write it on the board.

• Get SS to ask you *Have you been to …?* + places from your list. Drill the weak form /bɪntə/. Elicit *What's it like?*, and give an opinion of it (*Yes, I have. It's very nice. / I don't like it much.* etc.).

b • In pairs, SS ask each other about the places on their list using the model dialogue. If B answers *Yes, I have.*, A asks *What do you think of it?*

• Feedback any interesting answers.

■ PRONUNCIATION

a • ° 14 ° Tell SS they're going to listen to and remember five sentences. Play the tape once without stopping. In pairs, SS try to remember them.

• Play the tape again, pausing after each sentence.

• Elicit the answers onto the board.

> 1 I've been to China. 2 I haven't been to Japan.
> 3 Have you been to Brazil? 4 She's been to
> America. 5 She hasn't been to England.

b • ° 15 ° SS listen and repeat words with English sounds /h/ and /v/. Remind SS that nearly all words beginning with *h* are pronounced /h/ (common exception *hour* = /aʊə/) (see **Sound bank WB** *p. 81*).

c • ° 16 ° SS listen and repeat more irregular verbs.

have	had	had
hear	heard	heard
make	made	made
meet	met	met
read	read	read
see	saw	seen

4 Personalization: Experiences

• Tell SS to look at the pictures. Ask *What can you see?*

• Focus on the model dialogue. Teach *Me too. / neither.* Illustrate that *Me too.* is used to agree with a `+` sentence, *Me neither.* with a `−`.

• Ask individual SS the question for each picture, plus follow-up questions, e.g.

> T *Have you seen Casablanca?*
> S1 *Yes, I have.*
> T *Me too. Did you like it?*
> S1 *It was great.*
> T *How many times have you seen it? / Did you see it at the cinema or on TV?* etc.

• Get SS to brainstorm onto the board other questions about films, records, food, places, etc. that they know. Write up cues, e.g. *eat / octopus, use / Internet.*

• SS ask and answer in pairs. Monitor and help.

• Feedback any interesting information.

Lesson notes

Present perfect (experience) *English File 1* includes an optional final lesson which presented this use of the present perfect, so some SS may have seen it before. This lesson assumes no previous knowledge of this tense. In **2A** the present perfect is contrasted with the past simple.

ever The question *Have you ever…?* is taught in **File 2A**.

been / gone The difference between *been* and *gone* is explained in the **Grammar focus** in this lesson.

Extras

Unusual things I've done SS think of one unusual thing they've done, e.g. *I've been to Iceland.* SS mingle and tell the others, who have to remember what everyone's done.

Find somebody who … `P` *p. 149* Do after **ex. 4**. SS try to find people who have done different things and ask what they're like. Instructions *p. 128*.

Books-closed presentation

Present perfect / past participles For flashcard presentations, see **Introduction** *p. 11*.

• Do before **ex. 1**. Copy the pictures from **Picture bank 1D** *p. 205*. Localize by writing the name of a popular film currently showing.

• Use the first picture to teach the question *Have you been to London?* and the short answers *Yes, I have. / No, I haven't.* Drill pronunciation.

• Use the other pictures to present and drill *Have you been to McDonald's? / tried Chinese food / met a famous person / seen (a film) / heard Bolero?*

• Write up the six questions and the short answers for SS to copy. Then start **ex. 1**.

■ Learner-training

Get SS to start learning irregular verbs by looking again at **Irregular verbs A** *p. 141*. Test them in the next class.

■ Homework

SS do **WB 1D** *p. 13* and **Listen and speak 1D**.

1 🧳 *Getting there*

Lesson aims

Function	Checking in, arriving, losing your luggage
Vocabulary	Airport: *customs*, etc.
Revision	Question auxiliaries, *Would you like…? Could you…?* colours
Optional materials	A large travel bag and contents, a mock boarding pass (Books-closed presentation)

Lesson plan

■ Warmer: Airport vocabulary

- Copy this on the board.

- In pairs, SS have two minutes to add more words.
- Elicit words onto the board.

> **Suggested words:**
> plane ticket, passport, luggage, boarding pass, departures, duty free shop, customs, etc.

1 Presentation: Baggage security

- Books open. Elicit the meaning of the title (*getting there* = travelling to your destination).
- Tell SS to look at the photo. Ask *Where are they?* (at an airport check in). Explain that the traveller is Dutch (from Holland) and that he's on a business trip.
- Focus on the **Baggage security** sign. Elicit / explain the meaning of *baggage security*.
  ⚠ *baggage* = *luggage* (cases / bags) *baggage* is used in airport signs. *luggage* is used in conversation.
- ⦿17⦿ SS complete the questions with the right auxiliary. Play the tape once. SS listen and check.
- Play the tape again. SS tick the questions when he says *Yes* and cross them when he says *No*. Check answers.

> A Good afternoon. Your ticket and passport, please.
> B Just a moment. Here you are.
> A Thanks. **Is** this your baggage? (✓)
> B Yes, it is.
> A **Did** you pack it yourself? (✓)
> B Yes. Yes, I did.
> A **Are** you carrying anything for anyone else? (✗)
> B No, I'm not.
> A **Have** you had it with you at all times? (✓)
> B Yes, I have.
> A **Do** you know what's in it? (✓)
> B Yes, I do. I packed it.
> A OK, and … **does** it contain any electrical items? (✗)
> B Electrical items? I don't think so. No. No, it doesn't.

2 Presentation and practice: Checking in

a
- Focus on the boarding pass. Check SS understand *destination*, *gate*, and *aisle* /aɪl/.
- ⦿18⦿ SS listen and complete the information.

> Flight: BA617   Destination: London   Time: 10.20
> Gate: 12   Seat: 6F   window   non-smoking

b
- In pairs, SS read and try to complete the extracts from the dialogue.
- Elicit their guesses, then play the tape again to check.

> A **Do you have any** hand luggage?
> B **Only this** bag.
> A That's fine. **Would you like** smoking or non-smoking?
> B Non-smoking. **Could I have** a window seat, please?
> A Let me see. [Yes, that's OK, seat 6F. Right, here's your boarding pass. Flight number BA 617 to London. Board at 10.20 at gate number 12. Enjoy your flight.]
> B I'm **sorry. Could** you **repeat** that?
> A Yes, [look. Seat 6F, flight number BA 617 to London. Board at 10.20.]
> B Sorry, which **gate** is it?
> A **Gate** number **12**. [OK?
> B Yes, thanks.
> A You're welcome.]

> *Tip* Only the key language is on the **SB** page. Like all the gap-fill dialogues, this dialogue isn't in the **SB Listening** section. Write up on the board any other phrases SS have trouble understanding.

c
- Books closed. In pairs, SS roleplay the dialogue. A works at British Airways check-in. B's travelling to London. Then swap roles.

> *Tip* In roleplays, it's best to demonstrate first with a stronger student. You play the harder role (in this case the BA official). Then two SS can do it before everyone does it in pairs.

3 Listening: Airport announcement

- ⦿19⦿ Tell SS there's a problem with the flight. Play the tape. They listen to an airport announcement and note the two changes to the boarding pass information. SS check the tapescript if necessary.

> New departure time: 12.15
> New gate number: 21
> Tapescript **SB Listening** *p. 126*

- Ask *Have you ever had this problem?*

4 Presentation and practice: Arriving

a
- Tell SS the passenger has now arrived in London, at Gatwick Airport. Ask *Have any of you been there?* (it's about 32km south of London and is London's second biggest airport, after Heathrow.)
- ⦿20⦿ Tell SS to listen for why he's in England. Ask *Is he on holiday?* Play the tape once. Elicit that he's there on business.

b • Write on the board:

Passport control	Baggage reclaim
passport / holiday	Excuse / trolleys?
business	over
fine / enjoy	change? / coin / trolley here Thanks

• Elicit the meaning of *Passport control* (where they check your passport) and *Baggage reclaim* (where you collect your luggage).
• Play the tape again, and elicit the dialogue. SS remember and practise in pairs. Finally, get SS to write the dialogue.

5 Presentation and practice: Losing your luggage

a • Tell SS he's now at **Baggage reclaim**. Ask *What do you think has happened?* (one of his suitcases hasn't arrived) *What's he going to do?* (tell the airline).
• Focus on the **BA lost luggage** form. Ask SS to predict possible answers for Colour / Size / Contents.
• ° 21 ° SS listen and complete the form. Play the tape twice and check answers.

BA lost luggage report
Colour **black**   Size **big**
Contents **clothes and important documents**
Name **Pieter Okker**
Home address **29 Beethoven Straat, Amsterdam**
Temporary address **Hilton Hotel**
Tel. **0171 689 5022**   Staying until **October 5th**

Tapescript **SB Listening** *p. 126*

b • SS listen again and note down the woman's questions. Pause the tape after each question to give SS time to write. Elicit the questions onto the board. SS check the tapescript if necessary.

Can I see your ticket, please?
What colour is your suitcase?
What's it like?
What's in it?
What's your name?
And **how do you spell your surname?**
And your home address?
And **where are you staying in London?**
Do you know the phone number?
And **how long are you going to be there?**

c • SS roleplay the dialogue. Get them to imagine they are travellers, and to note down the details of their luggage (description and contents).
• Demonstrate the roleplay with one student, using the **Lost luggage report** and the questions on the board.
• In pairs, SS roleplay using an invented name, address and phone number. Then SS swap roles.

> *Tip* Reduce the questions on the board to prompts for each question, e.g. see / ticket? What colour / suitcase? What / like? What / in it? / name? / home address? Where / staying / London? How long / be there?

6 Vocabulary: Travel phrasebook

• SS turn to **SB** *p. 132*. Explain that this is a **Travel phrasebook** where SS record the most useful 'survival' phrases from the lesson and memorize them. Tell SS they will be able to use it when they travel abroad.
• SS translate the key phrases from the lesson.

Lesson notes

Learning English as the international language of foreign travel is an important motivation for many students. This is the first in a series of core lessons called **Travel with English**, which promote confidence and fluency in practical situations. There is one per File. The lessons focus on speaking and listening in common travel situations and include authentic travel texts for SS to deal with. Apart from learning the basic language for each situation, SS also learn to cope with typical problems that may arise, e.g. losing luggage. After each **Travel with English** lesson, SS complete their **Travel phrasebook**. The **Travel with English** lessons are based around the travels of a Dutch businessman, Pieter Okker. In this first lesson, SS see him checking in, arriving at Gatwick airport, and reporting his missing suitcase.

Pronunciation People everywhere respond better to a foreign speaker if he / she uses friendly intonation. Encourage SS to use a wide voice range and give plenty of intonation practice.

Extras

At the airport 🅟 *p. 150* Do after **ex. 5c**. A pair work activity. SS describe pictures of an airport to find ten differences. Instructions *p. 129*.

Books-closed presentation

Checking in

• Bring in a travel bag or case. Tell the class that you work for British Airways and to imagine they're at the airport. Give the bag to a good student. Then tell him / her that this is their bag, and to come up and check in. Ask for his / her ticket and passport and work through the security questions in **ex. 1**.
• Ask if he / she has got any hand-luggage, wants smoking or non-smoking, and then give him / her a 'boarding pass' and explain the departure times. Then say *Have a good flight.*
• Tell SS that today they're going to learn to communicate at an airport. Then start **ex. 1**.

■ Learner-training

Encourage SS to memorize key phrases from the **Travel phrasebook**. Remember to test SS on the key phrases at the beginning of the next class. Regular testing really motivates SS to learn vocabulary.

■ Homework

SS do **WB 1** 📖 *p. 14* and **Listen and speak 1** 📖.

Lesson aims

Revision	**File 1:** All tenses, routines, study habits, family, weather, places
Skills	Study skills

Lesson plan

■ Warmer: Progress chart

- Books closed. Ask *Can you remember what the lessons in File 1 were about? What grammar and vocabulary did we learn?* Elicit from SS anything they can remember (e.g. that **1B** was about Anthony Hopkins, and the main grammar point was the revision of the present simple).
- Now tell SS to look at the **Progress chart** (**SB** *p. 8*) and to tick the lessons they've studied.
- Tell them that this is the revision lesson for this File, and that they can then do the **Vocabulary** and **Grammar files** (**SB** *pp. 24, 25*) to further revise the language of the File.

1 Revision: Past simple, (be) going to

- SS in pairs, **A** and **B**. SS turn to ✎ **Activities A** *p. 134* and focus on the pictures.
- Elicit the past tenses of the verbs, e.g. *wake up – woke up*. Ask for negative sentences too, e.g. *I didn't …*
- Demonstrate the activity. Tell SS what you did yesterday, using the ✎ pictures (*I woke up at about 7.00 but I didn't get up until 7.20. Then I got dressed. I had breakfast at 7.45.* etc.) Add in extra details too (e.g. *I had coffee and toast.*)
- **A** uses the pictures to tell **B** what he / she did yesterday. **B** listens and helps / corrects. Monitor and note down any common mistakes.
- When they finish, write any mistakes on the board for SS to correct.
- Now tell SS that **B** is going to talk about tomorrow. Elicit the right form of the verb (*I'm going to wake up …*) and a negative (*I'm not going to …*)
- **B** tells **A** what he / she's going to do tomorrow / at the weekend. **A** listens and helps / corrects.

Tip Encourage SS to use connectors and add extra information. Fast finishers can swap roles on each tense to give the rest time to finish.

2 Revision: All tenses

a • Focus on the names of the tenses (a – g). Tell SS to read sentences 1 to 7 and match each one to the correct tense, as in the example.

> **2** e **3** a **4** d **5** g **6** b **7** c

b • Get individual SS to tell you the ☐ − ☐ forms of sentences 1 to 7.

> **2** She hasn't been **3** We aren't going
> **4** He isn't looking **5** They aren't often
> **6** I didn't go **7** She wasn't

- Tell SS to change sentences 1 to 7 into questions with *you*, e.g. *Do you live near here?* SS interview each other.

> **2** Have you been …? **3** Are you going to buy …?
> **4** Are you looking …? **5** Are you often …?
> **6** Did you go …? **7** Were you …?

Tip Make sure **B** closes his / her book and that **A** asks all the questions first. When they swap, get **B** to ask them in a different order.

3 Practice: All tenses, speaking

- Focus on the photos. Ask *What are they?* (a ring file, a highlighter pen, *Easy Readers* (= simplified stories in English)). Tell SS that all these things can help them study more effectively.
- Get SS to read quickly through the questionnaire. Point out that each section practises a different tense. Elicit whether the tense in each section is past, present, or future.
- SS in pairs, **A** and **B**, **B** with books closed. Set a time limit of about five minutes. **A** interviews **B** and notes the answers. Then swap roles.

Tip Encourage SS to ask follow-up questions whenever possible.

- Feedback. Ask *Who has more contact with English,* **A** *or* **B***?* Tell SS they should get some good ideas for improving their English from the questionnaire.
- Get useful information about your SS by quickly asking the class some of the questions, e.g. *Who spoke English on holiday?* and getting SS to put up their hands.
- Use this opportunity to encourage SS again to get a ring file to organize their work, a good bi-lingual dictionary, and a highlighter pen to highlight grammar rules and new words in a text.

4 Personalization: Talk about you

- SS in groups of three. Tell each student in the group to choose a different topic. Give them two minutes to think about what they're going to say, which tense they need to talk about their topic (e.g. my plans for the weekend = (*be*) *going to*) what vocabulary they're going to need, etc.
- Show SS your own 'thinking' by making notes on the board about one of the topics. Then demonstrate by talking for exactly a minute. Get a student to time you. Emphasize that the important thing is to keep talking and not to worry about making mistakes.
- The first student in each group starts talking. When the minute is over, the others in the group ask one question each.
- Then the next student speaks for a minute, etc.

Tip Monitor the groups but don't interrupt unless a student really needs help. Tell SS that if someone is still talking after a minute, to let them finish. Make a note of any common errors, (e.g. NOT ~~the last summer~~). When all SS have spoken, write any errors on the board and ask SS to correct them.

Lesson notes

This non-core revision lesson consolidates the main language points of **File 1**: revision of present tenses, *(be) going to*, past simple, and present perfect. The aim is to get the main tenses clear in SS' minds. As well as revising tenses, the questionnaire should provide you with valuable feedback about your SS contact with English. The lesson also recycles key word families from **File 1**.

⚠ SS may ask you about the *will / won't* future. Explain that this will be taught later in the course, in **File 4**.

Talk about … Remember that the emphasis in these sections should be on fluency rather than accuracy. Try to avoid interrupting / correcting unless it's really needed.

Extras

Who are you? 🎲 *p. 210* A revision guessing game.

Glug 🎲 *p. 208* A game to revise tenses.

Yesterday and tomorrow P *p. 151* Picture prompts for SS to talk about the past and the future. Instructions *p. 129*.

■ Homework

Choose from the **End-of-file options below**.

End-of-file options

There are no specific **Workbook** practice pages for the **Revision and extension** lessons. Instead, take time to introduce and do or set for homework **Vocabulary file 1** and **Grammar file 1** (SB *p. 24, 25*). These pages revise and summarize the vocabulary and grammar content of each File. They can be done in class or set as homework. You can:

– use them all at once at the end of a File.
– use exercises or grammar summaries to consolidate specific points during a lesson.

Student's Book

■ Vocabulary file 1 *p. 24*

● Do this in class or set it for homework. However, even if SS do the rest of the page at home, you should try to go quickly through the introductory text and **Organize your vocabulary learning!** in class.

Organize your vocabulary learning! Emphasize that the best way for SS to record words is in two columns so they can cover one and test themselves by looking only at the other. They can record the right-hand column in various ways: a translation, a phrase, a picture, etc., as in the example.

Try it! Tell SS (in pairs or for homework) to find six new words that they want to learn from 1🔊 *p. 20*, including the tapescripts. They then follow steps **a** to **c**, deciding how to record the words.

1b ✏ Prepositions A
  1 in front of **3** next to **4** between **5** near
  6 under **7** opposite **8** outside **9** inside
3 Grammar words
  2 h **3** i **4** f **5** a **6** c **7** d **8** g **9** b
  Encourage SS to cover the grammar words and try to remember them from the examples.
4 Prepositions
  2 to **3** for **4** with **5** of **6** near **7** In
  8 on **9** at **10** until **11** before **12** after
5 Key words
  2 Yes, she plays like Monica Seles.
  3 Reading and swimming. **4** Milk and sugar?
6 Word-building
  fog rain snow cloud wind

■ Grammar file 1 *p. 25*

Explain the tick-off system. SS read each grammar summary and the rules, then tick off each box when they're satisfied they understand it. This is the moment for SS to voice any doubts they have, in L1 if they can't express them in English. Try to go through this first **Grammar file** with the whole class. Once they've got the idea, they can easily do later ones alone.

Workbook

■ Grammar check 1 *p. 15*

● This is a page of exercises revising the **File 1** grammar. Tell SS to do the page with **Grammar file 1** (SB *p. 25*) open in front of them. They use the check exercises to test they understand each grammar point, referring back to **Grammar file 1** as necessary. SS can check their answers with the **WB** key.

■ Read and write 1 *p. 61*

The first in the eight-stage guided writing syllabus.

● SS write a letter to introduce themselves to a penfriend, following a model.
● Briefly explain the exercises and model letter. Emphasize the need to read and follow the instructions carefully and compare their final letter with the model. Use L1 if you need to. Remind SS that they have a key to the exercises, but that you're going to collect and correct their letters.

Lesson aims

Pronunciation   English sounds, word stress, sentence stress, intonation

Lesson plan

■ Warmer: Introduction to pronunciation

- Book closed. Ask *Why is good pronunciation important?* Elicit some answers, e.g.
- you feel more confident and are more likely to speak.
- if you know how words are pronounced you will understand better.
- Tell SS that in this lesson you are going to look at ways of improving their pronunciation. This means working on three things: sounds, stress and intonation.
- Books open. Read the introduction together.

Sounds

- Ask *How many different sounds are there in English?* (44) Compare this number with SS' L1 if you / they know it.
- If you have the **English sounds** poster up in the classroom, point to it, or show SS the chart in the **Word bank** (**SB** *p. 142*).

■ *Tip 1*

- SS read the tip. Explain / translate *tip* (= a useful idea telling you how to do something better).
- Explain that:
- it's important to concentrate on sounds which are different from their own language.
- being able to recognize phonetic symbols helps when SS look up a new word in the dictionary.
- Write on the board *friendly* and the phonetic transcription /'frendlɪ/. Elicit from the transcription that *i* is not pronounced.

1 Presentation: English sounds

- **a** • SS turn to 📖 **English sounds** *p. 142* and focus on the pictures and example words for the vowel sounds.
  - Go through the sounds and get SS to repeat them.
  - Call out the picture numbers. SS say the word.
    T 5   **S** *clock*

    Tip If SS have trouble with a particular sound, show them the correct mouth position.

  - In pairs, SS test each other. **A** points at a picture and **B** says the word. Then they swap.
- **b** • Focus on the symbols in the pictures. Get SS to repeat just the sound (not the word) after you. Ask *What do you think the two dots mean?* (a long sound).
  - Practise by calling out numbers. SS say the sound.
- **c** • Now SS focus on the consonants. Repeat the procedure you followed for vowels.
- **d** • Elicit the seven symbols which are <u>not</u> like letters of the alphabet (/ʃ/, /ʒ/, /θ/, /ð/, /tʃ/, /dʒ/, /ŋ/) and /j/ not pronounced like *j*.

■ *Tip 2*

- SS read the tip. Tell SS that although many common words are irregular (e.g. *live, women, bread*), the majority of English words (more than 70%) follow a regular pattern.

2 Practice: Sound / spelling patterns

- **a** • This exercise focuses on five different pronunciations of the letter *a*. SS look at the headwords and complete the chart headings.

cat   horse   car   computer

  - ∘22∘ Ask SS to pronounce the words in each group. Listen and check.
  - SS repeat after the tape.
  - Focus on the words in each group and highlight the common pronunciation / spelling rules:
  - /eɪ/ = *a* + consonant + *e*, *ai*, *ay*
  - /æ/ = consonant + *a* + consonant
  - /ɔː/ = *al*, *aw*
  - /ɑː/ = *ar*
  - /ə/ = words where the *a* syllable is not stressed
  - Get SS to mark the stress on the words.
  - If time elicit more words with these spellings. (See also **Sound bank WB** *p. 81*.)
- **b** • 🎵 *Every breath you take* Focus on the photo and song text. Ask *Do you know this song / singer?*
  - Focus on the words in the box. Ask *Which sound do all these words have?* (/eɪ/).
  - In pairs, SS put the words into three groups. Don't worry about the meaning of the words yet.
  - Check answers.

/eɪ/	/eɪs/	/eɪk/
play	embrace	make
say	replace	take
stay	trace	aches

- **c** • ∘23∘ Play the song. SS listen and write in as many words as they can. Check answers in pairs.
  - Play the song again verse by verse. SS complete any gaps they still have. Tell SS that all the words in each verse rhyme, e.g. *take, make*, etc.

1 take   make   break   take
2 day   say   play   stay
3 aches
4 trace   face   replace   embrace

  - Tell SS to read the song with the **Glossary**. Ask *What's the song about?* A man who misses his ex-lover and thinks about her all the time.

Word stress

- Students read the introduction and focus on the dictionary extract. Highlight the dictionary symbol (ˈ) for syllable stress. Tell SS that it always comes before the stressed syllable.

- Tell SS this is probably more important for communication than pronouncing sounds correctly. If you stress the wrong syllable in a word it can be very difficult to understand.

■ *Tip 3*

- SS read the tip. Demonstrate by saying a few words exaggerating the stressed syllable, e.g. *English*, *pronunciation*, *cassette*, etc.
- Highlight the importance of SS underlining the stress on all new words.

3 Practice: Word stress

- In pairs, SS underline the stressed syllable. Get them to say the words aloud to help them.
- ◦24◦ Play the tape. SS check answers.
- Feedback, with individual SS saying each word aloud and exaggerating the stressed syllable.
  ⚠ Many SS will stress *interesting* /ˈɪntrəstɪŋ/ incorrectly.

tomato	seventy	interesting
picture	important	begin
beautiful	yesterday	angry
nationality	Friday	engineer
sixteen	July	police

Sentence stress

- Write on the board:

  > I'd like a cup of coffee, please.

- Say the three sentences stressing all the words equally. Ask *Is my pronunciation correct?* (it isn't) *Which words do we stress when we speak?* (the words that carry important information).
- Elicit which words to stress.
- Ask *What kind of words are not usually stressed?* (pronouns, articles, and prepositions, e.g. *I, a, of*).

■ *Tip 4*

- SS read the tip. Get them to practise repeating **ex. 4** question 1 a few times.

4 Practice: Sentence stress

a
- ◦25◦ SS listen and underline the stressed words.
- SS check in pairs. Play the tape again.
- Check answers, getting SS to exaggerate the stressed words and to repeat after the tape.

2 What type of music don't you like? I don't like opera.
3 Where do your parents live? They live in Brazil.
4 Have you got any brothers or sisters? I've got two sisters.
5 Have you been to Switzerland? Yes, I have.
6 What did you do last night? I went to a concert.

b
- SS practise in pairs, using the same questions but giving true answers.

Intonation

- SS read the introduction. Explain that English goes up and down more than most other languages.

■ *Tip 5*

- SS read the tip.
- Give examples of friendly and unfriendly intonation with some simple greetings, e.g. *Hello, How are you?*

5 Practice: Intonation

a
- Tell SS they're going to hear two people saying the same sentence. They have to decide which sounds friendly, **A** or **B**.
- ◦26◦ Play the tape. SS write down the number and **A** or **B**. Check answers.

1 Nice to meet you. **A = friendly**
2 What do you do? **B = friendly**
3 What are you going to do tonight? **B = friendly**
4 Did you have a good weekend? **A = friendly**

b
- In pairs, SS turn to 1 🗂 *p. 132*. **A** says a sentence, trying to make the intonation friendly or unfriendly. **B** says *friendly* or *unfriendly*.
- **A** continues with all the phrases. Then they swap.

■ *Tip 6*

- Ask *How can you practice pronunciation outside class?* Elicit some ideas.
- SS read the tip and the four suggestions. Ask *Do you do any of these things?* Encourage SS to try them out, and remind them regularly.

Lesson notes

This lesson is the first in a series of four optional **Focus on ... skills** lessons. Many SS think of pronunciation as a difficult area of English. This lesson looks systematically at the main aspects of good pronunciation and offers practical tips to help SS.

English sounds (SB *p. 142*) The chart provides SS with a reference for the pronunciation of the forty-four sounds of English. It also helps SS to recognize phonetic symbols when they look up words in the dictionary. Use the **classroom poster** (available from OUP) to help SS correct their pronunciation by pointing to the example words.

This lesson will take more than an hour. You could do half the lesson (up to the end of the song) in one class, and do stress and intonation in another class.

Sound bank (WB *p. 81*) This will help SS learn common sound / spelling patterns.

■ Learner-training

Encourage SS to always underline stressed syllables when they record new words, and to mark the pronunciation of words which have an irregular pronunciation, either using a phonetic symbol or a similar sound from their own language.

■ Homework

- SS learn the **English sounds** pictures (SB *p. 142*), and test themselves.
- SS refer to the **Sound bank** (WB *p. 81*) and find more examples of sound / spelling patterns.

Classical experiences

> *Have you ever broken a bone?*
> *Yes, I broke my leg last year.*

Lesson aims

Grammar	Present perfect v. past simple
Vocabulary	*ever / never*, irregular past participles, classical music
Pronunciation	/əʊ/, /e/, /ʌ/, /ɪ/
Revision	Past simple

Lesson plan

■ Warmer: ® Irregular verbs
- SS revise 📖 **Irregular verbs A** *p.141*. In pairs, SS test each other. A: *go.* B: *went*

1 Presentation: Irregular past participles
- SS turn to 📖 **Irregular verbs B** *p.141*, and complete the chart with more irregular past participles.
- Check the meaning and drill pronunciation of those with phonetics.

■ PRONUNCIATION
- Check SS remember the four headwords and sounds.
- Focus on and elicit the vowel sound in each past participle. SS match two past participles to each headword.
- 🔊 **1** SS listen and check.

phone	spoken	**up**	done	drunk
egg	read	said	**fish**	driven written

2 Skills: Reading
- Focus on the photo. Ask *What's he doing?* Elicit / teach *He's conducting (an orchestra).* Ask *Can you play an instrument?*
- Give SS a minute to read the introduction to the magazine article and answer the four questions.
- Check answers.

> 1 He was a (professional) pianist.
> 2 He's a conductor.
> 3 Austria.
> 4 Two months a year only.

3 Presentation: *Have you ever…?*
a
- SS quickly read four extracts from an interview with Jan Latham-Koenig and match each extract to a picture, A to D. Give them a two minute time limit.
- Use the pictures / mime to check SS understand <u>hitch</u>-hike (*v.*), <u>dangerous</u>, <u>ankle</u>, <u>crutches</u>, <u>logic</u>, <u>agent</u>, <u>training</u> = professional education

> 1 B 2 C 3 A 4 D

b
- Focus on the questions in the interview. Pre-teach *bone, at first sight*, and *audience*.
- SS complete the interview with the missing questions, as in the example.

- Check answers.

> 2 Qii Have you ever fallen in love at first sight?
> 3 Qiii Have you ever broken a bone?
>   Q What did the audience think?
> 4 Qiv Have you read any Sherlock Holmes stories?
>   Q Which one did you like best?

- Focus on **V** *ever / never*. Check SS understand that *ever / never* = at any / no time in your life. Highlight that *ever* is used with a ⊟ verb and *never* with a ⊞ verb NOT ~~I haven't never …~~

4 Practice: *Have you ever …?*
a
- Tell SS to cover the extracts and look at the pictures. Elicit the four *Have you ever…?* questions (i to iv blue). Drill pronunciation, making sure SS stress the important words, e.g. *Have you <u>ever</u> <u>broken</u> a <u>bone</u>?*

b
- SS ask you the questions. Try to answer *Yes, I have.* to one question, even if it's not true. When you say *Yes, I have.*, get them to ask you follow-up questions. They then stand up and ask other SS the questions to try to find someone who has done each thing.
- Feedback. Ask *Who has …?* Find out from individual SS a bit more about their experiences. The emphasis should be on communication. Don't worry about mistakes at this stage.

■ GRAMMAR FOCUS
Present perfect or past simple?
a
- SS focus on all the questions in the four extracts, and answer grammar questions 1 and 2.

> 1 Present perfect.   2 Past simple

b
- Go through the rules, and get them to translate the examples. Ask *Is your language similar?*

  Tip To make the concept clear you could at this point refer SS to the time lines and explanations in **Grammar file 2 (SB** *p.37*) and go through the examples there with them.

PRACTICE
a
- SS write three true sentences in the present perfect about their experiences. They shouldn't mention 'when'. They then write a second sentence in the past simple saying when they did each thing.
- SS compare their sentences. Check answers.

b
- SS complete the dialogue with verbs in the past simple or present perfect.
- SS compare with a partner. Check answers.

> 1 been   2 went   3 Did you enjoy   4 was
> 5 seen   6 saw   7 took   8 was
> 9 loved

5 Practice: Present perfect and past simple

a • On the board, write a list of six countries/cities, three you've been to and three you haven't, in jumbled order. Get SS to ask you *Have you ever been to …?* If you say *Yes, I have.*, elicit the question *When did you go there?* Elicit some more follow-up questions, e.g. *Did you like it?* etc. Help SS with prompts if necessary, e.g. */ like it? Who / go with? Where / go? How / get there?.*

 • SS write their own list of six places (cities or countries). Remind them to jumble the order.

b • SS exchange lists with a partner. Focus on the example dialogue, and get them to have similar conversations about the places on their partner's list. They take turns to ask questions.

 • Feedback to find out any interesting places they've been to.

6 Skills: Listening

a • Tell SS to look at the photo. Ask *Who do you think it is?* (Jan Latham-Koenig) *When?* (a long time ago). Tell SS they're going to hear him talking about an experience he had in Barcelona.

 • Give SS a minute to read through the multiple-choice questions. Elicit the meaning of *port*, *ferry captain*, *birth certificate*, and *driving licence*.

 • ˚ 2 ˚ Play the tape. SS choose the right answer and compare in pairs. Play the tape again to check.

> 1 c 2 b 3 a 4 b 5 c
> Tapescript **SB Listening** *p. 126*

b • Ask *What happened in the end?* (he caught his ferry - just!).

 • If time, SS check the tapescript. What didn't they understand?

7 Personalization: Interesting experiences

 • SS in pairs, A and B. SS turn to ▶◀ *Have you ever …?* A *p. 120*, B *p. 123*. Give them a minute to read the instructions and questions, and check that they understand them.

 • A asks B the first *Have you ever …?* question. If B answers *Yes, I have.*, A asks further questions in the past simple. B then asks a question, etc.

 Tip Fast finishers can swap roles and interview each other with their partner's list. Make sure they ask the questions in a different order.

 • Feedback. Asking SS to talk about interesting experiences their partners have had, e.g. *Igor won the lottery last year. He bought a new car.*

Lesson notes

In this lesson, SS move on from **1D** (present perfect questions and answers) to *Have you ever …?* + follow-up questions in the past simple, e.g. *When did you …?*

Present perfect or past simple? Conversations in English often start with a present perfect question and then continue in the past simple. Common error *Have you ever been to Africa? ~~When have you been there?~~* The distinction to get clear in SS minds is that, in the first question, you are asking about an experience at any time in the past, but that in the follow-up questions you are talking about a specific time, and must use the past simple, e.g. *When did you go there?*

been* and *gone SS may still have problems with this. Refer them back to the **Grammar focus** in **1D** *p. 19*.

ever / never These adverbs are often used with the present perfect, referring to at any / no time in your life. Common error *~~I haven't never been to Italy~~ i.e. using two negatives.*

Extras

True or false! SS in pairs, A and B. Tell As to note down six interesting experiences they've had, three true and three false. Then A tells B about the experiences as if they were all true, e.g. *I've been to Chile. I went there in 1990.*, etc. B listens to A and asks a lot of questions to find out which three are false. Then they swap. Demonstrate yourself first and elicit questions from the class to see if you're telling the truth.

Have you ever …? P *p. 152* Mingle activity. *Have you ever…?* questions with past tense follow-up questions. Instructions *p. 129*.

Books-closed presentation

Present perfect v. past simple For flashcard presentations, see **Introduction** *p. 11*.

 • Do after **Pronunciation**. Copy the pictures from **Picture bank 2A** *p. 205*.

 • Show the six pictures in turn, asking *Have you ever …?* Elicit *Yes, I have. / No, I haven't.* Then show picture 1 again. Ask *Have you ever been to Africa?* If any SS answer *Yes, I have.*, ask *When did you go? Where did you stay?*, etc.

 • Repeat this procedure with the other pictures.

 • Show the class the flashcards again one at a time. SS ask you the questions. Make sure their follow-up questions are all in the past simple.

 • Stick the cards onto the board. SS ask and answer in pairs.

 • Elicit and write-up the six questions. Then start **ex. 2**.

 ■ **Learner-training**

Remind SS to read the relevant part of the **Grammar file** after each lesson. It often has a fuller explanation of the **Grammar focus**, with more examples.

 ■ **Homework**

SS do **WB 2A** *p. 16* and **Listen and speak 2A**.

> *I don't have to get up very early.*

Lesson aims

Grammar	*have to* / *don't have to* (obligation)
Vocabulary	Jobs: adjectives (*well-paid*, etc.), verbs (*earn*, etc.), nouns (*uniform*, etc.)
Pronunciation	/f/, /ə/, /hæftə/
Revision	Jobs, present simple
Optional materials	P What do they have to do? (**ex. 5**)

Lesson plan

■ Warmer: *job* or *work?*

● Write these gapped sentences on the board:

> 1 What's your _____?
> 2 Where do you _____?
> 3 I can't go out tonight. I've got a lot of _____ to do.
> 4 My brother's got a very good _____.

● SS copy the sentences and complete with *job* or *work*.
● Check answers. Highlight that *job* is a countable noun, but that work is either a verb or an uncountable noun NOT ~~a work~~.

> **1** job **2** work **3** work **4** job

1 Revision: Jobs

a ● Focus on pictures 1 to 5. Elicit the jobs. Write them onto the board, and mark the stress.

> **1** dentist **2** (concert) pianist **3** taxi-driver
> **4** chef/cook **5** police-officer

b ● In pairs, SS list five more jobs (or more).
● Feedback all their answers onto the board. Ask *Which jobs would you (most) like / hate? Why?*

2 Presentation: *have to* / *don't have to*

a ● SS read the introduction to the article. Focus on the photos. Ask *Can you guess their jobs?*
● SS read the article and complete the sentences with 'Carla' or 'Danielle'. Encourage SS to guess the meaning of new vocabulary from context.
● Check answers. Be prepared to explain / translate *uniform, concentrate, at least, get the chance, carry, still, both, including, although.*

> **1** Danielle **2** Carla **3** Danielle **4** Carla
> **5** Danielle **6** Carla

b ● ·3· Ask *What do you think they do?* Write SS' suggestions on the board. Play the tape. SS listen and check. Elicit the spelling and pronunciation of *interpreter* /ɪnˈtɜːprɪtə/.

> Carla's a bus driver.   Danielle's an interpreter.

3 Presentation: Job adjectives

a ● In pairs, SS read the text again to find ten adjectives which describe the two jobs. They decide if they're ⊞ or ⊟, as in the examples.
Elicit the adjectives onto the board in two columns and elicit the stress / correct pronunciation.

⊞	⊟
fun	tiring
important	badly-paid
well-paid	dangerous
satisfying	stressful

⚠ Explain that *tiring* = makes you feel tired.

b ● In pairs, SS look at the list of jobs from **ex. 1** on the board. They choose an adjective to describe each job. Elicit a few examples, e.g. *dentist – well-paid.*
● Feedback to see if SS agree.

■ GRAMMAR FOCUS

have to / *don't have to*

a ● SS circle five examples of *have to* in the article, and translate the phrases into their language.

b ● SS complete the chart. Drill an example of each form. Focus especially on the use of *don't* / *doesn't* and *do* / *does* in ⊟, ❓, and ✓✗.

don't **have** to	Yes, I **do**.
has to	No, he **doesn't**.

c ● Get SS to read the rules and look at the examples.

PRACTICE

a ● SS choose and write six sentences based on the items in the chart, as in the example. Check answers.

b ● Drill the question form with the expressions.

> T *get up early*
> SS *Do you have to get up early?*

● Elicit short answers from some SS. Ask one student a follow-up question, e.g. *Why?* Elicit a response.

> B *Do you have to get up early?*
> S *Yes, I do.*
> T *Why?*
> S *Because I start work at eight o'clock.*

● In pairs, SS ask each other the questions. Tell them to ask follow-up questions when they can.

■ PRONUNCIATION

a ● ·4· SS listen and repeat. Elicit a few more words with the sounds, e.g. /f/ co**ff**ee **F**riday li**ft** geogra**ph**y, /ə/ pictur**e**, wat**e**r, Octob**e**r, mirr**o**r.
● Highlight that the typical spelling for /f/ is *f*, but can also be *ph* (*gh* as in *enough* is less usual).

- Explain to SS that /ə/ is the most common sound in English. It often occurs before or after an unstressed syllable, e.g. arrive, banana, student, photographer, etc. It can be spelt by almost any vowel (see **Sound bank WB** p.142).

b • ˙5˙ SS listen and write three sentences. Check answers.

> 1 I have to get up early every day.
> 2 We don't have to come to class tomorrow.
> 3 Does she have to work on Saturdays?

c • Play the tape again. Ask *How do you pronounce 'have to'* (/ˈhæftə/).

4 Practice: Listening

a • Tell SS they're going to listen to a radio quiz show.
  • ˙6˙ SS listen to the introduction and answer two questions to check they understand the rules.

> 1 ten 2 Yes, No, or Sometimes.
> Tapescript **SB Listening** p.126

  • Ask some more questions, e.g. *What happens if they guess his job? What happens if they don't guess his job?*

b • Focus on the **Job analysis** form. Be prepared to explain / translate *analysis, responsibilities, qualifications, equipment, manage* (v.).
  Explain that in the quiz, the panel can ask only ten of the questions on the form. Get SS to listen and say which questions they ask. Then they tick if Martin answers *Yes*, or cross if he answers *No*.
  • ˙7˙ Play the tape once. SS compare answers.
  • Play the tape again. Check answers by getting SS to say, e.g. *He doesn't have to get up early.*

> get up early ✗   work outside ✗
> work at weekends ✓   travel ✗
>   (sometimes)   speak other languages ✓
> work at night ✓   (sometimes)
> wear a uniform ✓   well-paid ✗
> have special   tiring ✓
>   qualifications ✗
> Tapescript **SB Listening** p.126

c • In pairs, SS guess Martin's job. Elicit different guesses onto the board.
  • ˙8˙ Play the last part of the show. SS listen and check if they guessed right.

> B Time's up. What's his job?
> N We think he's a hotel receptionist.
> B Sorry panel, that's not the right answer. So what do you do, Martin?
> M I'm **a waiter**.
> B Congratulations Martin. You win £500.

5 Practice: Game

- SS in groups of three. A chooses a job, and B and C use the form to ask ten questions. A can only answer *Yes, No,* or *Sometimes*. B and C try to guess the job.
- SS swap roles. Encourage short answers (*Yes I do. / No it isn't.* etc.), not just *Yes. / No.*

Tip You could use the pictures in P **What do they have to do?** (see **Extras**) to help SS choose a job. If most of your SS work, you could use the **Job analysis** form for them to interview you or each other about their own jobs.

6 Personalization: Writing

- SS write a paragraph about their job, or about a friend / family member's job, using the article as a model. Remind them to use third person *has to / doesn't have to* with the latter. Set a time limit, e.g. ten minutes.
- When SS finish writing tell them to check for mistakes, and then to exchange with another student to read and check for mistakes.

Lesson notes

SS learn to use *have to / don't have to* to talk about obligations in the context of jobs.

have to / don't have to SS usually find the form more difficult than the meaning. Common errors ~~I've to wear a uniform. He hasn't to work on Saturdays.~~

must / have to SS may ask about the difference between *must* and *have to*. Explain that in ＋ (*must* and *have to*) they are very similar, although *must* is not normally used to talk about general obligations, e.g. at work. In － (*mustn't* and *don't have to*) they are completely different. Compare *You mustn't tell Mary.* = *Don't tell Mary.* and *You don't have to tell Mary.* = *It isn't necessary to tell Mary. must / mustn't* are taught in 8☐.

Extras

What do they have to do? P p.153 Twenty job cards. SS define what each person has to do. Instructions p.130.

Books-closed presentation

have to / don't have to (**obligation**) For flashcard presentations, see **Introduction** p.11.
- Do before **ex.2**. Copy the pictures from **Picture bank 2B** p.206.
- Show the pictures in turn and ask *What does he / she do?* to quickly elicit the jobs.
- Then show picture 1 again. Ask *What does a nurse have to do?*. Elicit and drill *She has to (wear a uniform)*.
- Repeat with the other pictures.
- Stick the cards on the board. SS ask and answer in pairs.
- Elicit and write the six *have to* sentences. Then do **ex.2**.

■ Learner-training

Remind SS to write down and learn jobs and job adjectives. Test them at the beginning of the next class.

■ Homework

SS do **WB 2B** p.17 and **Listen and speak 2B**.
Writing: **ex.6** SS write a paragraph about their job.

Going back to the past

*They can eat hot dogs
but they can't have TVs.*

Lesson aims

Grammar	*can / can't* (permission), impersonal *you*
Vocabulary	Appearance: *short hair*, etc., clothes
Pronunciation	*can / can't*: weak / strong forms, sentence stress
Revision	*have to*, colours, clothes

Lesson plan

■ Warmer: ® Jobs / job adjectives

a ● Test SS on the job vocabulary from the previous lesson. Give definitions of five jobs for SS to guess, e.g. *He isn't very well-paid. He wears a black and white uniform. He works in a restaurant.* (a waiter). SS write them down. Check spelling.

b ● SS write five + and five − adjectives for jobs.

1 Introduction: Reading about the Amish

a ● Focus on the photo. Ask *Where are they?* (on a farm / in the USA) *Do you know anything about the Amish* /ˈeɪmɪʃ/? (they're a sect) *Have you seen the film 'Witness'?* (a 1985 film starring Harrison Ford and Kelly McGillis, which takes place in an Amish community).

b ● SS read paragraph 1 to find out three things about the Amish. Encourage them to guess new vocabulary from the context.

● SS to cover the text. Elicit what they remember, e.g. *The Amish come from Pennsylvania. They live together on farms.* etc.

● Go through paragraph 1. Be prepared to explain / translate *although, turn their backs on, technology, strict.*

2 Presentation: *can / can't* (permission)

a ● Tell SS the Amish have some unusual rules. Give them a minute to read about them in paragraph 2.

b ● SS cover the text and, in pairs, complete the chart from memory with the words and appropriate verbs.

● Check answers. Be prepared to explain / translate *oil lamps, light* (v.), *allowed* (= can), *tractors, baseball, religious.*

They can …	They can't …
eat hot dogs	use electricity
go to the doctor's	have a phone
play baseball	have a TV
use banks	

■ PRONUNCIATION

a ● · 9 · Focus on the sound in the three headwords. SS listen and repeat the sounds and sentences. They <u>can't</u> <u>drive</u>. /ɑː/ car can't

They can <u>use</u> <u>horses</u>. Can they <u>play</u> baseball? /ə/
computer can
Yes, they <u>can</u>. /æ/ cat /æ/ can

● Highlight the three pronunciations of *can.* When stressed it's pronounced /kæn/ in + short answers, and /kɑːnt/ in − . When *can* is not stressed (in + and ?) it's pronounced /kən/.

● SS say the sentences again. Encourage them to exaggerate the long /ɑː/ sound in *can't*, and to stress both *can't* and the following verb.

b ● Tell SS they're going to hear six sentences with *can* or *can't.* Get SS to write down the numbers 1 to 6. They listen and write + (for *can*) or − (for *can't*), as in the example.

● ·10· Play the tape twice. Check answers.

Tip You could do this as a dictation and get SS to write the sentences. Pause the tape after each sentence to give SS time to write.

1 You can use my phone.	+
2 We can't go tonight.	−
3 You can park here.	+
4 I can do it for you tomorrow.	+
5 The Amish can't drive cars.	−
6 She can't wear jeans at work.	−

For extra practice, SS say the same sentences to their partner, making them positive or negative. Their partner has to decide if they are saying a positive or a negative sentence.

■ GRAMMAR FOCUS
can / can't (permission)

a ● Focus on the examples. Check SS understand *allowed* (use L1 if necessary or SS can use their dictionaries). Remind SS that *can / can't* is followed by the infinitive without *to*, and is the same for all persons.

● Read the rule.

b ● Elicit the other uses of *can.* e.g. *Can I have a copy, please? I can't play the piano.*

Tip Refer SS to ⊙◄◄9 (**SB** *p. 4*) for full tables and rules if necessary.

PRACTICE

● SS read the sentences and complete with *can / can't.*

● Check answers. Get SS to read the sentences aloud, focusing on the pronunciation of *can / can't.*

1 can 2 can't 3 Can / can't 4 can't	
5 Can, can 6 can	

3 Presentation: Appearance and clothes

a ● In pairs, SS turn to ▯ **The body A** *p. 136.* They match the words and pictures, and test a partner on colours. Drill pronunciation of the words with phonetics.

> **B** long / straight / dark hair   **C** short / fair / curly hair   **D** beard   **E** moustache

> **2** a T-shirt   **3** a shirt   **4** a sweater   **5** a belt
> **6** a button   **7** a zip   **8** a pocket   **9** a mini-skirt
> **10** a dress   **11** trousers   **12** jeans   **13** pants
> **14** socks   **15** shorts   **16** a bra   **17** tights
> **18** a suit   **19** a tie   **20** a (leather) jacket
> **21** a (rain)coat   **22** a scarf   **23** a tracksuit
> **24** shoes   **25** trainers

> **1** black   **2** brown   **3** gold   **4** green   **5** grey
> **6** orange   **7** pink   **8** purple   **9** red   **10** silver
> **11** white   **12** yellow   **13** blue   dark / light

- In pairs, SS stand back to back and describe from memory to their partner what he / she's wearing.

b
- SS look at the photo of the Amish again and describe what they're wearing.
- Feedback. Ask *Do you like their clothes? Why do you think they wear these kinds of clothes?*

4 Practice: *can / can't*

a
- SS read the eight sentences in pairs and guess if they're true or false. Make sure they don't look at the rest of the text.

b
- SS read paragraphs 3 and 4 and check answers.
- Feedback. Ask SS to correct the false sentences. See if any pairs guessed all eight correctly. Encourage SS to guess the meaning of new words from context. Be prepared to explain / translate *curl* (v. from *curly*), *wedding*, *higher education*, *neighbour*, *old-fashioned*, *habits*, *destroy*, *community*, *grow*.

> **1** T   **2** F   **3** F   **4** T   **5** T   **6** T   **7** F   **8** F

- Ask *What do / don't you like about the Amish way of life? Would you like to live in an Amish community?*

5 Practice: Reading and listening

- Focus on the incomplete rules. Get SS to look at the cartoon, and read quickly through the rules. Ask *Which rule is this?* (rule 2).
- Elicit the meaning and pronunciation of *vote* (v.), *motorway*, *helmet* /ˈhelmɪt/ and *prison* /ˈprɪzn/.
- In pairs, SS try to guess which countries the rules are from.
- Feedback to see if the class agrees on the answers. There are sure to be different opinions.
- ○ 11 ○ Play the tape for SS to check.

> **2** Iceland   **3** Japan   **4** Germany   **5** Australia
> **6** Sweden   **7** Britain   **8** Israel   **9** Singapore

■ Grammar box: Impersonal *you*

- Write on the board:

> How do you spell it?
> You can buy stamps in a post office.
> You don't have to work on public holidays.

Ask *What does 'you' mean in these sentences?* (= people in general). Contrast with the personal *you*, e.g. *How are you?*

- Focus on the **Grammar box**. Get SS to read the example.

6 Personalization: Talk about rules

- **1** Read out the first rule from **ex. 5**. Ask *Is the rule the same in your country?* If it's different, ask SS to explain how.
- **2** Ask *Do you think this rule is good or bad? Why?*
  - SS discuss the other rules in pairs or small groups.
  - Feedback on rules they agreed / disagreed with. Get a class vote on the silliest / most sensible rule.
  - Ask *What rules have you got at home and at school / work?* SS tell each other about their rules and feedback to see out who has the strictest rules.

Lesson notes

SS have already learned *can / can't* for requests and ability. In this lesson they learn to use it for permission in the context of rules governing the Amish community.

Impersonal *you* This use of *you* e.g. *How do you spell it?* is very common, as English does not have an impersonal pronoun.

Extras

Find twelve differences P *p. 154* An information gap activity to revise body and clothes vocabulary, and describing people. Instructions *p. 130*.

Books-closed presentation

can / can't **(permission)** For flashcard presentations, see **Introduction** *p. 11*. Do before **ex. 1**. Books closed. Copy the pictures from **Picture bank 2C**.

- Ask *Where can you see these signs?* (in the street, a hospital, etc.). Point to each sign in turn and ask *What does this mean?* Elicit the six *can / can't* sentences.
- Drill pronunciation, especially weak /kən/ and strong /kɑːnt/. Ask *What does 'can' mean in these sentences?* (it is / isn't allowed).
- Elicit the sentences onto the board for SS to copy. Then start **ex. 1**.

■ Learner-training

SS have learnt a lot of new words from the ✏. Give SS some ideas for revising the words, e.g. *Cover the words and test yourself. / Write any words you find hard to remember on pieces of card, with a translation, and use them to test yourself.*

■ Homework

SS do **WB 2C** *p. 18* and **Listen and speak 2C**

> *A civil servant is a person who works for the government.*

Lesson aims

Grammar	Relative pronouns: *who / which / where*
Vocabulary	Shapes: *round*, etc., materials: *wood*, etc.
Revision	article: *a/an*, small objects
Optional materials	A bag of objects of different shapes and materials: round, square, rectangular, plastic, wood, glass (Books-closed presentation)

Lesson plan

■ **Warmer: ℞ Facial features, clothes**

- In pairs, SS test each other on ▯ **The body A** *p.136*.
- SS describe what their partner's wearing.

1 **Presentation: Shapes / materials**

- Books open. Focus on pictures 1 to 5. Ask *What are they?* (a ring, a table, a plastic bag, a mirror, a CD case).
- Focus on **V** **What shape is it?** Ask the question and illustrate by pointing to the pictures to teach *It's round / square / rectangular*. Drill pronunciation by miming a shape and getting SS to say the words.
- Teach *What's it made of?* Drill *It's made of metal / wood / plastic / glass.* by pointing to things in the class (a key, the door, a ruler, pencil, the window, etc.).
- In pairs, SS make sentences about pictures 1 to 5 using a noun and an adjective.
- Check answers.

> 1 It's round. It's made of metal.
> 2 It's square. It's made of wood.
> 3 It's rectangular. It's made of plastic.
> 4 It's rectangular. It's made of glass.
> 5 It's square. It's made of plastic.

2 **Presentation: *who / which / where***

a
- Draw a stick figure labelled STUDENT on the board. Ask *What's a student? Is it a person, thing, or place?* Elicit *It's a person.* Ask *What does he / she do?* Elicit *He / she studies.* On the board, show SS how to join the two sentences:

> A student is a person. He or she studies.
> A student is a person <u>who</u> studies.

- Do the same for *which* and *where*, using CAMERA (= a thing which takes photos) and ZOO (= a place where animals live).
- ·**12**· Tell SS to listen to the rules of a game. Play the tape twice and ask *How do you play the game?* (one person has to define/explain six words on a card to another person – he / she can't use any of the words on the card – the other person has to try to guess the words).

- Check SS understand *define*. Teach the noun *definition*.

> Tapescript **SB Listening** *p.127*

b
- ·**13**· Tell SS they're going to listen to two people playing the game and write down the six words that the man describes. Tell SS to write 1 to 6 on a piece of paper. Explain that the correct answers have been replaced by a bleep on the tape. Play it at least twice.

> Tapescript **SB Listening** *p.127*

- Check answers. See if SS can remember the definitions.

> 1 a civil servant 2 a chemist's 3 a watch
> 4 a zebra 5 a church 6 a taxi-driver

■ GRAMMAR FOCUS

Relative pronouns

a
- Focus on the examples. SS complete the gaps with *who*, *which*, or *where*.

> It's a person **who** works for the government.
> It's a thing **which** tells you the time.
> It's a place **where** you can buy aspirins.

- Refer SS to the key phrase at the top of the page.
- Highlight the silent *w* in *who* /huː/.

b
- Focus on the rule and example. Explain that we use relative pronouns to make one longer sentence from two shorter ones.

PRACTICE

- In pairs, SS complete the sentences with *who*, *which*, or *where* and one of the words.
- Check answers.

> 1 a cooker / which   2 a cook / who
> 3 a trainers / which
> 4 a thief / who   an estate agent's / where

- Drill the pronunciation of *thief* /θiːf/ and *estate agents* /ɪsˈteɪtˈeɪdʒənts/.

3 **Practice: Puzzle**

- Elicit / teach *puzzle* and *clues* (you could mime a detective looking for clues).
- In threes, SS complete the crossword and discover the mystery word.

Tip If SS are having problems with a particular clue, give them the first letter(s) of the word to help.

> | 1 END | 2 HOTEL |
> |---|---|
> | 3 LIFTS | 4 PICTURE |
> | 5 ORANGE | 6 DENTIST |
> | 7 CREDIT CARD | 8 BORING |
> | 9 BUTTONS | 10 THANK YOU |
>
> The mystery word is DEFINITION.

- Get SS to cover the clues and look only at the crossword. In pairs, they try to remember the ten clues. Then elicit the clues from the class.

4 Practice: Writing definitions

- Focus on **V** Definitions. Check that SS understand all the expressions.
- In pairs, SS use the expressions in the **V** box to write definitions of the six words and phrases. Do 1 and 2 with the class on the board first.
- Elicit SS' definitions onto the board.

> **Suggested definitions:**
> 1 **sleep** It's a verb you do when you're tired, with your eyes closed.
> 2 **a bus stop** It's a place where you wait for a bus.
> 3 **a banana** It's a noun. You can eat it. It's a kind of fruit. It's yellow.
> 4 **a knife** It's a thing which you use to cut things. It's made of metal. You can use it when you eat.
> 5 **Excuse me.** It's an expression. For example, you use it when you want to talk to a person in the street.
> 6 **nurses** They're people who work in a hospital. They look after sick people.

- Explain to SS that this language is very useful when they don't know a word in English.

5 Practice: Giving definitions

- In pairs, SS turn to ▶◀ **Crossword** A *p. 120* B *p. 123*. They should sit so that they can't see each other's books.
- Both SS have the same crossword but with different words filled in. Make sure SS understand *across* and *down*. They have to ask each other for definitions of their missing words, without saying the word itself.

> A What's 1 down?
> B It's a person who ...
> A Is it ...?
> B Yes, that's right. What's 2 down?

- Give SS a minute to check they understand the words they have to define. Remind them to ask *How do you spell it?* if they aren't sure.
- When they've both finished, tell them to compare their crosswords and check each others' answers.

Lesson notes

Students learn to use *who, which,* and *where* to join two sentences in relative clauses, through the context of a describing game and a crossword puzzle. The lesson also teaches SS some language to define / explain words. This is a very useful language skill which helps SS to keep going in a conversation when they don't know a word in English.

***that* / omission of the relative pronoun** In conversation *that* often replaces *who* or *which* in defining relative causes. However, at this level it's a good idea to get SS to use *who* and *which*. Omission of relative pronouns in sentences like *He's the man I love* is not taught here.

Extras

The describing game 🎲 *p. 208*

- In pairs, SS play the game modelled in **ex. 2**. Use the following words:

  A zip   sunbathe   an airport   a mouse
     a farmer   jewellery

  B a pocket   a beard   go sightseeing
     a flight attendant   university   purple

  Tip If your classroom doesn't allow your SS to sit back to back, write the words on pieces of card, or use P **What's the word?**

What's the word? P *p. 155* Picture and word clues to use in **The describing game** above. Instructions *p. 130*.

Books-closed presentation

Shapes / materials
- Books closed. Copy these shapes on the board:

- Teach the question *What shape is it?* Elicit *It's round / rectangular / square.* Drill pronunciation.
- Now use classroom objects, e.g. a key, the table, a pen, the window, to teach and drill *What's it made of? It's made of metal / wood / plastic / glass.* (Alternatively, you could bring in objects from home to do this presentation.)
- Drill both questions with more objects, e.g. a cassette box, a coin, the door, etc. Write both questions and answers on the board. Then start **ex. 1**.

  Tip Write up the key words in phonetics to drill pronunciation before you write up the words themselves.

■ Learner-training
Get into the habit of giving SS definition of new words (rather than a translation) when they ask what a word means. This will encourage SS to become familiar with the technique and use it with more confidence themselves.

■ Homework
SS do **WB 2D** *p. 19* and **Listen and speak 2D**.

Writing: Clues SS write five clues for words / phrases to be used in the next class for other SS to guess.

Lesson aims

Function	Changing money, getting a train / taxi
Vocabulary	High numbers, money
Revision	*What time ...? this / that / these / those*

Lesson plan

■ Warmer: Prices

- Write these prices in pounds sterling and US dollars on the board:

£1.00	$1
1p	1c
10p	10c
£1.50	$1.50
£15	$15
£100	$100

- Check that SS recognize the dollar and pound symbols. SS practise saying them correctly.
- Elicit the answers, together with the following rules:
  - p = /piː/ BUT c = cents NOT /siː/
  - We don't say 'p' for amounts over a pound (£1.50 = one (pound) fifty) OR 'cents' for amounts over a dollar ($1.50 = one dollar fifty).

a / one pound	a / one dollar
one p	a / one cent
10p	ten cents
one pound fifty	a / one dollar fifty
fifteen pounds	fifteen dollars
a / one hundred pounds	a / one hundred dollars

- Highlight the hyphen in two figure numbers, e.g. seventy-five.
- In pairs, SS write amounts in pounds and dollars for their partner to say.
- You may want to focus quickly on the English pronunciation of different currencies, e.g. /fræŋks/, /pəˈseɪtəz/, /ˈlɪərə/, etc.

1 Presentation: High numbers

a
- ⟨·14·⟩ Books open. Focus on 1 to 5. SS listen to five short extracts and circle the number they hear. Play the tape once.
- SS check in pairs.
- Play it again and check answers. Ask *Where is she? / are they?* for each situation.

> **1** 15 (at an airport)   **2** $60 (at a theatre box office)
> **3** 17G (on a plane)   **4** 40 (at a station)
> **5** £2.90 (in a cafe)
> Tapescript **SB Listening** *p.127*

b
- SS turn to 📖 **High numbers** *p.135* and complete the numbers.

- Check answers and drill pronunciation as necessary. Highlight:
  - *a* or *one hundred* (both are possible but we normally say *a*).
  - *and* after *hundred* e.g *a hundred and twenty*.
  - the singular form of *hundred*, *thousand*, and *million*. NOT ~~two millions~~.

> two   and ten   hundred and   and thirty-three
> six hundred and forty-four
> seven thousand and thirteen
> eleven, eight hundred   12,555
> fourteen thousand
> sixty-six thousand seven hundred and seventy-nine
> thousand   million   8,750,382

- Write some high numbers in words and figures on the board for SS to say.

2 Presentation and practice: Changing money

a
- Focus on the photo. Ask if SS remember the Dutchman from **1**📖. Ask *Who is he?* (Pieter Okker) *Where was he before?* (at Gatwick airport) *What happened to him there?* (one of his suitcases didn't arrive) *What's he going to do now?* (change some money).
- In pairs, SS read the dialogue and guess the missing words.
- Feedback, eliciting SS' ideas for each of the eight gaps onto the board. Don't confirm yet.
- ⟨·15·⟩ Play the tape for SS to check.

> P Hello. Can I **change** 300 US dollars, **please?**
> A Certainly, sir. Could I have your passport, please?
> P **Here** you are. **What's** the **exchange** rate?
> A A pound is one dollar fifty. **That's** £200.
> P Thanks ... **How** do I **get** to the station?

b
- Drill the dialogue, especially certainly /ˈsɜːtənlɪ/ and exchange /ɪksˈtʃeɪndʒ/.
- Practise with the class. Play the role of the clerk and change their money for them. Then play Pieter.
- SS roleplay the dialogue using the four amounts on the page. They swap roles.

> **Tip** Don't allow SS to get bogged down by maths. If the exchange rate between pounds and the SS' own currency makes for simple mathematics use sensible amounts of local currency instead.

3 Skills: Reading

- Ask if SS remember where Gatwick airport is (about 30km south of London). Tell SS *You're at Gatwick airport. You've changed some money. What do you have to do next?* (get to the city centre / to the hotel) *How can you get there?* (by train, bus, or taxi).
- Give SS a minute to read the text and answer the three questions.

- Check answers. Be prepared to explain / translate *service*(s), *journey*, high *frequency*, *required*.

> 1 Every 15 minutes during the day, every 30 minutes early in the morning / late at night.
> 2 35 minutes.
> 3 No.

4 Skills: Listening

a
- Tell SS Pieter's going to buy a ticket for the Gatwick Express. Get them to look at the chart. Check SS understand *destination*. They predict answers for 1 and 6 from what they've just read.
- ·16· Play the tape once. SS listen and complete the information.
- Play the tape again. Check answers.

> 1 Victoria station
> 2 single
> 3 £9.80
> 4 at 11.20, in ten minutes
> 5 platform 7
> 6 about half an hour
> Tapescript **SB Listening** *p. 127*

b
- Elicit the dialogue from the SS. Ask *Who's speaking?* (Pieter / ticket clerk). Ask *Who speaks first?* (Pieter) *What does he say?* (The centre of London, please.) *What does the ticket clerk say?* (All trains go to Victoria station). Continue with the rest of the dialogue. SS will need help with the last question *How long does it take?*
- In pairs, SS practise the dialogue. Let them read the tapescript if necessary.

> **Tip** Write P, A, etc. on the board and write up word cues for each line to help SS remember.

5 Presentation and practice: Getting a taxi

a
- Books closed. Tell SS Pieter's now arrived at Victoria station in London. Ask *Can you remember the name of his hotel from 1*⌂*?* (the Hilton).
- ·17· Play the tape once. SS listen to Pieter and the taxi-driver. Ask *What's the problem?* (the taxi-driver hasn't got any change).

b
- SS read the dialogue. Focus on the words in *italics*. Ask *What do they mean?*
- Check answers. Refer SS to ⊙◄◄ 22 (**SB** *p. 7*) if necessary.

> these – Pieter's cases
> that – the cost of the journey
> this – a large note (= money)

c
- Tell SS to cover the dialogue and look only at the word prompts to the left. Elicit and drill the dialogue line by line.
- In pairs, SS use the prompts to practise.

6 Vocabulary: Travel phrasebook 2

- SS turn to **SB** *p. 132* and translate the phrases.

> **Tip** Whenever you've got time at the end of these lessons, ask SS to tell you what phrases they think are in the Travel phrasebook before they turn and do it.

Lesson notes

We follow Pieter from Gatwick airport into London by train. SS learn common expressions for changing money, and for travelling by train or by taxi. They also read part of an authentic leaflet about the *Gatwick Express*.

How long does it / the journey take? This expression is introduced here as a set phrase but is focused on grammatically in **3C**.

Extras

High number dictations Dictate five high numbers for the class to write in figures. Then get SS in pairs to dictate five more numbers over 100 to each other.

From London to Amsterdam [P] *p. 156* Do instead of **ex. 4b** or for revision later. An information gap activity with authentic train, bus, ferry and plane times and prices from London to Amsterdam. Instructions *p. 130*.

Books-closed presentation

Changing money
- Do before **ex. 2**. Write on the board:

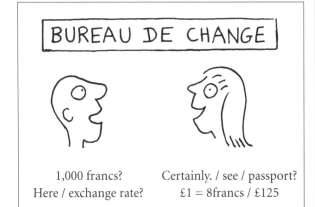

> BUREAU DE CHANGE
>
> 1,000 francs?   Certainly. / see / passport?
> Here / exchange rate?   £1 = 8francs / £125

- Use the picture and word prompts to elicit this dialogue.
  A: Can I change (1,000 francs), please?
  B: Certainly. Can I see your passport, please?
  A: Here you are. What's the exchange rate?
  B: A pound is eighty francs. That's £125.
  (Use your local currency instead of francs)
- Drill and practise the dialogue with the whole class and then in pairs. Then start **ex.2**.

■ Learner-training

Encourage SS to memorize the ⌂ dialogues (coloured grey in the SB), as these contain most of the key exchanges they need. Many SS enjoy learning this way and need to be reassured that memorization is a valid technique.

■ Homework

SS do **WB 2**⌂ *p. 20* and **Listen and speak 2**⌂.

Lesson aims

Revision	**File 2:** present perfect, *have to*, *have* / *have got*, *can* (permission), job vocabulary
Optional materials	🄿 🎵 *You don't have to say you love me*

Lesson plan

▪ Warmer: Progress chart

- Books closed. Ask *Can you remember what the lessons in File 2 were about? What grammar and vocabulary did we learn?* Elicit from the SS anything they can remember.
- Now tell SS to look at the **Progress chart** (SB *p. 8*) and to tick the lessons they've studied.
- Tell them that this is the revision lesson for this File, and that they can then do the **Vocabulary** and **Grammar files** (SB *pp. 36, 37*) to further revise the language of the File.

1 Revision: Reading

a ● Focus on the photo of Cristina. Ask *How old do you think she is? Where do you think she's from?*

  Tip If you are teaching in Spain, some SS may know who she is. Get them to write down her name rather than shout it out and spoil it for the others.

- Give SS two minutes to read quickly about Cristina. Tell them to ignore the gaps in the text and to read for the general idea. In pairs, SS try to guess her job.
- Feedback. Write suggestions on the board.

b ● Check SS understand the words in the list (*ready* and *nearly* are new).
- SS read the text again and complete.
- Check answers. Be prepared to explain / translate *hard* (= difficult), *hairdresser*, *team*, *put on*, *make-up*.

  > 2 stressful 3 nearly 4 let 5 train 6 every
  > 7 only 8 earns 9 wear 10 who 11 ready
  > 12 afraid

- See if they have any more ideas about her job. If nobody has guessed, give them the clue that she's Spanish, and her job is usually considered a man's job.

c ● ·18· Play the tape. SS hear Cristina in action.

  > She's a bullfighter.

- Ask *Would you do this job for £30,000? Why (not)?*

2 Presentation: Four uses of have

a ● Focus on the examples of the verb *have* (blue) in the text. SS write them in the right place in the chart, as in the example. Check answers.

  > 1 She's **travelled** a lot. present perfect
  > 2 She **has to** train. obligation
  > 3 She **has** lunch. have = eat / take, etc.

- Highlight key points. Write on the board:

+	−	?

  Elicit examples of each as you go through.
  - 1 *have* is an auxiliary verb (*has travelled*)
  - 2 *have to* is a main verb. It needs *do / does* for − and ?.
  - 3 *have* is a main verb. It needs *do / does* for − and ?.
  - 4 There is another form of *have* in the text which is used for possession. Elicit *have got*. Both *have* and *have got* are used for possession. *have* needs *do / does* for − and ?, *have got* doesn't.
- Ask *When can you contract 'have'?* (in 1 and 4 with *have got* only).
- SS find and classify other examples of *have* in the text 1, 2, 3, or 4. Check answers.

  > She **has** been to nearly every city in her country. 1
  > **I've** tried other jobs – **I've** worked as a hairdresser and as a secretary. 1
  > she also **has** to wear special clothes 2
  > … and **has** got two sisters 4

b ● SS classify further examples. Check answers.

  > I always **have** coffee for breakfast. 3
  > **I've done** all the exercises. 1
  > He**'s got** / He **has** a new car. 4
  > She **has to** work on Saturdays. 2

3 Practice: *have*

- SS complete the sentences with the right form of *have*. Remind SS to decide from the context which form they need and to use contractions when they can.
- Check answers.

  > 2 've got / have 3 do, have 4 've 5 does, have
  > 6 Has, got / Does, have

4 Practice: Speaking

- Focus on the four blocks of questions. First get SS to ask you some of the questions. Answer with a short answer, and elicit a follow-up question each time.

  > S1 *Have you been to an opera?*
  > T *Yes, I have.*
  > S2 *Which opera?*
  > T *Tosca.*
  > S3 *Did you enjoy it?*

- SS in pairs, A and B, sitting face to face. B book closed. A interviews B for three minutes. They swap roles. Monitor, and remind them to ask follow-up questions.

  Tip Tell SS to ask questions in random order so their partner has to listen carefully. Fast finishers can add more questions to each group.

5 Skills: Listening

a • Tell SS they're going to hear three short conversations. The first time they listen, they only have to try to identify where the conversation is taking place, and who the people are.

   • ·19· Play the tape once. SS check answers in pairs.

b • SS to listen again to check, and find out what the conversations are about. Check answers.

> 1 In a shop, customer and shop assistant. She wants to buy a corkscrew (to open a bottle of wine).
> 2 In a pub / office, woman and man having an interview for a job in a pub.
> 3 In a restaurant, waiter and customer. The waiter doesn't want to give the customer a table because he isn't wearing a tie / smart trousers.
> Tapescript **SB Listening** *p. 127*

■ ·20· ♫ *You don't have to say you love me*

The words to this song are on ⏸ *p. 157* (see **Extras**). If you can't make photocopies, exploit the song as follows.

• Write on the board:

> You _____ _____ to _____ you _____ me
> Just _____ close at _____
> You _____ _____ to _____ forever
> I will _____

• Tell SS that this is part of the chorus of the song that they're going to hear, and that it's repeated several times. Elicit / teach the meaning of *close* (*adj.* = near). Tell SS to listen and write down as many of the missing words as possible.

• ·20· Play the song once. Feedback. Play the song again to get any more words that are still missing.

Lesson notes

This revision lesson brings together and revises the four different uses of *have* (possession / auxiliary verb / main verb / *have to* for obligation). SS often confuse these forms. Their main problem is knowing when to use *do* / *does* to make questions and negatives and when to contract *have*. SS also recycle key language from **File 2**.

Extras

You don't have to say you love me ⏸ *p. 157* A song by Dusty Springfield. Instructions and answers *p. 131*.

Interview for a job ⏸ *p. 158* A roleplay to revise the key language of **File 2**. Instructions *p. 131*.

■ **Homework**

Choose from the **End-of-file options below**.

End-of-file options

Student's Book

■ **Vocabulary file 2** *p. 36*

• Do this in class, or set it for homework. However, even if SS do the rest of the page at home, you should try to go quickly through the introductory text and **Organize your vocabulary learning!** in class.

Tip Tell SS to bring dictionaries to this class.

Organize your vocabulary learning! Emphasize the importance of having a good bi-lingual dictionary. Recommend a locally-available compact one if you can.

Try it! Tell SS (in pairs or for homework) to find the spelling mistakes and correct them.

> 1 **Dictionary abbreviations**
>   2 somebody 3 noun 4 adjective 5 verb
>   6 preposition 7 adverb 8 pronoun
> 2 **Prepositions**
>   1 for 2 to 3 after 4 with 5 as 6 to
>   7 at
> 3 **Word-building**
>   1 con<u>duc</u>tor 2 psy<u>chol</u>ogist 3 <u>chem</u>ist
>   4 in<u>ter</u>preter 5 <u>hair</u>dresser 6 <u>law</u>yer
>   7 <u>bus</u> <u>driv</u>er 8 <u>sail</u>or 9 <u>jour</u>nalist
>   10 <u>sci</u>entist
> 4 **Key words**
>   1 ever 2 Although 3 only 4 also 5 still
> 5 **Pronunciation**
>   2 ticket 3 climb 4 motorway 5 earn
>
> **Try it!**
>   1 <u>jew</u>ellery 2 <u>hel</u>met 3 quali<u>fic</u>ations
>   4 <u>sal</u>ary 5 <u>con</u>centrate 6 <u>mot</u>orway

■ **Grammar file 2** *p. 37*

• If you can, spend ten minutes going through this with the class, answering any queries. SS tick each box when they're satisfied they understand it.

Workbook

■ **Grammar check 2** *p. 21*

• Remind SS to do this with **SB** and **WB** open in front of them, and to refer back to **Grammar file 2** as necessary. SS can check their answers with the **WB** key.

■ **Read and write 2** *p. 62*

• SS write a formal letter of application for a job, either in a hotel or as an au pair, following a model.

• Briefly explain the exercises and model letter. Emphasize the need to read and follow the instructions carefully and compare their final letter with the model. Highlight the key differences between an informal letter (**Read and write 1**) and a formal letter

■ **Quicktest 1** *p. 83*

   These are regular multiple-choice progress tests after **Files 2, 4, 6,** and **8**. They revise the language of the previous File(s). They complement the photocopiable 'surprise' tests in the **TB** which come after **Files 3, 6,** and **9**. SS have a key to check their answers.

Lesson aims

Listening skills / strategies	Listening for the general idea / focus on key words, listening for specific information, practising outside class

Lesson plan

■ Warmer: Problems with listening

- Write on the board:

reading	writing	speaking	listening

- In pairs, SS number them 1 to 4 in order of difficulty, (1 = the most difficult). Feedback. How many SS put 'listening' first?
- Ask *What do you find difficult about listening?* Elicit several different answers onto the board.

■ Introduction: SS' problems with listening

- Books open. SS read the introduction and quotes 1 to 3 from foreign students. Be prepared to explain / translate *conversation, impossible, clearly*. Give examples of weak forms, e.g. /hæftə/= *have to*, etc.
- Ask *Which ones do you agree with? What other problems are there?*
- Ask *Why do you think we use cassettes / videos in class?* Elicit reasons, e.g. so they experience listening to different voices / accents apart from yours, hear English in real-life situations, e.g. in a shop, in a restaurant, etc.
- Get SS to read the last paragraph to confirm this. Make sure they understand *accent*, and *situation*. Emphasize the importance of practice – the more they listen the more they'll understand.

Listening for the general idea

■ Tip 1

- SS read the tip. Tell the class that SS often don't understand as much as they could simply because they feel tense and stressed. Emphasize that when they listen to a tape in class they'll always have more than one opportunity to hear it, so it's very important to relax the first time, to get used to the speakers' voices, and just get a general idea of what they're listening to.

1 Listening for gist

- Books closed. Tell SS they're going to listen to a radio programme. Tell them to relax, listen and not to write.
- ◦21◦ Play the tape once. Ask *What kind of programme is it?* (the news) *How did you know?* (the introductory music, the way the newsreader speaks, the key words in the content – *news, weather*, etc.). Emphasize that 'non-linguistic' clues can often help them a lot.

> Tapescript **SB Listening** *p.127*

■ Tip 2

- Books closed. Write KEY WORDS on the board. Elicit

the meaning of *key* (= important). Demonstrate the importance of key words by saying (quite fast with correct intonation I <u>went</u> to a <u>fantastic</u> <u>party</u> at a <u>friend's</u> <u>house</u> on <u>Friday</u> <u>night</u>. Ask *What was I talking about? Which words did you hear clearly?* Elicit the sentence onto the board. Ask *Which words didn't you hear clearly? Were they necessary to understand?*

- SS read the tip about key words and listening for important information to give them the general idea.

2 Listening for key words

a
- In pairs, SS listen again and number the topics 1 to 4. Remind them that key words will help them.

The weather 4	Sport 3
International news 1	Business news 2

b
- SS copy down the four headings in **ex. 2a** onto a piece of paper. Tell them they're going to hear the news again twice. They have to write any key words they hear under each heading.
- Play the tape again twice. In pairs, SS compare the words they've written, and try to work out the general idea in each extract.
- Write the four headings on the board and elicit words under each heading.

> **International news**
> plane, crashed, South Korea killing 180 people etc.
> **Business news**
> pound, fallen, dollar, second day etc..
> **Sport**
> German, racing driver, Schumacher etc.
> **The weather**
> today, dry, sunny, all, country.

- Feedback.

■ Tip 3

- SS read the tip. Ask *When can you listen and also read the words?* (pop songs, *Easy Readers* which are also on cassette, textbooks, some ELT magazines, sub-titled films / videos, etc.)

3 Checking for key words

a
- SS look at the tapescript (**SB Listening** *p.127*) where all the key words are highlighted. They compare this with their own lists from **ex. 2b**. Ask *Are there many key words you didn't understand? Which ones?*
- Help SS to see why they didn't understand some of the words (because they didn't know them, they didn't recognize the pronunciation, the words were 'linked' to other words / they weren't important words and were swallowed by the newsreader, etc.)
- SS look at the other non-highlighted words. Ask *Can you understand the text without them?* Establish that the non-key words aren't really important to the meaning and the general idea of the text can be understood without them.

Tip Demonstrate by getting SS to cover the text and listen to you. Read aloud the key words only, as if a telegram (*plane crashed South Korea*, etc.).

b • Tell SS they're now going to listen to a story and put the strategies they've learned into practice.
   • Tell SS they're going to hear the story three times.
   – the first time they should relax.
   – the second time they should write key words and compare with a partner, and then feedback to you.
   – the third time they'll listen for answers to general questions about the story.
   • ⟨·22·⟩ Play the tape twice. Then explain *commit suicide* (= kill yourself). Write on the board:

   > 1 Why did he want to commit suicide?
   > 2 How did he plan to do it?
   > 3 Why didn't he do it?
   > 4 What did he find when he went back to his car?

   • SS answer in pairs.
   • Check answers. SS check the tapescript. Ask *Which words didn't you hear?* Discuss again why SS couldn't hear / didn't understand certain words.

   > 1 He was very depressed because he lost his job.
   > 2 He planned to jump off the tenth floor of a building.
   > 3 Because the police stopped him.
   > 4 A parking ticket.
   > Tapescript **SB Listening** *p.127*

Listening for specific information
■ Tip 4

   • SS read the tip. Be prepared to explain / translate *specific information*, *concentrate*.

4 **Listening for detail**

a • Tell SS to look at sentences 1 to 4 and predict what the missing information is.

   > **1** a time **2** a number **3** a place **4** a price

   • ⟨·23·⟩ Confirm with SS that they know what information to listen for. Play the tape twice.
   • Check answers. Encourage SS to use their common sense, i.e. if they're not sure whether they heard 16 or 60 in number 2, ask them which they think is more logical for a platform number.

   > **1** 9.00 a.m. **2** 16 **3** outside the British Museum
   > **4** £85
   > Tapescript **SB Listening** *p.127*

   • Write these questions on the board:

   > 1 Is the office open on Saturdays?
   > 2 Does the train stop at Gatwick airport?
   > 3 Does she know where the British Museum is?
   > 4 When can you get a cheaper room?

   • Play the tape again. SS answer, then compare in pairs.

   • Check answers. If SS have got most of them right, ask more comprehension questions, e.g. *What time does the office close on Saturdays?*

   > **1** Yes, in the morning.   **2** Yes.
   > **3** Not exactly (but she'll find it).
   > **4** On Friday and Saturday nights.

b • SS check the tapescript to see if there's anything they didn't understand.

Practising outside class
■ Tip 5

   • Books closed. Ask *How can you practise listening outside the class?* Elicit their ideas onto the board.
   • SS read the tip. Ask *Which of these do you do?* Get a show of hands for each one.

5 **Practising outside class**

   • Tell SS to try out a new idea for homework this week. ⚠ Although watching films in English is good practice SS are often demotivated by how little they understand. Point out that this is often because the sound quality can be very bad, especially in video copies.

   Tip Help SS by finding out local information, and guiding them to any English teaching programmes that are on TV / English films with subtitles in the cinema or on TV / what time satellite news is on, etc.

Lesson notes

The second of the series of **Focus on …** skills lessons. Listening is often the skill which SS find most difficult. This is mainly because English is a stress-timed language, with many weak forms and contractions. SS find listening to cassettes in class especially difficult. This lesson explains why listening can be difficult. It gives them strategies to help them to cope, and to develop their listening skills. Practice is given both in listening for gist and listening for specific information. It's important to give SS plenty of encouragement when they do listening exercises to build their confidence.

Cassette players Make sure the cassette player you use in class is in good working order, and that the heads are cleaned regularly. Experiment with the volume and the tone. Try sitting at the back of the class yourself to check if you can hear the cassettes clearly.

■ Learner-training

Check after a week if SS have tried out any of the suggestions in Tip 5, and remind them to do so.

■ Homework

   • SS choose and try out one of the outside class activities from **ex.5**.
   • SS use the **'Listen and speak' Student's cassette** and do the 'Listen again' activities if they haven't already done so.

> *Whose are these keys?*
> *They're mine.*

Lesson aims

Grammar	Possessive pronouns
Vocabulary	*Whose …?* or *Who's …?*
Pronunciation	/s/ or /z/, *whose …* (linking / sentence stress)
Revision	Possessive *'s*, possessive adjectives, clothes, possessions
Optional materials	A large plastic bag (ex.5)

Lesson plan

■ Warmer: ® apostrophe s

- Write these sentences on the board:

  > 1 Anne's got two children.
  > 2 Who's going to the party tonight?
  > 3 Andrew's brother works in a hospital.

- SS copy the sentences, and underline *'s*. In pairs they decide what it means in each sentence.
- Check answers.

  > **1** has **2** is **3** possessive *'s*

1 Skills: Reading

- Books open. Focus on the article and the photo on the top right. Ask *What's an auction? Have you ever been to one?*
- SS read a magazine extract about Christie's. Ask comprehension questions, e.g. *When did Christie's open?* (in 1766) *Who opened it?* (James Christie) *What's the name of the painting in the photo?* (*Sunflowers*) *Who painted it?* (Van Gogh). Encourage SS to guess from context the meaning of words they don't know. Be prepared to explain / translate <u>antiques</u>, <u>paintings</u>, <u>world record</u>, <u>belonged</u> (to).

2 Presentation: *Whose is this / that? It's …*

a
- SS look at the photos of seven famous musicians and their possessions.
- Drill the question forms *Whose is (the guitar)? / Whose are (the boots)?* with choral and individual repetition. Encourage SS to stress *Whose* and *guitar / boots* and to link *Whose is* /huːzɪz/ and *Whose are.* /huːzə/.
- Focus on the model dialogue. In pairs, SS ask and answer *Whose is / are …?* and try to guess which object belonged to each person. Get them to agree and write down their guesses.
  ⚠️ If you didn't do the **Books-closed presentation**, remind SS that for names which end in /s/ you have to add an extra syllable which is pronounced /ɪz/, e.g. *It's Nikolas's.* /nɪkləsɪz/. Revise possessive *'s* and pronouns with **G◄◄ 20** (SB *p.7*) if necessary.

b
- ○ 1 ○ SS listen to the beginning of the auction to check their answers. Play the tape twice.

- Check answers. SS check the tapescript if necessary.

  > 1 John Lennon's glasses 2 Elvis Presley's guitar
  > 3 Michael Jackson's hat 4 Elton John's shoes
  > 5 Keith Richard's jacket 6 Prince's boots
  > 7 David Bowie's watch
  > Tapescript **SB Listening** *p.127*

3 Presentation: Possessive pronouns

- Focus on the photo of Elvis Presley on the album cover. Ask *What do you know about him?* (born on January 8th 1935, died August 16th, 1977, probably of a drugs overdose, USA, known as 'the King (of rock 'n roll)'). Ask *Do you know the names of any of his songs?*
- ○ 2 ○ 🎵 SS listen to and read his song *Love me tender* (1956). They complete the song from the word list. Don't explain the difference between *my – mine / your – yours*, etc. at this stage.
- SS compare answers in pairs. Play it again to check.

Verse 1	me	me	me	You	my	I	you
Chorus	me	me	my	my	I	you	I
Verse 2	me	me	me	your	I		
Verse 3	me	me	me	you	mine	I	yours

- Ask *What kind of song is it?* (a love song) *Do you like it?* SS read through the song and check the meaning of each line using the **Glossary**.

  Tip With a mono-lingual class, you could get them to translate the song for homework and compare versions next lesson.

■ GRAMMAR FOCUS
Possessive pronouns

a
- SS complete the chart. They should be able to guess *ours* from the pattern of the other pronouns. Ask *What's the difference between possessive adjectives and possessive pronouns?* (pronouns aren't used with nouns). Refer them to verse 3 of the song where there are examples of both.

your	his	her	their	mine	ours

- Drill pronunciation. SS answer the two questions.

  > 1 mine 2 possessive pronoun

b
- Highlight that:
  - we use *Whose …?* to ask a question about possession.
  - each pronoun only has one form (singular and plural are the same, e.g. *It's / They're mine*).
  - we don't use *the* with possessive pronouns NOT *It's the mine.*
  - the possessive *'s* form can be used with or without a noun, e.g. *It's John's car. / It's John's.*

PRACTICE
- SS complete the sentences, and check in pairs.

- Check answers.

> **1** hers Her **2** our ours **3** your mine Yours
> **4** his her **5** my theirs **6** Our theirs their

- Drill *yours / mine / his / hers* round the class. Pick up SS' objects and ask *Whose is this?* Pick up your book and elicit *It's yours.*, ask different SS for *It's mine.*, and point to two SS' books for *They're theirs.*, etc. (omit this stage if you've done the **Books-closed presentation**).
- Focus on **V** *Who's or Whose?* Look at the two examples to check they understand the grammatical difference between *Who's* (= Who is) and *Whose is* (= Who is the owner of).
- Highlight that *Who's* and *Whose* are pronounced the same /huːz/.

■ PRONUNCIATION

a • · 3 · SS listen and write sentences. Pause the tape after each one to give them time to write.

> **1** Who's going to be at the party?
> **2** Whose is this bag?
> **3** Whose is that car?
> **4** Who's that girl over there?
> **5** Who's going to pay?
> **6** Whose are those books?

b • Focus on the headwords and elicit the sounds they represent. Remind SS of the difference between /s/ and /z/. /s/ is unvoiced, i.e. a sound produced without using the voice-box in the throat. /z/ is voiced.

> **Tip** Get SS to say /z/ and feel their throat vibrate. When they say /s/ it doesn't.

- Tell SS to look at sentences in **a**. Ask which words contain /s/? (1 this, 6 books).
- · 4 · SS listen and repeat the words to tell you if they contain /s/ or /z/. They mark each one either /s/ or /z/, as in the example.

> this /s/ these /z/ those /z/ miss /s/
> books /s/ sing /s/ chairs /z/

- Highlight that:
- s is almost always pronounced /s/ at the beginning of words.
- s + consonant and double s is always pronounced /s/ (*stay, boss*).
- z is always pronounced /z/ (*zoo, zip*).
- s before or after a vowel is usually /z/ (*music, easy*) (see **Sound bank WB** *p. 82*).

4 Learner-training: Classroom language

- SS turn to ▮ **Classroom language B** *p. 143*. Check SS understand all the phrases. In pairs, SS agree and write in a translation of each phrase.
- Give the class two minutes to memorize all the phrases. Then, books closed, SS try to recall them all.
- SS translate and learn the phrases for homework. Remind them how to test themselves (or a partner) by covering one column.

5 Personalization: Game

- Play *Guess whose.* Ask each student to give you an object secretly so the rest of the class can't see it, e.g. a

lighter, some earrings, etc. Tell them to choose something that isn't too obviously theirs. Put their objects in a large supermarket bag.
- Show SS the objects, either one at a time from the bag, or all at once on your desk.
- In pairs, SS say whose each thing is and note down the name of the object and the owner, e.g. *car keys – Hussain / old yellow pencil – Silvia.*
- When SS have finished guessing, pick up each object and ask *Whose is this? / are these?* Elicit guesses from different SS.
  - S1 We think it's / they're Hussain's.
  - S2 No, we think it's / they're Tina's, etc.
- Check by asking the named SS.
  - T Hussain, are the car keys yours?
  - H Yes, they're mine. / No, they aren't.

Lesson notes

SS learn *Whose ...?* + possessive pronouns in the context of an auction of famous singers' possessions and an Elvis Presley song. They also revise possessive *'s* and possessive adjectives.

Whose is that car? You may also want to teach the alternative word order *Whose car is that?*

Possessive pronouns These are very similar to possessive adjectives and SS often confuse the two forms. Common errors *It's my. They're hers books.*

Extras

■ **Grammar auction** ▰ *p. 159* SS bid for right and wrong sentences. Instructions *p. 131.*

Books-closed presentation

Whose ... / possessive pronouns

- Pick up objects belonging to you. Ask *Whose is this?* Elicit *It's yours.* Say *It's mine.*
- Pick up SS' objects (singular and plural), e.g. a bag, pen, books, glasses. Ask *Whose is this (bag)? Whose are these (books)?* Elicit answers with SS' names, e.g. *It's Maria's., They're Danny's.*, etc. On the board, highlight the change from *It's Maria's bag.* to *It's Maria's.*
  ⚠ Remind SS that for names which end in /s/ you have to add an extra syllable which is pronounced /ɪz/, e.g. *It's Nikolas's.* /ˈnɪkləsɪz/.
- Pick up SS' objects again, and ask *Is this yours?*, sometimes of the wrong owner. Elicit *Yes, it's mine. / No, it's hers / his / yours.*
- Write a big question mark on the board. Elicit the question *Whose is / are ...?* and answers onto the board for SS to copy. Then do **ex.1.**

■ Learner-training

Tell SS that they should use the phrases from ▰ **Classroom language** in class in English from now on, and that they should memorize and practise them. Test them on the phrases next lesson.

■ Homework

SS do **WB 3A** *p. 22* and **Listen and speak 3A.**

43

> *What are you doing on Sunday?*
> *I'm going to Vienna.*

Lesson aims

Grammar	Present continuous (future), invitations: *Would you like to …?*
Vocabulary	Verbs: *arrive in / at, leave*, etc.
Pronunciation	Intonation in invitations
Revision	Dates

Lesson plan

■ Warmer: Ordinal numbers 1st to 31st

- Quickly revise ordinal numbers round the class:
  T   *first*
  S1 *second*, etc.

1 Revision: Dates

- Ask *What's the date today?* Make sure SS answer correctly (*It's the (8th) of (December)*).

a • Books open. SS look at and say five dates showing four different ways to write the date. Highlight:
  – that you say **the** third **of** May, but you don't write *the/of*.
  – that you can also say *May the third*.
  – Ask SS *When's your birthday?*

b • SS match the list of travel verbs to their collocates.
  • Check answers.

> **2** meet **3** leave **4** arrive in **5** arrive at
> **6** have **7** stay

- Focus on **V** *at, in*. Look at the examples to explain *arrive* **at** (a place) but *arrive* **in** (a town / country).

2 Presentation: Present continuous (future)

a • SS focus on the photos of Debbie and Tim and read the short text. Ask *Where's Debbie going? Who's Tim?*
  • ◦5◦ SS listen and answer the three questions.

> 1 (She's going there) next Sunday.
> 2 She's going to a conference at the university.
> 3 (She's staying) for a week.
> Tapescript **SB Listening** *p.127*

b • Focus on the travel agent's form.
  • ◦6◦ SS listen to Debbie's second message and fill in the form. Check answers.

> Date of journey: Sunday March 14th
> Arr. Budapest 10.30 (local time)
> Flight number: MA209
> Hotel: The Danube Hotel
> Phone number: 0161 855 907
>
> Tapescript **SB Listening** *p.127*

c • In pairs, SS read Debbie's postcard.
  • Play the tape again. SS listen and complete the postcard. Ask *Why does Debbie want to see him?*

- Check answers.

> **2** leaving **3** 7.45 **4** arriving
> **5** 10.30 **6** staying **7** Danube
> **8** staying **9** flying **10** Maler
> **11** MA209

■ GRAMMAR FOCUS

Present continuous (future)

a • Get SS to look at Debbie's postcard again and highlight the verbs she uses to talk about her trip. e.g. *I'm going to Budapest soon.* Ask:
  1 *What tense is it?* (the present continuous).
  2 *Is she talking about now or the future?* (the future).
  • Highlight the future time expressions she uses, e.g. *soon, on (March 14th), for a week*, etc.

b • Focus on the examples and the rule. Highlight that *future arrangements* = e.g. things you write in a diary.

c • SS translate the examples in the box. Ask *What tense do you use in your language?*
  • Remind SS that the present continuous is also used to talk about actions happening now.

PRACTICE

- Focus on Tim's diary for next week. In pairs, SS use the present continuous to make sentences about his diary arrangements.
- Check answers.

> On Monday he's going to the dentist's.
> On Tuesday he's playing squash.
> On Wednesday he's meeting Viktor at the university.
> On Thursday, he's going to see *Terminator III*.
> On Friday evening he's having dinner with Erika.
> On Saturday he's going to the ballet.

3 Practice: Listening

a • ◦7◦ Play the tape twice. SS listen and answer, then compare.

> 1 Sunday, because Tim's going to Vienna, Monday because Debbie's busy, Tuesday, because Tim's playing squash.
> 2 Wednesday.

> D Hello?
> T Debbie, it's Tim.
> D Tim! Great to hear from you!
> T And you! I got your message and your postcard.
> D Great! When can we meet then? **What are you doing on Sunday night?**
> T **Well actually, I'm going to Vienna** on Sunday.
> D Oh no! How long for?
> T Only for the day. I'm coming back on Sunday night, but late.
> D I'm busy on Monday night. **Are you free Tuesday evening?**

T No, I'm playing squash. What about Wednesday?
D Wednesday? **Yes, that's fine. Would you like to have dinner?**
T **I'd love to. Where can we meet?** At the hotel?
D **Fine.** What time?
T 8.00?
D Great. I can't wait to see you, Tim. Two years is a long time!
T See you next week, then. Bye.
D Bye.

b • Focus on the **Invite / suggest / Accept / refuse** chart. SS listen again and complete the expressions. They tick the answer they hear.
• Check answers. Check vocabulary and drill pronunciation. *actually* (= to tell you the truth)

(See **bold** text in tapescript **ex. 3a** above).

■ PRONUNCIATION

a • ° 8 ° SS listen and repeat key phrases.
• Drill the intonation.
b • ° 9 ° SS listen to six invitations and practise accepting and refusing. Pause the tape after each invitation. With a strong class, individual SS can answer straight away. With a weaker class, ask SS what the invitation was first and then elicit answers from a selection of SS.

1 Would you like to go to the cinema tonight?
2 Would you like to go to the opera tomorrow?
3 Would you like to come to a party on Saturday night?
4 Would you like to have dinner with me?
5 Would you like to go for a walk on Sunday afternoon?
6 Would you like to come to my house for coffee after class?

• In pairs, SS invent their own invitations and practise accepting / refusing.

4 Practice: Making arrangements

• Focus on the blank diary page. Tell SS note to their arrangements for any three of the seven evenings.
• Demonstrate the activity with SS in the class.
  T *Are you free on (Wednesday evening)?*
  S1 *Yes, I am. / No, I'm going to the theatre.*
  T *What are you doing on Friday evening?*
  S2 *Nothing special. / Sorry, I'm meeting someone*, etc.
• If they're free, invite them to do something. e.g. *Would you like to (go out for a meal)?* If they say *yes*, they have to write the arrangement in their diary.
• SS mingle to try to fill their diaries. Monitor and help.
• Feedback to see what SS are doing next week.

5 Skills: Listening

• Tell SS they're going to hear Tim and Debbie meet. Ask *What's going to happen?*
• °10° Play the tape. Ask *What happened?* (Debbie still likes Tim, but he now has a Hungarian girlfriend, Erika).

T Hi Debbie.
D Tim! How are you?
T I'm fine. How are you?
D Fine. You haven't changed at all. You look fantastic.
T Thanks, so do you.
D Right, where are we going?
T I know a good restaurant near here.
D Great. Let's go.
T Well, actually we have to wait for Erika first.
D Erika?
T Yes, Erika. There she is. Debbie, this is Erika.
D Hi Erika.
E Debbie, nice to meet you. Tim has talked a lot about you.
T OK girls. Ready? Let's go!

6 Personalization: Talk about arrangements

• In pairs, SS ask the questions from the prompts. Demonstrate the activity first by getting SS to ask you.
• SS feedback to the class about their partner's plans.

Lesson notes

SS already know the present continuous to talk about ~~what's happening now. In this lesson~~ SS use the tense to talk about future arrangements. Common error ~~What do you do tonight? I go to the cinema.~~

going to **v. present continuous** (*be*) *going to* is used for future plans and intentions. The present continuous is used for definite arrangements, especially in the near future. The difference between the two is very small – in many cases both forms can be used.

Extras

Where are you going on holiday? [P] *p. 160* SS mingle to find a holiday partner. Instructions *p. 132*.

Books-closed presentation

Present continuous (future) For flashcard presentations, see **Introduction** *p. 11*.

• Do before the warmer. Copy the pictures and times from **Picture bank 3B** *p. 206*. Write tomorrow's date on the board.
• Show or point to the picture of the singer. Give the character a name.
• Tell SS they're going to see the singer's diary for tomorrow.
• Use the pictures one by one to present and practise *She's playing tennis at 7.00.* etc.
• Present the question form *What's she doing at (7.00)?*
• Write the six sentences on the board for SS to copy. Make it clear that the present continuous is being used here to refer to the future. Then start **ex. 1**.

■ Learner-training

Remember to ask SS regularly, e.g. *What are you doing this weekend?* and encourage them to ask each other.

■ Homework

SS do **WB 3B** *p. 23* and **Listen and speak 3B**.

3 C The slowest journey in history?

Finally he went across the sea to Ithaca.

Lesson aims

Grammar	*How long does it take? It takes …* , prepositions of movement: *along*, etc.
Vocabulary	Time: *half an hour*, etc. the country: *forest*, etc.
Revision	Daily routines: *get up*, etc. transport

Lesson plan

■ Warmer: ® Time expressions

- Books closed. Write on the board:

15 mins = a quarter of an hour	75 mins =
30 mins =	90 mins =
45 mins =	150 mins =

- In pairs, SS decide how to say the other expressions.
- Check answers. Highlight the use of *a / an*, the plural *s* and pronunciation problems, e.g. *quarter* /ˈkwɔːtə/, *half* /hɑːf/, *an hour* /ˈaʊə/.

a quarter of an hour	an hour and a quarter
half an hour	an hour and a half
three quarters of an hour	two and a half hours

⚠ Point out for times longer than two hours we say, e.g. *three and a half hours* NOT ~~three hours and a half~~.

1 Presentation: *How long does it take?*

- Books open. Take SS through ⓥ **Time** and check pronunciation.
- Focus on the competition. Read it with the class and check they understand *How long does it take?* and *round-the-world (adj.)*.
- In pairs, SS guess how long it takes to fly round the world from London via the five cities.
- Go through the possible answers. Highlight *twelve and a half hours* NOT ~~twelve hours and a half~~.
- Check answers. SS should give you full sentences.

> 1 c 2 b 3 b 4 a 5 b

■ GRAMMAR FOCUS 1
How long does it take? It takes …

- Focus on the example questions and answers. Highlight:

  fly to …
  drive to … OR get to … by plane
                                 bus

- *it* refers to the journey time + *takes* = third person singular.
  Compare the short answer (*about* + eight hours), and the full answer (*It takes about eight hours by plane*).
- *How long does it take you …? It takes me* is used for a personal question and answer.

PRACTICE 1

a
- Focus on the example. Elicit sentences with places: *How long does it take to get from* (your town) …?
- In pairs, SS write three true sentences.
- Feedback sentences from different pairs and see if SS agree with the times.

b
- Ask a few SS *How long does it take you to get to class?* Insist on full answers (*It takes me … minutes.*).
- SS ask about other personal times. First SS ask you the questions from the list. Make sure they understand *wake up in the morning* = to be completely awake, and the difference between *go to bed* and *go to sleep* (= fall asleep).
- In pairs, A asks B all the questions, with follow-up questions where possible. B answers with book closed. They swap roles.
- Find out who takes the longest to get to class.

2 Presentation: Prepositions of movement

a
- Write on the board:

Homer   Odysseus   Penelope

  Ask *Who are they? Why are they famous?* Homer wrote about Odysseus's famous adventures in *The Odyssey*, Penelope was Odysseus's wife.
- Focus on the map of the Aegean sea.
  ⚠ Don't worry about correct pronunciation of the Greek names.
- SS look at questions 1 to 3 and guess the answers.
- ▫11▫ SS read the text with the tape to check.

> **1** Ithaca, in Greece **2** About 500 km **3** ten years

b
- In pairs, SS read the text again and draw Odysseus's route on the map. The first stage is done for them. Encourage SS to guess new vocabulary from context. Be prepared to explain / translate *fought* (past of v. fight), *battle, island, blew* (past of v. blow), *giant, prisoner, adventure, escape, storm, sailed, goddess, kind (adj.), coast, deadly, mainland, monster, average*.
- SS compare routes in pairs. Check any queries.

46

GRAMMAR FOCUS 2

Prepositions of movement

- Focus on the examples and read the rule. Explain that in English you express movement and direction with a verb of movement (e.g. *walk, run*) + a preposition of movement (e.g. *up, round*).
- SS go through the text and highlight the verbs that go with each of the prepositions in blue, e.g. *blew round*.

PRACTICE 2

a
- SS turn to 🖉 **Prepositions of movement** *p. 135* and match the prepositions and pictures. Check answers and drill pronunciation.

10 along	**11** through	**12** up	**13** down			
14 over	**15** under	**16** past	**17** round			
19 to	**20** upstairs	**21** downstairs	**22** into			
23 out of						

- SS in pairs, A and B. A covers the words and is tested by B. Then swap.
  A (points to a picture and asks) *What's this?*
  B (answers with *go*, e.g.) *Go over.*

b
- SS cover the Odysseus text. In pairs, they take turns to describe Odysseus's journey using their maps. (To simplify the activity, tell SS to just use the verb *go* + prepositions of movement, e.g. *First he went round Crete. Then he went …*). A describes the route and B listens and corrects / helps A. Then swap.

3 Practice: Reading and listening

a
- Focus on the newspaper headline. Check SS understand *missing* (= they don't know where she is). Explain *Snowdonia* (an area of Wales).
- SS read the article quickly. Ask *Where's Pascale?*

> We don't know. She's missing somewhere in the mountains in north-west Wales.

- Ask a few comprehension questions, e.g. *What's the weather like? Where did she leave from? Who's looking for her?*

b
- SS match the pictures to the words in **Ⓥ The country**. Drill pronunciation, especially *field* /fiːld/, *mountain* /ˈmaʊntɪn/, and *castle* /ˈkɑːsəl/.

2 a castle	**3** a field	**4** a hill	**5** a lake
6 a mountain	**7** a path	**8** a river	
9 a valley	**10** a forest		

c
- 🔘12🔘 Play the tape twice. SS listen and tick the pictures they hear. Check answers.

> path   lake   path   field   forest
> valley   bridge   hill
> **Tapescript SB Listening** *p. 127*

d
- Tell SS to read the gapped directions. Ask *Can you remember any of the missing words?*

- SS listen again and complete the directions. Pause the tape after *Are you ready?* to make sure they are.

> Go **down** the **path**, **past** the **lake**.
> Go **along** the **path** for about 300 metres.
> Go **across** the **field** on your left.
> Go **through** the **forest** and then **down** into the **valley**.
> Go **over** the **bridge** and **up** the **hill**.

4 Personalization: ►◄ Describing a route

- SS in pairs, A and B, sit face to face and turn to ►◄ **Emergency** A *p. 120*, B *p. 123*. Elicit the names of the places on the map (they may not know *railway* (*line*)).
- Give SS time to read their instructions and draw their routes. Monitor to make sure they've understood and don't look at their partner's drawings.
- Tell As to imagine they have broken a leg, and to radio for help. A then 'radios' B and describes his / her route for B to draw. Then swap. Tell SS to compare maps.

Lesson notes

SS learn to say how long things take from an airline competition. From the context of Odysseus's journey back from Troy, they also learn to combine verbs and prepositions to express movement and direction.

How long does it take (you)? It takes (me) … SS probably won't use it confidently until they've had a lot of practice.

Prepositions of movement Some languages express movement and direction only with verbs (e.g. French *monter*) not verb + preposition as in English (*go up*).

Extras

How long does it take? 🄿 *p. 161*
A pairwork information gap activity. Instructions *p. 132*.

Books-closed presentation

How long does it take?
- Write this dialogue on the board.

A	B
How do you usually get here?	*I come by bus.*
How far is it?	*One and a half kilometres.*
How long does it take you?	*Ten minutes.*

- SS practise in pairs, then stand up and ask other SS. Then do **ex. 1**.

■ Learner-training

Tell SS to learn 🖉 **Prepositions** *p. 135* and test themselves and each other.

■ Homework

SS do **WB 3C** *p. 24* and **Listen and speak 3C**.

It was a cold, dark night ...

> *She was driving along the road when she hit a cat.*

Lesson aims

Grammar	Past continuous, contrast with past simple
Pronunciation	/ə/, /ɑ/, /ɜː/ weak / strong forms of *was* / *were*
Revision	Irregular plurals Prepositions of place / movement, the time

Lesson plan

■ Warmer: ℝ Irregular plurals

- Write on the board.

man	woman	child	person

- In pairs, SS write the plurals.
- Check answers and pronunciation, especially *women* /ˈwɪmɪn/ and *child* /tʃaɪld/.

men	women	children	people

1 Presentation: Vocabulary

- SS match the words and dictionary definitions. Tell SS to use the grammatical abbreviations to help.
- Check answers. Drill pronunciation.

  2 d **3** b **4** e **5** f **6** a

2 Presentation: Past continuous

- Focus on picture 1. SS describe what's happening in the picture of London, e.g. *It's raining.*, etc.
- SS read paragraph 1 and answer questions 1 to 3.

  1 It was raining.
  2 Because people were going home from work.
  3 She was driving to a friend's house (for dinner).

■ GRAMMAR FOCUS 1

Past continuous

a • SS focus on the four highlighted verbs. Elicit the name of the tense (past continuous). Point out that it's the past form of the present continuous.
- SS read and complete the rule.

  was   + -ing

b • SS complete the chart with the verbs in the past continuous.

were going home	Yes, it was.
were you going?	Were you studying?
wasn't raining.	No, we weren't.
Was it snowing?	

c • Focus on the rule. Tell SS we often use this tense to describe a scene, e.g. in a story.

PRACTICE 1

- In pairs, SS look again at the first picture and describe what else was happening at six o'clock.
- Feedback all the sentences from different pairs.

  A woman was buying a paper.
  Two people were waiting for a bus.
  A man was getting into a taxi.
  A man was smoking.
  Two men were going into the Underground.

■ PRONUNCIATION

- Explain that the pronunciation of *was* and *were* changes according to whether they are stressed or unstressed.
- Elicit the sound in each headword, /ə/, /ɒ/, and /ɜː/.
- ∘13∘ Play the tape. SS listen and repeat.
- Get SS to underline the stressed words in each sentence. Pause the tape after each sentence.

  1 He was <u>going</u> <u>home</u>. <u>What</u> were they <u>doing</u>?
  2 It <u>wasn't</u> <u>raining</u>. <u>Yes</u>, it <u>was</u>.
  3 They <u>weren't</u> <u>sleeping</u>. <u>Yes</u>, they <u>were</u>.

- Focus on the pronunciation of *was* / *were* in each sentence. Ask *When are <u>was</u> / <u>were</u> stressed?*

  They're only stressed in negatives and short answers (the same as *can* / *can't*).

- SS underline the stress in the past continuous sentences from **Grammar focus 1b** and say them correctly.

  I was <u>working</u>.
  They were <u>going</u> <u>home</u>.
  <u>Where</u> were you <u>going</u>?
  It <u>wasn't</u> <u>raining</u>.
  Was it <u>snowing</u>? <u>Yes</u>, it <u>was</u>.
  Were you <u>studying</u>? <u>No</u>, we <u>weren't</u>.

3 Presentation: Past simple or continuous?

a • In pairs, SS look at pictures 2 to 6 which continue the story. They're in the correct order. Then they read the jumbled story and match each paragraph to a picture. (The A1 is a main road from London to the north of England.)
- Check answers. Get SS to guess the meaning of any new words / expressions from context. Be prepared to explain / translate *suddenly*, *hit*, *farmer*, *doorbell*, *shout*. Paragraphs 4, 2, 3, 6, 5.
- In small groups, SS imagine how the story ends.
- Feedback their guesses.

b • Pre-teach *back of the car*.

- • `14` SS listen to the end of the story to check. Play the tape once and elicit what happened. Then play it again to check.

> DIANA Help, Help, Daniel! Open the door.
> DANIEL Diana! What's the matter?
> DIANA That man … he's the murderer! He wants to kill me!
> MAN Don't shoot! Please, don't shoot. Listen! I'm not the murderer. The murderer is in there, in the back of your car. When you stopped to look at the cat he got into your car. I saw him. That's why I was following you …
> DIANA What? He's in my car?
> DANIEL Oh my God … OK. Come out! With your hands up.

- • Get SS' reactions to the story. Ask *Do you think the story's true? Do you like driving at night?* etc.

■ GRAMMAR FOCUS 2

Past simple or past continuous?

- a • Get SS to highlight all the past continuous verbs in the story. Ask *What tense are the other verbs? Why?*
- b • Focus on the time line or draw it on the board. Explain that the arrows represent the two sentences. Highlight that one action interrupts the other. Ask *Which action was in progress when the other action happened?* (the past continuous sentence).
- c • SS read and complete the rules.

> continuous   simple

- • To test they've understood, write on the board:

> 1 When my friend arrived I was having dinner.
> 2 When my friend arrived, we had dinner.

Ask SS to translate the sentences and explain the difference in meaning.

> In 1, I was in the middle of having dinner when my friend arrived.
> In 2, I started having dinner after my friend arrived.

- • Ask *Do you use similar tenses in your language?*

PRACTICE 2

- a • SS write sentences with the verbs in the correct form, as in the example. Check answers.

> 2 killed, was driving   3 saw, was following
> 4 arrived, got, rang   5 was cooking, heard

- b • In pairs, SS cover the text and look at the pictures again. Elicit the whole story once round the class. Put up a few key phrases to help them with the end of the story (e.g. *murderer, stopped, got in the back, following, come out, hands up*).
  - • SS take it in turns to tell the story to their partner who listens and helps. A tells B the first half (pictures 1 to 3), then B completes the story with pictures 4 to 6. Fast finishers can swap roles.

4 Personalization: Speaking

- • Focus on the ten clocks. Elicit the times from the class, e.g. five past eight. Ask different SS *What were you doing at* (different times) *yesterday?* Ask follow-up questions too.
- • Get the class to ask you some questions. Encourage them to ask follow-up questions, with both the simple and continuous forms.
- • SS continue in pairs.

5 Personalization

- • SS have to make questions combining the two tenses. Demonstrate choosing any combination of words. Ask different SS some of the possible questions, e.g. *What were you thinking about when you got home last night?*
- • Get the class to practise asking you some questions. Then SS mingle and ask and answer the questions. Monitor and encourage follow-up questions.
- • If time, feedback any interesting answers.

Lesson notes

SS learn the past continuous in the context of a short mystery story, and contrast it with the past simple.

Past continuous or past simple? Emphasize that we use the past continuous to describe longer actions in progress. We use the past simple to describe consecutive finished actions.

Extras

Alibi 🎲 *p. 208* A class roleplay. SS act out a police murder investigation.

How Sally met Harry P *p. 162* A pairwork split reading story. Instructions *p. 132*.

Books-closed presentation

Past continuous For flashcard presentations, see **Introduction** *p. 11*.

- • Do after the warmer. Copy the pictures from **Picture bank 3D** *p. 206*. Write *yesterday* on the board.
- • Show the first picture of the man. Give the character a name).
- • Use the pictures one by one to present and practise *At seven o'clock he was sleeping.*, etc.
- • Present the question form *What was he doing at …?*
- • Write the six sentences on the board for SS to copy. Make it clear that *was + verb + -ing* refers to continuous actions in the past. Then start **ex. 1**.

■ Learner-training

Encourage SS to look at past tense forms when they read, and decide why some are in the continuous form and others in the past simple.

■ Homework

SS do **WB 3D** *p. 25* and **Listen and speak 3D**.

Lesson aims

Function	Checking into a hotel, calling Reception
Vocabulary	Hotel: *room service*, etc.
Revision	Ordinal numbers: *1st* to *7th*, polite requests: *Could you / I …?*

Lesson plan

■ Warmer: Hotel vocabulary

- Copy this framework for a HOTEL word map on the board:

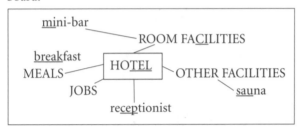

- SS copy it onto a page in their vocabulary file and suggest two words for each sub-group.
- Feedback all their words onto the board. Elicit and underline the word stress, and drill pronunciation.

1 Skills: Reading

- Books open. SS identify Pieter in the photo. Ask *What country is he in? Have you been there?*
- Tell SS to read the hotel guide for a minute then close their books and try to remember all the information.
- Ask *Would you like to stay there? Why (not)?* Feedback.
- Get SS to add some new words from the text to their HOTEL word map, e.g. *jacuzzi, sun terrace*, etc.

2 Presentation and practice: Checking into a hotel

a
- SS cover the dialogue and read questions 1 to 3.
- ° 15 ° Play the tape. SS listen once and decide the answers in pairs. Feedback.

> 1 a single room with a bath
> 2 three nights (the 5th, 6th, and 7th of November)
> 3 209 (on the second floor)

b
- SS uncover the dialogue, listen again, and complete it. Ask *Who's P?* (Pieter) *Who's R?* (the Receptionist).

Tip Get them to read the dialogue once first and remember / guess some of the missing words.

- Check answers.

> P Hello. I've got **a reservation**. My name's Okker. Pieter Okker.
> R Just a moment. **Can you spell that**, please?
> P O-double K-E-R.
> R Right Mr Okker. A **single** room with a **bath** for two nights, is that right?
> P No, it's **three** nights. From the **fifth** to the **seventh** of November.

> R No problem, I'll **change** it. May I see your passport, please? Thank you. **Could** you **fill** in this form, please?
> P Sure. **Have you got a pen**? Thanks.
> R OK. Here's your key, sir, room **209** on the **second floor**. The lift's over there.
> P Thanks. **What time's breakfast**?
> R From 7.00 to **10.00**. The dining-room's on the **first** floor.

- Elicit the meaning of *May I …?* (= *Can / Could I …* but a bit more formal / polite. It is only used with *I/we.*
- Highlight:
- *right* = OK (Right, Mr Okker.).
- *fill in* (*a form*) = complete.
- the use of *on* + *the* (*3rd*) *floor*. Practise with *What floor do you live on?*

c
- Ask SS to read the first line of the dialogue. Ask *Which do you think are the most important words to help you remember it?* (two or three only, e.g. *reservation, name's*).
- Get SS to write these words in the margin to the left of the first **P**.
- Do the same for the next line, etc.

> **Suggested answers:**
> P reservation / name's
> R moment / spell?
> P double K
> R single / bath / two?
> P three / fifth / seventh
> R change / passport / form?
> P Sure / pen?
> R key / floor / lift
> P thanks / breakfast?
> R 7.00 / dining-room

- SS cover the dialogue and practise it in pairs, using only their word prompts to help them. Make sure they swap roles. Tell them they don't need to remember the exact words of the dialogue.

3 Presentation: Calling Reception

a
- Focus on the pictures. Ask *What can you see in each one? Can you guess what each person is saying?*
- ° 16 ° Play the tape. SS listen, identify which person is talking, and write the correct room number under each picture. Play the tape again if necessary.
- Check answers.

> A 301 The TV doesn't work.
> B 637 There aren't any towels.
> C 418 For an alarm call.
> D 149 To order some food.
> Tapescript **SB Listening** *p. 128.*

b • SS listen again and complete requests 1 to 4. Drill pronunciation of *could* /kʊd/. Highlight that *l* is not pronounced.

• Get SS to check their answers / spelling in the tapescript.

> **1** Could I have a coke and a cheese sandwich, please?
> **2** Could you repair it, please?
> **3** Could you bring me one, please?
> **4** Could you wake me at 6.45 tomorrow morning?

• Elicit the meaning of other key language, e.g. *put it on my bill*, *(it) doesn't work* (= it's broken).

• Ask SS to find three ways of agreeing to requests. Elicit onto the board:
  – *Of course.*
  – *Certainly.* (= *Of course.*, but more formal)
  – *Right away.* (= immediately)

4 Practice: Speaking

a • SS look at the tapescript again and underline the key words in each dialogue.

b • Tell SS they're going to roleplay the four dialogues from ex.3 with some new vocabulary. Focus on the two role-cards. Elicit the meaning of *white <u>c</u>offee*, *<u>air</u>-conditioning*, *<u>blankets</u>*, and *<u>heating</u>*.

• Demonstrate first with you as the guest and a (strong) student as the receptionist. Tell SS to look at picture D. Pretend to phone Reception and ask *Could I have a white coffee (in my room), please?* Elicit a reply. Repeat with situation 2, if necessary.

• In pairs, **A** and **B**, SS now do the same, choosing different situations from their list and taking it in turns to be the guest. Fast finishers can invent situations of their own.

5 Vocabulary: Travel phrasebook 3

• SS turn to 📖3 *p.132* and complete and translate the phrases.

Lesson notes

Pieter has now moved on from the UK to Sweden. In this lesson, SS revise and extend the language of hotels. They practise checking into a hotel. They also practise reading an authentic hotel guide and call Reception to ask for various services.

Authentic reading texts These texts help SS to cope with authentic English in travel situations. Encourage them to guess vocabulary from the context or use dictionaries, but tell them not to worry about learning all the new words unless they want to.

can / could / may SS see all three forms for polite requests. Emphasize that *could* is a little more formal than *can* (although nowadays the difference is minimal). *May …* (used only with *I* and *we*) is much more formal and is used less frequently.

right This common word is used with different meanings in the lesson, i.e. *Right!* (= OK), *Is that right?* (= correct), *Right away* (= immediately). SS also know *right* (= opposite of *left*).

Extras

Hotel check-in 🅿 *p.163* Pair work role-cards. SS practise checking in and dealing with problems at a hotel. Instructions *p.132*.

Books-closed presentation

Checking in

• Do before **ex. 1**. Write on the board:

> HOTEL RECEPTION
>
> evening / rooms? single / double?
> How much / single? $65
> / much / double? $88 / taxes
>
> / rooms? Yes / private
> / like a … / fine. May / passport?

• Elicit and drill this dialogue line by line.

> **A** *Good evening. Have you got any rooms?*
> **B** *Yes, madam. Would you like a single room or a double room?*
> **A** *How much is a single room?*
> **B** *It's $65 a night.*
> **A** *And how much is a double room?*
> **B** *It's $88 a night, including taxes.*
> **A** *Is there a TV in all the rooms?*
> **B** *Yes madam, and all rooms have a private bathroom.*
> **A** *I'd like a (single room), please.*
> **B** *That's fine. May I see your passport, please.*

• Practise it in pairs, swapping roles. SS can decide for themselves if they want a single / double room and add extra questions like *How many nights would you like to stay?*, etc.

• When SS are comfortable with the dialogue, get them to write it in pairs.

• Elicit it onto the board for them to check spelling. Then do **ex. 1**.

■ Learner-training

Tell SS that maps are a good way to revise, record, and learn vocabulary. Refer them to another example in **Vocabulary file 3** (**SB** *p.50*).

■ Homework

SS do **WB 3**📖 *p.26* and **Listen and speak 3**📖.

Lesson aims

Revision	**File 3:** Present continuous (future), past continuous or past simple?
Skills	Listening, reading, speaking
Optional materials	P *Don't you want me baby?* ♫

Lesson plan

■ Warmer: Progress chart

- Books closed. Ask SS *Can you remember what the lessons in File 3 were about? What grammar and vocabulary did we learn?* Elicit from the SS anything they can remember.
- Now tell SS to look at the **Progress chart** (SB *p.8*) and to tick the lessons they've studied.
- Tell them that this is the revision lesson for this File, and that they can then do the **Vocabulary and Grammar files** (*pp.50, 51*) to further revise the language of the File.

1 Practice: Listening and speaking

a • ∘17∘ Play the tape all the way through once. SS listen to five dialogues and tell you what the people are doing tonight. Compare in pairs.

> 2 They're having dinner with her mother.
> 3 They're going to the cinema to see a French film.
> 4 She's flying to Berlin.
> 5 They're going to a football match.
>
> Tapescript **SB Listening** *p.128*

- Play it again, pausing after each one and checking answers. Ask other questions for each to see if SS understood everything, e.g.
  1 *What play are they going to?* (*Hamlet*)
  2 *Does the man want to go?* (no, he doesn't)
  3 *What film are they seeing?* (a French film with subtitles – she can't remember the name)
  4 *What time's he leaving?* (about 6.00)
  5 *What match are they going to?* (Liverpool and Manchester United)

b • Ask a range of questions to individual SS, e.g. *Are you doing anything special* (*tonight*)? *Where are you going? What are you doing tomorrow* (*morning*)? etc.

- In pairs, SS talk about their plans / arrangements for tonight, tomorrow, and next weekend using the present continuous.

2 Practice: Past simple or continuous?

a • Ask *Have you been to Scotland / Loch Ness?* Focus on the photos. Ask *What can you see?*
  ⚠ *Loch* is a Scottish word meaning *Lake*.

- Focus on the black and white photo. Ask *What is it?* (the 'Loch Ness monster' – it's never officially been seen, and this photo is a famous fake).

- SS revise past simple / past continuous contrast. They quickly read the newspaper article and tell you what happened to Mr Carner (he lost his bag in Loch Ness).
- In pairs, SS complete the text with the verbs in the correct past tense (simple or continuous).

> 2 was travelling   3 decided
> 4 was going   **5** fell   6 didn't expect
> 7 were exploring   8 were looking for
> 9 saw

- Check answers. Highlight the use of the conjunction *while* to show that two things were happening at the same time. Ask *What do you think the scientists saw?* Elicit answers (e.g. the monster, his passport, etc.).

b • ∘18∘ Tell SS they're going to hear Mr Carner telling the end of the story. Play the tape. Ask *What happened?* SS compare what they heard in pairs.

- Play it again for SS to check / revise their answers. Feedback their answers.

> The Scottish police found his bag and phoned him in Spain. A month later it arrived. The money, 47,000 pesetas, was in perfect condition. He was amazed, most of all, that the pen still worked.
>
> Tapescript **SB Listening** *p.128*

3 Practice: Listening

- ∘19∘ SS listen and make sentences to describe the sounds they hear. Play number 1 and use the example to show them what to do.
- Pause after each example and give SS time to work out a sentence in pairs. Elicit the answer onto the board.

> 2 She was having a shower when the phone rang.
> 3 They were playing tennis when it started to rain.
> 4 He was taking a photo when he fell into the pool.
> 5 They were having dinner when the baby cried.

4 Skills: Reading

- SS cover the text and focus on the photo. Ask *Who is it?* (Jack Charlton) *What do you know about him?* (brother of Bobby, a famous English footballer / manager, born on 8th May 1935, played for Leeds United and England more than 600 times, manager of the Irish World Cup team in the USA in 1994).
- SS read the introduction to the interview to confirm / find out about him.
- Focus on the four paragraph titles. Elicit the meaning of *news event* (a big news story, e.g. man walking on the moon, etc.) Give a good local example if you know one.
- SS read the interview and match the four titles to the paragraphs. Tell SS not to worry about words they don't understand, just to get the general meaning.

> 1 My first home   3 My first memory of a
> 2 My first best friend   news event
>   4 My first record

- Ask a few comprehension questions for each paragraph, e.g. *Why was Jack's first home uncomfortable?*

5 Personalization: Talk about your first …

- Elicit four questions from the **ex. 4** topics onto the board:

  > 1 Who was your first best friend?
  > 2 What was the first record that you bought?
  > 3 Where was your first home?
  > 4 What's your first memory of a news event?

- Ask individual SS each question. Ask follow-up questions too, e.g. 1 *Are you still friends?*, 2 *Have you still got it?* 3 *What was it like?*, 4 *How old were you?*, etc.
- In pairs / small groups, SS talk about them.
- Feedback any interesting information.

·20· ♫ *Don't you want me baby?*

The lyrics to all the songs are on photocopiable masters (see **Extras**). If you can't make photocopies, exploit the song as follows.

- Prepare 14 pieces of card / paper. Copy lines 1 and 2 of the song onto one piece, lines 3 and 4 onto another, and so on (line 15 should be on its own). If you have more than fourteen SS, make two or more sets of cards.
- Tell SS that they're going to hear a song by The Human League, about how the singer, Phil Oakley, met his wife. Ask *Where did your parents / couples you know meet? What were they doing?*. Elicit a few replies.
- Give one card to each student and get them to stand round the table. With a large class, put them in groups with a set of cards each (it doesn't matter if a student has more than one card). SS read the line(s) on their card.
- Tell SS that you're going to play the song, and that when they hear their line(s) they must put that card on the table in the right order.
- ·20· Play the song as many times as necessary for all SS to place their lines.
- Play it through a final time for the group to check.

Lesson notes

In this revision lesson, SS revise **File 3** through talking about their future arrangements, a true story about a tourist who dropped his bag in Loch Ness and then got it back 14 years later, and a text about Jack Charlton, one of Britain's most famous football managers. The lesson finishes with The Human League song *Don't you want me baby?*

while Introduced in **ex. 2** for SS to recognize. **when** can always replace *while* but not vice versa. *while* has to go with the continuous part of the sentence. NOT ~~They were having a party while the police arrived.~~ Don't go into this unless SS ask.

Extras

Don't you want me baby? P *p. 164* A song by The Human League. Instructions *p. 132*.

Revision conversations P *p. 165* A pair / groupwork activity to revise the key language of Files 1 to 3. Instructions *p. 133*.

■ Homework

Choose from the **End-of-file options** below.

End-of-file options

Student's Book

■ Vocabulary file 3 *p. 50*

- Do this in class, or set it for homework. However, even if SS do the rest of the page at home, you should try to go quickly through the introductory text and **Organize your vocabulary learning!** in class.

Organize your vocabulary learning! Emphasize the importance of recording words well, thinking how they're going to remember them, and regularly testing themselves.

Try it! SS do 📖 **Food A** *p. 137* and put the study tip into practice. Monitor how many words SS can remember over the next few classes.

> **1 Word groups**
> **a 2** 1 lorry 2 van 3 car **3** 1 motorway
>   2 road 3 path **4** 1 city 2 town 3 village
>   **5** 1 forest 2 tree 3 flower
> **2 Pronunciation**
>   **2** s **3** t **4** l **5** g **6** w **7** b **8** t
> **3 Key words**
>   1 Suddenly 2 even 3 while 4 actually
>   5 now
> **4 Verbs + prepositions**
>   2 get out of 3 get off 4 go upstairs
>   5 go over
> **Try it!**
>   A pear B grapes C spinach
>   D strawberries E chicken F lettuce
>   G mushrooms H carrots I salmon
>   J peach K sausage(s) L lamb chops
>   M prawns N pineapple O beans P peas
>   Q pork R cabbage S onions T steak

■ Grammar file 3 *p. 51*

- Spend ten minutes going through this with the class, answering any queries. SS tick each box when they're satisfied they understand it.

Workbook

■ Grammar check 3 *p. 27*

- Remind SS to do this with **SB** and **WB** open in front of them, and to refer back to **Grammar file 3** as necessary. SS can check their answers with the **WB** key.

■ Read and write 3 *p. 63*

- SS write the text for a story from prompts, following a model.
- Briefly revise the use of *After / After that*. Emphasize the need to read and follow the instructions carefully and compare their final story with the model. Remind SS that they have a key to the exercises, but that you're going to collect and correct their stories.

Teacher's Book

■ Test 1 P *p. 213*

Tell SS they're going to do a revision test next lesson and photocopy one per student. Instructions *p. 211*. (There are also photocopiable **TB** Tests after Files 6 and 9.)

Lesson aims

Reading skills	Recognizing different kinds of texts, skimming
	guessing meaning from context, using pronoun reference
Revision	Past tenses
Optional materials	A selection of locally-available *Easy Readers* (**ex. 1b**).
	Dictionaries (**ex. 4**)

Lesson plan

■ Warmer: Reading habits

- Books closed. Write on the board:

  > 1 Do you like reading in your language? Why (not)?
  >
  > 2 Where do you read? When? How often?

- In small groups, SS answer the questions. Feedback.

1 Presentation: Vocabulary

a
- Books open. Check vocabulary and drill pronunciation of the types of books. Elicit a few famous examples (local if possible) of some different kinds of books, e.g. thrillers – Agatha Christie's novels.

  ⚠ *thriller* = an exciting suspense novel

- Get SS to choose their top three and compare with a partner.

  Tip Ask for a quick show of hands for each type to find out the most popular.

- Feedback. Ask *What <u>don't</u> you like reading?*

b
- Ask *What do you read in English?* Elicit, e.g. songs, computer manuals, magazines, textbooks, etc.
- Ask *Have you ever read an Easy Reader? Did you enjoy it?*
- Take SS through **Question and answer 1**, and refer them to the photos of covers to make sure they understand what *Easy Readers* are.

  Tip Try to bring a selection of locally-available *Easy Readers* at SS' level, to show them what they are.

- SS read **Question and answer 2**. Make sure they understand *front / back cover*. Emphasize the importance of choosing a book that they find interesting.

2 Skimming

- SS quickly read through three extracts from *Easy Readers* and match them to the right cover.

  Tip The aim is to practise skimming (looking through a text quickly to see what it's about) as SS would in their own language. Set a short time limit, e.g. one minute. Tell them not to read every word.

- Feedback. Ask *What kind of books are they? Which one would you like to read?* Use a show of hands to see which is the most popular. Ask a few SS *Why?*

  > **Extract 1** Sherlock Holmes Short Stories (= detective stories)
  >
  > **Extract 2** Henry VIII and his Six Wives (= historical novel)
  >
  > **Extract 3** Rainforests (= non-fiction)

3 Choosing the right level

- SS read **Question and answer 3**. Check comprehension by asking *How do you know if an Easy Reader is too difficult?* (if it has more than eight words you don't know on the first page).
- SS read **Extract 1** in two minutes and underline all the words they don't know.
- They count them and choose **a**, **b**, or **c**. Feedback. There probably won't be more than eight that they haven't seen before or can't recognize from the context. Get SS to compare their underlined words in pairs. Don't explain the meaning of the words yet.
- Emphasize the importance of being able to read an *Easy Reader* quickly and easily. If SS have to read very slowly and frequently look up words, they won't enjoy reading nor get much from it, and will soon give up. It's much better to choose a book which is too easy rather than too difficult.
- Remind SS that most *Easy Readers* are numbered according to level. In the *Oxford Bookworms* series SS studying *English File 2* would normally be Level 2.

4 Guessing meaning from context

a
- Ask *What do you do when there are words in the story that you don't know?* Elicit their suggestions.
- Focus on **Question and answer 4**. Compare with SS' suggestions and go through the alternatives.
- Emphasize that SS should always try to guess the meaning of unknown words and keep on reading. They should only use a dictionary if they can't guess a word which seems important, or one which occurs more than once.
- In pairs, SS find the words from the list in the text (they'll probably have already underlined some or most of them) and guess what they mean from the context.

  Tip Get SS to tick the words on the list if they think they can guess what they mean.

b
- SS check to see if any of the words are in the **Glossary** at the bottom of the page (only five of them are there). Tell SS the **Glossary** is often at the back of an *Easy Reader*, and that it's like a mini-dictionary.
- SS tick any more words from the list they understand.
- Ask *How many words haven't you ticked?* Tell SS to look again at the context around these words. Then

ask *Are they very important to the story? Can you understand it without them?* This can help SS see that they can often continue reading without understanding everything.

c • Finally SS check the meaning of all the words from the list in their dictionaries.

5 Recognizing pronoun reference

- SS read **Question and answer 5**. Emphasize that when you read in English it's often quite difficult to know who's doing what. Remind SS that English adjectives, participles, etc. have no masculine / feminine or plural forms, and that the only words which tell you who is being spoken about are the pronouns. Elicit examples: *she* / *he* / *they, her* / *him* / *them*, etc.
- In pairs, SS read **Extract 2** again, look at the pronouns in italics, and decide who or what each one is referring to.
- Check answers.

which = the palace of Whitehall	he = Henry
them = her letters and books	it = the wooden box
it = the palace	them = the letters
his = Henry's	it = the letter
He = Henry	who = Anne Boleyn

6 Asking questions

- SS read **Question and answer 6**. Ask *Do you ask yourself questions when you read?*

  Tip Emphasize that this tip, together with trying to guess the meaning of unknown words from context, are the most important ones. SS have to try to read at a reasonable speed. But they must also stop at regular intervals and ask themselves *Do I understand this? What's happening?*

- SS read **Extract 3** and answer the three questions. Feedback.
  ⚠ SS will find answers 2 and 3 hard to formulate but should be able to express the idea to show they've understood what they've read.

  > 1 buy = North America, Europe, Japan
  >   sell = Latin America, Africa, Asia
  > 2 Because they don't want to destroy the rainforests.
  > 3 Rich countries / companies buy the rainforest land which is cheap. Then they cut down the trees, sell the wood, and use the land to produce meat cheaply.

7 Learning from Easy Readers

- Ask *How will reading Easy Readers help your English?* Elicit some answers, e.g. *Easy Readers* are good for revising grammar and vocabulary outside class, improve SS' ability to read texts in English.
- SS read **Question and answer 7**. Emphasize the importance of being selective, i.e. SS have to decide which words are important.
- SS read **Extract 3** again intensively and choose four words they think will be important throughout the book.

- SS compare with a partner to see if they agree. Feedback. Ask *Which are the four most common words?*

  Tip Point out that in *Easy Readers* most of the new words come in the first chapters and then these words are 'recycled' in the rest of the book. If SS write down the important words when they read the first chapter(s), they will be able to read more quickly later.

■ Building a class library

- SS read **Question and answer 8**. Get their reactions to the idea.
- If you're lucky enough to have a school library, take your SS there and help them choose an *Easy Reader* to read at home. If not, tell SS how much *Easy Readers* cost locally. If they like the idea and can afford it, collect the price of one book from each student. Buy a range of books that you think will interest them, then let each student choose one to read. When they finish, they can swap the books among themselves, e.g. at the end of each class or in the break.

  Tip You could take a student representative with you to choose the books.

Lesson notes

The third **Focus on ...** skills lesson, which encourages SS to start reading in English outside class. Some of your SS may already have to read / translate in English at a much higher level of difficulty than this coursebook, e.g. business correspondence, computer network, academic texts, etc.

The main aim is to interest SS in reading in English and improve their reading skills. *Easy Readers* provide one of the best ways of increasing your SS' contact with English in an enjoyable way.

Extras

A class reader

***Easy Reader* reviews** P *p. 166* A reading feedback form, similar to but more complex than the one in *English File 1*. Instructions *p. 133*.

***English File* reading chart** P *p. 167* SS record the *Easy Readers* they've read and write a brief, one-line review for other SS to read. Instructions *p. 133*.

■ Learner-training

Monitor and encourage SS reading. Keep the **English File reading chart** in your register or on the classroom wall, and get SS to record the titles they've read. Keep some spare copies of **Easy Reader reviews** with your register. Encourage SS to fill them in and show them to each other. Regularly review how they're getting on and perhaps offer a prize to each student who reads a certain number of titles.

■ Homework

See **End-of-file options**.

> London isn't as dangerous
> as San Francisco.

Lesson aims

Grammar	*as ... as, much / a bit* + comparatives
Vocabulary	Towns / cities: adjectives (*noisy*, etc.), nouns (*building*, etc.)
Pronunciation	/ə/: *er* endings, weak form of *as* and *than* sentence stress
Revision	Comparative adjectives, adverbs

Lesson plan

■ Warmer: Adjective rules

Write on the board:

> 1 He visited a lot of differents places.
> 2 It was an experience very interesting.

- In pairs, SS find one mistake in each sentence.
- Feedback. Elicit the basic rules for adjectives:
- – they have the same form in singular and plural.
- – adjectives go before the noun they describe.

> **1** different places.   **2** a very interesting experience.

1 Presentation: Vocabulary

a
- SS turn to 🔲 **Adjectives A** *p. 138* and match an adjective to each picture. Check answers.

> **1** dangerous **2** noisy **3** dirty **4** comfortable
> **7** modern **8** narrow **9** high **10** crowded

- SS match the adjectives with opposites from the box.
- Check answers, drilling pronunciation as necessary.

> dirty / clean   dangerous / safe   crowded / empty
> high / low   small / large   modern / old
> narrow / wide   noisy / quiet
> comfortable / uncomfortable

> ⚠️ Some adjectives have more than one opposite, e.g. the opposite of *empty* can be *full* or *crowded* (= full of people). Remind SS that *large = big*.

b
- Books open. SS focus on ❤ **Towns / cities**. SS look at the photos and find an example of each word.
- Ask *What can you see in the first photo?* Get the class to describe it using adjectives from **ex.1a**. Insist on full sentences.
- Do the same with the other three photos.

c
- SS identify photos of San Francisco or London.

> **A** (street car) and
> **C** (the Golden Gate bridge) = San Francisco
> **B** (Trafalgar Square / Nelson's Column) and
> **D** (Camden market) = London

2 Presentation: *as ... as / much / a bit* + comparative adjectives

- SS read the introduction. Ask questions e.g. *Where does Julie live? Where was she born?*
- Read sentences 1 to 4 to the class. Be prepared to explain / translate *violent*, *standard of living*. Ask them to predict if the sentences are true or false.
- Feedback, but don't tell them the answers.

3 Presentation: Reading

a
- SS in pairs, A and B. A reads the first two paragraphs only. B reads only paragraphs 3 and 4 . SS tell their partners about the differences. Tell them to do it without looking at the book.
- Feedback answers to **ex.2**.

> **1** True   **2** True   **3** False   **4** True

b
- SS read their partner's half of the text, then decide together which place Julie prefers for each of the four categories, and why.

> She prefers San Francisco in all categories except **Cities**.

- Encourage SS to guess new vocabulary from the context. Be prepared to explain / translate *architecture, stimulating, shopper's paradise, a fortune, quality, aggressive, fresh, choice, serve, disappointed*.
- Feedback. Ask *Where would you prefer to live? Why?*

■ GRAMMAR FOCUS 1
Comparatives

a
- Focus on the examples in the chart. Highlight:
- – the form of comparative= (see **Ⓖ◀◀ 13** *p. 5*).
- – *less* + adjective (without *er*) to reverse the comparison.
- – *as* + adjective + *as* in positive sentences to say two nouns are the same.
- – *not as* + adjective + *as* to say the first noun is *less* (adjective) than the second.

b
- Point out that we use:
- – *much* + comparative for a big difference.
- – *a bit* + comparative for a small difference.

PRACTICE 1

- Tell SS to write two comparative sentences about each pair of cities. Check answers.

> **2** Casablanca is hotter than Warsaw. Warsaw isn't as hot as Casablanca.
> **3** Tokyo is noisier than Helsinki. Helsinki isn't as noisy as Tokyo.
> **4** Chicago is more violent than London. London isn't as violent as Chicago.
> **5** The traffic in Bangkok is worse than the traffic in Venice. The traffic in Venice isn't as bad as the traffic in Bangkok.

■ PRONUNCIATION

- ◦ 1 ◦ SS listen and repeat six sentences from **Practice 1**.
- Elicit the headword for /ə/ (**comput**er). Ask *Is the /ə/ sound stressed?* (no).
- SS listen again. Pause after each sentence and ask *Which words are stressed?* (the cities and adjectives) *Which words aren't stressed?* (*as, than*). Elicit the pronunciation of *as* and *than* (= /ə/).

> 3 Casablanca is hotter than Warsaw.
> 4 Helsinki isn't as noisy as Tokyo.
> 5 Chicago is more violent than San Francisco.
> 6 The traffic in Venice isn't as bad as in Bangkok.

- Play the tape again and get SS to repeat the sentences with the right stress, producing the /ə/ sound correctly.

4 Presentation: Comparative adverbs

- Revise adverbs by writing on the board:

Adjective	Adverb
1 He's a bad player.	He plays badly.
2 They're a very good team.	They play _____.
3 I'm a slow reader.	I _____.
4 He isn't a fast runner.	He _____.
5 She's a hard worker.	She _____.

- In pairs, SS rewrite the sentences using adverbs.
- Check answers and spelling.

> 2 They play very well.   3 I read slowly.
> 4 He doesn't run fast.   5 She works hard.

- Ask *How do you form adverbs?* (adjective + *ly*). Remind SS that *well*, *fast*, and *hard* are irregular.
- Tell SS they're going to listen to Julie compare American and English lifestyles. Make sure they understand the seven phrases in the chart. Elicit / teach the meaning of *health* (*n.* from *healthy*), *stylishly*, and *freedom* (*n.* from *free*).
- ◦ 2 ◦ Play the tape twice. SS listen and tick under either the US or UK flag. Be prepared to explain / translate *vitamins*, *diet foods*, *outdoor activities*, *apart from*, *dependent*. Check answers.

> watch more TV – US
> worry more about their health – US
> do less sport – UK
> can't drink in bars until they're 21 – US
> dress more stylishly – UK   have less freedom – US
> leave home when they finish school – UK
> Tapescript **SB Listening** *p. 128*

■ GRAMMAR FOCUS 2
Comparative adverbs

a
- Focus on the chart. Highlight:
  - that regular comparative adverbs are formed with *more* / *less* + comparative adverb.
  - the six irregular forms. Elicit an example for each one, e.g. *I'm studying harder than last year.*

b
- Point out that comparative adverbs are used to compare two actions.

PRACTICE 2

- Focus on the example to see if SS agree. Elicit more sentences to compare how men and women drive, e.g. *Men drive more dangerously than women.*
- SS write five more sentences. Check they understand the meaning of *dress* (*v.*) and *logically*. Monitor and help, encouraging SS to use *a bit* and *much*.
- In pairs, SS compare their sentences to see if they agree.

5 Personalization: Talk about your town

- SS compare a city / town they know well to the place where they are now, using the six categories.
- Feedback from some SS. Ask *Which place would you prefer to live in? Why?*

Lesson notes

Through the context of comparing two cities, SS revise comparative adjectives and learn to compare using (*not*) *as … as*. SS also learn to form and use comparative adverbs. Revise with ⊕◄◄ 13 (**SB** *p. 5*) if necessary.

as and *than* Common error ~~as big than~~

Extras

Compare the pairs P *p. 168* Cards for SS to make comparative sentences. Instructions *p. 133*.

Books-closed presentation

Comparative (*not*) as … as
- Do after the **Warmer**. Think of a town / city which your SS will know (e.g. if you're in Florence, Siena). Ask *Has anyone been to (Siena)?* Then ask *Which is bigger, Florence or Siena?* to elicit *Florence is bigger than Siena.* Now ask *Which is more expensive?*
- Write on the board:

> 1 Florence is bigger than Siena.
>   Siena isn't _____.
> 2 Florence is more expensive than Siena.
>   Siena isn't _____.

- SS complete the sentences so they mean the same as the first ones. Elicit / teach *Siena isn't as big as Florence.* / *Siena isn't as expensive as Florence.* Then start **ex. 1**.

■ Learner-training

Get SS to asterisk (*) the adjectives in ◢ **Adjectives** *p. 138* which use *more* / *less* to form comparatives.

■ Homework

SS do **WB 4A** *p. 28* and **Listen and speak 4A**.

Writing: Two towns SS compare two towns, explaining which one they'd prefer to live in and why.

> *If I lend you my newspaper, we'll start talking.*

Lesson aims

Grammar	First conditional (*if ...* + *will* / *won't* + infinitive)
Vocabulary	Confusing verbs: *lend* / *borrow*, etc.
Pronunciation	/l/
Revision	Adjectives and their opposites
Optional materials	Pieces of paper with the first sentences copied (**ex. 6**)

Lesson plan

■ Warmer: ⓡ Adjectives

- In pairs, SS test each other on 📖 **Adjectives A** *p. 138*.

1 Presentation: First conditional

- SS read the list of places and mark the word stress. Check pronunciation, especially /ɪnˈʃʊərəns/. Elicit a local example of each.
- Focus on the five adverts. Ask *Where can you find these adverts?* SS match each one to a place from the list.
- SS compare in pairs, then check answers.

> **2** language school   **3** department store
> **4** insurance company   **5** travel agency

■ GRAMMAR FOCUS

First conditional

a • SS highlight the verbs in the adverts and look at the two examples in the chart. They complete the rule.

> if + **present simple** AND **will** / **won't** + infinitive

b • Read the rule of use. Make sure SS understand 'possible future situation'.

will / won't

c • SS complete the chart for *will/won't*.
- Check answers and drill pronunciation of the contracted forms.

> ⎯ **won't**   ？ **will**   ✓✗ **will, won't**
> Contractions **will**   **won't**

- Highlight that:
- there are two phrases in first conditional sentences.
- the *if*-phrase is always in the present simple NOT ~~If it will rain.~~
- the *if*-phrase can come first or second (*If it rains, we'll stay in.* = *We'll stay in if it rains.*)
- *'ll* is the contraction of *will* (c.f. *I'll*)

⚠ If SS ask about differences between *will* / *won't* and (*be*) *going to* and present continuous for future, tell them to use *will* / *won't* only in conditionals for now. Say that they're going to learn more uses of *will* / *won't* in **8B**.

• SS translate the two conditional sentences at the beginning of the **Grammar focus** (*If it rains ...*). Ask SS to compare how they express these phrases in their L1. Do they use similar forms?

PRACTICE

a • SS match the two halves of more adverts.
- Elicit the meaning of <u>dis</u>count (= cheaper price), book (*v.*), de<u>liver</u> (= take to your home).
- Check answers.

> **2** c   **3** e   **4** a   **5** b

b • SS read and complete the sentences.
- SS check answers first in pairs and then with you.

> **2** tell, won't tell   **3** drive, 'll be
> **4** 'll get, don't take   **5** doesn't work, won't pass
> **6** don't go, 'll be

■ PRONUNCIATION

a • ⟨3⟩ Focus on the headword (*leg*). Ask SS to tell you the sound it represents (/l/). SS listen and repeat the /l/ words.

b • ⟨4⟩ Focus on the example. Tell SS they're going to hear five more phrases with *will*, and to write them down. Play the tape once. Pause after each sentence.
- SS compare in pairs. Play the tape again to check.
- Feedback the sentences onto the board, checking / drilling pronunciation as necessary.

> **2** I won't be late.   **3** Will you meet me?
> **4** It won't be difficult.   **5** It'll be easy.
> **6** She'll help.

2 Vocabulary: Confusing verbs

- SS turn to 📖 **Verbs A** *p. 139*. In pairs, they complete the chart with the right pairs of verbs from the list.
- Check answers. For each pair, ask SS to describe the picture using the right phrase, e.g. 1 *The man has borrowed a book from the library.*

> **1** borrow / lend   **2** carry / wear
> **3** watch / look at   **4** win / earn   **5** meet / know
> **6** miss / lose   **7** say / tell

- Highlight:
- the difference between *Can **I** borrow your dictionary?* / *Can **you** lend me your dictionary?*
- that you can only *wear* clothes, jewellery, and glasses.
- that *watch* is normally used with TV.
- that we usually use *earn* for a salary.
- that *meet* is used only for people. We use it when people are introduced (*Come and meet my wife.*) or when people come together at a place (*Let's meet at the cinema.*).
- that you *can't lose* a bus/class.
- that *say* and *tell* have similar meanings but *tell* must be followed by an object, either a person or a story, etc. e.g. *Tell me a story.* NOT ~~Say me ...~~

Tip Suggest that SS record any other pairs of confusing verbs in the same way.

3 Practice: Reading / speaking

a • SS cover the pictures and quickly read the beginning of a short story called **An American in Paris**. After one minute, ask a few comprehension questions: *Who was on the train? Where were they going? Why was the American bored?*
• Ask SS to guess why the Frenchman doesn't want the American to read his paper. Elicit a few answers.

b • In pairs, SS look at pictures A to H and imagine the story.
• Feedback ideas about the story.

4 Practice: Reading and listening

a • In pairs, SS look at the pictures again and read and complete the story.

b • ◦5◦ SS listen to the story and check their answers. Pause the tape after each line and elicit the completed sentence.

> … we'**ll start** talking.
> If we **start** talking, we'**ll become** friends.
> If we **become** friends, I'**ll invite** you to my house.
> If I **invite** you to my house, you'**ll meet** my beautiful daughter, Yvette.
> If you **meet** Yvette, you'**ll fall in love** with her.
> If you **fall in love** with her, you'**ll run away** together.
> If you **run away** together, I'**ll find** you.
> If I **find** you, I'**ll kill** you.
> So, that's why I don't want to **lend** you my paper.

• Check the answers to the three questions.

> **1** She's the Frenchman's daughter. She lives in his house. **2** Because he doesn't want the American to fall in love with Yvette and take her away. **3** No, he doesn't.

5 Practice: Roleplay

• In pairs, SS roleplay the story. First demonstrate with you as the American and the class as the Frenchman.
• A is the Frenchman. He / She covers the text and looks only at the pictures. B, who is the American, has the text open, and helps and corrects A. Then they swap.

6 Game: *If …*

• SS in groups of four. Give each student a number between 1 and 4.
• Write on the board:

> 1 If I go out tonight, …
> 2 If it rains at the weekend, …
> 3 If I learn to speak English well, …
> 4 If I can't find my house keys, …

(If you need a group of five, write up five first sentences.) Give each S in the group a 'first sentence.'
• Explain to SS that they're going to write stories in their group. Demonstrate the game using another sentence e.g. *If I lose my wallet, …*
Elicit a possible continuation, e.g. *I'll go to the police.* Elicit the next sentence of the story, e.g. *If I go to the*

police, they'll lend me some money. Continue with a couple more sentences.
• SS complete their first sentences, and then pass the paper to the student on their left.
• SS look at the paper they've now got, and write another conditional sentence beginning with the second half of the previous sentence. Then they pass the paper again.
• When the pieces of paper have been passed round the group once or twice the SS read their 'chain stories' to the rest of the group.
⚠ SS may make the common mistake *I'll can*. If this comes up, tell them it's wrong, and teach *I'll be able to*. This is taught in **8B**.

Lesson notes

SS learn the first conditional through advertisements, then practise it with an 'if' chain story. In *English File* SS have so far seen *will / won't* in travel phrases and lines from songs, but this is the first time SS formally study it. Other functions of *will* (instant decisions, offers, promises, and predictions) are taught in **File 8B**.

First conditional SS may put *will / won't* in the *if*-phrase, e.g. ~~If it will rain tomorrow …~~ They also need help with the pronunciation of the *'ll* contractions and *won't*.

will / won't Emphasize the use of *will / won't* for conditionals and that we don't use it for future plans, e.g. ~~This weekend I'll go away.~~

Extras

If … 🄿 *p.169* A board game. SS complete first conditional sentences. Instructions *p.133*.

Books-closed presentation

First conditional (*will / won't*)
Do after the **Warmer**.
• Write on the board the name of a local newspaper, and underneath the name of your school and *If you come to (your school), you'll …*
• Tell SS they're going to write an advert for the school. Elicit possible ways of finishing the sentences, e.g. *learn English quickly, find a better job*, etc.
• Teach / elicit that *'ll* is the contraction of *will*, and expresses the future.
• Highlight the tenses in the two parts of the sentence. Tell SS that this is the first conditional and we use it to talk about a possible future event.
• Teach / elicit the negative form *will not = won't* and add an example to the advert, e.g. *It won't cost a lot of money.* Then start **ex. 1**.

■ **Learner-training**

Emphasize the importance of SS revising what they've done in class at home, e.g. reading their lesson notes and vocabulary lists, doing **Workbook** exercises and using the 'Listen and speak' cassette.

■ **Homework**

SS do **WB 4B** *p.29* and **Listen and speak 4B**.

| 4 | C | *Somebody told me* |

> *I don't want to do anything tonight.*

Lesson aims

Grammar	*something / anything / nothing*, etc.
Vocabulary	*else*
Pronunciation	/ʌ/, /əʊ/, /ɑ/, /ɔː/
Revision	*some / any*, present perfect

Lesson plan

■ Warmer: ℝ *some / any*

- Write these sentences on the board:

> 1 I haven't got _____ money.
> 2 There are _____ biscuits in the cupboard.
> 3 There isn't _____ milk.
> 4 Have you got _____ brothers or sisters?
> 5 Are there ____ shops near here?
> 6 Could I have ____ aspirins, please?

- SS copy and complete them with *some* or *any*. Tell SS to be careful with number 6.
- SS compare in pairs, then check answers.

> **1** any **2** some **3** any **4** any **5** any **6** some

- Ask *Why is number 6 different?* Elicit that in most questions we use *any*, but we use *some* when we offer things (*Would you like some more coffee?*) or when we ask for things (*Can I have some more coffee, please?*)

1 Presentation: *something / anything / nothing*, etc.

a
- Cover the dialogue. Focus on the women in the photos. Ask *Where are they?* (at home / in an office).
- SS read the instructions for **ex.1a**. Ask *Who's Zandra?* (the woman in the office).
- ▫6▫ SS listen and answer the questions about Julie. Play the tape once and elicit answers.

> Julie calls Zandra because she's ill. She's going to stay at home / She isn't going to go to work.

- Play it again for SS to check .

b
- SS uncover the dialogue and complete it with the four missing sentences. Elicit / teach the meaning of *sound* (v.), *catch* (*an illness*), *cold* (n.), *flu, take care*.
- SS compare in pairs, then listen again to check.
- Check answers.

> 1 I think I've caught something.
> 2 Have you taken anything?   3 No, nothing.
> 4 Is there anybody to look after you?

■ GRAMMAR FOCUS
some / any / no + body / thing / where

a
- SS highlight the six *some / any / no* words in the dialogue.

> something, anything, nothing, something, anywhere, anybody

- Check answers. Tell SS to look at the sentences containing these highlighted words and decide if they're ☐+☐, ☐−☐, or ☐?☐. Then they complete the chart with the right forms.

People	somebody	anybody	**nobody**
Things	something	**anything**	**nothing**
Places	somewhere	**anywhere**	nowhere

- Highlight that we use these words when we don't know exactly who / what / where, e.g. *Somebody phoned you last night.* (= we don't know who).
- Drill pronunciation especially *nothing* /ˈnʌθɪŋ/ and *nobody* /ˈnəʊbədiː/.

b
- Focus on rules 1 to 4. SS find an example from the dialogue to illustrate each rule.

> 1 I think I've caught something. /
>   I'm going to take something.
> 2 Have you taken anything? / Is there anybody …
> 3 You can't go anywhere with a cold like that.
> 4 No, nothing.

- Highlight that
- we use *nothing, nobody*, etc. in one word answers NOT ~~anybody~~, and as a subject, e.g. *Nothing happened.* NOT ~~Anything happened.~~
- *body = one*, i.e. For *somebody / anybody / nobody* you can also say *someone / anyone / no one*.
- in rule 3 we don't use *no…* with a negative verb because in English we never use two negative words in a sentence, e.g. *I didn't do anything.* NOT ~~I didn't do nothing.~~

PRACTICE

a
- SS complete the sentences.
- Check answers.

> 2 anything 3 anybody 4 somebody
> 5 something

b
- SS answer the questions with the right *No-* word.
- Check answers.

> 1 Nothing. 2 Nowhere. 3 Nobody.

c
- SS write the same answers to the questions in **b** with a full sentence and the right *any-* word.
- Check answers.

> 2 I didn't go anywhere. 3 I didn't see anybody.

- Focus on **Ⓥ** *else*. Highlight that we don't use *more* here. NOT ~~Does anybody more want to come?~~

2 Practice: Listening

- 〔 ·7· 〕 Tell SS that Julie went back to work the next day. SS read the six sentences and listen to see if they're true or false.
- Play the tape again if necessary. SS compare in pairs, then check answers.

> **1** F **2** T **3** F **4** F **5** F **6** T
>
> Tapescript **SB Listening** *p. 128*

- Ask *Have you ever said you were ill when you weren't? What do you think of Julie's behaviour?*

3 Personalization: Speaking

a
- Focus on the questionnaire **How interesting is your life?** Check the meaning of *recently*, *funny*, and *exciting*.
- Focus on the example sentence and point out the change from 〔+〕 *some* to 〔?〕 *any*.
- Get SS to ask you. Encourage them to ask past simple follow-up questions if you answer *Yes, I have.*, or *Why not?* if you say *No, I haven't.*

b
- Drill the questions again. Then SS stand up and mingle to find a student who says *Yes* to each question. When they do, they write their name beside the question and ask follow-up questions.
- Monitor, help, and correct as necessary.
- Set a time limit and then see how many *Yes* answers they've found, or let the activity continue until someone can complete the questionnaire.
- Individual SS feedback any interesting answers.

■ PRONUNCIATION

- In pairs, SS say each word and cross out the one with a different pronunciation of the letter *o* in each group.
- Read the words aloud to SS. They listen and check answers.
- Highlight that:
- *o* + consonant + *e* is usually pronounced /əʊ/ or /ʌ/.
- *o* between consonants is usually pronounced /ɒ/.
- *or* is usually pronounced /ɔː/ but occasionally /ɜː/ e.g. *work*, *world* (see **Sound bank WB** *p. 81*).

> **1** all /ʌ/ except home   **2** all /əʊ/ except not
> **3** all /ɒ/ except door   **4** all /ɔː/ except work

4 Practice: Reading

a
- Focus on the pictures and ask *What's happening in picture 1?* etc. Elicit *lift* (SS may know *elevator* – US).
- Ask *Have you ever been trapped in a lift? Do you know anybody who has? What happened?*

b
- SS read and number the paragraphs, using the pictures to help them.
- SS check in pairs. Then check answers.

> **2** g **3** d **4** a **5** b **6** e **7** f

- Read the text to the class. Elicit the meaning / pronunciation of *not work* (= broken), *immediately*, *repair*, *extra*, *city council*.

Tip You could use this text to give SS practice in reading aloud or get SS to use the pictures only to re-tell the story in pairs.

Lesson notes

In this lesson SS learn the compounds of *some* / *any* / *no* in the context of a dialogue between a boss and an employee and then recycle the target language in a reading skills activity based around a newspaper story.

***something*/ *anything*, etc.** SS have seen these words already (e.g. *Anything else?*) but have not focused on the rules of use (which are the same as those for *some* and *any*).

***nothing*/ *nobody*, etc.** SS often have problems using these words in short answers and as the subject of a sentence. Common errors: *Who phoned?* ~~Anybody.~~ ~~Anybody phoned.~~ (see 〔Ⓖ◄◄ 18〕 **SB** *p. 7*).

Extras

Odysseus and the Cyclops 〔Ⓟ〕 *p. 170* A story with pictures for SS to reorder and tell. Instructions *p. 134*.

Books-closed presentation

***something*/ *anything*/ *nothing*, etc.**
- Ask individual SS *Are you doing anything on Friday night?* Elicit answers. If some SS answer *No, anything.*, elicit and teach the correct short answer, *No, nothing.* Then ask different SS *What about Saturday night?* Try to elicit various positive answers.
- Write on the board:

> A Are you doing _____ on Friday night?
> B No, _____. I'm not doing _____. But I'm doing _____ on Saturday.

- Tell SS to copy and complete the dialogue with *nothing*, *anything*, or *something*. Check answers. Highlight that the rules are the same as for *some* and *any*. Revise with 〔Ⓖ◄◄ 18〕 (**SB** *p. 7*) if necessary.

> A Are you doing **anything** on Friday night?
> B No, **nothing**. I'm not doing **anything**. But I'm doing **something** on Saturday.

- Rub out the dialogue bit by bit. In pairs, SS try to complete it from memory.
- Omit the **Warmer** and start **ex. 1**.

■ Learner-training

Tell SS to take 15 minutes after they've done their homework to organize their files, lesson notes, and vocabulary lists. Make sure SS are doing this.

■ Homework

SS do **WB 4C** *p. 30* and **Listen and speak 4C**.

The best and the worst

> *The most cosmopolitan city in Europe.*

pronunciation is /ɪst/ NOT /est/ and that it's never stressed. Play the tape again if necessary.

the most popular, the most beautiful, the best, the greatest, the friendliest, the oldest, the most famous, the happiest

Lesson aims

Grammar	Superlative adjectives, article *the*
Vocabulary	Adjectives, places: *cathedral*, etc.
Pronunciation	/ð/, /d/, /ðə/ or /ðiː/
Revision	Comparative adjectives
Optional materials	Magazine adverts / tourist brochures (**Warmer**)
	Large sheets of paper to make posters (**ex. 4c**)

Lesson plan

■ Warmer: Adverts

- Ask *What do you think of adverts on TV and in the street?* Elicit opinions.
- In pairs, SS decide which is their favourite advert.
- Feedback comparing ideas.

1 Presentation: Reading / Listening

- Focus on the key phrase in the speech bubble. Ask *Which city is it?* (London)

[a]
- Books open. Focus on the authentic advertising slogans. Read the first one to the class and ask *What do you think it's advertising?* Elicit their guesses onto the board, e.g. *Marlboro Lights, Rothmans, Benson & Hedges, Camel*, etc. Don't tell them the answers yet.
- In pairs SS read the other seven slogans and decide what products or places they're advertising. Elicit / teach the meaning of *popular, king size, filter, lager* /ˈlaːɡə/, *airline*, and *earth* /ɜːθ/.
- Feedback their guesses.

[b]
- ○8○ Play the tape twice. SS listen to the adverts and write the names of the products or places.
- Check answers. Elicit the correct spelling onto the board. After each one ask *Do you agree?*

1 **Rothmans** cigarettes. The world's most popular king size filter cigarette.
2 Try a taste of **Martini**. The most beautiful drink in the world.
3 **Carlsberg**, probably the best lager in the world.
4 **Gone with the wind**, the greatest film ever made.
5 Why don't you fly with **British Airways**, the world's friendliest airline.
6 Welcome to **Bologna** University, the oldest university in Europe.
7 And over there on your left you can see the **Empire State building**, the most famous building in the world.
8 Ladies and gentlemen, boys and girls, welcome to **Disneyland**, the happiest place on earth.

■ PRONUNCIATION

[a]
- ○9○ Play the tape. SS listen and repeat the superlative adjectives from the slogans. Ask *How do you pronounce E-S-T?* Highlight that the

[b]
- ○10○ Elicit the two headwords, /ð/ and /d/. SS listen and repeat the words and sounds. Elicit a few more words for each sound if you can (see **Sound bank WB** *p.82*).

[c]
- Write *the* on the board. Ask *When do we say* /ðə/*? When do we say* /ðiː/*?* (/ðiː/ before vowels). Ask SS to predict how to say the six phrases from the list.
- ○11○ Play the tape. SS listen, check, and repeat.

/ðiː/ the oldest   The End   the Italians
/ðə/ the world   the sun   the city centre

■ GRAMMAR FOCUS
Superlative adjectives

[a]
- Focus on the adjective chart. Elicit the first two lines from the class (*old–older–the oldest, big–bigger–the biggest*) to demonstrate, and teach the word superlative.
- In pairs, SS complete the chart. Remind them to look back at the slogans to help them. Monitor to make sure they use *the* before superlatives.
- Check answers and elicit the correct spelling onto the board. Drill pronunciation as necessary, especially /ˈfrendliːɪst/, /wɜːs/, and /wɜːst/.

older   the biggest   the friendliest
the most famous   more popular   the most popular
bad   worse   better   the best

[b]
- SS look at the first three superlative forms in their completed charts. Ask *What letters do you add to adjectives to make superlative adjectives?* (*est*). Ask *What happens to longer adjectives?* (you use *most*).
- SS read and complete the rules.
- Check answers.

est   + iest   most

- Write more adjectives on the board for SS to transform to test they've understood all three rules, e.g.

small   hot   fat   nice   fine   fast   dirty   easy
modern   boring   wonderful   comfortable

- Highlight that:
- the spelling rules are the same as for the comparative.
- the irregular forms are *best* and *worst*.
- 1-syllable adjectives all add *est*.
- 2-syllable adjectives use *the most* unless they end in *y*, which becomes *iest* (there are exceptions to this rule but it's not necessary to deal with them at this level).

– all adjectives of 3 or more syllables use *the most*.
– we use a superlative adjective (not a comparative) to talk about *the biggest / best*, etc. in a group. Common error ~~He's the better player in the team.~~

c • Focus on the use of *the* before superlative adjectives. You can also use a personal pronoun (*my*, etc.).

PRACTICE

a • SS read the sentences. Elicit / teach the meaning of (*ho*tel) *suite* /swiːt/, *astronomer*, *discover*, *star*, *galaxy*, *Sultan*, *koala bear*, *lazy*, *rugby*.
• SS complete the *Did you know ...?* facts with the superlative form of the adjective in brackets.
• Check answers.

> 1 coldest 2 youngest 3 richest 4 laziest
> 5 most dangerous 6 most expensive

b • SS read the facts in **Practice a** and match them with sentences **a** to **f**.
• Check answers.

> 2 f 3 d 4 b 5 a 6 e

• Elicit the meaning of: *injured*, *tip* (= money), *robot-servant*, *called* (= named).

2 Practice: Listening

a • Tell SS they're going to listen to six general knowledge quiz questions. Get them to read quickly through the answers to check they understand the choices, especially question 5 (= planets), and question 6 (*chimpanzees / dolphins*).
• ∘12∘ Play the tape twice. SS listen and circle the right answer, as in the example.

> **Tip** Get SS to compare in pairs, but don't check answers yet.

> 1 Where's the longest wall in the world?
> 2 What's the biggest country in the world?
> 3 What's the smallest country in Europe?
> 4 What's the noisiest city in the world?
> 5 What's the largest of our nine planets?
> 6 What are the most intelligent animals in the world?

b • SS listen to the questions again. This time they have to write their answer as a full sentence. Pause the tape after each one to give them time to write.
• Check answers.

> 2 The biggest country in the world is **Russia.**
> 3 The smallest country in Europe is **Vatican City.**
> 4 The noisiest city in the world is **Tokyo.**
> 5 The largest of our nine planets is **Jupiter.**
> 6 The most intelligent animals in the world are **chimpanzees.**

3 Personalization: Talk about the best in town

• SS in threes, A, B, and C. A and B are local residents, C is a tourist.
• Demonstrate yourself first. Pretend to be a tourist. Ask the class *Excuse me, what are the most interesting monuments in this town?*

• C asks A and B the first three questions in the same way. A and B have to agree an answer to each one.
• SS take it in turns to be the tourist, and swap roles for each group of three questions.
• Feedback. Try to agree on the top three attractions in your town.

4 Personalization: Writing

a • Focus on the advert for Edinburgh.
• SS read the advert for thirty seconds, then cover the text and, in pairs, remember the eight superlative claims. Elicit the meaning of *impressive*, *generous*, and *arts festival*. If any SS have been there, ask *Do you agree?*

b • Tell SS they're going to design a similar advert for their town. Ask *What photos would you use?*

c • In groups or pairs, SS write some slogans to go with their chosen images in **ex.4b**. Monitor and help with vocabulary. They create an advert-style poster.
• When they finish, get SS to read out their adverts.

Lesson notes

SS learn superlative adjectives through the context of advertising slogans.

Superlative adjectives SS can usually understand the superlative quite easily (they usually know *the best* already) but may have problems forming it. They may also confuse comparative and superlative sentences.

Extras

Do you agree? P p.171 Group activity to practise superlatives with prompts about TV and radio, the cinema, and music. Instructions *p.134*.

Books-closed presentation

For flashcard presentations, see **Introduction** *p.11*.
• Copy the pictures from **Picture bank 4D** *p.207*.
• Elicit that they represent Everest, the Nile, Russia, a giraffe, and a Rolls Royce.
• Ask *Why is Everest famous?* Elicit / teach *It's the highest mountain in the world*. Write it on the board.
• Repeat with the other pictures to elicit.
• Use the pictures to drill pronunciation. SS copy the six sentences from the board.
• Elicit / teach that the adjectives *highest*, *longest*, etc. are superlative adjectives. Then start **ex.1**.

■ Learner-training

Get SS to revise words from the **Words to learn** section in **WB Language practice 4A** to **D**. Test them in the next class.

■ Homework

SS do **WB 4D** *p.31* and **Listen and speak 4D**.

4 📧 *At the restaurant*

Lesson aims

Function	Ordering a meal (*I'll have …* / *I'd like …*), complaining
Vocabulary	Condiments, cutlery, ways of cooking, ®️ food
Optional materials	📄 **Going out for dinner** (ex. 6) A tea towel and blank mock menu card (Books-closed presentation)

Lesson plan

■ Warmer: Restaurant vocabulary

- Books closed. Write on the board:

  > What do you find on the table in restaurants?

- Elicit two or three examples, e.g. *plates, glasses, a tablecloth.*
- In pairs, SS list all the items that they know in English for a minute.
- Feedback SS' words onto the board in two groups, 'Food' and 'Other'. Underline the word stress.

1 Presentation: Vocabulary

- SS turn to 📖 **Food B** *p. 137* and match the words and photos.
- Check answers. Highlight the irregular plural *knives.*

  > **2** vinegar **3** pepper **4** salt **5** fork
  > **6** spoon **7** plate **8** knife

- Drill pronunciation, especially words with phonetics.
- SS add any other words from the **Warmer** to the **Word bank**
- Now focus on **Ways of cooking**. Elicit the meaning of the five adjectives. Drill pronunciation.
  ⚠️ *baked* and *roast* (= cooked in an oven). *Roast* is normally used only for meat or potatoes.
- Ask SS to copy the basic map into their vocabulary file. Then they think of another food for each category, and add it to the map, e.g. **baked**: bread, biscuits, apples / **boiled**: peas, spaghetti / **fried**: sausages, chips / **grilled**: chops, bacon / **roast**: lamb, potatoes, etc.

2 Practice: Reading a menu

- Ask *Where was Pieter last time?* (in Stockholm, Sweden) *Where was he staying?* (at Fogg's Hotel). Tell SS he's still in Sweden. Get them to read the introduction to **ex. 2**. Then they quickly read the menu and answer questions 1 and 2. Make sure they understand <u>dishes</u>, <u>vegetarians</u> and <u>kronor</u> (/ˈkrəʊnə/ = Swedish money).
- Check answers. Ask *What do you think of the menu?*

  > **1** three   **2** Yes, the soup, the salad, and the lasagne

3 Presentation: Ordering a meal

a
- Tell SS Pieter is with his two friends, Benni and Hana in the restaurant. SS listen and tick on the menu the food that they hear.
- ◦13◦ Play the tape twice. In pairs, SS listen and compare answers.
- Check answers by writing these chart headings (without the food words) on the board and see if SS can tell you what each person ordered:

	Starter	Main course
Pieter	salmon	roast chicken
Benni	soup	pepper steak
Hana	salad	roast chicken

b
- SS read quickly through the incorrect phrases. Explain that there's a word missing in each line.
- Get the class to predict the errors.
- SS listen and check, noting the missing words and their position in each sentence.
- Check answers.

  > Are you ready **to** order? **w**
  > What **do** you recommend? **c**
  > I'll have the pepper steak. **c**
  > Rare, medium, **or** well-done? **w**
  > The roast chicken **for** me, please. **c**
  > What **would** you like to drink? **w**
  > I'd like some mineral water too, please. **c**
  > Tapescript **SB Listening** *p. 128*

- Highlight the three ways of having your steak cooked (*rare, medium, well-done*). Ask *How do you like your steak?*

c
- SS read the sentences again and decide who says them. They write **c** (customer) or **w** (waiter) after each sentence. (See answers above.)
- SS find and underline three different expressions to order food.
- Check answers.

  > **I'll have** (the pepper steak).
  > The roast chicken **for me, please.**
  > **I'd like** (some mineral water too), **please.**

  ⚠️ Note that we use *I'll* here to order because it's a decision made at the moment of speaking rather than a plan. It's taught in **File 8B**.

4 Personalization: Roleplay

- SS roleplay ordering a meal. SS in groups of three. **A** is the waiter, **B** and **C** are customers.

  Tip Arrange the furniture so each group is sitting round a 'table' with enough space for the waiter to come and go. Use the menu in the SB or write it on the board.

- Demonstrate first with you as the waiter. Take one group's order and serve them their meal.
- SS continue in groups. Monitor and help as necessary.

5 Presentation: Complaining

a • Focus on the title **Complaining**. Elicit / explain the meaning (= say angrily that something is wrong).

• Ask *What kind of problems can you have in a restaurant? Have you ever had any problems?*

• Focus on pictures 1 to 5. Tell SS these illustrate five problems with the meal. Ask *Can you guess what the problems are?* Elicit ideas, but don't tell SS if they're right or wrong.

• °14° Tell SS they're going to hear five dialogues, one for each picture. Play the tape once. SS listen and check to see if they guessed the problems correctly.

> 1 The soup is cold.
> 2 The steak is rare, not well-done.
> 3 The glass is dirty.
> 4 She hasn't got a fork.
> 5 She ordered roast chicken.
> Tapescript **SB Listening** *p.128*

• Play the tape again and pause after each exchange. Elicit the five exchanges and write them on the board. Drill pronunciation as necessary.

• Highlight:
- the use of *for* after *ask*.
- how to apologize: *I'm (very) sorry.*
- the position of *you* in *I'll get you …, I'll bring you …,* and *I'll change it for you.*

b • On the board, rub out half the words in the dialogue leaving a skeleton:

> Excuse ___, ___. This soup's ____.
> I'm ___ ___. I'll ____ you ____ one.

• In pairs, SS practise the dialogues using the skeleton on the board and remembering the missing words.

• SS swap roles. Rub out all the words and SS do it once more from memory.

6 Practice: Listening

a • °15° Tell SS they're going to hear the end of the meal. SS listen and answer questions 1 to 4.

• Check answers.

> 1 True   2 False (Benni doesn't)
> 3 False (Benni pays)   4 True

• Ask *What was the mistake on the bill?* (they only had one bottle of wine).

b • Tell SS to read the ten phrases and try to remember exactly what they said.

• Play the tape again for them to check. SS complete the phrases. Check SS understand *get this* (= pay).

> W Would you **like any dessert?**
> P Just a black **coffee for me**. What about **you two?**
> H I'll have **a white coffee.**
> B Nothing for **me, thanks**. Oh, and could I **have the bill, please?** We're in **a hurry**.
> W Here you are sir.
> P How much is it, Benni? Please let me pay.
> B No, no, I'll **get this**. Hold on, there's a **mistake** here. Excuse me, I think the bill's **wrong**. We only had one bottle of wine.

Tip If time roleplay the whole situation in the restaurant. Give SS time to prepare / review what they're going to say. You can do this activity with [P] **Going out for dinner** (see **Extras**).

7 Vocabulary: Travel phrasebook 4

• SS turn to 📖4 *p.132* and translate the phrases.

Lesson notes

In **Travel with English 4,** Pieter's still in Sweden and goes out for dinner with some local friends. The lesson revises and extends the restaurant language that SS learnt in *English File 1*. SS practise ordering food and complaining. They also learn vocabulary for condiments, cutlery, and ways of cooking, and practise reading an authentic menu.

'll have … Used here for an unplanned / spontaneous decision. This is a common way of ordering food. Don't focus grammatically on the *will* form – if SS ask, tell them it's taught in **File 8**.

Extras

Going out for dinner [P] *p.172* A more detailed menu with prices, and a role-card for the waiter, for SS to roleplay restaurant language. Instructions *p.134*.

Books-closed presentation

Restaurant language

• Write RESTAURANT on the board. Tell SS to imagine they've just come into a restaurant with a friend. Roleplay the waiter. Go up to a pair of SS and elicit *Could we have a table for two?* Write this key phrase on the board. Now tell SS *You're sitting at the table.* Roleplay the waiter again. Elicit *Can I have the menu, please?* and *Have you got a menu in English?*

Tip Roleplay the waiter with a menu and a tea towel over your arm as props.

• Tell SS to imagine the menu. Tell them it's divided into different sections. Elicit / teach *starter*, *main course*, and *dessert*. Ask them to suggest some possible dishes for each section. Then start **ex. 1**.

■ Learner-training

Tell SS that next time they eat in a restaurant they could try asking for an English menu and see if they can understand it, or compare it to the menu in their language. They can do the same with, e.g. instructions for machines, on packets of food, etc.

■ Homework

SS do **WB 4** 📖 *p.32* and **Listen and speak 4** 📖.

Lesson aims

Speaking skills	Paraphrasing, fluency
Revision	Giving definitions, *There is / are …*, furniture, prepositions of place

Lesson plan

■ Warmer: Learning to drive

- Books closed. Ask *Who can drive? Do you remember learning to drive? What was it like? Describe how you felt. How long did it take?* etc. Ask *Can you see any other similarities between learning a language and learning to drive?*

  Tip If you know SS L1 and they want to express a complex opinion (here or with any of the other tips in the lesson), allow them to answer in L1 as this discussion can be very useful.

■ Introduction: Problems with speaking

- Books open. SS read the introductory paragraph. Ask *What can help you to speak better?* Elicit their ideas.
- SS read the quotes from five foreign students learning English. Teach / elicit the meaning of *embarrassed, express* your *personality, strange.* Ask *Which is your biggest problem?* Feedback.

Paraphrasing

■ Tip 1

- SS read the tip. Tell SS that if you want to say something but you don't know the exact word, you can usually find another way to say it.
- Give examples with words that SS know, e.g. *It's made of glass, and you put flowers in it* (= *vase*). Even if they don't remember the word they will know what you mean.

  Tip If you know SS L1, think of a word you don't know and define it to them in their language using words that you do know.

1 Dealing with unknown words

a
- SS read the five definitions and decide what each word is. If they don't know the word in English they can ask you *How do you say…?*, or use a bi-lingual dictionary.
- Check answers. Underline the stress and drill pronunciation.

  > 1 tiger   2 soap   3 <u>sun</u>bathe   4 <u>me</u>dals /medlz/
  > 5 <u>ner</u>vous

b
- SS in pairs, A and B. They now do the same with fifteen pictures of words which they probably don't know in English. Focus first on the key language they'll need from **ex. 1a** (*It's like …, It's bigger / smaller than …, They're made of …*, etc.) Remind

them of *a person who*, *a thing which*, and *a place where* from **2D**.

- Demonstrate yourself first with one of the pictures, e.g. *It lives in the sea. It's like a fish but it's much bigger. It's grey. It's very intelligent.* etc. (= *dolphin*) Get SS to say what it is when they are sure.
- SS continue. A describes one of the pictures to B without saying the word (even if they know it). B listens and then points to the right one when sure which it is.

  Tip Encourage A to say as much as possible before B points to the picture.

- Monitor and help as necessary. Don't over-correct as the objective is to show SS that they can communicate successfully.
- Feedback. Ask if they know any of the words. Be prepared to explain / translate *bottle-opener, corkscrew, factory, scream, compass, shark, skyscraper, whale, yawn, soldier.*

  > 1 bottle-opener   2 cathedral   3 corkscrew
  > 4 dolphin   5 factory   6 fireman   7 scream (*v.*)
  > 8 compass   9 shark   10 skyscraper   11 cry (*v.*)
  > 12 policeman   13 whale   14 yawn (*v.*)
  > 15 soldier

Oral fluency

■ Tip 2

- SS read the tip. SS usually worry a lot about being correct and this inevitably inhibits their fluency. Emphasize that, when they're speaking, the most important thing is to communicate. It doesn't matter if they make mistakes as long as the message is clear.

2 Communication

- Tell SS they're going to practise communicating. SS in pairs, A and B. They sit facing each other so they can't see the other's book.
- SS turn to ▶◀ **Find the differences** A *p. 121* B *p. 124*. Give them time to look at their picture of an office and read the instructions.
- Emphasize that:
  1 they have to find ten differences between their pictures.
  2 they can't look at the other picture.
  3 they have to speak only in English.
- Tell As to begin, and to describe their picture to B. Encourage Bs to ask questions to check the information.

  Tip If your SS aren't familiar with this kind of exercise, give them a few phrases / ideas to get them started, e.g. *In my picture, there is a / are some …* Tell them to focus on position, colour, and number.

- Monitor and help. If some pairs finish quickly, get them to write the differences.
- Check answers.

Picture A	Picture B
The bin is full.	The bin is empty.
There are some flowers on the desk.	There's a plant on the desk.
The drawer is open.	The drawer is closed.
There are some birds outside the window.	There aren't any birds.
There's an ashtray on the desk.	There isn't an ashtray.
The man has curly hair.	The man has straight hair.
The man's wearing a tie.	The man isn't wearing a tie.
The computer is on.	The computer is off.
There are two shelves.	There are three shelves.
The chair's black.	The chair's brown.

■ Tip 3

- SS read the tip. The aim is for them to see that by thinking for a minute before they speak, they can often say things better, feel more confident, and speak more fluently.

3 Confidence-building

a
- Tell SS they're going to describe their living-room to a partner. First they should imagine their room and think what words they're going to need. Put headings like furniture, possessions, colours, adjectives, etc. on the board to help them. Get them to ask you for any new words they need before they start.

  Tip SS could draw a small sketch of their room to help them. Show them by drawing a quick sketch of your living-room and describing it.

b
- In pairs, SS describe their rooms to each other. Monitor and help but don't over-correct, as the aim is to build confidence and fluency.

■ Tip 4

- SS read the introduction to the tip. Emphasize that, like learning to drive, you have to practise as much as you can if you want to be confident, and that without confidence you can't speak well.

4 Opportunities to practise

- Read the two **In class** tips (**a** and **b**) which emphasize the importance of speaking as much as you can in class. Tell SS that in pairwork, the best pair isn't the one that finishes first but the one that speaks most.
- Emphasize that it's SS' own responsibility. The teacher can make suggestions / provide help with strategies / techniques, but SS must act on these to improve.
- Read the three **Outside class** tips (**c** to **e**) which tell SS some of the ways they can practise for themselves. Highlight that:
  - it's important to learn the words that they will personally need to talk about themselves, their lives and their family.
  - the **Listen and speak** cassette gives them the opportunity to practise key language and pronunciation. Check who's already using it regularly.
  - they can get extra practice, e.g. before and after class, by talking to other SS in English.

- Ask *Which of these ideas have you tried? Which do you think are good ideas? Can you think of any other ways to practise?* (e.g. checking answers to WB exercises together, talking to tourists, recording themselves on cassettes, etc.).
- SS choose an 'outside class' activity, either from the list or that they have suggested, and try it this week. Ask SS individually *Which one are you going to do?* Remember to check that they actually do it and feedback how it went.

Lesson notes

This is the last in the series of **Focus on ...** lessons on specific language skills – this lesson is on speaking. The main aim is to show SS that speaking a foreign language is above all a question of confidence and technique, and that these only come with practice. The main emphasis of the lesson should be on getting the SS to communicate, without worrying about making mistakes. The lesson also highlights activities which SS can do outside class to practise on their own. If you can encourage SS to do some or all of them, the amount of practice they get will be greatly increased.

Extras

The describing game ⚃ *p. 208* SS define words to each other in pairs.

Talk for a minute P *p. 173* A game to practise free-speaking. Do here or after **4** ◁▷. Instructions *p. 134*.

■ Learner-training

Tell SS to try out at least one of the ideas in Tip 4. Remember to follow this up a week later to see how they got on.

■ Homework

See **End-of-file options** *p. 69*.

Lesson aims

Revision	**File 4:** First conditional, comparative and superlative adjectives, *some / any / body / nowhere*, etc.
Skills	Listening, reading, and speaking
Optional materials Dictionaries (**Vocabulary file 4**)	

Lesson plan

▪ Warmer: Progress chart

- Books closed. Ask *Can you remember what the lessons in File 4 were about? What grammar and vocabulary did we learn?* Elicit from the SS anything they can remember.
- Now tell SS to look at the **Progress chart** *p. 8* and to tick the lessons they've studied.
- Tell them that this is the revision lesson for this File, and that they can then do the **Vocabulary** and **Grammar files** (*pp. 64, 65*) to further revise the language of the File.

1 Revision: First conditional

a ● SS look at the photos. Ask *Who's the woman in the bottom right-hand corner?* (she's a politician) *What do you think she's talking about?* Elicit the topics of photos A to D (jobs / homeless people / education / old people).

b ● Focus on the handwritten notes. Elicit / teach the meaning of taxes, *education, pensions, create*.
- ⁚**16**⁚ SS listen to the politician speaking and take notes on what she promises to do, as in the example. Tell them just to write words, not full sentences.
- SS compare answers in pairs. Play the tape again if necessary.

> 2 build more houses and flats / no more homeless people
> 3 pay less tax / cut taxes by 10%
> 4 spend more / classes smaller, teachers better
> 5 pensions up by 20%

c ● SS listen again for her exact words. In pairs, they write four conditional sentences, as in the example.

> 2 If they win, they'll build more houses and flats.
> 3 If they win, they'll cut taxes by 10%.
> 4 If they win, they'll spend more on education.
> 5 If they win, pensions will go up by 20%.
> Tapescript **SB Listening** *p. 128*

2 Practice: Writing and speaking

a ● Tell SS to imagine they're politicians. Put them into small groups. They have to agree and write three promises for the next election, as in the example.

b ● Each group reads their three promises to the class. Tell the others to listen and decide which group's promises are the best.

Tip Once they've agreed their promises, you could get SS to decide the name of their party. Write these names on the board and, if time, have an 'election'. Get each student to 'vote' by writing the name of their preferred party on a slip of paper and then hand them to you. Count the votes and announce the winners, in reverse order.

3 Revision: Comparatives and superlatives

a ● Read question 1 and go through the two examples to show SS that they should be using both comparative and superlative forms. Elicit / pre-teach <u>con</u>tinent, a<u>ddic</u>tive, to<u>bacco</u>, spec<u>ta</u>tor sport. Explain *Finns* (= people from Finland).
- In pairs, SS read the quiz, circle the right answers, and decide the order of the other two options, numbering them 2 and 3.

b ● SS compare answers with another pair.
- Check answers. Read out the questions one at a time and ask individual SS what they think the answer is. Get them to give their answers with a superlative and a comparative, then tell them.

> **Answers in order from the most to the least:**
> 1 Switzerland USA Saudi Arabia
> 2 Asia Africa America
> 3 Chicago (O'Hare) London (Heathrow) Frankfurt
> 4 the Finns the British the Brazilians
> 5 alcohol tobacco coffee
> 6 the Swiss the Germans the Belgians
> 7 the Japanese the Spanish the Americans
> 8 basketball football golf

Tip You could get SS to add up their scores to see which group has the most correct answers – one point for each correct answer and one for each correct comparative / superlative.

4 Personalization: Talk about the best and the worst

- Focus on the example exchanges and sentence prompts. Ask *What do you think?* Get individual SS to tell you, e.g. *I think the most beautiful city in this country is* (…), then another to agree / disagree, etc. Pre-teach *attractive*.
- In pairs, SS make sentences.
- Feedback any interesting ideas / disagreements that arose.

Tip Tell fast finishers to continue by making sentences with the opposite meaning, e.g. the ugliest city / most unattractive person, worst place for a holiday, etc.

5 Revision: *some / any + body / where*, etc.

a ● ⁚**17**⁚ 🎵 SS listen to a Phil Collins song about homelessness in big cities. Focus on the picture. Ask *What can you see?* Elicit *She's a poor woman who lives in the street. She's asking for money.*

- Tell SS to read the song quickly. Avoid pre-teaching vocabulary as SS can guess most of it from the song and work out the rest with the **Glossary**.
- ° 17 ° Explain that they have to listen and choose the right missing word from the pair after each line, as in the example. SS listen to the song and circle the word they hear.

  ⚠ Make sure they don't start filling in the gaps until you've checked the answers.
- In pairs, SS compare the words they've circled. Don't check answers yet.

b
- Play the song again, this time in sections, and check answers after each section. Re-play any lines where SS can't agree on the right answer. SS then complete the gaps.

> l.2 can l.3 sleep l.4 tell l.5 look l.6 hear
> l.7 street l.8 Seems l.12 street l.13 crying
> l.14 feet l.15 walk l.16 anybody
> l.17 say l.18 face l.19 there l.20 place
> l.21 there

- SS read the song again with the **Glossary**. Deal with any remaining vocabulary problems.
- Ask *Why does the singer think 'it's another day for you and me in Paradise'?* Elicit the answer (that compared to the woman, our lives are like living in Paradise, and that we ought to think twice before we walk past without helping people who have no home).

c
- SS complete sentences 1 to 5 about the song using the right form of *some… / any…body*, etc.
- Check answers.

> 1 anywhere 2 somewhere 3 anything
> 4 Nobody 5 something

d
- Ask *What do you think of the song? Do you like it?*
- Tell SS that there are over 350,000 homeless people in England (of a population of about 60 million) especially in big cities like London and Birmingham. Ask *What about in your town / other towns in your country?*

Lesson notes

In this lesson, SS revise the new grammar from **File 4** through listening to a politician's election promises, a comparative / superlative quiz and discussion, and the Phil Collins song *Another day in Paradise*. SS cover the skills of listening, reading, and fluency.

Extras

Talk for a minute 🄿 *p. 173* A board game where SS talk for a minute about the topic on the square they land on. This can also be used after **Focus on speaking** *p. 61*. Instructions *p. 134*.

■ **Homework**

Choose from the **End-of-file options** below.

End-of-file options

Student's Book

■ **Vocabulary file 4** *p. 64*
- Do this in class, or set it for homework.
- *Organize your vocabulary learning!* Remind SS that a good dictionary will usually tell them if a word is only US and what the British equivalent is.
- *Try it!* SS use their dictionary to check five more words.

> **1 British and American English**
> 2 cookies 3 subway 4 gasoline
> 5 pharmacy 6 freeway 7 a check
> **2 Word groups**
>
> | Vegetables | Fruit | Meat and fish | Desserts |
> |---|---|---|---|
> | beans | peach | lamb | ice-cream |
> | peas | strawberry | salmon | apple pie |
> | | pineapple | chicken | cheesecake |
>
> **3 Restaurant**
> 1 menu 2 starter 3 main course 4 dessert
> 5 coffee 6 bill
> **4 Synonyms**
> 2 difficult 3 usually 4 perhaps 5 large
> 6 only 7 dirty 8 quickly 9 type
> **5 Key words**
> 1 else 2 as 3 probably 4 recently 5 than
> **6 Verbs**
> 1 tell 2 watch 3 miss 4 lend 5 meet
> 6 earn 7 carry
> **Try it!**
> 2–5 are American English. British equivalents:
> 2 lorry 3 lift 4 flat 5 holiday
> 6 is British English. US = fries

■ **Grammar file 4** *p. 65*
- Spend ten minutes going through this with the class, answering any queries. SS tick each box when they're satisfied they understand it.

Workbook

■ **Grammar check 4** *p. 33*
- Remind SS to do this with **SB** and **WB** open in front of them, and to refer back to **Grammar file 4** as necessary. SS can check answers with the **WB** key.

■ **Read and write 4** *p. 64*
- SS write a description of their town or city.
- Briefly revise adjectives for describing a place, and pre-teach any vocabulary you think your SS may need. Emphasize the need to read and follow the instructions carefully and compare their description with the model. Remind SS that they have a key to the exercises, but that you're going to collect and correct their work.

■ **Quicktest 2** *p. 84*
A multiple-choice progress test revising the language of Files 3 and 4. SS have a key to check their answers.

I've had this T-shirt for 15 years.

Lesson aims

Grammar	Present perfect + *for* / *since*
Vocabulary	Sport: *team* etc. possessions, *buy (for)*, *give (to)*
Pronunciation	/ɪ/ and /iː/, sentence stress, weak forms
Revision	*How long …?*, time and dates

Lesson plan

■ Warmer: Team sports
- Books closed. Write 'Team sports' on the board. Elicit examples of team sports onto the board, e.g. *football*.
- Ask *Have you ever played a team sport? Did you enjoy it? Why (not)? Have you ever won a trophy / medal?*

1 Presentation: Reading
- Books open. SS focus on the photo of Natalia. Ask *What's she doing?* (she's playing handball) *Have you ever played handball / seen a handball match?*
- SS read the text quickly and decide why the eight numbers are important in Natalia's life.
- In pairs, SS cover the text and tell each other.
- Feedback, eliciting answers in the past simple.

> She was born on the **17th**.   She was **twelve** when she first started playing handball.   When she was **sixteen** she became a professional player.   She won the Olympic bronze medal in **1988**.   In **1990**, she became world champion.   In **1991** she went to Spain.   She got married **ten** years ago.   Her daughter is **nine** years old.

- Read the text aloud to the SS. Get them to highlight any words they still don't understand. Be prepared to explain / translate *hard, former, star, bronze, medal, vote (v.), league* /liːg/, *champions*.

2 Presentation: *How long …? + for / since*

a
- SS complete the answers from the text. Remind them to use contractions. Check answers.

> **1** has / ('s) lived / since   **2** has / ('s) been / for

- Focus on the pronunciation of *since* /sɪns/.
- Ask *When do we use 'since' and when do we use 'for'?* (*since* is used with a point in time and *for* with a period of time).

b
- SS answer questions 1 and 2. Check answers.

> **1** Yes, she does.   **2** Yes, she is.

- ⚠ Highlight that Natalia <u>still</u> lives in Spain and she's <u>still</u> married.

■ GRAMMAR FOCUS
Present perfect + *for* / *since*, *How long …?*

a
- Focus on the time line and the question *How long has she lived in Spain?* (the answer will depend on the year you are in now).
- Focus on the alternative answer with *since*.
- SS read and complete the rules with *since* or *for*.

> **1** for   **2** since

b
- Highlight the rule. Use the present perfect (+ *How long? / for / since*) to talk about actions which started in the past and are still true now.

> **Tip** Get SS to translate the two sentences from the time line, and compare with the tense they use in their language.

⚠ SS may use the present tense in their L1. Emphasize that, in English, you can't use a present tense here. They may also try to use *ago*, which is normally used with the past simple.

PRACTICE

a
- Tell SS to copy the chart and put the time expressions into the right column. Check answers.

> **for:** three months   ten days   ages   a long time
> **since:** my last birthday   May   1960   a few weeks ago   I was eighteen

b
- Focus on the example. In pairs, get SS to write one present perfect sentence with *for* or *since* for each situation. Tell them to use contractions.
  ⚠ Highlight that they need to use the verb from the second sentence each time. Check answers.

> **2** We've had our car for two years.   **3** He's lived in Leeds since April.   **4** They've been married for six months.   **5** Italy's been a republic since 1946.

c
- In pairs, SS write questions for the other four sentences from **Practice b**. Check answers.

> **2** <u>How long</u> have you <u>had</u> your <u>car</u>?   **3** <u>How long</u> has he <u>lived</u> in <u>Leeds</u>?   **4** <u>How long</u> have they been married?   **5** <u>How long has Italy</u> been a <u>republic</u>?

■ PRONUNCIATION

a
- Focus on the two headwords. Ask *What's the difference between the two sounds?* (/tree/ is longer) *What tells you it's a long sound?* (the two dots).
- 🔊 **1** SS listen and repeat.

b
- SS put the words from the list in the right column. Check answers. Elicit other words with the same sound (see **Sound bank WB** *p. 81*).

> /fish/ live   chip   sit   it   /tree/ leave   cheap   seat   eat

- Highlight that:
  - common spellings for /iː/ are *ea* and *ee*.
  - *i* between two consonants is pronounced /ɪ/ unless there is a final *e*. (*live* (*v*) and *since* are exceptions).
- **c** • ⟨2⟩ Play the first sentence for SS to repeat, stressing the underlined words.
  - SS listen and write four more *How long?* questions. Pause after each sentence to give SS time to write.
  - Elicit the sentences onto the board. Elicit and mark the sentence stress. Drill pronunciation.

> 1 <u>How</u> <u>long</u> have they been <u>married</u>?
> 2 <u>How</u> <u>long</u> have you <u>had</u> your <u>car</u>?
> 3 <u>How</u> <u>long</u> has he <u>lived</u> in <u>Italy</u>?
> 4 <u>How</u> <u>long</u> have you <u>been</u> in this <u>class</u>?

3 Personalization: Speaking

- Focus on the chart and the example exchange. Ask several questions from the chart with *How long …?*
- Get individual SS to ask you some of the questions. Insist they stress the key words, e.g. <u>How</u> <u>long</u> have you <u>been</u> in this <u>school</u>? Elicit some follow-up questions.
- In pairs, SS take turns to ask questions.
- Feedback any interesting answers.

4 Practice: Listening

- **a** • Focus on the six photos. Ask *What are they?* (A an Olympic bronze medal, B a cup (= trophy), C a photo of two people, D a white BMW, E a gold <u>bracelet</u>, F a yellow sports T-shirt) *Whose are they are?* (Natalia's).
  - Focus on the title of the article. Ask *Why are the objects important?* (they're her favourite things).
  - ⟨3⟩ SS listen to Natalia and number the photos 1 to 6.
  - SS compare in pairs. Check answers.

> 1 D 2 F 3 B 4 A 5 E 6 C

- **b** • SS listen again, note how long she's had each thing, and where she got it from. SS check in pairs.
  - Elicit answers in note form onto the board but insist SS give you the information as complete sentences.

> **Tip** Write the chart headings in the key onto the board for SS to copy and complete as they listen.

	Has had it since	Got it from …
BMW	August /	Madrid
T-shirt	1980	Moscow Olympics
cup	1986	Amsterdam
medal	1988	Seoul Olympics
bracelet	last birthday / January	present from husband
photo	1991	from her parents
Tapescript **SB Listening** *p. 128*		

5 Personalization: Talk about your favourite things

- Focus on **V** *buy for* / *give to*. Check SS understand.

- Practise by asking individual SS about their possessions, singular and plural, e.g. *Where did you get that bag* / *those earrings?*
- Give SS two minutes to list their five favourite possessions. Help with vocabulary where necessary or get SS to use dictionaries. Make a list yourself.
- Demonstrate first with your list. Get SS to ask you questions, e.g. *How long have you had it* / *them? Where did you get it* / *them?*
- SS swap their lists and ask and answer in the same way.
- Feedback. Ask some SS to tell you about one of their partner's favourite possessions.

Lesson notes

SS learn to use the present perfect with *How long …? + for* / *since* for unfinished actions.

Present perfect + *How long?* Your SS may use a different tense in their language to express this concept. e.g. present simple.

for / *since* SS may have problems with the meaning / use of *for* and *since* (see **Grammar focus** notes) .

⚠ **Present perfect continuous** (*I have been living here for two years*) This is not taught in *English File 2*.

Extras

Who's going to get promotion? Ⓟ *p. 174* Information gap activity to practise *How long …? + since* / *for*. Instructions *p. 135*.

Books-closed presentation

Present perfect + *for* / *since*

- Write on the board, e.g. if you're working in Paris:

> I live in (Paris). I came to (Paris) in (1990).

- Tell SS that we can make one sentence which includes all this information, i.e. *I've lived in Paris since 1990*. Write the sentence on the board. Ask *What tense is it?* (present perfect) Elicit the meaning of *since*.
- Drill the pronunciation. To check the concept, ask *When did I come to Paris? Do I live in Paris now?*
- Now teach the alternative sentence *I've worked here for … years*. Ask a few SS *How long have you lived here?* ⚠ You'll probably need to teach *all my life*.
- Elicit and drill the question.
- SS mingle, asking *How long have you lived here?* to see who has lived in the town / city the longest. Then start the **Warmer**.

■ Learner-training

Tell SS to make a list of expressions in the grammar section of their ring file under the headings *for* and *since*.

■ Homework

SS do **WB 5A** *p. 34* and **Listen and speak 5A**.
Writing: My favourite things SS write about their favourite things.

I want to be free.

Lesson aims

Grammar	Verb + *to* + infinitive, *would like to* + verb or *like* + -*ing*?
Vocabulary	Age groups: *middle-aged*, etc., verbs + *to*: *want*, etc.
Pronunciation	/tə/ weak form, sentence stress
Revision	Time expressions present simple, present continous for future
Optional materials	P *I want to break free* 🎵

Lesson plan

■ Warmer: Ⓡ Present perfect + *for* / *since*

● Books closed. Write these sentences on the board:

> 1 How long are you a teacher?
> 2 I live here for ten years.
> 3 She has worked here since two years.
> 4 We've studied English here for 1996.

● In pairs, SS correct them.

> 1 How long **have** you **been** a teacher?
> 2 I**'ve lived** here for ten years.
> 3 She has worked here **for** two years / since (date).
> 4 We´ve studied English here **since** 1996.

1 Vocabulary: Age groups

a ● Books closed. Write on the board:

> get married   have children   retire

Elicit the meaning of *retire* (= stop working at 65).
● In pairs, SS decide what they think is the best age to do each thing.
● Feedback (and give your opinion too).
● Books open. Focus on photos A to F. In pairs, SS match each one to a word from Ⓥ **Age-groups**. Check answers and drill pronunciation as necessary.

> **A** a <u>tee</u>nager   **B** <u>mi</u>ddle-aged   **C** old   **D** a <u>ba</u>by
> **E** an <u>a</u>dult   **F** a child

● Explain *teenager* (= a young person between 13 and 19 – *teen* is the ending of numbers 13 to 19). We usually use *adult* for a person who is over 18.
● Ask SS for an approximate age for each of the six groups, e.g. *A baby is from nought to two.*, etc.

b ● Ask *How old is old?* Elicit opinions.

2 Presentation: Verbs + *to* + infinitive

a ● Focus on the title of the questionnaire. Ask *What makes you feel 'old' or 'young'?*
● Go though the questionnaire, making sure SS understand the questions. Be prepared to explain / translate *within*, *cholesterol*, *latest*.

● In pairs, SS take turns to interview each other with the questionnaire, and tick / cross their partner's answers. Make sure the SS being interviewed have their book closed.

b ● When both have finished, they look at the **Score** chart and work out their partner's scores. They read the result to their partner to see if he / she agrees.
● Feedback to see who's the youngest in spirit.

> **Tip** Get SS to ask you the questions or do the questionnaire yourself.

■ GRAMMAR FOCUS
Verb + *to* + infinitive

a ● SS look at the verbs in the questionnaire and answer questions 1 and 2.

> **1** would like   plan   hope   want   need   **2** like

b ● SS read and compare sentences 1 and 2. Ask *Which one is general?* (sentence 1 – *like* + gerund = enjoy) *When does 'like' = 'want'?* (sentence 2 – *would like* + infinitive = something you want to do).

PRACTICE

a ● SS complete the sentences with *to* + a verb from the list. Check answers.

> **2** to go, to rest   **3** to do, to study, to be
> **4** to bring   **5** to go cycling, to stay

b ● SS complete the sentences with a verb + *to* or -*ing*. Check answers.

> **1** to go out   **2** cooking   **3** to buy   **4** flying
> **5** to do

■ PRONUNCIATION

a ● ∘4∘ SS listen to the tape and write five sentences. Pause the tape after each one.
● In pairs, SS check. Elicit each sentence onto the board.

b ● Play the tape again for SS to check and mark the sentence stress, as in the example. Elicit the answers onto the board.

> **2** Do you <u>want</u> to <u>see</u> a <u>film</u>?
> **3** He <u>needs</u> to <u>find</u> a <u>new</u> <u>flat</u>.
> **4** I'm <u>hoping</u> to <u>go</u> <u>abroad</u> this <u>summer</u>.
> **5** They've <u>decided</u> to <u>get</u> <u>married</u>.

● Highlight that *to* is pronounced /tə/ not /tuː/ in these sentences because it's unstressed.

3 Personalization: Writing

● Focus on sentence stems 1 to 7. Elicit ways to complete the first sentence, e.g. *When I was young, I wanted to be an actor / actress.* etc.
● SS complete the sentences in any way they want.

- SS compare their sentences with a partner. Are any of them the same?
- Feedback, eliciting ideas for each one. Ask *Do anyone's answers surprise you?*

4 Personalization: Speaking

- Write on the board *Would you like to be very rich?*
- Drill the pronunciation, especially *would* = /wʊd/, making sure SS don't pronounce the *l* and that they stress the important words.
- Elicit the short answer *Yes, I would. / No, I wouldn't.*
- Ask some students the question. Say *Why (not)?* to elicit the answer *Because ...*
- SS in pairs, A and B. Turn to ▶◀ **Would you like to ...?** A *p. 121*, B *p. 124*. They read their instructions, the example exchange, and their list of prompts.
- SS ask and answer alternate questions, each time asking *What about you?* after they've answered.
- Feedback any interesting answers.

5 Practice: Listening

a
- Focus on the photo of Charles Bornat. Ask *How old do you think he is?* (he's 85 but don't tell SS that yet). Elicit ideas about his lifestyle. Ask *What do you think he does during the day? What hobbies do you think he has?* etc.

b
- Tell SS they're going to hear an interview with Charles. They listen for his age and his hobbies.
- ∘ 5 ∘ Play the tape once. Elicit answers.

> He's 85. He likes cooking and photography. He studies French and Spanish. He travels a lot. He likes classical and pop music.

- Ask *Do you think he's typical for a man of his age?* (no, because he's very active / busy, etc.).

c
- SS read the incomplete sentences about Charles's past present and future. In pairs, they try to remember some of his answers.
- SS listen again and note the information they need to complete the sentences.
- Get SS to compare in pairs, then play the tape again for them to check, pausing and replaying as necessary. Check answers.

> **Past** He was born in **France**.   When he was young, he wanted to be a **professional footballer**. Before he retired he was an **architect**.
> **Present** He's been retired since he was **65**. He's lived in Coventry since **1953**.   He likes **travelling**.   He's trying to **learn Spanish**. He likes listening to **music (classical and pop)**. He's a big fan of **Annie Lennox and Queen**.
> **Future** He wants to **speak Spanish well**.   He'd like to **travel more**.   He's hoping to **go to New York next winter**.
> Tapescript **SB Listening** *p. 129*

- Ask *What else do you know about him?* to elicit any other information. Finally, SS can read the tapescript.

∘ 6 ∘ ♫ *I want to break free*

The lyrics to this song are on P *p. 175* ***I want to break free*** (see **Extras**). If you can't make photocopies, exploit the song as follows.

- Write on the board:

But I have to be sure	I don't want to live alone
But life still goes on	I've fallen in love
I don't need you	It's strange but it's true

- Tell SS they're going to hear the song *I want to break free* by Queen. Ask *What does the title mean?* Tell them that the six lines on the board all come in the song.
- ∘ 6 ∘ Play the tape. SS listen and number the lines 1 to 6 in the order they hear them.

But I have to be sure 4	I don't want to live alone 6
But life still goes on 5	I've fallen in love 2
I don't need you 1	It's strange but it's true 3

Lesson notes

SS learn some common verbs + infinitive through the context of a light-hearted questionnaire about age. SS may prefer not to say their *real* age.

to + infinitive SS already know *want* and *would like* as verbs which are followed by *to* + infinitive.

like / would like *would like* + *to* + infinitive for a specific wish / ambition is contrasted with *like* + *-ing* for general likes and dislikes.

⚠ ***like*** This verb can also be followed by *to* + infinitive (although with a slightly different meaning, c.f. *I like to go to the dentist once a year* (= I think it's a good idea) and *I like going to the dentist* (= I enjoy it). Emphasize that *like* + *-ing* is the most common way to express *like* = enjoy.

Extras

I want to break free P *p. 175* A listening activity based on the·song by Queen. Instructions *p. 135*.

An Indian legend P *p. 176* A story for SS to uncover and read / predict what happens next. Instructions *p. 135*.

Books-closed presentation

***like* + verb + *-ing* / *would like* + *to* + infinitive**

- Do after the **Warmer**. Ask individual SS *Do you like going to the cinema?* Elicit answer.
- Elicit the names of several films currently showing, and write them on the board. Ask individual SS *Would you like to see* (name of film)? Elicit the answer *Yes, I would. / No, I wouldn't.* Ask *Why (not)?*
- Elicit the two questions from the class and write them on the board.
- In pairs, SS ask each other about the different films on the board. Then start **ex. 1**.

■ Learner-training

Tell SS to record the verbs which take *to* + infinitive and those which take the gerund (*-ing* form) under separate headings in their vocabulary file or notebook.

■ Homework

- SS do **WB 5B** *p. 35* and **Listen and speak 5B**.
- SS learn key verbs with *to* + infinitive.

> *He thought she was dead
> so he killed himself.*

Lesson aims

Grammar	*so / because, had to / didn't have to*
Vocabulary	Connectors: *then*, etc.
Pronunciation	/ə/, word stress
Revision	Story-telling

Lesson plan

■ Warmer: ℞ Verb + *to* + infinitive?

- Write on the board:

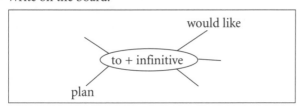

Brainstorm verbs and write them on the spidergram,
e.g. *want, need, hope, plan* etc.

- Write on the board:

> Would you like …?
> Do you want…?
> Are you hoping…?
> Are you planning…?

- Elicit a possible continuation for each question using a verb in infinitive form, e.g. *Would you like **to go out tonight?***
- SS copy and complete the questions and ask a partner.

1 Vocabulary: Pre-teaching

- Books open. SS in pairs match the eight words to the correct definitions. Check answers.

> **2** e **3** a **4** h **5** d **6** b **7** c **8** g

- Use some examples with *pretend* to make sure they understand the meaning, e.g. *She pretended to be ill* (= said she was ill) but she wasn't really.
- Encourage SS to use the phonetics and word stress and say the words correctly. Drill as necessary.

2 Presentation: *so / because*

a
- SS cover the text and focus on pictures A to J. Tell them they're going to listen to a famous love story (don't tell them the name of the story). Tell SS that the pictures are in the right order, but there is one extra picture which doesn't belong to the story.
- ⟨ **7** ⟩ Play the tape once. SS follow the story with the pictures and cross out the wrong picture. SS compare in pairs. Ask *Which is the extra picture?* (G) *What's the name of the story?* (Romeo and Juliet) *Do you know the story? Have you seen the play / film?*

b
- Play the tape again. SS read and listen to the story to check. Tell them not to fill in the gaps yet. Be

prepared to explain / translate *afraid, balcony, drug, hurry* (v.), *marriage* /ˈmærɪdʒ/, *himself / herself*.

■ GRAMMAR FOCUS 1

so / because

- Focus on the examples. SS read and complete the rules. Highlight the difference between *reason* and *result*.

> **1** because **2** so

PRACTICE 1

a
- SS complete the gaps in the story with *so* or *because*. Focus first on examples 1 and 2 which are done for them, then tell them to do the other eight in pairs.
- Check answers.

> **3** because **4** so **5** because **6** so **7** because
> **8** so **9** so **10** because

b
- In pairs, SS complete the sentences about the story. Correct this orally with the whole class – there are several possible answers.

> **Suggested answers:**
> 1 he went to her house (after the party).
> 2 he (had) killed his wife's cousin / didn't want to be caught.
> 3 he didn't get the message.
> 4 (she thought that) her husband was dead.

■ PRONUNCIATION

a
- Focus on and elicit the picture word, computer, /ə/. Remind SS that this is the most common and important sound in English.
- ⟨ **8** ⟩ Play the tape. SS listen and repeat some words from the lesson with the /ə/ sound.
- Ask *Is the /ə/ sound stressed?* (no, it never is – it occurs before or after a stressed syllable).

b
- ⟨ **9** ⟩ SS look at some more words from the lesson and underline the stressed syllable. Get them to circle the /ə/ sound. Listen and check.

> hus**band** **a**fraid im**me**di**a**tely **fi**n**a**lly to**ge**th**er**
> a**gain**

- Highlight that many different spelling combinations can produce the /ə/ sound, but it's always unstressed. Get SS to list some from the examples above.

(See also **Sound bank WB** *p.81*)

3 Practice: Story-telling

a
- Tell SS they're going to tell the story of Romeo and Juliet. Focus on the connectors highlighted in **bold** in the story. Get SS to copy the correct ones onto each picture, as in the example *One night*. Check answers.

> **B** That night **C** the next day
> **D** The following day **E** later **F** Then
> **G** When **H** When **I** Finally

b • SS in pairs, **A** and **B**. SS cover the text, look only at the pictures and connectors and tell half the story each. **A** retells pictures A to E, **B** then finishes the story with pictures F and H- to J.

> **Tip** Emphasize that SS should tell the story in their own words. They don't have to memorize the text.

■ GRAMMAR FOCUS 2
had to / didn't have to

a • Focus on the example. Elicit that *had to* is the past tense of *have to* (refer SS to **2B** if necessary).
   • SS complete the 'present to past' chart. Check answers.

> I had to go   Did he have to go?

b • Emphasize that *had to* is used for past obligations. Give a couple of personal examples, e.g. *Yesterday I had to go to the bank because I didn't have any money.*

PRACTICE 2

a • In pairs, SS read and match the pairs of sentences.
   • Check answers.

> **2** g **3** f **4** a **5** b **6** d **7** e

b • Ask individual SS to say the sentences in **a** as one sentence, using *so* or *because*, as in the example.

> **2** I had to borrow an umbrella **because** I couldn't find mine.
> **3** I didn't go away in August **because** I had to work.
> **4** I didn't have to work yesterday **because** it was a public holiday.
> **5** I missed the last bus **so** I had to get a taxi.
> **6** I had to go to the post office **because** I needed some stamps.
> **7** The hotels were full **so** I had to stay at a Youth Hostel.

4 Personalization: Story-writing

   • Tell SS they're going to imagine and write their own short love story in groups. Quickly ask them if they know any famous love stories (films or books), and list a few on the board (e.g. *Love story, Pretty woman, Jane Eyre, Anna Karenina,* etc.). Ask *Do you like these kinds of stories?*
   • Focus on the 'story-telling framework'. Tell SS to imagine the characters and storyline and fill in as many details as they can for each section.
   • SS in small groups brainstorm and write their stories. Monitor, help, and correct as necessary. Give them a time limit and make sure they finish their story.
   • Feedback. Get one member of each group to read out their story to the rest of the class. SS decide on the most original story.

> **Tip** Alternatively get each student to write down their own copy of the story. Put a student from one group with a partner from a different group to tell their stories.

Lesson notes

so / because SS already know how to use *because* in answer to questions beginning *Why …?* Here they learn to use it to connect a result with its cause, and to use *so* to connect a cause with its result. They also learn to express past obligation with *had to / didn't have to* (*have to* was introduced in **File 2B**). The lesson is based on *Romeo and Juliet.* SS get both oral and written practice in story-telling.

Extras

Finish the sentences [P] *p. 177* Cards with half sentences for SS to finish with *so* or *because*. Instructions *p. 135.*

Books-closed presentation

so / because
• Write on the board:

> 1 I went to bed early _____ I was tired.

   Ask SS to tell you the missing word(*because*).
• Now write:

> 2 I was tired _____ I went to bed early.

Ask *What word can I put here so that it means exactly the same as sentence 1?* Elicit / teach the missing word (*so*). Then start **ex. 1**

■ Learner-training
Get SS to update their vocabulary files with ten key new words from this lesson.

■ Homework
SS do **WB 5C** *p. 36* and **Listen and speak 5C**.
Writing: Love story SS write their own love story based on a book or a film, using the Romeo and Juliet text / the notes from **ex. 4** as a model.

> Who said: 'I'm the greatest'?

Lesson aims

Grammar	Questions with / without auxiliaries
Vocabulary:	Verbs: *invent* etc.
Pronunciation:	Introduction in *Wh-* words
Revision	Past simple, dates

Lesson plan

■ Warmer: ℝ Superlatives

- Write on the board:

> THE 20TH CENTURY
> the most famous:
> film? _____
> actor / actress? _____
> athlete? _____
> singer? _____
> politician? _____
> writer? _____

- Elicit the pronunciation of *20th*. Check SS understand <u>century</u> (= 100 years), *20th century* (= 1900 – 1999).
- Books closed. In pairs, SS write one for each category.
- Quickly feedback their answers and see if the class agrees on any of them.

❶ Presentation: Questions with / without auxiliaries

- SS look at the pictures around the quiz. Ask *What can you see in each one?* (Ayrton Senna the Brazilian who died in a crash in 1994, Humphrey Bogart in the film *Casablanca*, Gene Kelly the American dancer / singer, the Berlin Wall coming down, Ben Johnson and Carl Lewis in the 1980 Olympic 100m final).
- Divide the class into small groups to do the quiz. Tell SS to agree and write down their answers to questions 1 to 10. Be prepared to explain / translate <u>championship</u>, <u>athlete</u>, <u>resign</u>, <u>literature</u>, <u>novel</u>, <u>solitude</u>. Check answers and scores for each group.

> **1** b **2** a (in Terminator 2) **3** a
> **4** c (Lewis came second but won the gold medal after Johnson was disqualified for drug-taking)
> **5** b **6** c (in 1990 and 1994) **7** c **8** a **9** b
> (Tolstoy wrote *Anna Karenina*, Dostoevsky wrote *The Idiot*) **10** a

■ GRAMMAR FOCUS

Questions with / without auxiliaries

a
- Write **Q A S I** on the board. Elicit what the letters represent (**Q**uestion–**A**uxiliary–**S**ubject–**I**nfinitive, i.e. the normal word order of questions).
- Focus on example questions 1 and 2. Ask *What's the difference?* (the first has an auxiliary, *did* and infinitive verb, *say* the second has no auxiliary and a past tense verb, *said*).

- Write question 1 on the board under headings like this:

Q	A	S	I
What	did	Humphrey Bogart	say?

Ask What's the subject in sentence 1? (Humphrey Bogart).
- Focus on sentence 2. Show that it doesn't fit into the **QASI** chart.
Ask What's the subject in sentence 2? Elicit that the subject is the question word *Who?*
- Elicit / teach that we use *did* for all questions except when the subject of a question is the question word.

Tip SS usually need to translate the sentences to find the subject.

b
- SS read and complete the rules.

> **1** use **2** don't use

- Highlight that:
- **QASI** is the normal order, i.e. most questions in the past tense are formed with the auxiliary *did*.
- questions without an auxiliary are also possible with the present tense (*Who likes The Beatles?*)
- SS have already seen questions without auxiliaries, e.g. *What happened? Who knows the answer?*
- In pairs, get SS to look back at questions 3 to 10 in the quiz and highlight the subject in each question.

> **3** Ayrton Senna **4** Which athlete **5** Gene Kelly
> **6** Which singer **7** Germany **8** Who
> **9** Boris Pasternak **10** Who

PRACTICE

- Focus on the two examples. In pairs, SS write the questions for each answer, using the question word in brackets. Check answers.

> **3** Who sang *Blowing in the Wind* in 1965?
> **4** When did Albert Einstein win the Nobel prize for physics?
> **5** Where did Anwar Sadat die (in October 1981)?
> **6** Which scientist invented the TV in 1926?
> **7** Which ship hit an iceberg in 1912?

- Remind SS that in *Wh-* questions in English the intonation usually falls at the end. Drill with **Practice** questions 1 to 7.

❷ Practice: Quiz questions

- In pairs, SS write a quiz question for the rest of the class to answer. Give an example or two yourself first, based on information which is local or well-known to your SS. Monitor, help, and correct as necessary.
- Ask each pair to read their question to the class twice to make sure they all hear and understand it. Then ask for the answers.

Tip You could make this activity part of the 20th century quiz in **ex. 3**. At the end of the quiz each group writes one or two extra quiz questions for the other group to answer.

3 Practice: Class quiz

- Tell SS you're going to have a quiz about famous events in the 20th century. Put SS into three groups A, B, and C, turn to ▶◀ **20th century quiz** A *p. 121*, B *p. 124*, C *p. 125*) and read the instructions. Each group has six questions to write from the answers, similar to **Practice**. Monitor and help as necessary.
- When they're ready, hold the quiz. One person from team A reads out a question. Team B have 30 seconds to confer and answer for 2 points. If they get it wrong, the question is passed to team C for 1 point. Then team B ask a question, and C have the first opportunity to answer, etc.
- Keep the teams' scores on the board. If the final score produces a draw and you have time, ask tie-break questions yourself until you have a clear winner.

Tip Tell SS that the questions will only be repeated once, to encourage them to listen. Tell them not to shout out an answer before they have conferred, as the first answer will count. It's a good idea to appoint a 'captain' to speak for each team.

Lesson notes

SS learn to recognize and use questions without auxiliaries in the context of a general knowledge quiz based around 20th century facts.

Questions without *do* / *did* SS should by now be fairly confident forming questions using the pattern **QASI** (= **Q**uestion **A**uxiliary **S**ubject **I**nfinitive). Here they learn that some questions in English are formed without an auxiliary (e.g. *What happened?* NOT ~~*What did happen?*~~) when the question word is the subject of the sentence. Both question types (with and without an auxiliary) are presented using the same verb in the quiz so that SS can see the difference clearly.

Extras

Hollywood quiz 🅿 *p. 178* Quiz question prompts for questions with and without an auxiliary. Instructions *p. 136*.

Books-closed presentation

Questions with and without an auxiliary

- Think of a famous event which your SS would know, but which is not in the quiz, and write it on the board, e.g. *Mitterand died in 1996.*
- Write up:

    > 1 Mitterand? In 1996.

    Elicit the question *When did Mitterand die?*
- Write up:

    > 2 Which French president _____ in 1996? Mitterand.

    Elicit / teach *Which French president died in 1996?*
- Get SS to compare the two questions and see if they can work out the difference, i.e. one uses the auxiliary *did* and the other doesn't.
- Elicit the subject of each sentence (sentence 1 = Mitterand, sentence 2 = Which (French President)?) Then start **ex. 1**.

■ Learner-training

Remind SS to revise the **Words to learn** from the **WB** for **File 5** for a test next class. Remember to test them.

■ Homework

SS do **WB 5D** *p. 37* and **Listen and speak 5D**.

Writing: Quiz questions Get SS to write two more questions about the 20th century to ask the class at the beginning of the next lesson.

Lesson aims

Function	Giving directions, asking the way
Vocabulary	Buildings and places in a town
Revision	Preposition of place / movement
Optional materials	P Could you tell me the way to ...? (ex. 5)

Lesson plan

■ Warmer: New York

- Books closed. Ask *Where was Pieter last lesson?* (at a restaurant in Stockholm). Write NEW YORK on the board and say that Pieter is there now. Ask *What do you think of when someone says 'New York'?* Brainstorm some ideas onto the board, e.g. *Broadway, the Empire State Building, Central Park, sky-scrapers, The Statue of Liberty*, etc. Try to elicit *Manhattan* and *Wall Street*. Ask *Have you been there? Would you like to go there? Do you know why Wall Street is called Wall Street?* (because there used to be a wall there which divided the city).

1 Presentation: Giving directions

- **a** • Elicit possible problems asking directions, e.g. dealing with different accents (the American accent / the many English speaking immigrants), the speed of reply, etc.

  Tip If anybody in the class has been to New York, you could ask *Did you ask the way when you were there? Did you have any problems understanding?*

  - Focus on pictures A to H. Tell SS they're directions and they have to match each picture to the right phrase, 1 to 8. Check answers and drill pronunciation, especially *straight* /streɪt/ and *opposite* /ˈopəzɪt/.
    Highlight:
  - that you can say (*It's*) *on* **the** OR **your** *left / right*.
  - the meaning of *Take the first turning* (= turn at the first side street going off from the road you are on)
  - that *Go* **up** / **down** / **along** are all used synonymously when a street is flat.

2 G	3 A	4 D	5 F	6 B	7 C	8 H	

- **b** • SS cover the phrases and test each other only with the pictures.

2 Practice: Asking the way

- **a** • Tell SS that Pieter's in New York on business but he's spending the afternoon sightseeing in Manhattan. They're going to hear him asking for directions (the place he wants to go to has been replaced in the dialogue by a bleep). Focus again on the list of directions in **ex. 1a**.
  - ○**10**○ Play the tape once. SS listen and tick the five expressions that they hear.

- SS compare in pairs. Play the tape again to check. Check answers.

  1 Go along / up this street for about (400 metres).
  2 Take the first turning on the right.
  3 Go straight on until you get to (Exchange Place).
  4 Turn left into (Nassau Street).
  5 It's on the / your left.

- **b** • Focus on the map. SS listen again. This time they mark the route on the map and find out where Pieter wants to go. Make sure SS know where they're starting from. Play the tape again, pausing and re-playing parts if necessary. Check answers.

  He wants to go to Federal Hall (the place where George Washington became the first US President).

  Tip To check, get SS to give you directions to Federal Hall using the route they've drawn. Don't worry about the pronunciation of place / street names.

- Ask *What three questions did Pieter ask?* Elicit the answers. Play the tape again if necessary.

  Excuse me, could you tell me how to get to (Federal Hall)?
  Can you tell me the way to (Federal Hall)?
  Can you show me on the map?
  Tapescript **SB Listening** *p. 129*

3 Practice

- Focus on the incomplete dialogue. Tell SS they're going to listen to another tourist asking for directions. Ask the class to guess the missing words.

  Tip Tell them not to write in the spaces, or to write in pencil until they've checked the answers.

- ○**11**○ Play the tape. SS listen and check.

  A Excuse me, please. Is **there** a post office **near** here?
  B Yes, the nearest **one**'s at the **end** of Fulton Street. Go **up** this street and **turn** left. Go **over** the traffic **lights**, and take the **third** turning on the **right**. It's **on** the corner **on** the left, **next** to the market. You can't **miss** it.

4 Personalization: Asking for / giving directions

- **a** • Focus on the map again. Give SS directions from the World Trade Center to a chosen place on the map, e.g. *Start outside the World Trade Center in West Street. Turn left and go along this street, then turn right into Broadway*, etc. SS follow your directions and say where they get to.
  - Now tell SS to write directions from the World Trade Center to any other place on the map. Monitor, help, and correct as necessary.

Tip Encourage SS not to use street names too much as this makes it too easy, and in real life, people usually don't use / know street names all the time when giving directions.

b • SS in pairs, A and B. A reads his / her directions to B, who follows them on the map and says where A gets to. Then they swap roles. Fast finishers can swap partners or write new directions.

5 Practice: Listening

a • ◦12◦ Tell SS Pieter now wants to go somewhere else. Play the tape once. SS listen and say where he wants to go, and count how many people he speaks to. Check answers.

> the Metropolitan Museum of Art   seven
> Tapescript **SB Listening** *p. 129*

b • SS read statements 1 to 7 again and check they understand.
• Play the tape again. SS listen and mark true or false. SS compare answers in pairs.
• Check answers, pausing and re-playing as necessary. Ask SS to tell you the correct answer for all the false ones.

> 1 F (It's 100 blocks away)   2 F (4, 5, or 6)
> 3 T   4 T   5 T   6 F (he's lost too)   7 T
> Tapescript **SB Listening** *p. 129*

• Ask *What happens in the end?* (when he gets there the museum is closed).
• For further practice, SS can roleplay giving directions, either in New York with this map, or locally from the school to various places (see also **Extras Could you tell me the way to …?**)

6 Vocabulary: Travel phrasebook 5

• SS turn to ⬚5 *p. 133*, and complete and translate the phrases.

Tip Before looking, get SS to guess the phrases that will be in the phrasebook.

Lesson notes

In **Travel with English 5** SS revise and extend the language of asking the way, and understanding / giving directions. Pieter's now in New York, asking directions to some famous places. As SS usually need to understand directions much more than give them, the emphasis in this lesson is on listening.

⚠ As the lesson is set in New York there are a few Americanisms – *subway* (= underground), *block* (= distance between streets), *center* (US sp. = *centre*).

Extras

The way to my home

In pairs, SS give each other directions from the school to their house, including get on / off the bus, etc. Tell SS not to actually tell their partner their address, to see if they can work out from the directions more or less where their partner lives.

Could you tell me the way to …? 𝖯 *p. 179* SS ask for / give each other directions using maps with some unmarked buildings. Instructions *p. 136*.

Books-closed presentation

Asking for / giving directions

• Pretend you're a tourist. Ask *Excuse me, could you tell me the way to …?* (a well-known local place within walking distance from the school) and elicit directions.
• Pretend to keep checking you understand by echoing the directions. Finally ask *Is it far? Can I walk there?*
• Elicit the questions you asked onto the board. Then elicit the phrases the SS used to direct you. Correct where necessary.
• Elicit other phrases the SS know to give directions and add them to those on the board.
• Now start with the **Warmer**.

■ Learner-training

Show SS how to test each other using **Travel phrasebook 1** to **5**. SS can:
– write sentences with (a) missing word(s).
– mix the order of words in phrases.
– ask for translations from L1 to English.

■ Homework

SS do **WB 5**⬚ *p. 38* and **Listen and speak 5**⬚.

Lesson aims

Revision	**File 5:** Present perfect and past simple, questions with / without auxiliaries.
Vocabulary	Events in your life: *be born*, etc.
Skills	Reading, speaking

Lesson plan

■ Warmer: Progress chart

- Books closed. Ask *Can you remember what the lessons in File 5 were about? What grammar and vocabulary did we learn?* Elicit anything they can remember.
- Now tell SS to look at the **Progress chart** on *pp. 8-9* and to tick the lessons they've studied.
- Tell them that this is the revision lesson for this File, and that they can then do the **Vocabulary** and **Grammar files** (*pp. 76-77*) to further revise the language of the File.

■ Vocabulary: Life stages

- Focus on ⓥ **Events in your life**. SS number the expressions 1 to 13 in a usual order, beginning with *be born*, as in the example.
- SS compare in pairs, then check answers. There are several possible variations.

> **Suggested answers:**
> 1 be born 2 go to school 3 leave school
> 4 fall in love 5 go to university
> 6 leave university 7 start work 8 get engaged
> 9 get married 10 have children
> 11 get divorced 12 retire 13 die

② Introduction: Famous detectives

a
- Focus on the detectives' names. Ask *Do you recognize any of them?* SS match them with photos A to E. Check answers.

> 1 C 2 E 3 A 4 B 5 D

- Ask if SS recognize any of the actors playing them (A = Joan Hickson B = Peter Cushing, C = Peter Ustinov, D = Humphrey Bogart, E = Peter Sellers,).

b
- Ask *Do you like detective stories / films? Which ones? Who's your favourite detective / detective writer?* SS tell a partner the name of a detective story they've read / seen / heard of.
- Ask *Who created the characters Hercules Poirot and Miss Marple?* (Agatha Christie).

③ Skills: Reading and speaking

a
- Focus on the photo of Agatha Christie. Ask *What do you know about her? Have you read any of her books? Which ones?*
- SS in pairs, **A** and **B**. **A** reads **Part 1** of her biography and **B Part 2**. They try to remember all they can

about her life. Give SS plenty of time to read their text and tell them to ask you for vocabulary they don't know / can't guess. Be prepared to explain / translate:
Part 1: *poison, mysteriously, suffer, amnesia*
Part 2: *archaeologist, create, play(s)(n.), pen name*

b
- Focus on the lifelines for **Parts 1** and **2** of the text. SS use the lines to tell their partner everything they remember about Agatha Christie. Tell SS not to worry about making mistakes – the important thing is to communicate. Monitor and help as necessary.

④ Revision: Questions with / without an auxiliary

a
- Focus on the answers and the two example questions. In pairs, SS write questions 3 to 8 in the same way. Check answers.

> 3 When did she begin to write? 4 What happened in 1928? 5 Why did she disappear?
> 6 What did her second husband do?
> 7 How many detective stories did she write?
> 8 How old was she when she died?

> **Tip** If SS find this difficult, give them the first word of each question to help them.

b
- Focus on ⓥ **Kinds of books**. SS complete the words from the text. Check answers.

> romantic novels   detective stories   thrillers
> novels   plays

- Ask *What kinds of books do you most like reading?* Get a quick show of hands for a class survey.

⑤ Revision: Present perfect or past simple?

a
- Focus on the photo of Ruth Rendell. Ask *Do you know who she is? Have you read any of her books?*
- SS read her biography and complete with the verbs in the past simple or present perfect.
- SS compare in pairs, then check answers.

> 1 was born   2 left   3 worked   4 got
> 5 published   6 was   7 has written
> 8 has published   9 has won   10 has lived

- Be prepared to explain/translate *re-marry, immediate, success, psychological, best-seller*, and *highest-earning*.

b
- Ask *How is Ruth Rendell's life similar to Agatha Christie's?* Focus on the example. SS find four more similarities. (She's English. Ruth Rendell has also got married twice. She's got one child. She's written under a pen name.)

c
- Ask *Why is Agatha Christie's biography all in the past simple but Ruth Rendell's in the past simple and present perfect?* (because Ruth Rendell is still alive, whereas Agatha Christie is dead).

6 Revision: *How long …? + for / since*

a • SS use the answers and complete the three questions about Ruth Rendell.

> 1 How long **has she been** a writer?
> 2 **How long has she been** married?
> 3 **How long has she lived in a** farmhouse?

b • Focus on Ruth's lifeline. Ask *Why were these dates important in her life?* Elicit answers onto the board.

> **1930** She was born.
> **1950** She got married.
> **1964** She published her first novel.
> **1973** She got divorced.
> **1977** She re-married her husband.
> **1986** Since then she has lived in the farmhouse.

7 Personalization: Talk about your lifeline

• Draw a similar lifeline on the board with five important dates for you. Get SS to ask you questions:
> ss *What happened to you in 1979?*
> т *I was born in 1979, on October 4th.*

• Elicit follow-up questions, e.g. *Where were you born?*
• SS do the same in pairs. First they draw their lifeline with five important dates, then they swap lines and ask and answer questions they can about each other's dates.
• Monitor, help, and correct as necessary.

Tip Tell SS who finish quickly to add more dates and information.

Lesson notes

In this lesson, SS revise the main new language from **File 5**. They read the biographies of two famous detective writers and then tell their own. The biographies highlight the difference between the present perfect (for someone who is alive) and the past simple (for someone who is dead). Most SS will know of Agatha Christie. Ruth Rendell's novels are now translated into many languages and British television have made several TV adaptations which SS may have seen.

Extras

Eva Perón – Evita P *p. 180* A pairwork information gap activity based on the life of Eva Perón. Instructions *p. 136.*

May and June P *p. 181* A short story by Ruth Rendell. Instructions *p. 136.*

Who were you? 🎲 *p. 210* A guessing game to practise the past simple.

■ **Homework**

Choose from the **End-of-file options** below.

Writing: Biography SS write a short biography either of a member of their family, e.g. a grandparent, or of a famous person.

End-of-file options

Student's Book

■ **Vocabulary file 5** *p. 76*
• Do this in class, or set it for homework.

Organize your vocabulary learning! Remind SS to be selective about the vocabulary they learn, and to choose and record words which are useful for them.

Try it! SS put the tip into practice with words from 5 ◁▷.

> **1 Word groups**
>   **Suggested answers:**
>   Jewellery: <u>necklace</u>, ring, etc.
>   Age groups: <u>teenager</u>, <u>adult</u>, etc.
>   Family: son, wife, etc.
>   Connectors: then, next, etc.
>   Kinds of books: <u>thrillers</u>, <u>novels</u>, etc.
>   Verbs + *to* + infinitive: need, hope, etc.
> **2 Prepositions**
>   1 to 2 on 3 at, to 4 on 5 on
> **3 Key words**
>   1 nearly 2 immediately 3 together
>   4 as well 5 soon 6 exactly
> **4 Verbs**
>   a 2 lose 3 disappear 4 leave 5 be married
>   6 die 7 sell 8 finish / end
>   b 2 paint 3 direct 4 invent 5 win
>   6 become
> **5 Word-building**
>   1 tracksuit 2 military service
>   3 detective story 4 fruit juice
>   5 phone call (/service) 6 traffic lights
>   7 table tennis 8 car park (/lights)
>   9 tin opener 10 coffee table
> **6 Pronunciation**
>   2 heart 3 wear 4 meat 5 team

■ **Grammar file 5** *p. 77*
• Spend ten minutes going through this with the class, answering any queries. SS tick each box when they're satisfied they understand it.

Workbook

■ **Grammar check 5** *p. 39*
• Remind SS to do this with **SB** and **WB** open in front of them, and to refer back to **Grammar file 5** as necessary. SS can check their answers with the **WB** key.

■ **Read and write 5** *p. 65*
• SS write about a favourite photograph.
• Briefly revise the tenses SS may need. Emphasize the need to read and follow the instructions carefully. Remind SS that they have a key to the exercises, but that you're going to collect and correct their work.

> *Trying to shop with young children is a nightmare.*

Lesson aims

Grammar	Verb + *-ing* (= gerund), gerund or infinitive?
Vocabulary	Housework: *ironing*, etc., shopping: *bargain*, etc.
Pronunciation	/ŋ/, /g/, /dʒ/
Revision	*like / love*, etc. + *-ing*, *would like* + *to*, adjectives of opinion

Lesson plan

■ Warmer: *love / enjoy*, etc.

● Copy this chart on the board:

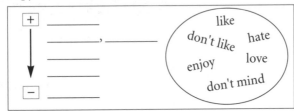

● SS complete the chart with the verbs, from most positive to most negative.
● Check answers. Elicit the meaning of *don't mind* (= neither like nor dislike).

+					−
love	like, enjoy	don't mind	don't like	hate	

1 Presentation: Housework vocabulary

a ● SS turn to 🔖 **Activities C** *p. 134* and match the words and pictures. Ask *What's the difference between 'housework' and 'homework'? Which do you prefer doing?* Check answers. Drill pronunciation of *iron* /ˈaɪən/.

> 13 do the washing-up   14 tidy my room
> 15 do the washing   16 clean the floor
> 17 cook

b ● Elicit other types of housework and pre-teach *vacuum*.

● ∘ 1 ∘ Play the tape once. SS listen and complete the chart, as in the example. SS compare in pairs.
● Play it again and check answers, especially the spelling of *ironing, shopping, cleaning*, and *vacuuming*. Elicit the other details they understood. Ask *Who's the most similar to you? Why?*.

> 1 doesn't like cleaning, hates washing-up.
> 2 enjoys cooking, doesn't mind vacuuming, hates ironing.
> 3 likes shopping, doesn't mind ironing, doesn't like cleaning.
> 4 doesn't mind washing-up, hates shopping.
> 5 loves cooking, enjoys cleaning.

Tapescript **SB Listening** *p. 129*

c ● Focus on the example. Ask *What do you think of washing-up?* etc.
⚠️ Highlight that SS must use *it* after *like / don't mind / hate*, when they don't repeat the verb, e.g. *I like **it**.* NOT ~~*I like.*~~
● Elicit onto the board a few more adjectives to describe housework, e.g. *tiring, boring, necessary*, etc.
● In pairs, SS talk about the activities in the chart. Monitor, help, and correct as necessary.

Tip Find out what is the favourite / least favourite housework activity in the class.

2 Presentation: Uses of verb + *-ing* (gerund)

a ● Focus on the magazine article. Elicit the meaning of *pain / pleasure* (= boring / enjoyable). Read the introduction with the class. Ask *Do you think shopping is a pain or a pleasure?* Elicit answers from men and women in the class.
● Focus on the two cartoons. SS read the article quickly (in two minutes) and match the pictures to the correct two people.
● Check answers.

> **A** Simon   **B** Aisha

b ● SS read the article again, this time more intensively, and complete questions 1 to 4. Avoid explaining the new words yet as this comes in step **c**.
● Get SS to compare in pairs. Check answers.

> 1 Ivan   2 Rosa   3 Aisha and Simon
> 4 Aisha and Rosa

c ● In pairs, SS find words which fit the definitions.
● Check answers and underline the stress. Be prepared to explain / translate *collection, taste, (TV) channel*.

> 1 <u>night</u>mare   2 fun   3 on my own
> 4 <u>ward</u>robe   5 <u>cat</u>alogue   6 <u>crow</u>ded
> 7 the sales   8 <u>bar</u>gain

■ GRAMMAR FOCUS
Verb + *-ing* (= gerund)

● Tell SS that the verb + *-ing* form in English has a special name – the *gerund*.
● Tell SS to highlight six different gerunds in the texts about Aisha and Simon. Then they read rules 1 to 3 and the examples and match each gerund to its rule of use.

> shopping 1   Trying 3   spending 2   shopping 3
> going 1   making 2   buying 2

● SS translate the examples from rules 1 to 3. Ask *What form of the verb do you use in your language?*

PRACTICE

a ● SS complete the sentences truthfully with a verb + *-ing* making sure no one can see what they write.

- In pairs, SS try to guess how their partner has completed each sentence.
- Ask *How many answers did you guess correctly? How many of your answers were the same?*

  Tip If SS have problems remembering the spelling rules of verb + -*ing*, refer them back to $\boxed{\text{G}\blacktriangleleft\blacktriangleleft\,3}$ (**SB** *p. 2*).

3 Personalization: Talk about shopping

- Get the class to go through the questionnaire and ask you some of the questions. In small groups, SS answer each of the questions in turn and try to ask follow-up questions where appropriate.
- Feedback the answer to question 6 with a show of hands, by asking *Who's like Aisha / Simon?* etc.

■ PRONUNCIATION

a ● $\boxed{\circ\,2\,\circ}$ SS listen and repeat the sound, headwords and examples for each sound.
- Ask *Can you see any spelling rules for each sound?* Highlight that:
  - /ŋ/ is usually spelt *ng*.
  - /g/ is always a single or double *g*.
  - /dʒ/ can be spelt *age*, *j*, *dge*, or *gy*.
- $\boxed{\circ\,3\,\circ}$ Do this as a dictation. Get SS to draw three columns headed /ŋ/, /g/, /dʒ/, or use the headwords 'singer', 'girl', and 'jazz' if you prefer. SS listen to thirteen words and write them in the right column.

  Tip Pause after each word to give SS time to write.

- In pairs, SS compare answers and spelling.
- Play the tape again and elicit the answers into a three-column chart on the board (see also **Sound bank WB** *p. 82*).

/ŋ/	along	song	speaking	tongue
/g/	bigger	foggy	bag	together
/dʒ/	dangerous	imagine	village	strange

■ Grammar box: Gerund or infinitive?

- SS read the rules and examples. Highlight that:
  - the first verb decides the form of the second verb.
  - some verbs are followed by *to* + infinitive: verbs of intention (*want*, *hope*, etc.)
  - some verbs are followed by a gerund (verb + -*ing*): verbs of emotion (*love*, *like*, etc.)

4 Practice: Gerund or infinitive?

- SS complete the sentences in pairs, using the grammar box as a reference. Check answers.

1 to come, going	2 to work, getting up
3 Studying	4 to buy, living	5 travelling, flying
6 running, swimming	

5 Personalization: Speaking

a ● Focus on the cartoon. Ask *Do you agree?*
- Highlight the position of *not* before the gerund.
- SS complete the three sentences however they like. Monitor and help with any new vocabulary.

- SS stand up and move around the class comparing their sentences, e.g. *This summer I'd like to go to the USA. And you?* Join in yourself and help as necessary.
- Feedback answers.

Lesson notes

Through the context of shopping, SS learn three different uses of verb + -*ing* (= gerund) i.e. when the verb is used as a noun, after prepositions, and after certain verbs (e.g. *like*). SS also learn vocabulary of housework, and revise the verbs *like / love / hate*.

Spelling rules (-*ing* form) The spelling rules are the same as for the present continuous (see $\boxed{\text{G}\blacktriangleleft\blacktriangleleft\,3}$ **SB** *p. 2*). SS will need to be reminded of these rules.

Gerund or infinitive The gerund is contrasted with verb + *to* + infinitive, which SS studied in **File 5B**. SS will need reminding when to use a gerund and when to use an infinitive.

Extras

Do you agree?
- Prepare a series of statements using the -*ing* form as a noun, e.g. *Jogging is good for you. Seeing films on video is better than seeing them in the cinema.* Write them on cards or on the board.
- In pairs, SS discuss them and say if they agree / don't agree and why.

Free-time activities $\boxed{\text{P}}$ *p. 182* Picture prompts for SS to talk about free time activities they enjoy / don't enjoy doing. Instructions *p. 137*.

Books-closed presentation

Verb + -*ing* (= the gerund)

Do before the **Warmer**. Write on the board:

> 1 <u>Smoking</u> is bad for your health.
> 2 Always use the shower before <u>getting</u> into the water.
> 3 If you like <u>skiing</u>, you'll love the Swiss Alps.

- Ask *Where could you see these sentences?* (1 on a packet of cigarettes 2 at a swimming pool 3 in a travel agency or travel brochure).
- Then ask *What have all the underlined verbs got in common?* (they all end in -*ing*) *Why?*
- Elicit / teach the three uses of -*ing* form (see Lesson notes) Then start the **Warmer**.

■ Learner-training

Tell SS to keep a record of verbs which are followed by *to* + infinitive and verb + -*ing*, with example sentences.

■ Homework

SS do **WB 6A** *p. 40* and **Listen and speak 6A**.

> *He looks friendly.*
> *He looks like an actor.*

Lesson aims

Grammar	*look* or *look like*?
Vocabulary	Adjectives of personality: *shy*, etc., zodiac signs: *Aries*, etc.
Pronunciation	/eə/, /ɪə/
Revision	Describing people, age, jobs, likes
Optional materials	Magazines or personal photos of people (Books-closed presentation)

Lesson plan

■ Warmer: ® Adjectives to describe people

- Write on the board:

Hair	Body	General Appearance
long	tall	good-looking

- In pairs, SS brainstorm adjectives for two minutes.
- Feedback onto the board.
- Suggested answers
  hair: long, short, curly, dark, etc.
  Body: tall, slim, short, strong, etc.
  General Apperance: good-looking, ugly, attractive, etc.

1 Revision: Describing people

- Focus on the lesson title. Check SS understand *first impressions* (= what you think of someone the first time you meet). Ask *Are your first impressions usually right?*
- Focus on photos A to F. Ask SS to describe them, as in the example. Elicit sentences for the first two onto the board, then get SS to do the other four in pairs.
- Feedback answers onto the board. Highlight any common errors, especially with articles, e.g. NOT ~~He's got a long hair.~~ etc.

2 Presentation: *looks* or *looks like*?

a • Ask *How old do you think they are?* Elicit guesses. Tell SS to use *He / She looks* (= appears) *about … .*

b • In pairs, SS guess their jobs, using *He / She looks like a / an …* Remind SS to use a/an for jobs.
- Feedback answers, then tell them the real answers.

> **A** Dawn French (actress) (born 1957)
> **B** Paul Boateng (politician) (born 1951)
> **C** Helen Steward (university teacher) (born 1958)
> **D** Usha Patel (police officer) (born 1968)
> **E** Nigel Kennedy (violinist) (born 1956)
> **F** Greg Rudeski (tennis player) (born 1973)

3 Vocabulary: Adjectives of personality

a • In pairs, SS turn to 📖 **Adjectives B** *p. 138* and match the adjectives and definitions.
- SS match each adjective to its opposite.

- Check answers and drill pronunciation as necessary

> **1** selfish (opp. unselfish)   **2** generous (opp. mean)
> **3** lazy (opp. hard-working)   **4** talkative (opp. quiet)
> **5** shy (opp. extrovert)   **6** friendly (opp. unfriendly)   **7** intelligent (opp. stupid)

b • Focus on photos A to F again. Tell SS to guess their personalities, using adjectives from the **Word bank**.
- Elicit answers using *He / She looks …*

  Tip Remind SS to use *really / very*, *quite*, *a bit*.

■ GRAMMAR FOCUS
look or *look like*?

a • Focus on the two examples. Elicit when we use *look* and when we use *look like*. SS complete the rule with 'adjective' or 'noun'. Check answers.

> adjective   noun

- Highlight that:
  – *He **looks** intelligent* is a different meaning from *He **looks** at his watch.*
  – We use *look* + an adjective (*intelligent*) or age (*about 40*).
  – We use *look like* + a noun.
- Give further practice in a drill:
  T *friendly*
  SS *He looks friendly.*
  T *a pop singer*
  SS *He looks like a pop singer.*, etc.

b • Focus on the rules of use. Remind SS of the meaning of *impression* (= what you think) and contrast this with *fact* (= what you know).

PRACTICE
- SS complete the sentences with *look* or *look like*.
- Check answers.

> **1** look   **2** looks like   **3** looked   **4** looks
> **5** look like   **6** looks like

■ PRONUNCIATION

a • ⌐4⌐ SS listen and repeat the sound, headword, and examples.
- Highlight that:
  – /eə/ is usually spelt *air*, *are*, or *ere* (e.g. *hair*, *care*, *there*).
  – /ɪə/ is usually spelt *ear*, or *eer* (e.g. *clear*, *engineer*) (see **Sound bank WB** *p. 81*).

b • ⌐5⌐ SS listen to the four 'tongue twisters' and write /eə/ or /ɪə/ after each sentence, according to the sound they're practising. Check answers.

> **1** /eə/   **2** /ɪə/   **3** /ɪə/   **4** /eə/

4 Practice: Question formation

a • Focus on the magazine article. SS read the

introduction about the personal column in *Marie Claire* (a woman's magazine).

- Focus on the photos of Jerry and Anna. Ask SS to describe them using *be / have got / look / look like.* Ask *Would you like to meet these people? Why (not)?*

b • Focus on the chart. Elicit onto the board the questions you need to find out the information.

> How tall is he / she?   What does he / she do?
> Where does he / she live?   What car has he / she got?   Does he / she smoke?   Who's his / her favourite actress / actor?   What are his / her ideal weekend activities?   What's his / her star sign?
> What's he / she like?

- Focus on **V** *be like / look like*. Remind SS of the difference.
  ⚠️ SS may use *How is (she)?* Explain that this means *Is she well? / How is she feeling?*
- Teach SS how to say their height, e.g. *I'm one metre eighty-five* (we don't say *centimetres*).

5 Practice: Asking about / describing people

a • Tell SS they're going to read about Jerry and Anna and complete the charts. SS in pairs, A and B, turn to ▶◀ **Jerry and Anna** A *p. 121* B *p. 124.* They read their descriptions. (They complete half the chart on *p. 81*.)
- B asks A the questions to complete the information for Jerry. Then they swap and A asks B the questions to complete the chart for Anna.
- Monitor and help as necessary. Check answers.

	Name	
	Jerry Dowles	**Anna Malik**
Age	34	26
Height	*1m 85*	*1m 71*
Job	architect	doctor
Home	flat in west London	small house in north London
Vehicle	Fiat Uno	1959 Mercedes
Smoker	yes (about five a day)	no
Favourite actress	Isabella Rossellini	Isabella Rossellini
Favourite actor	Mel Gibson	Jeremy Irons
Ideal weekend activities	going out, listening to jazz	eating out, going to the theatre
Star sign	Taurus	Gemini
Personality	open, generous	intelligent, extrovert

b • SS look at their completed charts. Give them a minute to decide in pairs if Jerry and Anna will get on well if they meet. Feedback. Ask *Why (not)?*

6 Skills: Listening

- ∘6∘ Tell SS Anna and Jerry met for an evening and were then interviewed. SS listen and note the four

adjectives that each uses to describe the other. Play the tape twice.
- SS compare in pairs. Check answers.

> **Anna is** extrovert   talkative   generous hard-working
> **Jerry is** friendly   shy   talkative   mean
> Tapescript **SB Listening** *p. 129*

- Ask *Were you right? Do they want to meet again?* (he does, she doesn't)

7 Personalization: Talk about people

a • Focus on the chart. Describe somebody you know well. Get SS to ask you the questions for each heading in the chart to get the information. Encourage them to ask follow-up questions. When they've asked at least one question for each heading, ask *Would you like to meet him / her? Why (not)?*
- Tell SS to choose a family member or friend and think about what they're going to say for three minutes. Help with vocabulary.

b • In pairs. SS ask and answer about each other's person to decide if they would like to meet him / her. Feedback.

Lesson notes

SS revise language of physical descriptions and learn to use *look / look like* to describe people. They also learn and practise adjectives of personality.

What's he / she like? SS learned *What's it like?* in **File 1**, but they are still likely to have problems with this useful question. SS commonly confuse *How is she?* and *What's she like?*

Descriptions SS probably still have problems with articles and confuse *is / has*.

Extras

Magazine photos Use magazine photos of people to practise *look / looks like* and physical descriptions.

Are you a good matchmaker? 🅿 *p. 183* A questionnaire about a friend or family member. Instructions *p. 137*.

Books-closed presentation

look / look like

- Do before the **Warmer**. Find some large magazine pictures of men and women (not famous people) or some photos of your family or friends.
- Show them to the class one by one. Ask *How old do you think he / she is?* Elicit / teach *He / She looks about* (25).
- Then ask SS to guess their jobs. Elicit teach *He / She looks like a* (*teacher*). Then start **ex. 1**.

■ Learner-training

Remind them that it helps to record adjectives with their opposites.

■ Homework

SS do **WB 6B** *p. 41* and **Listen and speak 6B**.

What's in your rubbish?

He doesn't drink much fruit juice.

Lesson aims

Grammar	*a lot of* / *much* / *many* / *a little* / *a few*
Vocabulary	Food, containers / packaging: *packet*, *plastic*, etc., agree / disagree, the environment: *recycle*, etc.
Pronunciation	Linking, weak form /əv/
Revision	Countability, high numbers
Optional materials	Magazine photos of countable / uncountable food (**Practice b**)

Lesson plan

■ Warmer: ⓡ Adjectives of personality

- SS quickly write three adjectives of personality on a piece of paper (the first ones that they think of).
- SS compare their three adjectives with a partner.
- Then tell them that this is a psychological test. The first adjective is how they see themselves, the second is how other people see them, the last is how they really are.

1 Revision: Countability

- Remind SS of the difference between countable and uncountable nouns (see Ⓖ◄◄ 18 **SB** *p.6*). Highlight that:
- – all countable words have a plural form (formed with an *s* except irregular plurals like *people*, *men*, etc.).
- – uncountable nouns don't have a plural and so don't usually end in *s*. Elicit a few examples of both.
- SS turn to 🔖 **Food B** *p.137*. In pairs, they decide if the words are countable or uncountable, and label the uncountable nouns with **U**.

> The condiments are all **U**: oil, pepper, salt, vinegar. plate(s), knife(knives), fork(s), spoon(s), are **C**

2 Presentation: Containers

- SS do 🔖 **Food C** *p.137*, matching the words and pictures.
- Check answers. Drill pronunciation as necessary.

> **9** a jar of jam **10** a can of Coke
> **12** a packet of biscuits **13** a bottle of water
> **14** a tin of tuna **15** a box of tissues

- Highlight that:
- – we say *a* (*box*) *of* (*tissues*) and that the noun (*tissue*) is always plural if it's countable.
- – we say *half a* / *a quarter of a* (*kilo*) *of* NOT ~~a half kilo of~~ / ~~a quarter kilo of.~~
- – we use *can* for drinks NOT ~~tin.~~
- SS test each other in pairs.
- Write on the board:

> beer   matches   fruit juice
> marmalade   cigarettes   soup

- Ask *How do you usually buy these things?* (a bottle/can of beer, a box of matches, a carton of fruit juice, a jar of marmalade, a packet of cigarettes (a carton = 200), a tin of soup.

■ PRONUNCIATION

- ∘ **7** ∘ Play the tape. SS listen and repeat sentences.
- Focus on the linkers (marked ‿). Explain that we always link words when a vowel sound and a consonant sound come together at the beginning / end of a word.
- SS say the sentences again quickly, trying to link the words together. Drill any they find especially difficult.
- Play the tape again. Ask *Is 'of' pronounced* /ɒf/, /ɒv/, or /əv/? (/əv/).

3 Presentation: Quantifiers (*a lot of*, *much*, etc.)

a
- Focus on the photo of Jack Nicholson. Ask *Who is he?* (an American actor. Films include *One flew over the cuckoo's nest*, *Batman*, *Wolf*, etc.).
- Tell SS to read the introduction to the magazine article and answer the two questions.
- Check answers.

> Bruno and Pascal are journalists. They looked in famous peoples' rubbish bins for information about them.

b
- Focus on the photo. Ask *What can you see?* Elicit answers. Encourage SS to use linkers. Elicit / teach *bar* (*of chocolate*), *lollipop*, *bacon*, *frozen* (*peas*), *corn chips* (= American crisps), *ginger beer*, *wrapper* (= empty packet).

> four bottles‿of champagne   seven bottles‿of beer
> seven bottles‿of ginger beer
> two bottles‿of mineral water   a can‿of seven-up
> two bottles‿of French wine   a packet‿of coffee
> a carton‿of orange juice   a packet‿of bacon
> a packet‿of corn chips   a packet‿of frozen peas
> two lollipop wrappers   two chocolate bar wrappers
> four packets‿of Camel cigarettes

c
- SS read the article and answer questions 1 to 5.
- Check answers. Be prepared to explain / translate *obviously*, *occasionally*, *surprisingly*, *instead of*, *as for*, *except for*.

> **1** A lot.   **2** No (only a little).   **3** A few.
> **4** Yes, a lot.   **5** Probably not because he drinks and smokes a lot, and eats very little fresh food.

■ GRAMMAR FOCUS
Quantifiers (*a lot of*, *much*, etc.)

a
- SS highlight *a lot of* / *much* / *many* / *a little* / *a few* / *very few* in the article and in **ex. 3c**.

b ● SS study the nouns which follow each highlighted word and then complete the rule chart.

		Countable	Uncountable
For large quantities	+	a lot of / lots of	**a lot of /** lots of
	− ?	**(not) many**	(not) much
For small quantities	+ −	a few very few	**a little** **very little**
Questions		**How many?**	**How much?**

⚠ Remind SS that *lots of* = *a lot of,* and that we don't say *of* after *lot* at the end of the sentence.

PRACTICE

a ● Focus on the example. Ask *Why is 'much' wrong?* (because we use *a lot of* in positive sentences). SS read the sentences and cross out the words which are grammatically wrong, as in the example.
● Check answers. Elicit why each one is right / wrong.

> **2** How much tea   **3** a little meat   **4** Do you drink much coffee?   **5** Yes, I drink a lot.   **6** I don't eat many vegetables.   **7** I only eat a few sweets

b ● Focus on the food in the picture. Ask *What can you see?* SS name the food (**a few** sweets, **some** meat, **some** pasta, **some** fish, **a bottle of** beer, **some** fruit, **a jar of** / **a cup of** coffee).

Tip Use magazine pictures of your own here.

● Focus on **V** Short answers. Check SS understand.
● SS interview you first, and you demonstrate the short answers. Then ask individual SS *How many (sweets) / How much (fish) do you eat?*
● In pairs, SS interview their partner in the same way, using *How much …? / How many …?* and the food. Tell them to note the quantities their partner eats of each thing, using the short answers.
● Highlight that we use *none* (= not one / not any).

c ● SS write six sentences about their partner's diet.
● Ask *Whose diet is healthier? Why?* Elicit answers.

Tip You could collect SS lists of sentences and read them out. The class has to guess who wrote each.

4 Practice: Listening

● ◦8◦ Books closed. Tell SS they're going to listen to a radio programme about rubbish. Write the title on the board, **The throw-away society**. Elicit the meaning of *throw away* (rubbish). Play the tape once. SS listen and write all the numbers that they hear (as figures).
● SS compare in pairs / small groups. Play it again for them to check.
● Books open. Read the text to the class and elicit each missing number onto the board. SS complete the text.

> **2** 7   **3** 1   **4** 7,000,000   **5** 80,000,000   **6** 50
> **7** 60   **8** 45   **9** 300,000   **10** 173

● Ask *Do any of the statistics surprise you?* Elicit SS' reaction to the text.

5 Personalization: Talk about the environment

a ● Focus on the expressions in the speech bubble.

● Drill pronunciation. Make sure SS don't over-stress *so.*
● SS read five tips to help the environment. Be prepared to explain / translate *bottle bank*, *paper bank*, *re-use*, *recycled*, *packaging*.
● SS in small groups. Ask *Which do you think is the most important tip? Why?*
● Feedback. Encourage SS to justify their choice if they can, using the expressions from the speech bubbles.

b ● Ask the class *Which ones do you do?* Get a quick show of hands to see how many do each one. Ask those SS who answer yes *How often?* etc. Elicit answers.

Lesson notes

Through the context of the contents of Jack Nicholson's rubbish bin, SS revise countability and *How much / many ..?* and learn to use more quantifiers. SS also learn the vocabulary of common condiments and food containers.

much / many / a lot of Although the rules are clear, SS will have problems putting them into practice.

⚠ Native speakers are increasingly using *a lot of* in − and ? sentences.

a little / a few SS already know *a little,* and here learn *a few* used with countable nouns.

Extras

Magazine pictures of food
Use in **Practice b** to drill *How much / many …?*

Food, food, food P *p.184* A pairwork questionnaire. Instructions *p.137.*

Books-closed presentation

much / many / a lot of / none

● Do after the **Warmer**. Ask *What do people usually keep in their fridge?* Elicit suggestions, e.g. *eggs, milk,* etc.
● Write their suggestions on the board in two columns according to whether they're countable or uncountable.
● When you have six words in each column, stop and ask *Why are they in two columns?* Elicit that one column is countable nouns and the other uncountable nouns.
● Write the headings **countable / uncountable** on the board. Elicit the two question forms *How much* and *How many,* and three possible answers for each column: *a lot / not much / many,* and *none.*
● In pairs, SS ask and answer *How much (milk) have you got in your fridge?* etc.
● Feedback. Ask *What does this tell you about their lifestyle?* (e.g. she's got a lot of fruit and vegetables. She's very healthy). Then start **ex.1**.

■ Learner training

Discuss ways SS revise vocabulary and share ideas. Tell SS to revise the vocabulary of 🗎 **Food** *p.137* for a short test at the beginning of the next class.

■ Homework

SS do **WB 6C** *p.42* and **Listen and speak 6C.**

The day the birds died

> There are too many people
> and there isn't enough fresh air.

Lesson aims

Grammar	*too much / many, (not) enough*
Vocabulary	Town facilities and problems: *car park, traffic*, etc., *n. / v. / adj. /* families: *pollute*, etc.
Pronunciation	Word stress in word families
Revision	countability, *too* + adjective, comparative adjectives

Lesson plan

■ Warmer: ® Quantifiers

- Write on the board:

> 1 I eat much potatoes.
> 2 I don't eat many meat.
> 3 Do you drink many milk?
> 4 I only drink a few wine.

- SS correct the mistake in each sentence.

> 1 I eat **a lot of** potatoes.
> 2 I don't eat **much** meat.
> 3 Do you drink **much** milk?
> 4 I only drink **a little** wine.

- Check answers, reminding SS of the rules (see **File 6C Grammar focus**).

1 Presentation: Uncountable nouns

- Focus on ⓥ Cities. Make sure SS understand all the words.
- SS complete the column headings with *'s* or *are*. Ask *Why are they different?* (because the words on the right are uncountable).

> are   's

- Highlight that many words in English, not just food words, are uncountable (you can't add an *s* to them), e.g. *work, traffic, unemployment, information*.
  ⚠ *people* is an important exception. It has no *s* but it's countable. We say *people are* NOT ~~*people is.*~~
- Practise quickly by asking SS to give you a few sentences about the town where you are, e.g. *There's a lot of traffic. There aren't many jobs.* etc.

2 Skills: Reading

- **a**
  - Focus on the photos of Mexico City. Ask *What can you see?* Encourage SS to answer with *There is / are …*
  - Ask *Have you been there? What's it like? / Would you like to go there? Why (not)?*
- **b**
  - Tell SS they're going to read about Mexico City. Focus on the phrases in the list. Ask *Why do you think they're in the text?* Elicit suggestions, e.g. *22 million = the number of birds in Mexico City.* Don't confirm if their answers are right or wrong yet.

Tip Books closed. Write the seven phrases on the board to discourage them from reading ahead.

- **c**
  - SS read the text quickly to see if they were right. Try to avoid explaining new words yet. Check answers.

> 22 million = the population of Mexico City
>
> Mexico City is three times bigger than New York City
>
> 2,255 metres = the height of the city above sea level
>
> the Aztecs = the people who first built the city
>
> 40 cigarettes a day = breathing the air has the same effect as smoking this
>
> thousands of birds died on a single day in the 1980s because of the pollution
>
> 30 million = the expected population of the city in the year 2010

3 Presentation: *too much / many, (not) enough*

- **a**
  - In pairs, SS read the text again to find words which fit definitions 1 to 8. Do the first one with them.

    Tip If your SS are finding this is taking a long time, help them by telling them the line number for each word.

  - Check answers and drill pronunciation as necessary.

> 1 over (l.4)   2 unem<u>ploy</u>ment (l.9)
> 3 over-<u>pop</u>ulation (l.9)   4 snow-capped (l.11)
> 5 smog (l.12)   6 <u>traf</u>fic jam (l.14)
> 7 <u>breath</u>ing (l.14)   8 im<u>prov</u>ing (l.17)

Encourage SS to guess other new vocabulary from context. Be prepared to explain / translate *magical, extremely, situated, surrounded by, volcanoes, enormous, factories, endless, solve (a problem).*

- **b**
  - SS complete the sentences with one word. Elicit answers.

> 1 people   2 traffic   3 jobs   4 big / large
> 5 dirty / polluted

- Check SS understand *enough* /ˈɪnʌf/ (= sufficient, the right amount) and *too / too much / many* (= more than enough). Drill pronunciation of sentences 1 to 5.
- **c**
  - Ask *Does (your capital city) have any similar problems?* Elicit answers from the class with phrases similar to those in **ex. 3b**.

■ GRAMMAR FOCUS
(not) enough, too, too much / many

- **a**
  - Tell SS to look carefully at the sentences in **ex. 3b** and complete the rules in the box with 'C nouns', 'U nouns', or 'adjective'.

> *too* + adjective   *too much* + U nouns
> *too many* + C nouns   *(not)* adjective + *enough*

b • Focus on the pairs of sentences. Ask *Which of the two sentences is more negative?* Check answers.

> 1 The film was **too** long.   2 She eats **too much**.
> 3 We haven't got **any** money.

• Highlight that:
– *too* + adjective and *too much* / *many* (= more than necessary) have a negative meaning. Compare *My house is very big.* / *My house is too big.*
– *not enough* (= less than necessary) is the opposite of *too much* / *many*.
– *enough* goes after an adjective but before a noun.

PRACTICE

a • SS complete sentences 1 to 7 with *too* / *too much* / *too many*, or *enough*. Check answers.

> 1 too much   2 enough   3 too   4 too much
> 5 too many   6 enough   7 too / too many

b • Focus on the four cartoons. Tell SS in pairs to write two sentences for each one with *too, too much* / *many*, or *enough*, as in the example.
• Monitor and help as necessary, then check answers.

> **Suggested answers:**
> 1 There are too many boxes. The van isn't big enough.
> 2 There's too much smoke. The music is too loud.
> 3 The box is too heavy. They aren't strong enough. They're too weak.
> 4 There are too many people. The car isn't big enough. The car is too small.

4 Practice: Listening

• SS to look at the photo and read about Jean François. Ask *Have you been to this part of France? What do you think is negative / positive about living in a very small village?*
• ∙9∙ SS listen and note down two positive and two negative points in two columns.
• SS compare answers with a partner and listen again.
• Check answers with a two-column chart on the board. Ask *Would you like to live there? Why (not)?*

> ＋ quiet   old beautiful houses   surrounded by lovely fields and forests   close to Nature / grow own food   friendly / everybody knows everybody
>
> － 20 kms to nearest big town   no shops / bars very cut off   no cinema   difficult to have a private life / no secrets
>
> Tapescript **SB Listening** *p. 129*

5 Personalization: Talk about your town / city

a • In small groups SS answer the questions together and talk about the items in the list. Give some examples to start them off, e.g. *Do you think there are enough parks? Do you think there's too much traffic?*
• Monitor, help and correct as necessary.
• Feedback. Ask *Which three things most need to be better in your city / town?*

Lesson notes

This lesson continues the notion of countability. SS learn to use *too, too much* / *many*, and (*not*) *enough* in the context of environmental problems facing cities nowadays, and compare this with life in a small village.

Uncountable nouns SS have only explored countability with food words, and here apply the rules to abstract nouns such as *work* and *unemployment*. Watch out for errors with *people*, which looks uncountable but isn't. Common error ~~people is~~.

too, too much / many SS already know *too* + adjective. They may try and use *too much* + adjective (*It's too ~~much expensive.~~ etc.*) SS may also confuse it with *too = also*.

enough SS have problems with the position and pronunciation of *enough*. They may also confuse *enough* and *quite*.

Extras

Talk about … television P *p. 185* A questionnaire for SS to talk in pairs about television. Instructions *p. 137*.

Books-closed presentation

too much / *too many*   For flashcard presentations, see **Introduction** *p. 11*.
• Do after the **Warmer**. Copy the pictures from **Picture bank 6D** *p. 207* onto cards / the board.
• Ask *Do you like living in a city? / Would you like to live in a city?* (according to where you are), *What are the problems of living in a city?*
• Use the pictures one by one to present and practise *There are too many (cars).* etc.
• Write the sentences on the board for SS to copy. Ask *Why do we use 'much' with pollution / 'many' with cars?* Elicit *much* + uncountable nouns / *many* with plural countable nouns. Then start **ex. 1**.

■ **Learner-training**

Encourage SS to learn and record words in grammatical 'families'. Tell them to mark the stress At the end of the lesson get them to record, e.g.
po<u>llute</u> (*v.*), po<u>lluted</u> (*adj.*), po<u>llution</u> (*n.*)
em<u>ploy</u> (*v.*), (un)em<u>ployed</u> (*adj.*), (un)em<u>ployment</u> (*n.*)

■ **Homework**

SS do **WB 6D** *p. 43* and **Listen and speak 6D**.

■ **Writing**

SS could write about the problems in their town.

Lesson aims

Function	Buying food / clothes, taking things back
Grammar	*(Which) one / ones?*
Revision	*this / that / these / those*, food, clothes, colours, numbers
Optional materials	Pairs of objects (yours or SS') (Books-closed presentation)

Lesson plan

■ Warmer: ® Shopping vocabulary

- Books closed. Ask *Where was Pieter last time?* (New York) *What was the lesson about?* (asking the way).

  In pairs, SS test each other on the phrases in **Travel phrasebook 5** *p. 133* (in a mono-lingual class, SS use *How do you say … in English?* / in a multilingual class SS can quickly revise the expressions individually or test each other with cloze sentences).

- Quickly revise shopping vocabulary from **6A** with these definitions:
  1. a person who works in a shop (shop assistant)
  2. a person who buys something from a shop (customer)
  3. the time when everything in the shops is cheaper (sales)
  4. something you bought at a very good price (bargain)
  5. a magazine with pictures of things you can buy (catalogue)
  6. where you can go shopping in the street (a market)

1 Practice: Reading about shops

- Books open. Ask *Where's Pieter now?* (he's still in New York). SS look at the extract from Pieter's guidebook and read about the two shops. Focus first on *Zabar's*. Tell SS to look at the photo of Zabar's. Elicit / teach the meaning of *delica̱tessen*, *vari̱ety*, *qua̱lity*, *brea̱thtaking*.
- Focus on **The Original Levi Store**. Elicit the meaning of *store* (= shop, US) and *are limited to* (= can only buy).
- Ask *Do you know any similar shops? Which would you prefer to go to?*

2 Presentation: Buying food

a
- ⟨ 10 ⟩ Play the tape. SS cover the dialogue and listen to Pieter shopping at Zabar's. Ask *What does he buy? How much does it cost?*
- Check answers.

Half a kilo of cheese.	$8.50

- SS focus on the dialogue and try to remember some of the missing words.

b
- Play the tape again. In pairs, SS check and complete the dialogue.
- Check answers. Re-play any parts of the dialogue if SS have missed anything or got something wrong.

P Can I **have** some of that **cheese**, please?
A Which one? This **one**?
P No, **that** one.
A Ah, this **one**. How much **do you want**?
P **Half** a **kilo.**
A Anything **else**?
P No, thanks. How **much** is **that**?
A **$8.50**.
A **Here** you are. **Thanks.**

- Highlight the use of *How much is that?* to ask for the total price in a shop. Compare with *How much is it? How much are they?* to ask the price of individual things.

■ Grammar box: *one / ones*

- Focus on the first four lines of the dialogue. Look at *one*. Ask *What does it mean here?* (cheese).
- Read SS the first four lines of the dialogue, repeating *cheese* instead of *one*.
- Focus on the grammar box. Highlight that:
  - we use *one* (singular) and *ones* (plural) to avoid repeating a noun, e.g. *These biscuits are nice. Would you like one?*
  - we use *one(s)* with or without an adjective, e.g. *Can you pass me that coat? Which one? This one? No, not that one, the brown one.*
- Model more examples using SS' possessions, e.g. *Which is your bag? The brown one?* etc.
  ⚠ In your SS' language they may be able to use an adjective without a noun, e.g. *Do you want the big or the small?* In English you must add *one(s)*.

3 Practice: Roleplay

a
- Ask SS to imagine Pieter wants to buy some apples. Tell them to change the dialogue as necessary. Elicit the first four lines onto the board and drill pronunciation of *these* and *those ones*:

  P Can I have some of those apples, please?
  A Which ones? These ones?
  P No, those ones.
  A Ah, these ones. How many do you want?

  ⚠ Highlight that *How much is that?* doesn't change as it still refers to the total money (which is uncountable, so takes a singular verb).

b
- In pairs, SS roleplay the dialogue using the four food items on the list. If there's an odd number of SS, either join in yourself or have two customers with one shop assistant. Get them to swap roles each time.
- Monitor, help and correct as necessary.

4 Presentation: Buying clothes

a
- ⟨ 11 ⟩ Tell SS that Pieter's now at the Levi Store. Play the tape twice. SS listen and complete what he buys, the colour, size, and price. Check answers.

> Clothes: **jeans**   Colour: **black**
> Size: **34**   Price: **$49.95**
> Tapescript **SB Listening** *p. 129*

b
- Focus on the word prompts. Tell SS they're going to write the dialogue using these prompts.
- SS in pairs. Play the tape again, and they write the dialogue. Re-play the tape as many times as SS need.

  Tip Tell SS to leave any lines they can't remember, and wait till they hear the dialogue again. Pause the tape after each line to help them.

- Tell SS to look at the tapescript, compare it with their version, and check spelling.

c
- SS cover their completed dialogues and look only at the word prompts. Elicit all the dialogue from them and correct where necessary.
- In pairs, SS practise the dialogue. Monitor and help as necessary. If they get stuck, let them look back quickly at their written version. Fast finishers can swap roles.
- SS roleplay the dialogue again but this time tell them that they want to buy a *shirt*. Elicit how the dialogue will change and teach *small*, *medium*, and *large*.

> Have you got **this shirt** in my size?
> Which **one**?
> The (**dark blue one**).
> What size are you?
> I'm (**large**).
> Let's see. Here you are.
> Can I try **it** on?
> Yes, there's a changing room over there.
> **It**'s a bit too (**big**). Have you got a (**smaller**) size?
> **This one is medium.**
> Yes, **this is** fine. OK, I'll take **it**.
> Would you like anything else?
> No, thanks. How much **is it**?
> It's $34.

- In pairs, SS roleplay the dialogue. Then swap roles.

5 Presentation: Taking things back

a
- Elicit the meaning of *taking things back* (= returning things to a shop because there's a problem). Ask *Have you ever taken anything back to a shop? Why?*
- °12° Tell SS to cover the phrases in **ex. 5b** and listen to three people taking things back to a shop. Ask *What did they buy?* Check answers.

> **1** jeans   **2** a radio   **3** a shirt

b
- SS listen again and complete what the customer says. Check answers.

> **1** The zip's **broken** on **these jeans**. Can I **change** them?   **2** **The** volume control doesn't **work**. I'd **like** my **money back**.   **3** **There's** a button **missing** on this shirt. Have **you** got **another** one?
> Tapescript **SB Listening** *p. 130*

- Check SS understand *broken*, a new use of the verb *work* (= function), *have my money back*, *missing*, and *another one*. Drill pronunciation.
- For extra practice SS can roleplay the three situations with prompts on the board.

6 Vocabulary: Travel phrasebook 6

- SS turn to 🕮6 *p. 133* and translate the phrases. Before they look, ask them to look through the lesson and predict what important phrases will be in the phrasebook.

Lesson notes

In **Travel with English 6** Pieter's still in New York and goes shopping. He buys some food at a delicatessen and some clothes from a large store. The lesson revises and extends shopping language and SS learn useful expressions for taking defective things back to a shop.
They also practise reading an authentic guidebook extract.

one / ones In many other languages an adjective can be used as a noun e.g. *Do you want the big or the small?* but in English *one(s)* must be added to the adjective.

Extras

I'd like my money back! ⟦P⟧ *p. 186* Role cards for SS to roleplay complaining in a shop. Instructions *p. 138*.

Books-closed presentation

Which one? This one. / That one. / The blue one. etc.
- Do after the **Warmer**. Bring to class some pairs of (different) objects e.g. pens, cassettes, watches, books, credit cards, sweaters, etc. Offer them to the class and say *Which one do you prefer, this one or that one?*
- Get individual SS to point to one or the other and say *That one.* Pretend to be confused and say *This one?* Elicit *No, that one.*
- Write the new language on the board.
- Now pretend to offer SS a choice by holding an object in either hand and ask *Which do you prefer, the blue one or the red one? / the big one or the small one? / the cheap one or the expensive one? / the English one or the Italian one? / the wooden one or the plastic one?* etc.
- SS answer according to their preferences.
- Write some examples on the board. Highlight that you can't use an adjective without adding a noun or *one*. Then start **ex. 1**.

■ Learner-training

Get SS to revise a selection of phrases from **Travel phrasebook 1** to **6**. Give them a test next class. Write some situations on the board, e.g. *You're lost in New York and you want to find Wall Street.* Ask *What do you say?*

■ Homework

SS do **WB 6**🕮 *p. 44* and **Listen and speak 6**🕮.

Lesson aims

Revision	**File 6:** Gerunds, quantifiers: *too, too much / many, (not) enough,* describing people
Vocabulary	*go / do / play* + sports

Lesson plan

■ Warmer: Progress chart

- Books closed. Ask *Can you remember what the lessons in File 6 were about? What grammar and vocabulary did we learn?* Elicit from the SS anything they can remember.
- Now tell SS to look at the **Progress chart** *p. 9* and to tick the lessons they've studied.
- Tell them that this is the revision lesson for this File, and that they can then do the **Vocabulary** and **Grammar files** (*pp. 88-89*) to further revise the language of the File.

1 Presentation: Sports vocabulary

a
- Focus on the chart. Check vocabulary. Elicit the difference between *bat* and *racket* (a racket has strings / a bat is solid).
- Drill the eight sports in the list. SS put two of them into each column, as in the example, then add one more to each.
- Draw the empty chart on the board and elicit their answers. Ask for more suggestions. Mark the stress.

Ball sports	Racket / bat sports	Water sports	Other
rugby	table-tennis	scuba-diving	gymnastics
squash		sailing	jogging

- Focus on **V** *go / play / do.* Go through the three rules and elicit more examples for each, e.g. *go* (*skate-boarding / roller skating / climbing*), *play* (*basketball / tennis*), *do* (*aerobics / judo*). ⚠ *boxing* is an exception (= *do*).

b
- Ask *Which verb goes with each of the sports in the chart in ex. 1a?* Elicit the answers.

We use **play** with column 1 / 2, **go** with column 3 and *jogging,* and **do** with *gymnastics.*

2 Personalization: Talk about sports

- Focus on the cartoon. Ask *Does this look like anyone you know?*
- Focus on the questions. Get SS to ask you them in a random order. Help them make follow-up questions.
- ⚠ Highlight the difference between watching *live* /laɪv/ (*adj.*) (= at the stadium) and *on TV.*
- In pairs, SS answer the questions together. Monitor and help as necessary.
- Ask each pair *Which one of you watches most sport? / does most sport? Does anyone hate sport?*

3 Revision: *many / a lot / a few*

a
- Focus on the statistics for sports in Britain. Use the illustrations to teach / elicit the meaning of *darts* and *snooker* (similar to billiards, played with a cue, seven coloured balls, and fifteen red balls on a large table).
- SS read the statistics. Ask *Do any of them surprise you?*

b
- SS in small groups. Ask *What are the three most popular sports in your country / countries a) on TV, b) that people do?*
  Give SS a minute to decide. Elicit answers from each group. Do they agree?

c
- In groups, SS write five sentences about their country / countries using the sports from the chart about Britain, as in the example.

  Tip SS can swap their sentences with a student from another group to read and compare them, look for grammatical errors, etc.

4 Revision: *look / look like*

a
- In pairs, SS describe the four people in photos A to D for a few minutes.
- Elicit a description of each person in the photo from individual SS.

b
- Ask *Do you know who they are?* (they're all international sportspeople). Ask the class to guess their nationalities and sports, as in the example.

  1 Jeremy Guscot (a British rugby player)
  2 Kimiko Date (a Japanese tennis player)
  3 Merlene Ottey (a Jamaican runner)
  4 Marco Pantani (an Italian cyclist)

  Tip If SS already know who the people are, tell them not to tell the others.

5 Skills: Listening

a
- Focus on the photo. Tell SS they're going to listen to a report about Arantxa Sanchez-Vicario, a professional tennis player. Ask *Have you heard of her? What do you know about her? Describe her.*
- °13° Play the tape. SS listen and make notes about her training routine and her diet, then compare in pairs. Play the tape again.
- Elicit their answers onto the board in note form.

  1 **her training routine:** wakes up at about eight o'clock, trains six days a week, every day except Sunday, trains on the tennis court for four and a half hours every day, spends one and a half hours in the gym, goes to bed at ten o'clock every night.
  2 **her diet:** quite strict, eats a lot of pasta and salads, doesn't eat many sweet things, occasionally eats a little chocolate, doesn't smoke, never drinks coffee, never drinks alcohol, except champagne if she wins a championship.

  Tapescript **SB Listening** *p. 130*

- Get SS to look at the tapescript and see how much they understood.
- Ask *What else did you find out about her?*

b • Ask *Would you like to be a professional sportsperson? Why (not)?*

Lesson notes

In this lesson, SS revise the new grammar from **File 6** in the context of sport. SS also learn the vocabulary of sports using the verbs *play*, *go*, and *do* and listen to a radio programme about the tennis player, Arantxa Sanchez-Vicario.

Extras

Too much football P *p. 187* A formal letter of complaint about the amount of sport on TV with errors for SS to correct. Instructions *p. 138*.

■ **Homework**

Choose from the **End-of-file options** below.

End-of-file options

Student's Book

■ **Vocabulary file 6** *p. 88*
- Do this in class, or set it for homework.

Organize your vocabulary learning! Encourage SS to find their own best way of remembering difficult words, and to experiment with different methods.

Try it! Give SS a test on ⬧ **Food** *p. 137* the following class. Find out which words they're still having problems remembering, and help them to find a way to learn them.

> **1 Remembering verbs**
> **b 1** do housework **2** do your homework
> **3** do aerobics **4** do military service
> **5** do an exercise **6** do an exam
> **7** make the bed **8** make a mistake
> **9** make lunch **10** make a cake
> **3** *go, play,* or *do?*
>
> | go | play | do |
> |---|---|---|
> | swimming | football | yoga |
> | cycling | tennis | aerobics |
> | | basketball | karate |
>
> **4 Word-building**
> unemployed empty unselfish shy lazy
> quiet uncomfortable unfriendly old
> untidy
> **5 Key words**
> **1** really **2** again **3** another **4** other
> **6 Prepositions**
> **1** at **2** in **3** about **4** of **5** at
> **7 Odd one out**
> **1** potatoes (countable) **2** cycling (go)
> **3** want (+ to) **4** quiet (adj. of personality)
> **5** kilo (weight) **6** selfish (negative)

■ **Grammar file 6** *p. 89*
- Spend ten minutes going through this with the class, answering any queries. SS tick each box when they're satisfied they understand it.

Workbook

■ **Grammar check 6** *p. 45*
- Remind SS to do this with **SB** and **WB** open in front of them, and to refer back to **Grammar file 6** as necessary. SS can check their answers with the **WB** key.

■ **Read and write 6** *p. 66*
- SS write a description of a person.
- Briefly revise vocabulary for descriptions. Emphasize the need to read and follow the instructions carefully. Remind SS that they have a key to the exercises, but that you're going to collect and correct their descriptions.

■ **Quicktest 3** *p. 85*

A multiple-choice progress test revising the language of **Files 5** and **6**. SS have a key to check their answers.

Teacher's Book

Test 2 P *p. 215*

Tell SS they're going to do a revision test next lesson, and photocopy one per student. Instructions *p. 211*. (There is also a photocopiable **TB** test after **File 9**.)

> *I've already done it.*

Lesson aims

Grammar	Present perfect + *yet* / *already* / *just*
Vocabulary	More irregular verbs, travel verbs: *book (a hotel)*, etc.
Pronunciation	/j/ and /dʒ/
Revision	Past participles, irregular verbs

Lesson plan

■ Warmer: ⓡ Irregular verbs

- SS in pairs. A turns to 📖 **Irregular verbs** *p. 141*. B book closed. A tests B on **Irregular verbs A** as follows:
  A *hear*
  B *heard, heard*
- Swap. B tests A on **Irregular verbs B**.

1 Presentation: More irregular verbs

- SS stay on *p. 141* and do **Irregular verbs C** by putting the past participles in the chart.
- Check answers and drill pronunciation of those with phonetics.

  Tip Ask SS if they can see any patterns, e.g. *drink* / *drank* / *drunk* and *swim* / *swam* / *swum*. It will help SS to remember these verbs together.

2 Presentation: Present perfect + *already* / *yet*

a
- Focus on the photo. Ask *What can you see?* (a business woman looking at a filofax and talking on her mobile phone to a man in a tidy office).
- ⚬1⚬ Tell SS they're going to hear a conversation between Louise (the woman) and Andy (the man). Play the tape. SS listen once and answer the three questions. Check answers.

  > 1 She's in her car (on her way to London).
  > 2 He's her secretary.
  > 3 Yes, because he's organized / has done most of the things she wanted him to do.

b
- Focus on the list for Andy in her filofax. SS listen again and tick the things Andy has done and cross those that he hasn't done.
- SS compare answers in pairs. Check answers.

  > book hotel ✓   pick up tickets ✗ (going this afternoon)   confirm flight ✓   rent car ✓
  > send fax to Brazil ✗ (finished but not sent yet)
  > write report ✓   find passport! ✓
  > Tapescript **SB Listening** *p. 130*

- Ask for other information they can remember, e.g. *When's he going to pick up the tickets? Has he finished the fax yet? Where's she going? Where was her passport?*

■ GRAMMAR FOCUS 1

Present perfect + *already* / *yet*

a
- Focus on the extract from the dialogue. SS highlight *already* and *yet*, and complete the rules.

  > 1 already   2 yet   3 already   4 yet

- Focus on pronounciation *yet* /jet/ and *already* /ɔːlˈrediː/.

b
- Go through the rules. Highlight that:
  – *already* is used to emphasize that someone has done something, e.g. *I've already seen that film.*)
  – *yet* is used:
    1 to ask if someone has done something, usually when you expect it to be done, e.g. *Have you done your homework (yet)?*
    2 to emphasize that they haven't done something, e.g. *He hasn't finished yet.*
- Get SS to translate the sentences and compare the equivalent words and verb forms in their L1.

PRACTICE 1

a
- SS write sentences about Andy from Louise's filofax notes, using *already* / *(not) yet*.
- Go through the first two examples. Then SS write the other five sentences. Check answers.

  > 2 He hasn't picked up the tickets yet.   3 He's already confirmed the flight.   4 He's already rented the car.   5 He hasn't sent the fax to Brazil yet.
  > 6 He's already written the report.   7 He's already found her passport.

b
- Focus on the example dialogue. SS roleplay the conversation in pairs using only the notes

■ PRONUNCIATION

a
- ⚬2⚬ Focus on the two picture words. Ask *What sounds are they?*
- SS listen and repeat the words.

b
- SS put the words from the list in the right sound group.
- Check answers (see **Sound bank WB** *p. 82*).

  > /j/ young   new   music   use
  > /dʒ/ June   job   jam   jogging

- Highlight that:
  – the letter *y* at the beginning of a word is always pronounced /j/.
    ⚠ The phonetic symbol looks like the letter *j* (pronounced /dʒ/), which can confuse.
  – /j/ is often added before the sound /uː/ as in /juːnɪˈvɜːsɪtiː/.
  – the letter *j* at the beginning of a word is always pronounced /dʒ/. This sound can also be spelt with the letter *g*, e.g. *gym, Germany*.

3 Practice: List of jobs

- Ask *What do you have to do before you go on holiday?* Elicit suggestions. Pre-teach *grass* and *water* (v.).
- In pairs, SS turn to ►◄ **Have they done it yet?** *p. 121* and look at the picture for one minute to remember the details.
- SS now turn to ►◄ *p. 124* and look at the list of jobs to do. They take turns to ask and answer about the things on the list and tick or cross each thing.
  - A *Have they washed the car yet?*
  - B *No, they haven't. Have they put the bikes in the garage?*
- From memory SS write eight sentences using *yet / already*, e.g. *They haven't washed the car yet.*
- Elicit answers onto the board.

> They haven't washed the car yet.
> They've already put the bicycles in the garage.
> They haven't repaired the garage door yet.
> They've already closed the windows.
> They've already cut the grass.
> They haven't watered the plants yet.
> They haven't ironed the clothes yet.
> They've already been to the supermarket.

- Feedback to see which pair got the most right.

4 Presentation: *just* + present perfect

a
- ○3○ Tell SS Louise has now arrived in Lisbon and is phoning Andy. SS cover the dialogue, listen once, and answer the questions. Check answers.

> She's lost her bag. She left it in a taxi on the way to the hotel. She asks Andy to phone the bank and cancel her credit cards.

b
- SS read the dialogue and try to remember the words
- SS listen again and check / complete the dialogue. Check answers.

> L Andy, is that you? It's Louise.
> A Yes, where are you?
> L I've **just** arrived in Lisbon. But I've **done** something really stupid.
> A What?
> L I've **lost** my bag. I **left** it in the **taxi** when I was **going** to the hotel.
> A Oh no! What **was** inside it?
> L Everything. My **wallet** with my credit cards, my **tickets**, my **passport** …
> A Have you called the police **yet**?
> L Yes, I've **just spoken** to them. **Could** you phone the bank and cancel my **credit cards**?
> A Don't worry. I'll do it right now.

- Ask *Has this ever happened to you / anyone you know?*

■ GRAMMAR FOCUS 2 *just*

a
- Focus on the examples. Highlight that:
  - just is pronounced /dʒʌst/, or /dʒəst/ unstressed
  - we use *just* + present perfect to say that something happened very recently, e.g. *I've just arrived.*

b
- Highlight that we mainly use *just* in positive sentences.

⚠ Warn SS not to confuse this meaning of *just* with other meanings, e.g. *only* (*I've just got one sister.*)

PRACTICE 2

- SS look at pictures 1 to 6 and write sentences with *just*, as in the example.
  ⚠ Remind them to contract the auxiliary *have* where appropriate.
- SS compare in pairs, then check answers.

> **2** They've just got married.
> **3** She's just had a shower.
> **4** The film's just finished.
> **5** They've just arrived (at the hotel).
> **6** He's just got up. / woken up.

5 Practice: *just*

- ○4○ Tell SS they're going to hear some sounds. They have to imagine what has just happened. Play the tape once. Encourage as many different answers as possible.

> **Suggested answers:**
> **1** Someone's just given / bought the man a drink.
> **2** They've just had an argument.
> **3** Jeremy and Miriam have just met.
> **4** She's just seen a mouse.
> **5** A show's just finished.
> **6** Someone's just won the lottery.

Lesson notes

SS learn to use the present perfect with *yet / already / just*. This is the third lesson on the present perfect. SS learnt present perfect for experience in **File 1D** and **File 2A** and with *How long …? + for / since* in **File 5A**.

yet / already SS may have problems with the exact equivalent and word order in their language.

just This use of *just* with the present perfect may be expressed with a different verb / tense in SS' L1.

Extras

I haven't done it yet P *p. 188* A pair work activity. SS ask and answer questions using *yet*, *just*, and *already*. Instructions *p. 138*.

Books-closed presentation

just + present perfect

- Do before **ex. 4**. Go to the board and clean it. Ask *What have I just done?* Elicit / teach *You've just cleaned the board.* Write the sentence on the board. Highlight the tense and the position of *just*. To reinforce the concept, ask *When did I clean the board?* Elicit *A minute ago*.
- Repeat with different actions to elicit more sentences with *You've just …* Then start **ex. 4**.

■ Learner-training

Remind SS to learn verbs in phrases (see **V** box).

■ Homework

SS do **WB 7A** *p. 46* and **Listen and speak 7A**.

> He went to Romania
> to help in the orphanage.

Lesson aims

Grammar	*Why …? To* + verb / *For* + noun
Vocabulary	Aid organizations: verbs: *feed*, etc.
Pronunciation	/ʃ/ and /tʃ/, word stress
Revision	*Because* + subject + verb

Lesson plan

■ Warmer: ⓡ just, yet, already

- Write on the board:

> 1 Romania just been I've to
> 2 I Russia been haven't yet to
> 3 I've to been Poland already

- SS order the sentences. Check answers.

> **1** I've just been to Romania.
> **2** I haven't been to Russia yet.
> **3** I've already been to Poland.

① Presentation: Vocabulary

- SS read and match the definitions to the right word.
- Check answers and pronunciation.

> 2 c 3 e 4 a 5 b

② Presentation: *Why …? To* + infinitive

- Write 'Romania' on the board. Ask *Where is it?* (in Eastern Europe) *What's the capital?* (Bucharest) *What do you know about it? Have you been there?* etc.

a • Focus on the questions. SS read the article quickly to find the answers. Check answers.

> Negru Voda is in Romania, on the border with Bulgaria.
>
> The people there needed money to look after the children in the orphanage.
>
> John Keeping is a builder who went to Romania with an aid organization.

b • ⟨ 5 ⟩ In pairs, SS listen to an interview with John and answer the questions.

> **1** To give him an award.
> **2** To get money and medicine.
> **3** They had to rebuild the orphanage.
> **4** To work with the children.
> **5** About five years.
> **6** The mayor of Negru Voda.
> Tapescript **SB Listening** *p. 130*

- Play the tape again to check. Elicit further details. Refer SS to the tapescript if necessary.

■ GRAMMAR FOCUS 1

Why …? To + infinitive

a • Focus on the two examples. Highlight that we use *to* + infinitive to answer the question *Why?*
⚠ SS may say *for learn English*

- Ask *Why do you come to English classes?* Elicit answers with *Because I want / need to …*

b • Focus on the example with *Because* + subject + verb. Highlight that there is no difference in meaning between … *to rebuild the orphanage* and … *because they wanted to rebuild the orphanage.* The first sentence is just a shorter version of the second.

PRACTICE 1

a • SS match the sentence halves to make six sentences.

- SS compare in pairs. Check answers from individual SS. Insist they give you a full sentence with *to*.

> **2** He's gone to the bank to order some dollars.
> **3** I'm going back to the hotel to have a rest.
> **4** He drove to the airport to pick up his friend.
> **5** We phoned the travel agency to confirm our flight.
> **6** She sent a fax to cancel her ticket.

- For more practice, ask SS to think of as many reasons as possible why they come to English classes.

b • Write a list of local places that you've been to on the board. Elicit various *When?* and *Why?* questions. Encourage follow-up questions too.

- Focus on the **recently** / **soon** list. Tell SS to write the two headings down and list three places that they've been to recently and three they're going to soon. Give them a minute to write their lists.

- In pairs, SS swap lists with their partner. SS ask *When?* and *Why?* for each one, as in the example.

- Monitor, help, and correct as necessary.

■ PRONUNCIATION

a • ⟨ 6 ⟩ Focus on the picture words. SS listen and repeat the sounds and words.

- Ask *Do you have these sounds in your language?* Drill the sounds further if they are difficult for your SS (see **Sound bank WB** *p. 82*).

b • SS listen again and underline the word stress.

> organi<u>za</u>tion inter<u>na</u>tional <u>dic</u>tionary
> pro<u>fes</u>sion <u>sta</u>tion <u>chil</u>dren church <u>na</u>tural
> beach <u>fu</u>ture <u>pic</u>ture

- Ask *Where do we stress words ending in -tion / -sion?* (always on the penultimate syllable). *Can you think of more examples?* (e.g. infor<u>ma</u>tion, re<u>cep</u>tion, etc.)

c • ⟨ 7 ⟩ Focus on the nine words. Elicit / teach any that SS don't know. In pairs, they mark the word stress, as in the example.

- Play the tape. SS listen and check.

<u>a</u>nimals	<u>e</u>lephant	<u>me</u>dical
envir<u>o</u>nment	dis<u>a</u>ster	<u>nu</u>clear
salary	pro<u>vi</u>de	

3 Presentation: *Why …? For* + noun

a
- Focus on the four aid organizations symbols. Ask *What do you know about them?*
- SS quickly read and complete the four paragraphs. Check answers. (We usually refer to the Red Cross movement as the Red Cross.)

> 1 UNICEF 2 Greenpeace
> 3 Medecins sans frontières 4 The Red Cross

b
- SS read the texts again carefully. In pairs, they complete the chart. Encourage SS to guess the meaning of new words. Be prepared to explain / translate *fund*, <u>collect</u>, <u>protect</u>, <u>danger</u>, *whale*, <u>tiger</u>, <u>victim</u>, <u>natural</u>, <u>wounded</u>, <u>civilian</u>, <u>crescent</u>.
- Monitor and help as necessary. Check answers.

> UNICEF: New York 1946 To help children after World War 2.
>
> Greenpeace: British Columbia 1971 To stop US nuclear testing.
>
> Medecins sans frontières: Belgium 1971 To provide help for victims of war / natural disasters.
>
> The Red Cross: Switzerland 1863 To help soldiers wounded in war.

■ GRAMMAR FOCUS 2
to or *for*?

- Focus on the two example sentences which describe UNICEF. Ask SS to highlight similar examples of *to* and *for* in texts 2 to 4 and describe the other three organizations. Check answers.

> **2** to stop to protect **3** to provide for victims for no salary **4** to help for both soldiers and civilians

- SS complete the rules with *to* or *for*.

> **to** + a verb **for** + a noun

- Highlight that:
- *to* is followed by an infinitive.
- *for* is always followed by a noun.
  NOT ~~for to help children~~ ~~for help children~~.
- Get SS to translate the examples and compare with their own language.

PRACTICE 2
- SS complete sentences 1 to 7 with *for* or *to*. Check answers.

> **1** for **2** to **3** to **4** for **5** to **6** for **7** to

4 Personalization: Writing game

a
- Focus on the example stem *I gave him some money* and the *to* / *for* endings. Elicit other ways to finish this sentence with *to* or *for*.

- In small groups, SS write as many endings as they can for sentences 1 to 4 with *for* and *to*.
- Monitor, help, and correct as necessary.

b
- Check answers. Get each group to read out all their endings to sentence 1, then ask other groups to add any others that they've got. They all get one point for each correct one.
- Repeat this procedure with sentences 2 to 4. Then find out which group is the winner.

Lesson notes

SS learn to use *to* + verb and *for* + noun, e.g. *I need English to travel / for my job.* The context is the true story of a builder who transformed the lives of some orphaned children. SS also read a text about aid organizations.

***to* + verb / *for* + noun** SS may confuse these patterns. Common errors ~~I come here for learn English.~~ / ~~for to learn English~~.

Extras

The long sentence game 🎲 *p. 209* SS make *to* / *for* sentences with places and reasons.

I went to the supermarket to … [P] *p. 189* A board game. SS make sentences with *to* + infinitive. Instructions *p. 139*.

Books-closed presentation

***To* + verb**
- Do after the **Warmer**. Copy the pictures from **Picture Bank 7B** *p. 207*, or write the places on the board.
- Tell SS these are all the places you went to yesterday. Ask *Why do you think I went to the post office?* Elicit / teach a *To* + verb sentence, e.g. *To buy some stamps.*
- Point to the other five pictures / words one by one. Elicit / teach the five sentences. Drill round the class.
- Write the six sentences on the board for SS to copy. Then start **ex. 1**.

***For* + noun** Do before **ex. 3**. Repeat with the same pictures but elicit answers with *For* + noun, e.g. *For some stamps.* Then start **ex. 3**.

■ Learner-training

There are several poly-syllabic words in this lesson. This is a good moment to remind SS of the importance of marking the stress on all new words and of noting patterns, e.g. all words ending in -*ion* have the stress on the previous syllable.

■ Homework
SS do **WB 7B** *p. 47* and **Listen and speak 7B**.

What should I do?

Lesson aims

Grammar	*should / shouldn't* (advice / opinion)
Vocabulary	Feelings, *-ed* or *-ing* adjectives: *bored / boring*
Pronunciation	/ʊ/, silent *l*
Revision	Personality adjectives

Lesson plan

■ Warmer: ® Adjectives

- In pairs, SS turn to 🗐 **Adjectives B** *p. 138* and test each other.

1 Presentation: *ed* and *-ing* adjectives

a
- SS look at 🗐 **Adjectives C** *p. 138* and match the words and pictures.
- Check answers. Drill pronunciation.

> **1** surprised **2** embarassed **3** frightened
> **5** annoyed **6** bored **8** stressed **9** interested
> **10** pleased **11** excited

> ⚠️ Point out that the *-ed* endings are pronounced like regular past simple verbs, e.g. bored /bɔːd/.

- SS cover the pictures and test each other.
- Focus on ♥ **bored** or **boring**? Highlight that:
- most *-ed* adjectives also exist in the *-ing* form, e.g. *interested / interesting*.
- *-ed* adjectives are used to describe how people feel.
- *-ing* adjectives are used to describe things (and sometimes people) which produce the feeling, e.g. *an **interesting** film makes you feel **interested**.*

b
- SS choose the correct adjective and cross out the wrong one. Check answers.

> **2** exciting **3** interested **4** worrying
> **5** embarrassed **6** depressed

2 Presentation: *should / shouldn't*

a
- Tell SS that many British people write to magazines with their problems and that 'Problem pages' are often the most popular page in a magazine.
- Focus on the problem page extracts. Ask *Who's the woman in the photo?* (Maggie, the woman readers write to for help). SS may be amused to know that the name for this job is an *agony aunt*.
- Get SS to read the introduction. Elicit the meaning of *solve* and (*practical*) ad*vice*.
- SS quickly read letters A to D and match an adjective to each writer.
- Check answers.

> **A** selfish **B** forgetful **C** annoyed **D** shy

b
- SS quickly read Maggie's answers (1 to 4) and match them to the problems.

> **1** C **2** D **3** B **4** A

- Go through each letter and Maggie's reply one by one. Be prepared to explain / translate *any more*, (*centre of*) *attention*, *set* (*an alarm clock*), *keep* (*a list*), *unsure* (*of herself*), *madly*, *rose* (= a flower), *get to know*.
- After each one, ask *Do you agree with Maggie's advice? Have you got any better advice for the person?*
- Elicit SS' opinions and any better answers.

■ GRAMMAR FOCUS
should / shouldn't

- SS find and highlight the six examples of *should / shouldn't* in Maggie's answers.
- SS focus on the verbs after *should* and complete the grammar rule.

> infinitive

- Highlight that:
- *You should / shouldn't* = I think it's a good / bad idea.
- *should / shouldn't* is the same for all persons.
- Drill the pronunciation with the three examples (*should* /ʃʊd/ and *shouldn't* /ˈʃʊdnt/).

> **Tip** Get SS to cross out the *l* in *should* to show that it is not pronounced.

> ⚠️ *advice* is uncountable in English. You have to say *some advice / a piece of advice* NOT ~~an advice~~.

PRACTICE

a
- SS cover Maggie's answers. Ask *Can you remember her advice?* Elicit sentences with *should / shouldn't* for each reply.

b
- Focus on the five problems in the speech bubbles. Elicit sentences with *should / shouldn't* for the first one (e.g. *You should have a hot bath before you go to bed. You shouldn't drink coffee in the evenings.* etc.)
- In pairs, SS write two pieces of advice for each of the other situations (ideally one with *should* and one with *shouldn't*).
- Elicit answers onto the board.

> **Suggested answers:**
>
> | | You should | You shouldn't |
> |---|---|---|
> | **1** | have a hot bath before you go to bed | drink coffee late at night |
> | **2** | go to England / study more at home | speak your language in class |
> | **3** | do yoga / try not to worry | work too much / think about work at home |
> | **4** | join a club / go out more | stay in every night. |
> | **5** | go to bed early / wear your best clothes | be late be nervous |

■ PRONUNCIATION

a ● ◦ 8 ◦ SS listen and write five sentences with *should / shouldn't*.

● SS check spelling in pairs and then match each sentence to the right problem from **Practice**, 1 to 5.

> **Tip** Tell SS to write down, not shout out, the answers.

● Elicit the sentences and answers onto the board.

> You should wear a suit. 5
> You shouldn't drink coffee in the evenings 1
> You should go to Britain. 2
> You should go out more. 4

b ● ◦ 9 ◦ Focus on the headword /ʊ/. Elicit the word and sound, and write the phonetic symbol on the board.

● Tell SS to read the six words in phonetics and write them as words, as in the example.

● Check answers. Emphasize the silent *l* again in could, should, would.

> **2** could   **3** should   **4** put   **5** shouldn't
> **6** wouldn't

● Drill pronunciation again.

3 Practice: Listening

a ● Focus on the photo. Ask *What's Maggie doing?*

● Tell SS that the agony aunt, Maggie, also works on the radio. They're going to hear a listener phone her with a problem.

● ◦ 10 ◦ Play the tape. SS listen and tell you the woman's problem.

> Her husband has bought a dog and now he's only interested in the dog and not in his wife. He's obsessed with his new dog.
> Tapescript **SB Listening** *p. 130*

b ● Focus on Ⓥ **Giving advice**. SS read three typical expressions for giving advice / making suggestions.

● Tell SS that Maggie uses these three expressions to give advice. They listen again and complete what she says.

● Check answers. Refer SS to the tapescript if necessary.

> Why don't you **go with him?**
> What about **buying another dog for you?**
> I think you should **talk to your husband.**

● Highlight the use of the gerund (verb + *-ing*) after the preposition in *What about …?*

● Ask *Can you think of any other advice?*

4 Personalization: Giving / accepting advice

● SS in groups of three, A, B and C. If your class doesn't divide exactly, have one or two pairs.

● SS turn to ▶◀ **What should I do?** A *p. 121*, B *p. 124*, C *p. 125*. Give them a minute to read and memorize their two problems. Elicit / teach the meaning of *share* (a flat) and *get fit*.

● A tells B and C the first problem. B and C listen, then give advice using the phrases *I think you should … /*

Why don't you …? etc. A chooses the best suggestion. Continue.

> **Tip** Encourage the people with the problems to reject the first piece of advice. This will make the other two students have to think up more advice.

● SS swap roles. Monitor and help as necessary.

Lesson notes

SS learn *should / shouldn't* + infinitive for advice in the context of a magazine Problem page and a radio phone-in programme. They learn two other common phrases for advice: *What about + -ing* and *Why don't you …?* and look at adjectives ending in *-ed* and *-ing*, e.g. *bored / boring*.

should / shouldn't (advice) The meaning is usually made clear from the context, but watch out for pronunciation errors. Highlight that the pronunciation is the same as for *could / would*, i.e. /ʊd/, and that the *l* is not pronounced.

bored / boring The difference in meaning between the *-ed / -ing* ending of adjectives is an important one. Common error ~~The film was excited. I am boring.~~

Extras

I need some advice [P] *p. 190* A group activity where SS pick a problem card and ask other SS for advice. Instructions *p. 139*.

Books-closed presentation

● Do after the **Warmer**. Invent a problem and dramatically tell your class, e.g. *I've got a problem. Can you help me? I want to lose some weight quickly.* or *It's my mother's birthday and I don't know what to buy her.*

● Elicit suggestions. SS will probably try to use the imperative. When they do, teach *You should + infinitive … / You shouldn't …* Get them to rephrase their answers.

● Invent reasons why you can't follow their advice so they get a lot of practice.

● Write some of the sentences on the board for SS to copy. Drill pronunciation of *should* /ʃʊd/ and *shouldn't* /'ʃʊdnt/. Then start **ex. 1**.

■ Learner training

Tell SS to keep a list of words with silent letters, e.g. *could, should, answer, Wednesday, island*, etc. and add to the list every time they learn a new example. An awareness of silent letters will help improve SS' pronunciation.

■ Homework

SS do **WB 7C** *p. 48* and **Listen and speak 7C**.

Writing option: Problem page letter SS write a letter to Maggie with an invented problem. Take in the letters and correct them. In the next class redistribute the letters and get SS to write an answer to them giving advice. Then return the letters and advice to the writers and ask what they think of the advice given.

> *They turned off the gas and picked up the canary.*

Lesson aims

Grammar	Phrasal verbs + object
Vocabulary	Phrasal verbs: *turn off*, etc.
Revision	Story-telling

Lesson plan

■ Warmer: Pets

- Ask *What is a pet?* (= domestic animal, e.g. *dog*)
- In pairs give SS two minutes to write down as many pets as possible, e.g. *cat, dog, fish, snake, horse, budgerigar* (= *budgie*). If it doesn't come up, teach the word *canary*.
- Ask *What pets have you got? What do you think is the best animal for a pet? Why?*

1 Presentation: Phrasal verbs

a
- Focus on pictures A to D. SS look at picture A. Ask *What can you see? What's happening?* Remind SS to use the present continuous, e.g. *There are two men and an old lady in a living-room. One man is carrying a bag*, etc. Continue with the other three pictures. Pre-teach *gasmen, gas fire, gas, cage, perch, scream*.

b
- Tell SS that this is a true story. SS read the beginning of the story and in pairs try to put the other five sentences in order, 1 to 6, using the pictures to help.
- ◦11◦ Play the tape twice. SS listen and check their answers.

> **2** They repaired the fire and turned on the gas.
> **3** They forgot to turn off the gas and they went into the garden. **4** The gasmen came back. They turned off the gas. **5** They picked up the dead canary and put it on its perch. **6** The old lady saw the canary and screamed.
> Tapescript **SB Listening** *p. 130*

c
- Ask *Why do you think the old lady screamed?*
- ◦12◦ SS listen to the end of the story.

> **GM** What's the matter?
> **OL** I don't believe it. My canary!
> **GM** Your canary? What's the problem?
> **OL** It died this morning before you came – and now it's alive again!

Tip You can elicit the end of the story onto the board in dialogue form, writing up words / phrases that SS have understood.

■ GRAMMAR FOCUS 1
Phrasal verbs

- Focus on the three highlighted verbs in the story (*turned on, picked up, turn off*). Remind SS of the literal meaning of the verb *turn* (in *turn left / turn right*) or demonstrate by turning the door handle, or miming.

- Focus on the chart. Explain that sometimes when we add a preposition or adverb to a verb it then has a new, non-literal meaning, and that these kinds of verb are called 'phrasal verbs'. Focus on the new meaning of *turn* when we add *on / off* to it (= stop a machine). Focus on the meaning of *turn on / off* and *pick up*.
⚠ Particle (= a preposition or adverb).

PRACTICE 1

a
- SS turn to ✐ **Verbs B** *p. 139* and match the verbs and pictures. Check answers.

> **A** turn off **B** turn down **C** turn on **E** put on
> **F** take off **G** turn up **H** throw away
> **2** take out **3** look after **4** fill in **5** try on
> **6** look up **7** get on with **8** look for

- In pairs, SS test their partner. **B** covers the list of words. **A** asks *What's picture (C)?* **B** replies (*turn on*). After a minute they swap roles.

b
- In pairs, SS complete sentences 1 to 6 with a phrasal verb in the correct tense. Check answers.

> **2** looks after **3** looking for **4** took off, put on
> **5** look up **6** fill in

2 Presentation: Word order of phrasal verbs

a
- Focus on stories 2 and 3. Tell SS to cover the text and look at the pictures. In pairs, **A** describes picture 2 to **B**, then **B** describes picture 3 to **A**.
- Monitor, help, and correct as necessary. Elicit / teach the meaning and pronunciation of *businessman* /ˈbɪznɪsmən/ and *dressing-gown* /ˈdresɪŋɡaʊn/.

b
- SS quickly read the story for their picture. Tell them they're going to tell the story to their partner, so they should read it carefully and memorize the details.
- In pairs, SS cover the text again and tell each other their story. Monitor and help as necessary. Encourage the listeners to ask questions if anything is unclear.
- Then get SS to read their partner's story.

c
- In pairs, SS read and answer the questions. Feedback their ideas. Don't say if they're right or wrong.
- ◦13◦ Play the tape. SS listen to the end of the two stories. After playing each one, ask *What happened?* Re-play the tape if necessary.

> **Story 2** Because the man showed him his business card with his home address in Copenhagen, not the hotel address. **Story 3** It was her sister who she had come to visit.

> **Story 2** The taxi-driver stopped. 'I'm looking for the address on this card,' he said. 'What's the problem?' The businessman looked at the card. It wasn't the card of his hotel in Frankfurt. It was his own business card with his home address in Copenhagen. It was the most expensive taxi journey he'd ever made.

Story 3

N That's strange. There's somebody in your bed.

W Yes, that's my sister. I've just come to visit her.

N Oh no! I'm, terribly sorry.

W That's OK. That's the nicest bath I've had for a long time.

- Ask *Which of the three stories do you like best?*

■ GRAMMAR FOCUS 2
Word order of phrasal verbs

a
- Focus on the examples *He took out this wallet. / He took it out.* Ask *How has the word order changed?*
- Focus on the list of verbs. SS find and highlight the verbs in stories 2 and 3, then circle their objects.
- Check answers, writing them on the board with each object circled.

> take (him) back   took out his wallet   was looking after (a room of elderly patients)   take off (your clothes)   put on (this dressing gown)

b
- Tell SS to look carefully at the examples from the story and the **Grammar focus** and complete the rule.

> pronoun

c
- Use the example to illustrate that with most phrasal verbs, if the object is a noun, you can put it between or after the verb and particle.
- Go through the examples from the story again, and elicit the possible forms, e.g. *take the man back / take back the man / take him back*, etc.
- Highlight that when the object is a pronoun it always goes between the verb and particle.

  ⚠ *look after, look for*, and *get on with* are exceptions. Their object always goes <u>after</u> the preposition or adverb even when it's a pronoun, e.g. *A nurse looks after people.* NOT ~~A nurse looks people after.~~ These are the only three examples in *English File 2*. If SS ask, tell them that there are a few others, but to learn each one as it comes up.

PRACTICE 2

a
- Focus on cartoons 1 to 4. SS complete the questions for each picture. Emphasize that they can put the preposition before or after the object and elicit both versions for all four sentences. Check answers.

> 1 try on this dress OR try this dress on   2 take off your shoes OR take your shoes off   3 turn on the light OR turn the light on   4 Give back my towel OR give my towel back

b
- Now ask individual SS to say all four sentences with object pronouns instead of nouns. Make sure they put them all between the verb and particle.

> 2 Can you take them off, please?
> 3 Could you turn it on?   4 Give it back!

3 Personalization: Talk about your habits

- In pairs, SS read through and answer the questions together, comparing their answers and noting any differences.

Tip Tell SS to make full sentences not just one word answers to get more practice.

- Monitor and help with vocabulary as necessary (e.g. *tap, switch*, etc.)
- Feedback a selection of answers to each question.

Lesson notes

Phrasal verbs, i.e. verbs which combine with an adverb or preposition with a new, often non-literal meaning, e.g. *look up* (*a word in the dictionary*) are an important feature of English. A verb such as *turn* can combine with different 'particles', e.g. *turn on / off / up / down*. A phrasal verb is technically different from simple verb + preposition combinations, e.g. *speak to someone* or verb + preposition of movement, e.g. *go away*. This lesson introduces an area of English which SS will focus on in more detail at intermediate level and beyond. The verbs in the lesson are all high frequency, and SS have seen most before. SS learn the three basic patterns of phrasal verbs: 1 Turn on the light, 2 Turn the light on, 3 Turn it on.

Extras

Find somebody who … P *p. 191* A mingle activity to practise phrasal verbs in different tenses. Instructions *p. 139*.

Books-closed presentation

Phrasal verbs

- Put a (music) cassette into the cassette player and turn the volume control right down.
- Pretend the cassette doesn't work. Say *What's the matter? What should I do?*, etc. Ask SS to give you instructions. Elicit / teach *Turn it on*. Turn the cassette on. The SS can't hear anything. Elicit / teach *Turn it up*.
- Now turn the volume right up and elicit *Turn it down!* Finally do a mime to elicit *Turn it off*.
- Write the four phrases on the board for SS to copy.
- Tell SS that the verbs *turn on / off / up / down* are phrasal verbs and that they're going to learn some more in this lesson. Then start **ex. 1**.

■ Learner-training

Tell SS always to learn phrasal verbs in a clear example sentence. Give an example to show them how, e.g. *look after* (*When I lived at home I often had to look after my younger brothers and sisters.*) Recommend that they start a list in their vocabulary file and learn each one as it comes up.

■ Homework

SS do **WB 7D** *p. 49* and **Listen and speak 7D**.

7 💼 Talking on the phone

Lesson aims

Grammar	Using the phone, leaving a message on an answerphone
Vocabulary	Phone verbs: *put through*, etc., hotel services: *laundry*, etc.
Revision	Requests, *will* for unplanned decisions

Lesson plan

■ Warmer: ® Travel with English 1 to 6

- Books closed. Copy these phrases from the **Travel phrasebook** onto the board:

> 1 Could I have a window _____, please?
> 2 Can I _____ $100, please.
> 3 The TV in my room doesn't _____.
> 4 I'll _____ the soup to start, and then the steak.
> 5 Could you tell me the _____ to the bank, please?
> 6 Can I _____ them on?

- In pairs, SS complete the phrases.
- Check answers. Ask *Where would you say it?* for each one.

> **1** seat (at an airport) **2** change (at a bureau de change) **3** work (in a hotel) **4** have (in a restaurant) **5** way (in the street) **6** try (in a shop)

- Ask *Where was Pieter last time?* (in New York). Write 'Sugar Loaf Mountain', and 'Copacabana beach' on the board. Tell SS that Pieter's now in a hotel, and he can see these. Ask *Where is he?* Elicit *Rio de Janeiro, Brazil*. Ask *What do you know about Rio? Have you been there? Would you like to go? Why (not)?* etc.

1 Practice: Reading phone instructions

- Books open. Focus on **Telephone information**. Tell SS to read the introduction. Ask *Where do you find this kind of information?* (in a hotel room, next to the phone). Ask a few questions: *What's the name of the hotel?* (Copacabana) *What number should he dial to speak to the hotel operator?* (0), etc. Elicit / teach *require* (= need), *assistance* (= help), *laundry* (= where they wash your clothes), *(phone) line*.
- SS read the dialling instructions and answer questions 1 to 4.
- Check answers.

> **1** 82 **2** 84 **3** 3217
> **4** 900 + country code + area code + number

2 Practice: Listening

- SS focus on the three questions. Tell SS they're going to hear Pieter make three calls.

- ⟨ 14 ⟩ SS listen and answer the questions.
  ⚠ 'Varig' is the national airline of Brazil. **Call 1** begins in Portuguese. They ask *How can I help you?*
- Play the tape again if necessary. Check answers.

> **Call 1** To confirm his flight to Bangkok. **Call 2** Anna (Ronald's wife). Late, but she isn't sure when. **Call 3** Simone (his partner) because it's a reverse charge call. It's 3.00 a.m.

Tip Don't forget to set the counter to 0 on your cassette player as you have to replay the dialogue several times.

3 Presentation: Using the phone

a
- In pairs, SS read through dialogue extracts 1 to 3 and remember some of the missing words.

  Tip Do this orally, or get SS to complete the gaps in pencil.

- Quickly elicit SS' guesses but don't confirm whether they are right or wrong.

b
- SS listen again and complete the phrases. Then they write **P** against the lines that Pieter says as in the example. Re-play as necessary if SS can't hear / agree on the missing words. Check answers.

> **1 P** Hello, is **that** Varig Airlines?
> **P** **Can I have** Reservations please?
> Just **a** moment, I'll **put** you through.
> Sorry, it's **engaged**. Can you **hold**?
>
> **2 P** Can I **speak to** Ronald please?
> **Who's** calling?
> **P** **This is** Pieter Okker.
> **P** What time **will** he be **back**?
> **P** Can **I leave** a message?
> **P** Can you **tell** him I called?
> **P** I'll **call back** later.
>
> **3 P** I'd **like** to **make** a **reverse** charge call to Holland.
> Hold the **line**, please **caller**.
> Go **ahead**, caller. **You're** through **now**.
>
> Tapescript **SB Listening** *p. 130*

- SS turn to the tapescript. Play the tape again and tell SS to underline all the phrases not on the lesson page. This is to help them remember them for the next stage.

  Tip It's better to do this dialogue by dialogue, or SS may not remember the extra words by the time they get to dialogue 3.

- Now tell the class to turn back to the lesson, look at the four phrases, and try to remember and practise the rest of the first dialogue.
- Get SS to do the same in pairs for dialogues 2 and 3.

4 Practice: Speaking

- SS in pairs, A and B, turn to ▶◀ **On the phone** A *p. 122*, B *p. 124* and read their instructions carefully.
- Demonstrate by taking the part of A and roleplay the dialogues yourself with a good student B.

  ⚠️ Make sure SS understand exactly what they have to do. Remind SS that if they don't hear / understand what their partner says to say *Sorry?* or *Pardon?*
- Monitor, help, and correct as necessary. Then they swap roles. Fast finishers can start again.

  Tip Get SS to mime talking on the phone. If it's easy to rearrange chairs get SS to sit back to back.
- Feedback any problems. You can ask pairs of SS to roleplay one of the dialogues to the class.

5 Presentation: Leaving a message on an answerphone

- Ask *Have you got an answerphone? What does your answerphone say when people call? Do you like leaving messages on answerphones? Have you ever left a message on an answerphone in English?* etc.
- ◦15◦ Tell SS that Pieter left Ronald a message. Play the tape. SS listen to the message and complete Ronald's notes.
- SS listen again and compare in pairs. Check answers.

> Here until **Tuesday**
> Staying at the **Copacabana hotel**, room **307**, phone **780780**
> Call him between **8.00 and 9.00 p.m.**
> Tapescript **SB Listening** *p. 130*

6 Personalization: Speaking

a
- Tell SS they're going to leave a message in English on an answerphone. Demonstrate yourself. Invent a message using your name, city, hotel, and room number.

  Tip Tell SS that if they have to leave a message on an answerphone in English, it's a good idea to write it first. A lot of native speakers do this anyway.
- SS write and then memorize their message. Monitor and help as necessary.

b
- SS in pairs, A and B. A tells B their message at normal speed. B listens and take notes, like Ronald did. If they don't understand all the message, tell them to 'rewind the answerphone', in other words to ask A to say it again. A should repeat the whole message each time.
- SS swap roles.

7 Vocabulary: Travel phrasebook 7

- SS turn to 📖 *p. 133.* and translate the phrases. As usual, get SS to predict what phrases are in the **Travel phrasebook** before they look.

Lesson notes

In **Travel with English 7** SS practise the language they need to make phone calls in English. Talking on the phone is one of the most difficult things to do in a foreign language and the activities in this lesson should give SS more confidence. Pieter is now in Rio de Janeiro; he phones the airline, makes a local call to a friend, makes an international reverse charge call, and leaves a message on an answerphone. SS learn important phone vocabulary.

Extras

What's the problem? [P] *p. 192* A group game. Typical traveller's problems on cards to mime for others to guess the exact words. Instructions *p. 139*.

▪ Learner-training

Remind SS that many of the 📖 dialogues are on the '**Listen and speak**' cassette. They can practise the dialogues, trying to answer before the 'traveller' each time.

▪ Homework

SS do **WB 7**📖 *p. 50* and **Listen and speak 7**📖.

Lesson aims

Revision	**File 7:** Present perfect + *just / already / yet*, *should / shouldn't*, collocates of *do* and *make*
Vocabulary	Verb *get*

Lesson plan

■ Warmer: Ways of communication

- Books closed. Draw the central circle <u>only</u> of this word map on the board:

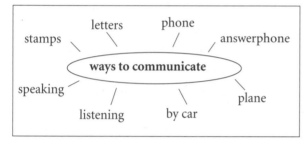

- Elicit from SS as many ways to communicate as possible and write up suggestions.
- Tell SS *Imagine you're on a desert island. How could you communicate?* Elicit *a message in a bottle.*
- SS copy the word map into their vocabulary files.

  Tip Remember to go through the Progress chart in the usual way either at the beginning or end of this lesson.

1 Skills: Reading

a
- Tell SS to cover the text and look at the map. Ask *What countries can you see?*
- Ask *What can you see in the photo? What do you think the article is about?* Elicit guesses but don't confirm if they're right.
- SS read the article and number the paragraphs in order, 1 to 6.

  Tip Set a time limit of about four minutes to encourage SS to try to read quickly.

- SS check answers in pairs. Elicit the correct order.

  2 F   **3** A   **4** C   **5** E   **6** D

- Read the text aloud to the class. Be prepared to explain / translate <u>almost</u> (= nearly), <u>attic</u> (= a room in the roof of the house), <u>curious</u> (= interested to know something), <u>honeymoon</u> (= a holiday for people who have just got married).

  Tip Whenever possible, explain new words by giving a definition in English, or get SS who know the words to give a definition or example of when they would say them. Don't be afraid to elicit / teach the meaning in L1 if necessary / you are able to. Get SS to record the word.

- Ask *What do you think of the story? Have you ever sent or found a message in a bottle?*

b
- In pairs, SS order the sentences, then decide if they're true (T) or false (F)? Do the first one with the class as an example. Check answers.

  1 Karen has already replied to the letter. F
  2 The two women haven't met yet. T
  3 Emilie has just got married. F
  4 Emilie has just found the bottle in the attic. T
  5 Karen's daughter hasn't written to Emilie's son yet. T

2 Revision: Different meanings of *get*

a
- SS find and circle five examples of *get* in the story, then match them to the meanings. Check answers.

  1 get = receive Karen **got the reply** she was waiting for (Para A)   Karen didn't **get an answer** (Para F)
  2 get = become I **got** very **excited** (Para D) The letter **got lost** (Para E)
  3 get = arrive When they **got to the beach** (Para B)
  4 get = phrasal verb I'm sure I'll **get on with** her very well (Para D)

b
- SS turn to 📖 *Do, Make, Get* **B** *p. 140* and match the expressions and pictures.

  A get married   **C** get a letter
  D get a new car   **E** get to work   **F** get up
  G get lost   **H** get a job   **I** get a taxi.

- Check answers. Highlight:
- that *get* is one of the most common and important verbs in English.
- its different meanings with the groups of words in the **Word bank**. Write on the board for SS to copy:

  get = become e.g. get wet / lost / married
     = buy e.g. get a new car / camera
     = find e.g. get a job / flat
     = travel by e.g. get a taxi / a bus
     = receive e.g. get a fax / a letter
     = arrive e.g. get to work / school / home
     = phrasal verb e.g. get up / get on with

3 Practice: *get*

a
- SS complete the sentences with a phrase using *get*.
- Monitor and help as necessary, then check answers.

  2 get lost   **3** get   **4** get up   **5** get   **6** get

b
- Ask two SS questions 1 and 2 and ask a follow-up question where appropriate.
- In pairs, SS interview each other.

  Tip Tell **A** to close his / her book and listen while **B** asks the questions. When they swap roles, tell **B** to ask the questions in a different order.

- Feedback by asking questions, e.g. *Who often gets lost? Who gets up the latest on Sundays?* etc.

4 Revision: *should / shouldn't*

- SS in pairs, A and B, turn to ▶◀ **I'm sorry I don't agree** A *p. 122* B *p. 125*. SS read out some controversial statements with *should / shouldn't* to their partner, who agrees or disagrees.
- Demonstrate with A's first sentence. Write on the board *I think people shouldn't get married until they're over 30. Do you agree?* Elicit opinions from the class. Then do the same with B's first sentence.

  Tip Remind SS of *I agree. / I don't agree.*

- Monitor, help, and join in as necessary.

5 Revision: Game

Play *Noughts and crosses* 🎲 *p. 209* to revise the language of the File that your SS need.

🎵 *Message in a bottle*

The words of the song are on P **Message in a bottle** *p. 193* (see **Extras**).

- If you can't make photocopies. Write on the board:

```
_____ _____ _____ _____ _____ _____
_____ _____ _____ _____ _____
_____ _____ _____ _____
```

- Tell SS they're going to hear a song by The Police. They have to listen for the chorus, and try to write down any words they hear.
- ° 16 ° Play the first verse and chorus. Elicit any words the SS have heard and write them in the right place on the board. Play the chorus as many times as necessary for SS to complete the words. Then play the whole song.

  > I'll send an SOS to the world
  > I hope that someone gets my
  > Message in a bottle

- Ask *What's the song about?*

Lesson notes

SS revise and extend **File 7**, looking at present perfect + *just / already / yet*, and *should / shouldn't*. They read a true story about a message in a bottle and look in detail at the verb *get*.

The verb *get* Perhaps the most flexible verb in English with several important meanings. SS have already seen most of these but in the lesson they are brought together, both in the story and in the **Word bank**.

Extras

Telepathy 🎲 *p. 210* Revises infinitive of purpose.

Message in a bottle P *p. 193* A song by The Police. Instructions *p. 139*.

***get* questionnaire** P *p. 194* A group or pairwork activity to revise *get* and language from **File 7**. Instructions *p. 140*.

■ Homework

Choose from the **End-of-file options** below.

End-of-file options

Student's Book

■ Vocabulary file 7 *p. 100*

- Do this in class or set it for homework.
- ***Organize your vocabulary learning!*** Remind SS that many words in English have more than one meaning. A dictionary will usually give the meanings in order of frequency, but they need to check which one is correct by deciding if it's a noun, adjective, etc. and by looking at the context.
- ***Try it!*** SS look up five words in their dictionary.

> **1 Verbs**
> become / buy / travel / receive / arrive + phrasal verbs
> **2 Key words**
> 2 a   3 a   4 b   5 c
> **3 Word-building**
> 2 decision   3 protection   4 information
> 5 revision   6 reservation   7 pollution
> **4 Pronunciation**
> 1 accident   2 annoyed   3 environment
> 4 flight   5 honeymoon
> **5 Phrasal verbs**
> 1 up   2 after   3 on   4 up, away   5 off, on
> 6 out   7 in
> **6 Adjectives**
> 2 stressed   3 bored   4 depressed   5 worried
> 6 embarrassed
> **Try it!**
> 1 let = rent   2 saw = a tool to cut wood
> 3 fine = money you have to pay if you do something wrong   4 safe = a secure box
> 5 engaged = going to get married

■ Grammar file 7 *p. 101*

- Spend ten minutes going through this with the class, answering any queries. SS tick each box when they're satisfied they understand it.

Workbook

■ Grammar check 7 *p. 51*

- Remind SS to do this with **SB** and **WB** open in front of them and to refer back to **Grammar file 7** as necessary. SS can check their answers with the key.

■ Read and write 7 *p. 67*

- SS write a second informal letter to invite a friend from abroad to visit their town.
- Briefly revise the language and layout of informal letters (SS have already written one in **Read and write 1**). Emphasize the need to read and follow the instructions carefully. Remind SS that they have a key to the exercises, but that you're going to collect and correct their letters.

> *I love westerns. Do you? So do I.*

Lesson aims

Grammar	Echo questions, *So / Neither do I.*
Vocabulary	Types of film
Pronunciation	Intonation in echo questions, stress in disagreeing
Revision	Auxiliaries, all tenses, adjectives of opinion
Optional materials	[P] Talk about the cinema (ex.6)

Lesson plan

■ Warmer: ℝ Auxiliary verbs

- Write on the board:

  AUXILARY VERBS

- Elicit examples e.g. *did / didn't, am (not), have (n't), can('t), will /won't, should.*
  ⚠ *Can, will,* and *should* are modal auxiliaries.

1 Presentation: Types of films

- Focus on the photos and Ⓥ **Types of film**. Highlight *What type of …?* (= What kind of …?) Ask *What type of film is picture A?* (an adventure film). In pairs, SS match three more words to photos B to D. Check answers.

  B a horror film **C** a musical
  D science fiction

- Check SS understand the meaning of the other words in the **vocabulary box**. Drill pronunciation, especially *ad**venture*** /əd'ventʃə/, *science fiction* /'saɪəns 'fikʃən/, and *western* /'westən/.

2 Practice: Reading

[a] • Focus on the film poster for *Cyrano de Bergerac* but covering the text. Ask *What type of film is it?* (a love story) *What's it about?* Try to elicit a very simple description (It's about a man, Cyrano de Bergerac, who's in love with his cousin. She's in love with another man and Cyrano helps him write love poems for her. Cyrano never tells his cousin that he loves her until he's dying. She then realises that she also loves him, but it's too late.)

[b] • Focus on the text. Teach the word *review.*
- SS read the review. Elicit / teach *superb, version, brave, classic, deeply-moving, portrayal, spectacular.*
- Ask *Does the reviewer like it?* (yes, very much).

  Tip Ask SS who've seen the film if they agree with the review.

3 Presentation: Echo questions

[a] • ∘ **1** ∘ Tell SS two people talking about the film *Cyrano de Bergerac.* .

- Ask *Do the two people agree?* (no).

[b] • SS listen again and complete the dialogue.
- Check answers.

  Did you? Didn't you? Don't you? Do you?

- SS listen and repeat after the tape, line by line, copying the intonation.

■ GRAMMAR FOCUS 1
Echo questions

[a] • Focus on the examples. Highlight that:
  - echo questions are so called because the listener 'echoes' what the speaker has just said.
  - echo questions use the same verb tense as the speaker.
  - with a ⏤ auxiliary, the echo question is also ⏤.
  - with a ⧾ verb, the auxiliary in the echo question is also ⧾.
  - the echo question always uses a pronoun (*you*, etc.).

[b] • Elicit that we use echo questions to show interest in or surprise.

PRACTICE 1

- SS write echo questions for sentences 1 to 8.
- SS quickly compare their answers in pairs.

■ PRONUNCIATION

[a] • ∘ **2** ∘ SS listen to **Practice** sentences 1 to 8 and check their answers. Then they listen again and repeat, copying the intonation.

  1 Don't you? **2** Can't she? **3** Are they?
  4 Has he? **5** Were you? **6** Did he?
  7 Have you? **8** Is it?

- Invent and drill a few personal or locally relevant sentences to make sure they've got the idea, e.g.
  T *I'm getting married next month.*
  SS *Are you?*
  T *I can't swim.*
  SS *Can't you?*

[b] • ∘ **3** ∘ SS respond to eight more sentences. Demonstrate with the first example on tape. Encourage them to use a lively interested intonation.

  Tip Pause the tape after each sentence for SS to give the answer before they hear it.

  2 I didn't sleep last night. <u>Didn't</u> you? **3** I was awake all night. <u>Were</u> you? **4** I've got a big problem. <u>Have</u> you? **5** I often sleep badly. <u>Do</u> you? **6** I don't know what to do. <u>Don't</u> you? **7** I'm going to the doctor's tomorrow. <u>Are</u> you? **8** She's going to help me. <u>Is</u> she?

4 Personalization: Echo questions

a • SS complete the sentences truthfully about themselves. Demonstrate first by completing the sentences with information about yourself. Make a statement from your list, e.g. *I like reading in bed* and elicit an echo question *Do you?*

b • In pairs, SS do the same. Encourage them to ask follow-up questions too, as in the example.

5 Presentation: *So / Neither do I.*

a • Focus on the photo. Ask *Where are the people? What have they just done?*
  • ⚬ 4 ⚬ Play the tape once. SS cover **Conversations 1** and **2** and listen. Ask *Do they agree about the film?*
  • Check answers.

> In both conversations, the two women agree but the man doesn't.

b • SS uncover the conversations, listen again, and complete the gaps with the four phrases.
  • SS listen again and check answers.

> **1** So did I. I didn't.   **2** Neither did I. I did.

■ GRAMMAR FOCUS 2
So / Neither do I.

• Focus on the three example exchanges. Read them to the class once, then ask *Who agrees with the speaker?* (the first person / bubbles on the left) *Who disagrees?* (the second person / bubbles on the right).

• SS complete the rules with the ➕ or ➖.
  1 ➕   **2** ➖

• Go through the rules with SS. Highlight that:
  – *neither* is used to agree with a ➖ (not to disagree).
  – when you disagree using *I do / don't* etc. the pronoun is stressed (*I do.*)

PRACTICE 2

a • SS practise agreeing / disagreeing with *So / Neither do I* or *I do / don't*. Demonstrate by giving your opinions and eliciting agreement / disagreement from individual SS, e.g.
  T   *I like westerns.*
  S1   *So do I.*
  S2   *I don't.* etc.

  SS practise in pairs. Monitor and help as necessary. Encourage appropriate sentence stress, especially when SS disagree.
  ⚠ This is restricted to the present simple to help SS manipulate *so / neither*, etc. confidently.

b • Focus on the chart and example. In pairs, SS complete both columns for each statement. Check answers. Make sure SS stress the pronoun *I* when they disagree.

> **1** do   **2** do, do   **3** have, haven't   **4** can, can
> **5** So did, didn't   **6** Neither did, did
> **7** Neither have, have   **8** So am, 'm not

• SS in pairs, **A** and **B**. Tell **B** to close their book and listen to **A**. Tell **A** to read the sentences to **B** in a different order. **B** replies with his / her real opinion. They then swap roles.

6 Personalization: Speaking

• SS look again at **Practice 2** sentences 1 to 8. Focus on the words in italics. Get SS to change them to make true sentences about themselves.

  Tip Give SS a minute to write their replacements for the words in italics only, not write full sentences.

• SS in pairs, **A** and **B**. **A** makes eight true sentences. **B** agrees / disagrees. Then they swap roles.

• Monitor and help as necessary.

Lesson notes

In this lesson SS learn to use 'echo' questions to show interest, and to agree / disagree with statements using *So / Neither (do) I.* in the context of the cinema.

Echo questions A very natural feature of English requiring very fast manipulation of auxiliary verbs. SS should be encouraged to use them but at this level they are unlikely to use them with great confidence / fluency.

So (do) I. / Neither (do) I. SS can already agree / disagree with statements using the shorthand *Me too / neither.* *Neither* is pronounced /ˈniːðə(r)/ or /ˈnaɪðə/.

The alternative form *Nor do I.* is *not* taught here, but some SS may know this.

Extras

Do you? So do I. P p. 195 Mixed tense pairwork prompts to practise echo questions and *So / Neither*, etc. Instructions *p. 140.*

Talk about ... the cinema P p. 196 Questions to answer in groups about films and the cinema. Instructions *p. 140.*

Books-closed presentation

• Do after the **Warmer**. Think of or invent six facts about yourself that SS might not know, the more interesting the better. Use a range of tenses.

• Tell SS to listen and try to respond with interest. Say your first sentence. SS will probably respond, e.g. *Yes? Really? That's interesting.* Indicate that all these responses are correct / appropriate but try to elicit *Do you?* Write it up and drill intonation.

• Say your other sentences. Elicit / teach the correct echo questions
  Have you? Did you? Are you? Can't you? Would you?

• Elicit how the echo questions are formed (using the auxiliary). Then start **ex. 1**.

■ Learner-training

Take every opportunity to use echo questions and *so / neither*, yourself and elicit / revise these structures in natural contexts in class so that SS get used to hearing / using them.

■ Homework

SS do **WB 8A** *p. 52* and **Listen and speak 8A**.

We all make mistakes

> I'll pay you back tomorrow.

Lesson aims

Grammar	Uses of *will* / *won't* (offers, promises, unplanned decisions, predictions), future forms: *will be able to*, etc.
Vocabulary	*Possibly.* / *Maybe.* / *Perhaps.* etc.
Revision	Agree / disagree: *Do you?* / *I don't., So* / *Neither do I.* etc., weather, sport, fashion, films, politics
Optional materials	P Offers and promises (Practice 1) P *will* or *going to?* (Grammar focus 2)

Lesson plan

■ Warmer: ® First conditional

- Write these sentences on the board:

  > If there's nothing good on TV tonight, I …
  > If the weather's good at the weekend, …

- SS copy and complete the sentences.
- Feedback to see how many people wrote the same thing, and remind any SS who forgot to use *will* / *won't* after *if* + present simple (see **File 4B**).
- Now tell SS that in this lesson they're going to learn other uses of *will* / *won't*.

1 Presentation: Uses of *will* / *won't*

- In pairs, SS read and complete cartoons.
- Check answers and pronunciation.

  > 1 I'll have the steak.
  > 2 I'll take this one for you.
  > 3 I'll come back tomorrow.
  > 4 Shall I take a message?
  > 5 I'll pay you back tomorrow.
  > 6 I won't do it again.

■ GRAMMAR FOCUS 1
Uses of *will* / *won't*

a
- Focus on the chart and explain the uses of *will*, 1 to 3. Make sure SS understand *offer*, *promise*, and *unplanned decision* (= a spontaneous decision, made at the moment of speaking).
- In pairs, SS complete the chart with the other three sentences from the cartoons. Check answers.

  > 1 I'll take this one for you.   2 I won't do it again.
  > 3 I'll have the steak.

- Highlight that *Shall* (*I* / *we* …?) is a special form used only in the question form to make an offer, e.g. *Shall I help you?* (= Do you want me to help you?)

b
- SS translate the cartoons. Ask *Do you use the future tense in your language for all of them?* (some may use the present tense).

PRACTICE 1

- SS read situations 1 to 6. In pairs, write a suitable phrase using *will* / *shall* and one of the verbs from the list. Do the first one with the class as an example.
- Monitor and help as necessary. For extra help, highlight when to use a question (2, 4) and a negative (5, 6).
- Check answers.

  > 1 I'll pay 2 Shall I turn on 3 I'll have the roast chicken 4 Shall I answer the phone?
  > 5 I won't tell anybody 6 I won't forget

2 Presentation: *will* / *won't* for predictions

a
- Make a local / personal prediction, e.g. about which football team will win the league etc. Ask SS if they think your prediction will come true. Make sure they understand *prediction* (= something that you think will happen).
- Tell SS they're going to read some famous predictions which were wrong! Read the introduction and make sure they understand *expert*.
- Focus on the six photos. Ask *What can you see?*

  > 1 American soldiers (in Vietnam)
  > 2 Mrs Thatcher at 10 Downing Street
  > 3 a CD of Verdi's *Rigoletto* 4 an IBM computer
  > 5 the Beatles 6 an early plane (the one first flown by the Wright brothers in 1903)

- Focus on the list of names. Make sure SS understand *record producer* and *music critic*.
- Read the six predictions to the class. Highlight in number 2 that *there will be* is the future of *there is*, and *will be able to* in number 6 is the future of *can*.
- Ask *Who said what?* In pairs, SS try to match the predictions to the speaker, and the year from the list.

b
- ∘5∘ Play the tape. SS listen to check their answers.

  > 1 In 1971 **Richard Nixon**, President of the United States of America, said about the Vietnamese war 'I don't think we'll have another war. This one is probably the last.'
  > 2 In 1976 **Margaret Thatcher**, at that time British Minister for Education, said 'I don't think there'll be a woman Prime Minister in my lifetime.'
  > 3 In 1860 **James Davidson**, a music critic, said 'Verdi's *Rigoletto* will be famous for a day or two and then will be forgotten.'
  > 4 In 1943 **Thomas Watson**, chairman of IBM, said, 'There'll only be a world market for about five computers.'
  > 5 In 1961 **Dick Roe**, a London record producer, said about the Beatles, 'These boys won't be a success.'
  > 6 In 1907 **Lord Haldane**, the British War Minister, said, 'The aeroplane will never be able to fly.'

- Feedback to check whether they got them all right.

GRAMMAR FOCUS 2
will / won't (predictions)

a • SS look back at predictions 1 to 6 from **ex. 2** and highlight *will / won't* and the following infinitive verb.

b • Focus on the two examples. Tell SS that these predictions are personal opinions about the future .
   • Ask *Do you agree with the two example predictions?*

c • Focus on the rule. Highlight that for negative predictions, we use *I don't think + will*, e.g. *I don't think they'll come.* **NOT** ~~I think they won't come~~.
   ⚠ In *English File 1*, SS use *(be) going to* for predictions when there is some evidence, e.g. *Look at those clouds. It's going to rain.* Use 🅟 *will or going to? p.198* if you want to go into this (see **Extras**).
   • Highlight the future forms of *can* (= *will be able to*) and *there is / are* (= *there will be*).

PRACTICE 2

a • ◦6◦ Focus on the five topics (sport, politics, etc.). Tell SS they're going to hear five conversations. Play the tape once. SS listen and number the topics 1 to 5.
   • SS compare in pairs.
   • Ask *Do the speakers agree or disagree?* SS listen again and write A (= agree) or D (= disagree). Check answers.

> **1** films D   **2** politics A   **3** fashion A
> **4** the weather D   **5** sport D

   • SS listen again and identify the expressions the speakers use to agree / disagree.

> **1 A** I think Harrison Ford will win the Oscar for best actor this year.
>   **B** Do you? **I don't think so.** I'm sure Keanu Reeves will win it.
> **2 C** I don't think the Socialists will win the next election.
>   **D** **Neither do I. Definitely not.** They're finished.
> **3 E** I think people will wear longer skirts this winter.
>   **F** **I hope so.** It's too cold to wear mini-skirts.
> **4 G** I don't think it'll rain at the weekend.
>   **H** **I hope not.** I'm going away. But **I think it will.**
> **5 I** **I think** Real Madrid will lose to Barcelona next week.
>   **J** Do you? **I'm not sure.** Barcelona aren't playing very well at the moment.

   • Focus on **Ⓥ Agreeing / disagreeing with opinions**. Go through the expressions. Highlight that the first two columns are opposites, and that the third column is the usual response to a question. Ask *Which are the stressed words in each phrase?* Drill pronunciation. Make sure SS don't stress *so* in *I think / hope so.*

b • Tell SS to write a prediction for the five topics. Monitor and help with any vocabulary they need.
   • ⚠ SS may ask if we use *that* after *I think.* Tell them they can, but it's usually omitted.

c • Tell SS to stand up and mingle to find a student who agrees with each of their predictions.

③ Personalization: Talk about your future
   • Focus on the flowchart. Highlight that questions to the left include the word *ever* (= at any time in the future), but those on the right don't.
   • Demonstrate by asking individual SS a question from both blocks and respond to their answers with follow up questions, e.g.
     T *Do you think you'll stay in your present flat?*
     S *I don't think so.*
     T *Why not? Are you thinking of moving?* etc.
   • In pairs, SS continue. Monitor, help, and correct as necessary.

Lesson notes

SS practised *will / won't* in first conditional sentences in **File 4B**. Here they learn other uses to make offers, promises, predictions, and unplanned, spontaneous decisions.

will / won't SS who've learnt English before often think *will* is the main way to express the future in English. In fact *(be) going to* and present continuous for future (**3B**) are used much more to express future plans, e.g. *I'm going out tonight* **NOT** ~~I will go out tonight~~.

Shall I …? is used to make an offer, e.g. *Shall I make you a cup of coffee?*

Extras

Offers 🅟 *p.197* Do after **Practice 1**. A pairwork activity. SS choose offers for different situations. Instructions *p.140.*

will or going to? 🅟 *p.198* A gapped grammatical exercise. Do only if your SS are confusing the *will* and *going to.* Instructions *p.141.*

Books-closed presentation

Offers
• Mime to elicit you've got these problems:

> 1 I'm hot.
> 2 My bag is very heavy.
> 3 The phone's ringing.

   Write the sentences on the board.
• Ask SS to help you. Ask *What can you say?* Elicit / teach *I'll open the window / carry your case / answer it* or any other appropriate offers.
• Drill the sentences by repeating the mimes in a different order, or say sentences 1 to 3. Tell SS we always use *I'll +* infinitive to make offers. Write them on the board.
• Tell SS they can also make the offers as questions. Elicit / teach *Shall I open the window?*
• Drill the offers again using *Shall I …?* Omit the **Warmer** and start **ex. 1**.

■ Learner-training

Get SS used to looking closely at examples of *will* when they find them and decide which use it is. This is the best way for them to remember and pick up the different uses.

■ Homework

SS do **WB 8B** *p.53* and **Listen and speak 8B**.

A passion for chocolate!

Fifty Kit Kats are eaten every second.

Lesson aims

Grammar	Present passive
Vocabulary	Verbs: *produce*, etc., products: *uranium*, etc.
Revision	Verb *be*, countries, fruit
Optional materials	Magazine adverts of well-known products (Books-closed presentation)

Lesson plan

■ Warmer: ℝ Countries

- Books closed. Dictate this list of countries:
  1 Switzerland 2 Belgium 3 Germany 4 Norway
  5 Austria 6 Britain 7 France 8 The USA
  9 Canada 10 Sweden
- Elicit answers and spelling onto the board.
- Tell SS that the list shows the top ten countries for something, and ask them to guess what. Elicit ideas, and then tell them that they are the world's top ten chocolate-eating countries.

1 Personalization: Talk about chocolate

a
- Books open. Ask *Do you like chocolate?* SS name all the chocolate products in the photos plus any others they can think of. Elicit / teach *bar*, *drinking chocolate*, *powder*, *product*, and the correct pronunciation of *chocolate* /'tʃɒklət/.
- SS in small groups. Focus on the questions in speech bubbles. Drill the words *addict* and *addictive*. Demonstrate each question with individual SS, and answer yourself. Then SS ask and answer the questions together.
- Feedback each group's answers. Ask *Who has a passion for chocolate in your group. Is anyone an addict? Which are the most popular products?*

b
- Ask *Do you know where chocolate comes from?* Elicit answers.
- SS cover the rest of the article and read the introduction to the article about chocolate to check.
- Ask comprehension questions, e.g. *What continent did chocolate come from? Who was the first European who tried it? Where?* etc. Elicit answers and deal with any vocabulary problems.

2 Presentation: Present passive

a
- Ask *Do you know how chocolate is made?*
- Look at the photos again. Elicit / teach *cocoa beans*, *pod*, and *cocoa tree*. Drill *cocoa* /'kəʊkəʊ/.
- Focus on the verbs in the list. For each verb ask *Is it regular or irregular? What's the past participle?* Drill pronunciation of *bought* /bɔːt/ and the endings of the regular participles – *cooked* and *produced* (= /t/), *dried* and *used* (= /d/).
- SS read the **Did you know …?** article and complete the seven gaps with the past participles.

- Check answers. Elicit / teach new vocabulary *mainly*, *leaf(ves)*, *liqueur*, *(face) cream*, *recipe* /'resəpiː/, *chemical*, *brain*, *calories*.

  2 grown **3** dried **4** eaten **6** used **7** cooked
  8 produced **10** bought

b
- In pairs, SS cover the text and remember if sentences 1 to 6 were true (T) or false (F).
- Check answers. Get SS to correct the false sentences.

  1 T **2** F (mainly in Ghana, Nigeria, and Brazil)
  3 F (but the brain produces the same chemical as when you fall in love) **4** T **5** F (cocoa beans, sugar, and dried milk) **6** F (the Swiss, but the Belgians make the world's best chocolate by hand)

c
- Ask *Which fact(s) did you find most surprising?* Feedback.
  ⚠️ Make sure SS use the present tense after *I didn't know (that)* …

■ GRAMMAR FOCUS
Present passive

a
- Focus on the verb forms in the chart. SS complete the rule.

  be + past participle

b
- Ask the two questions. Elicit that the answer to both is *No*.

c
- SS circle the right rule.

  don't focus

- Get SS to translate the sentence *Chocolate is made from cocoa beans*. Highlight that the passive exists in all tenses. Other tenses are formed by changing the tense of the verb *be*.
  ⚠️ If your SS' language(s) uses an impersonal form, highlight that English often uses the passive where other languages use an impersonal form of the verb.

PRACTICE
- Focus on the example sentence. SS combine words from each group to make four more passive sentences, as in the example. Elicit / teach *mine* (*v.*) (= take out of the ground). Tell SS it's a regular verb. Check answers.

  2 Rice is grown in fields full of water.
  3 Gold and diamonds are mined in South Africa.
  4 145 McDonald's hamburgers are sold in the world every second.
  5 Many TVs and videos are made in Japan and Korea.

3 Practice: Speaking
- SS in pairs, **A** and **B**, turn to ▶◀ **Where are they made?** A *p. 122*, B *p. 125*. Both SS have question prompts about different products from around the

world and the information to answer them. Give them time to read their instructions and look through their prompts. Encourage SS to check meaning and pronunciation with you if they're not sure.

- **A** asks five questions and then **B**. Warn them to be careful with singular / plural forms of the verb *be*.
- Monitor, correct, and help as necessary.
- Feedback. Ask *What's the difference between 'grow', 'produce', and 'make'?* (we use *grow* for vegetables, fruit, etc., *produce* for by-products of natural products, e.g. wine, olive oil, and *make* for manufactured things, e.g. cars, clothes).

4 **Personalization: Writing**

- SS write five sentences about what's grown, produced or made in their country.
- Tell SS to swap sentences with SS from a different group, and read and correct the information.

   Tip In mono-lingual classes, ask each group to write about a different area of their country. Feedback each group's sentences and ask the others what they can add.

5 **Practice: Listening**

a
- Write 'chocoholic' on the board. Ask *What does it mean?* (Someone who is addicted to chocolate).
- Focus on **V** -**holic**. Look at the examples. Elicit what each problem is (addiction to alcohol, shopping, work).
   ⚠ SS will probably only find *alcoholic* in the dictionary.
- Tell SS that in Britain there's an organization called *Chocoholics Unanimous*. Ask them to read and guess the answers to the questions. Do the first one with the whole class. Don't check their answers yet.

b
- ° **7** ° Tell SS they're going to hear an interview with the organization's president. They listen and see if their guesses were right.
- In pairs, SS compare what they understood, and listen again to check.
- Check answers. Play the tape again if necessary.

> **1** For people who love / eat a lot of chocolate. (The name is a play on words echoing *Alcoholics Anonymous*, the organization which helps people who are addicted to alcohol.)
> **2** No, more women than men.
> **3** Several times a year.
> **4** Have dinner, with chocolate included in every course!
> **5** Most eat some every day. One member eats at least a half-kilo box every evening.
> **6** No. They don't worry about it.
> Tapescript **SB Listening** *p. 130*

- Ask *Do you know any chocoholics? Are you any kind of -holic? Do you know anyone who is?*

■ **Skills: Reading for pleasure**

SS read quickly **Death by chocolate**. Ask *Did he know she was poisoning him?* Be prepared to explain / translate *fatal* (= causing death), *courtier* (= member of the King's court), *hide* (= cover), *poison* (= a substance that can kill you).

Lesson notes

SS are introduced to the present passive through the topic of chocolate, its history, and how it is made.

Present passive (*is* / *are* + past participle) The passive voice is more formal than the active, and so is more common in written texts than in conversation. SS don't normally have problems with the form , but find it difficult to use correctly, especially if their language uses an impersonal verb form. At this level it's more important for SS to recognize and understand the uses of the passive than to expect them to use it correctly themselves. SS will cover the past passive in **File 8D**.

Extras

True / false dictation Dictate five facts for SS to write. SS guess the missing words and then decide if they're true or false, e.g.

1 More _____ is produced in Russia than any other country. (sugar, T)

2 _____ are grown under the ground. (peanuts, T)

3 A third of the world's _____ is found in Canada. (uranium, T)

See also P **Passive quiz** 8D *p. 199*. Instructions *p. 141*

Books-closed presentation

Present passive (*be* + past participle)

- Bring in some magazine advertisements of well-known products made in various different countries, e.g. Toyota cars (Japan), Chanel perfume (France), Cadbury's chocolate (Britain), Rolex watches (Switzerland), Carlsberg lager (Denmark), etc. If you can't find magazine pictures, simply write the names of the products on the board. Make sure you have a mixture of singular and plural products.
- Ask *Where are Toyota cars made?* Elicit / teach *They're made in Japan*. Continue with the other products.
- Write one singular and one plural question and answer on the board, e.g.

> Where are Toyota cars made?
>   They're made in Japan.
> Where's Chanel perfume made?
>   It's made in France.

- In pairs, SS ask and answer the questions for each product. Then start **ex. 1**.

■ **Learner-training**

As the present passive is very common in written texts, tell SS to look out for examples of this form when they read something in English, e.g. instructions for electrical products, university text books, etc. They should ask themselves *Why is it passive, not active?*

■ **Homework**

SS do **WB 8C** *p. 54* and **Listen and speak 8C**.

> *The White Tower was built by William I.*

Lesson aims

Grammar	Past passive + *by*
Vocabulary	Verbs: *build*, etc.
Pronunciation	/ɜː/
Revision	Definite article, *was / were*, ordinals
Optional materials	Photos of typical sights of London (**ex. 1**) An anecdote about an interesting building (**ex. 5**)

Lesson plan

■ Warmer: ℝ Ordinal numbers

- Count round the class with ordinal numbers, *first, second, third*, etc. If SS make a mistake (either the word or the pronunciation), they are 'out' and the next student begins with *first*. Stop when they've managed to get to *thirty-first* with no mistakes.

1 Personalization: Talk about London

- Ask *Have you ever been to London? When? How long for? What are the famous sights of London?*

  Tip Bring postcards, magazine pictures, or a book of photos of London if you can.

- SS in small groups. Ask *Which places have you visited / would you most like to visit? Why?*
- Monitor and help as necessary.
- Quickly feedback to see which is the most popular place.

2 Presentation: Past passive

a
- Books open. Focus on photos 1 to 6. They are all connected to the Tower of London. (the number one paying tourist attraction in London). Elicit the meaning of *Bloody* and *Henry VIII* (= Henry **the** eighth). Ask *Who's the present British Queen?* Elicit that we write *Elizabeth II* and say *Elizabeth **the** second*.
- Ask *What's the connection between the photos and the Tower of London?* Elicit anything SS may know.

  Tip With a strong class, you could play the tape here, and SS listen with the text covered for any information about the eight pictures.

b
- SS quickly read the text and find out what the pictures are.

  > 1 The Crown Jewels   2 The White Tower
  > 3 Henry VIII and Anne Boleyn   4 A museum in the Bloody Tower   5 A Beefeater and a raven
  > 6 The young princes, Edward II and the Duke of York

- Focus on the gaps in the text. Ask *What kind of words are missing?* (numbers or dates).
- ° 8 ° SS listen to a tourist guide and complete the text, then compare answers in pairs.
- Play the tape again for them to check.
- Elicit the answers onto the board. Highlight that *thousands* (gap 2) is a word not a figure, and that *I* and *III* (gaps 5 and 9) are roman numerals used for kings and queens.

> 2 thousands   3 2.5 million   4 1068   5 I
> 6 1285   7 17th   8 I   9 III   10 second   11 38
> 12 1536   13 hundreds   14 9

c
- Focus on the words. In pairs, SS find the words in the text using the line numbers, and guess what they mean.

  Tip Do this as a class activity if short of time, or if you want to avoid SS using L1 too much.

- Check answers. Use SS L1 here if you can / want to.

> <u>dai</u>ly (= every day), <u>Con</u>queror /ˈkɒŋkərə/ (= a leader who wins a war), the rest (= the other parts), prison (= a place where criminals are kept), kept (= made to stay), <u>ex</u>ecute (= kill), <u>sev</u>eral (= some), guard /gɑːd/ (= a person who looks after a building or prisoners), <u>bo</u>dyguard (= a person who protects a famous person), de<u>signed</u> /deˈzaɪnd/ (= planned), <u>king</u>dom (= land belonging to a king)

■ PRONUNCIATION

a
- Focus on the picture word. Elicit the word and sound (bird, /ɜː/).
- Tell SS to say the four words in each line aloud to themselves and cross out the word which doesn't have the sound /ɜː/.
- SS compare answers quickly in pairs.

b
- ° 9 ° Play the tape. SS listen and check.

> 2 fire   3 where   4 bored

- SS look carefully at the spelling of /ɜː/ in each group. Elicit the alternative spellings of /ɜː/.
- Highlight that:
- – the most common spellings of the /ɜː/ sound are *ir* and *ur* e.g. *girl, burn,* (but not when followed by *e*).
- – *er* in the middle of a word is also often pronounced /ɜː/, e.g. *person, certain* but not at the end.
- – *or* is occasionally pronounced /ɜː/, e.g. *word*, but is more usually /ɔː/.

3 Practice: Describing photos

- SS cover the text and look at the photos. Ask *What can you remember about The White Tower?* Elicit facts about it, e.g. *It's the oldest part of the Tower of London. It was built by William the Conqueror.* etc.
- In pairs, SS say what they can remember about each picture.
- Feedback asking different pairs.

■ GRAMMAR FOCUS

Past passive

a
- Focus on the two example sentences. Elicit that this tense is called the 'past passive'. Ask SS to find and highlight six more examples in the text.

> was visited   was completed   was used   were kept
> was executed   were designed

b • SS read and complete the rules.

> 1 was, past participle 2 by

c • Focus on the two sentences with *build*. Ask *In which sentence are we more interested in the person?* (the second = active) *In which sentence are we more interested in the building?* (the first = passive).

PRACTICE

a • Focus on the chart. Mark the word stress and drill the words / phrases.
  • Focus on the first one as an example. In pairs, SS make five more true sentences using one item from each group.
  • Monitor, help, and correct as necessary. Check answers.

> The 1994 World Cup was won by the Brazilians.
> The Pyramids of Giza were built by the Egyptians.
> Paper was invented by the Chinese.
> The Mona Lisa was painted by Leonardo da Vinci.
> The Olympic Games were started by the Greeks.

b • Focus on the categories, 1 to 5. In pairs, SS write one more sentence for each category. Give two examples relevant to your SS so they know exactly what to do.
  • Monitor, help with vocabulary and pronunciation, and correct as necessary.

c • Tell SS to work with another pair. Focus on the example. SS read the first part of their sentence to the other pair who have to complete it correctly.

> **Tip** This can be expanded into a class team quiz.

4 Practice: Listening

a • Focus on the diagram. In pairs, SS guess how the words or dates are connected to Anne Boleyn. Check the meaning of *ghost* and <u>innocent</u>.
  • Monitor, correct, and inject a few ideas if necessary, e.g. point out that the link between the two dates is 18 days, ask *What do ghosts usually wear?* etc.
  • Feedback, but don't confirm the answers yet.

b • ⎡10⎤ Tell SS to listen to the guide and see if their guesses were right.
  • Elicit answers. Play all or part of the tape again as necessary.

> 2 **2nd May, 1536** was her last day as Queen and the day she was arrested.
> 3 She was taken to **the Bloody Tower.**
> 4 She was imprisoned in the Bloody Tower for **18 days.**
> 5 On **19th May 1536**, she was taken from the room and executed.
> 6 Her **ghost** has been seen and heard many times in the Tower of London.
> 7 Her ghost wears **a long, grey dress, and a white hat.**
> 8 Some people have heard it crying, saying, '**I am innocent.'**
>
> Tapescript **SB Listening** *p. 131*

5 Personalization: Speaking

a • Tell the class about the most interesting or beautiful building that you've visited. Say where it is, why you

like it so much, and any history that you may know etc. Ask *Have you been there? Do you agree?*
  • Ask *Which is the most interesting or beautiful building you've visited?* Give SS a moment to think about which buildings they know and can talk about, based on the four questions.
  • SS tell each other about their favourite places.
  • When they finish, feedback which places SS chose. Ask *Did anyone choose the same place?*

b • SS write a paragraph about their chosen building as if for a guidebook, using the Tower of London text as a model.

Lesson notes

SS continue their study of the passive, moving from the present in **File 8C** to the past. Like the present passive, the past passive is more common in more formal (especially written) language than in conversation. The context is a guide book description of the Tower of London.

Past passive (*was* / *were* + **past participle**) SS may still have problems with *was* and *were*.

(built) by SS may confuse *by* and *for*.

Henry VIII SS may have problems with this use of the ordinal. Common error ~~Henry Eight~~.

Extras

Passive quiz ⎡P⎤ *p. 199* A quiz of unusual facts using present and past passive. Instructions *p. 141*.

Books-closed presentation

Past passive (*was* / *were* + **past participle**)
Do before **ex. 1**.
• Write on the board some famous works of art you think your SS will know:

1 Sunflowers	3 Psycho
2 Hamlet	4 the Colosseum

Underneath in a box, write these verbs:

> build direct paint write

• Ask *Who painted 'Sunflowers'?* Elicit *Van Gogh painted 'Sunflowers'.*
• Ask SS to change the sentences, starting *'Sunflowers' was …* Elicit *'Sunflowers' was painted by Van Gogh.*
• In pairs, SS make five more sentences.
• Check answers. Write the sentences on the board for SS to copy. Elicit that these are examples of the 'past passive'. Now do **ex. 1**.

■ Learner-training

Tell SS to look out for examples of the past passive in any written texts they read in English.

■ Homework

SS do **WB 8D** *p. 55* and **Listen and speak 8D.**

Lesson aims

Function	Describing illness, going to the doctor's
Grammar	*must / mustn't*
Vocabulary	Advice about illnesses
Revision	Advice / suggestions, parts of the body, travel verbs: *book* (*a hotel*), etc.

Lesson plan

■ Warmer: Travel problems

- In pairs, SS list problems they might have while travelling. Set a time limit of three minutes.
- Feedback. Ask *Have you had any of these problems? What did you do?*

> **Possible problems:**
> lose your luggage / passport / tickets, be robbed, miss a plane / train, hotel overbooked, bad weather, terrible hotel, get ill.

1 Vocabulary: Ⓡ Parts of the body

- SS in pairs, **A** and **B**, turn to 📖 **The body B** *p. 136* and test each other. Ask *Which ones didn't you remember?* Drill pronunciation of those with phonetics.
- Demonstrate yourself first. Point to a part of your body and get SS to remember the word in English. Then, still in pairs, books closed, SS do the same.

2 Presentation: Describing illness

a
- Focus on cartoons A to H. Drill the phrases 1 to 8. SS match them with the cartoons. Check answers.

> **A** 4 **B** 2 **C** 1 **D** 6 **E** 5 **F** 3 **G** 8 **H** 7

- Elicit the stress on *stomach-ache* and *headache*. Drill *temperature* /ˈtemprɪtʃə/ and *cough* /kɒf/.
- Highlight that:
- *stomach-ache* and *headache* are written as one word.
- *sore* is normally used with *throat*. Otherwise SS should say *My … hurts. / My …s hurt.*
  ⚠️ With some parts of the body you can also say *I've got a pain in my* (*back*).
- we use the article *a* with all these illnesses except *flu* (= *influenza* – flu symptoms are usually a combination of a cough, a cold, and a temperature).

b
- Mime a headache to the class. Elicit / teach *What's the matter?* Answer *I've got a headache.* Elicit their suggestions, e.g. *Why don't you take an aspirin? You should sit down.* etc.
- Repeat this a couple of times with *flu* and *shoulder hurts*. Elicit more suggestions.
- Focus on Ⓥ **Advice about illnesses**. Go through the expressions. Highlight:
- no article ~~the~~ before hospital.

- *take **an** aspirin* (= countable) but ***some** medicine* (= uncountable).
- Drill pronunciation of /ˈasprɪn/ and /ˈmedsn/.
- Focus on the model dialogue. Refer back to a few negative adjectives SS can use after *I feel …*, e.g. *awful, terrible, horrible.*
- In pairs, SS choose a picture and roleplay having different illnesses and making suggestions. Monitor and help as necessary.

> **Tip** Get a good pair to demonstrate first.

3 Presentation: Going to the doctor's

a
- Focus on the heading. Elicit the difference between *the doctor* (= the person) and *the doctor's* (= the place).
- Focus on the photo. Ask *Where is it?* (Bangkok). Tell SS Pieter's staying in Bangkok for a few days. Ask *What do you know about Bangkok? Have you been there?*
- Focus on the photo. Ask *What do you think's the matter with Pieter?*
- ∘**11**∘ SS listen and answer questions 1 to 4. Check answers.

> **1** It's 8.00. **2** He's in his hotel room. **3** He feels ill. **4** He should call / go and see a doctor.
> **Tapescript SB Listening** *p. 131*

b
- Focus on Pieter's notes. Tell SS they're going to hear Pieter phoning to make an appointment with a doctor. Check they understand what they have to listen for.
- ∘**12**∘ SS listen and complete his notes. Check answers.

> Dr Kriangsak   Tel: 7649763   Time 9.30 a.m.
> Take my passport and insurance documents.
> 428 Rama road

4 Presentation: *must / mustn't*

a
- ∘**13**∘ Tell SS Pieter's with the doctor. SS listen and find out what the matter is.
- Check answers. Ensure SS know the spelling / pronunciation of *virus*.

> He's got a really bad stomachache and a headache (= a stomach virus).
> **Tapescript SB Listening** *p. 131*

b
- SS listen again and complete the doctor's advice.
- Play the tape once or twice as necessary, then check answers.

> You've got a **stomach** virus.
> You must **rest for a few days**.
> Don't **try to do too much**.
> You mustn't **eat any fried food or drink any alcohol**.
> Come back **and see me tomorrow**.

■ Grammar box: *must / mustn't*

- Focus on the three example sentences. Highlight that:
- – *must / mustn't* is followed by the infinitive.
- – we use *must / mustn't* for strong advice and obligation. Compare it with *should*, e.g. *You should stay in bed.* (= it's a good idea to stay in bed) *You must stay in bed.* (= it's very important for you to stay in bed).
- – *must* has a weak and strong pronunciation. Compare *You must* /məst/ *rest*. and *You must* /mʌst/ *rest*. (= more emphatic).
- – the *t* is normally silent and is only pronounced when followed by a vowel, e.g. *You must͜ always read the instructions.*
- – *mustn't* is always stressed but the middle *t* is silent (mustn't = /ˈmʌsnt/).
  ⚠ SS may ask if they can use *have to* here. Tell them that in positive sentences the meaning is more or less the same, but in the negative, *you mustn't* (= it's prohibited) and *you don't have to* (= it's not <u>necessary</u> to do it).

5 Practice: Roleplay

- SS in pairs, **A**'s the patient, **B**'s the doctor. You can give SS pieces of paper with illnesses written on, or they can suggest an illness to another pair. Tell them to read the instructions and think for a minute about what they can say. Let them note down a few ideas if necessary.

  Tip If you haven't used the tapescript yet, rewind the tape and let them listen to and read ◦13◦ *p.131* again. This should give them confidence and a bit more time to think what they can say.

- Demonstrate yourself with a couple of strong SS first. Be the doctor the first time, then the patient.
- SS roleplay in pairs. Monitor / help as necessary.

6 Vocabulary: Travel phrasebook 8

- SS turn to 📖 *p.133* and complete and translate the phrases. If you haven't got time to do this in class, set it for homework.

Lesson notes

Travel with English 8 is set in Bangkok. Pieter becomes ill with a stomach virus. He goes to visit a local doctor. SS learn how to describe illness symptoms.

must / mustn't SS learn to use *must / mustn't* to give strong advice. This is the only use of this modal verb taught in *English File 2*. You may want to contrast *must* with *should* (**File 7C**). *Must* is stronger than *should*.

must* or *have to As SS usually tend to over-use *must* once it has been taught, and under-use *have to*, *must* has been introduced late, and its use restricted to strong advice. SS should not now forget to use *have to / don't have to* for general obligations. Try to avoid contrasting these two modals more at this stage.

Extras

Travel with English revision [P] *p.200* A pairwork activity to revise phrases from 📖1 to 8. Instructions *p.141*.

Books-closed presentation

What's the matter? I've got a (headache). etc.

- Do after **ex.1**. Mime looking ill, holding your head, etc. Say *I don't feel very well.* Elicit / teach *What's the matter?*
- Mime a headache and say (twice) *I've got a headache.*
- Mime a stomach-ache and say (twice) *I've got a stomach-ache.*
- Mime and present in the same way *I've got a cold / sore throat / cough / temperature. / My back hurts.*
- Now ask *What's the matter?* Mime the symptoms again. Elicit the phrases with *You've got …*
- Write up the sentences on the board for SS to copy. Drill pronunciation.

Then start **ex.2**.

■ Learner-training

Practising understanding authentic English is a valuable activity. Tell SS to use any written information in English included with any products they have, e.g. medicines, electrical goods, computer manuals, etc. Encourage them to try to understand them, compare with their L1, learn a few key words, etc.

■ Homework

SS do **WB 8**📖 *p.56* and **Listen and speak 8**📖. This is the last 'Listen and speak' lesson, so discuss with SS ways for them to use it to revise the course, e.g. listening to the whole tape in their cars, re-doing exercises and improving, doing the extra tasks in the **WB** again, etc.

Lesson aims

Revision	**File 8:** Echo questions, *So / Neither do I.*, uses of *will / won't*, passives
Vocabulary	Verbs: *execute*, etc.
Optional materials	Personal anecdote of a coincidence (**ex. 3b**) P *Imagine* ♫

Lesson plan

■ Warmer: Progress chart

- Books closed. Ask *Can you remember what the lessons in File 8 were about? What grammar and vocabulary did we learn?* Elicit from the SS anything they can remember.
- Now tell SS to look at the **Progress chart** *p. 9* and to tick the lessons they've studied.
- Tell them that this is the revision lesson for this File, and that they can then do the **Vocabulary** and **Grammar files** (*pp. 112, 113*) to further revise the language of the File.

1 Listening: ℝ Echo questions

a
- Focus on pictures A to D. Ask *What can you see?* (A two pints of lager and a coke B a newspaper headline about a tiger escaping from a zoo C a poster advertising a football match D a restaurant).
- °**14**° Tell SS they're going to hear four dialogues. Play the tape once. SS listen and match each one to a picture.
- SS compare in pairs. Check answers.

> **1** B **2** C **3** D **4** A

b
- Teach *coincidence* with an example (e.g. *my mother and I have the same birthday*). SS listen again and note the four coincidences. Feedback answers.

> **1** A tiger has escaped from Bristol zoo and the man's parents live next to it. **2** They've both just got tickets for the same football match. **3** Two old friends meet in a restaurant where they are having dinner. **4** Both order the same drink.
>
> Tapescript **SB Listening** *p. 131*

- Ask *Can you think of any examples of coincidences?*

2 Revision: Echo questions, *So / Neither do I.*

- Focus on the title. Make sure SS understand *in common* (shared situations or interests).
- SS in pairs, A and B, turn to ▶◀ **What have you got in common?** A *p. 122* B *p. 125*. They do part **a**.
- Tell SS to read part **b** but don't let them begin yet. Make sure everyone understands what they have to do.
- Demonstrate yourself first. Make some statements in answer to the prompts for individual SS to respond to you. Make sure they ask a follow-up question too, e.g.

T *I really like Indian food.*
S1 *Do you? I don't. It's too hot. I prefer Chinese. Do you like Chinese food?*
T *Not very much.* (to S2) *I can play the guitar very well.*
S2 *Can you? So can I. What kind of music do you play?*

- SS do the same in pairs to try to find as many things as possible that they have in common. Monitor and help as necessary.
- Feedback any coincidences.

3 Revision: Past passive

a
- Focus on the photos. Ask *Who are they?* (Abraham Lincoln and JF Kennedy) *What do you know about them?* (both were US presidents, both were assassinated, etc.).

b
- In pairs, SS read the text, choose the right verbs, and cross out the wrong ones, as in the example.
- Monitor and help as necessary. Be prepared to explain / translate *elected* (= voted), *shoot* (*shot*), *assassinate* (= kill), *assassin*, *hide* (*hid* / *hidden*), *warehouse* (= a large building where things are kept), *succeed* (= follow).
- Check answers.

> **2** was called **3** were shot **4** were assassinated
> **5** shot **6** hid **7** was shot **8** was found
> **9** was shot

c
- Focus on the chart. Check SS understand the information they need to find. Elicit / teach *accompanied by* (= the person with him).
- In pairs, SS complete the chart with notes. ⚠ Remind SS that *notes* = a word or two, not a sentence.
- Elicit the answers onto the board in columns:

	Lincoln	Kennedy
elected in	1860	1960
secretary's name	Kennedy	Lincoln
shot in the back of his	head	head
accompanied by	his wife	his wife
on (day)	a Friday	a Friday
assassin was from	the South	the South
succeeded by (who)	Andrew Johnson	Lyndon Johnson
who was born in	1808	1908

- Ask *Which coincidences do you find strangest? Do you know any other strange coincidences?*

4 Personalization: Talk about the future

a
- Focus on the predictions in bubbles. Check SS understand *fashionable* / ˈfæʃənəbl/, *illegal* /ɪˈliːɡəl/, and *except* /ɪkˈsept/. Drill pronunciation.
- SS read quickly and tick those they agree with.
- SS in pairs or small groups. Tell each pair to choose the three predictions that they think will come true in their lifetime and say why.

- Monitor and help as necessary. Insist they choose three.

b • SS compare with other pairs. Ask *Do you agree or disagree? Why?*

- Feedback, asking SS to justify their choices.

■ ·15· ♫ *Imagine*

- The words to this song are on ⓟ *Imagine* p.201 (see **Extras**). If you can't make photocopies, exploit the song by copying part of it onto the board for SS to listen to and complete.

Lesson notes

This lesson revises and extends the language of **File 8** through the theme of coincidences.

Extras

Talking circle

- Draw this 'talking circle' on the board. Add / adapt categories as required:

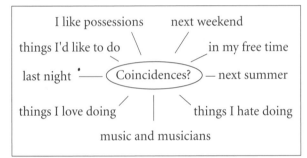

- SS talk to a new partner (i.e. someone they don't know well) about the subjects in the circle.
- In three minutes SS see if they can find any coincidences.

  A *In my free time I like travelling.*
  B *Do you? So do I. Where was the last place you went?*
  A *Turkey.*
  B *That's a coincidence. I went to Turkey last summer.* etc.

Revision questions ⓟ *p.202* Question prompts to revise the main structures in *English File 2* and generate mini-conversations. Instructions *p.142.*

Imagine ⓟ *p.201* A song by John Lennon. Instructions *p.141.*

■ **Homework**

Choose from the **End-of-file options** below.

End-of-file options

These are the last **Vocabulary** and **Grammar files** in *English File 2* (there are none for **File 9** as it's largely revision). Tell SS that if they've learnt and can use the language of **Files 1** to **8** they now have a good level of English and should have no problems with the **End-of-book test**. Encourage them to check back to the **Progress chart** for **Files 1** to **8** and identify any areas they're still unsure about.

Student's book

■ **Vocabulary file 8** *p.112*

- Do this in class or set it for homework. Note that SS can always learn from English around them, not only books / papers, but also product information, etc.

  Ex.3 Highlight that the verb is stressed on the second syllable, the noun on the first. More examples include *import, export, record*, etc.

  Ex.5 Get one student to point at a consonant picture for the other to remember the word and sound.

Organize your vocabulary learning! Tell SS to look back through the **Vocabulary file** tips in pairs and say how useful they think each one has been. Remind them to try and use the tips regularly.

> 1 **Word groups**
>   2 novel 3 jump 4 tip 5 queen 6 teeth
>   7 grow 8 menu 9 winter
> 2 **Word pairs**
>   2 quiet 3 half an hour 4 legs 5 borrow
>   6 can 7 turn on 8 vegetable 9 down
>   10 do
> 3 **Word-building**
>   be<u>gin</u> <u>pro</u>duct con<u>tain</u> pre<u>dic</u>tion
>   in<u>ven</u>tion e<u>lect</u>
> 4 **Prepositions**
> a 1 by 2 for 3 about 4 by 5 without
>   6 about 7 back 8 since 9 at 10 on
>   11 in 12 for
> 5 **Pronunciation**
> b 2 bird 3 phone 4 car 5 jazz 6 shower

■ **Grammar file 8** *p.113*

- Spend ten minutes going through this with the class, answering any queries. SS tick each box when they're satisfied they understand it.

Workbook

■ **Grammar check 8** *p.57*

- Remind SS to do this with **SB** and **WB** open in front of them, and to refer back to **Grammar file 8** as necessary. SS can check their answers with the **WB** key.

■ **Read and write 8** *p.68*

- SS read an advert for and a fax to a language school in Bath, analyse the different steps and then write their own fax to the same school.
- Quickly go through the model in class so SS understand what to do. Remind SS that they have a self-check key to ex.1 to 3 but that you're going to collect and correct their faxes.

■ **Quicktest 4** *p.86*

A multiple-choice progress test revising the language of **Files 7** and **8**. SS have a key to check their answers.

Lesson aims

Revision	All tenses
Skills	Reading

Lesson plan

■ Warmer: Ⓡ Word bank

- In pairs, SS choose a page from the **Word bank** and test their partner, e.g. by covering the words and pointing to pictures, asking him / her to say the opposite adjective, giving the past tense and past participle of an irregular verb, etc.

1 Revision: Reading

- Focus on the photo of Somerset Maugham /mɔːm/. Ask *Have you heard of him? Have you ever read any of his stories?* (e.g. *Of Human Bondage, The Razor's Edge*). He was often called 'the English de Maupassant'.
- Tell SS they're going to read a short story by him. First they read some facts about him.
- Ask *Why did some of his friends get angry with him?* (because he wrote about some of them in his books) *When was he born / did he die? Where did many of his stories take place? Would you like to appear in a novel?* etc.

2 Vocabulary: Definitions

- Focus on the six pairs of words. In pairs, SS explain the difference to each other.
- Elicit answers from individual SS. Use L1 if you want to / can to make sure SS know the exact difference in meaning.

> 1 **get engaged** = when you promise to marry someone / **get married** = when you marry someone.
> 2 **a stranger** = somebody you don't know / **a foreigner** = somebody from another country.
> 3 **a journey** = when you travel from one place to another / **a trip** = a short excursion
> 4 **a boat** = a vehicle for travelling on water / **a ship** = a big boat
> 5 **a servant** = somebody who works for a rich family / **a civil servant** = somebody who works for the government
> 6 **terrible** = very bad / **terrified** = very frightened

3 Skills: Reading

- Focus on the photos. Ask *What can you see?* (an old-fashioned steam train, travellers on a 1920s passenger ship) Ask *What do you think of when you see these photos?* Help SS express the answers, e.g., the past, the British Empire, colonialism, etc.
- Focus on the map. Ask *Have you been to any of these countries?*

  Tip All the story is on tape so you can do the whole story as listen and read, or save the listening till the

end for SS to listen to all the story after they've read it. Make sure SS always keep the next part of the story covered so they can't read ahead.

- ∘ **1** ∘ SS listen and read **Part 1** of the story. Encourage them to guess unknown words from context, and to ask you any they can't guess.
- SS cover the text and answer questions 1 to 3 in pairs from memory.
- SS read **Part 1** again to make sure they didn't miss anything. Quickly check answers, especially to question 3.

> 1 He was a civil servant working in Burma and Mabel was his fiancee – they met in England when he was on holiday.
> 2 Her father died, the (First World) War started, and George had to go to an area which was dangerous for a white woman.
> 3 Suggested answers: Because he hadn't seen her for seven years / didn't really want to get married / met somebody else / thought she might have changed, etc.

4 Skills: Reading

- Ask *What do you think happened next?* Elicit suggestions.
- ∘ **2** ∘ SS listen and read **Part 2** to see if they were right.
- Ask *What do you think he decided to do?*

5 Skills: Reading

- ∘ **3** ∘ SS listen and read **Part 3**. Tell SS to find where George went on the map (Singapore).
- Ask *What do you think of George? What kind of person is he? What do you think Mabel did?*

6 Skills: Reading

- ∘ **4** ∘ SS listen and read **Part 4**, then draw the route of George's journey on the map. Check answers.

7 Skills: Reading

a
- Ask *What do you think George is going to do next?* Elicit suggestions.
- SS read and work out the telegrams using the words in the list.
- ○ **5** ○ SS listen and read **Part 5** to check.

> **Telegram 1** SORRY I DIDN'T SEE YOU AT
> MANILA
> **Telegram 2** ARRIVING SOON

b
- SS continue to draw in George's journey on the map.
- Check answers (see **ex.6** above).
- Ask *Where do you think he went next?*

8 Skills: Reading

a
- In pairs, SS read **Part 6** and guess the missing words from the first letter, following the example. Tell SS to note their guesses on a piece of paper / in the margin and not to complete the text yet. They will probably come up with several answers. Check all their guesses but don't confirm them yet.

b
- ○ **6** ○ SS listen and check. Pause the tape after each word to help them.

> **2** spring **3** boat **4** impossible **5** road **6** safe
> **7** relax **8** find **9** friend **10** lazy **11** weeks

- SS complete the rest of George's journey on the map.
- Check answers (see **ex.6** above).

9 Skills: Listening

- Ask *How do you think the story ends?* Elicit suggestions.
- ○ **7** ○ SS listen and check. Play the tape more than once if they want.

> She finds him , and this time they get married.
> Tapescript **SB Listening** *p. 131*

10 Speaking: Talk about the story

- Ask *Did you enjoy the story? Why (not)? How do you imagine the characters? What do you think George and Mabel looked like? Which character did you prefer? Why? Do you think they were real people? Do you think many people get nervous before they get married? Why?*

Lesson aims

Revision	All tenses, question formation
Optional materials	P *Nothing compares 2U* ♫

Lesson plan

■ Warmer: ® Musical tastes

- Books closed. Ask SS about their musical tastes. Revise different types of music / musicians. Ask *What's your favourite record?*
- Play the opening verse of *Nothing compares 2U*. Ask SS *What kind of song is it? Who's singing?* (Sinead O'Connor). Then start **ex.1**.

1 Practice: ® Question formation

- Books open. Focus on the photo. Get SS to describe Sinead O'Connor. Ask *How old do you think she is? What do you think she's like?* (she's a strong feminist and famously outspoken).
- **b** Ask *What does 'Profile' mean?* Elicit what a profile of someone includes (i.e. brief details about name, place of birth, etc.).
  - SS read the **Profile** .
  - Get SS to cover the text and ask them some comprehension questions, e.g. *Where's she from? Where / When was she born?* etc.

2 Revision: All tenses

- **a** Focus on Sinead O'Connor's answers, 1 to 10. In pairs, SS imagine and write the questions.

  Tip Tell SS to cover the questionnaire itself to discourage them from reading ahead, or write Sinead's answers 1 to 10 on the board and get SS to close their books and write the questions.

  - Feedback SS answers. Accept all correctly-formed relevant questions as possibilities, but don't tell SS the answers yet.

- **b** SS read the questionnaire to see if their predicted questions were right. Get them to underline any answers that they find surprising as they read. Be prepared to explain / translate *granny* (= grandmother), *passionate*, *loving*, *mothering*.
  - Ask *Which questions did you guess correctly? Do any of her answers surprise you?*

3 Revision: Question formation

- Focus on the four sections of the questionnaire: Your tastes / habits / personality / future. Get SS to ask you some of the questions from each category.
- In pairs, SS add another question to each category.
- Monitor and help as necessary. Get SS to ask you their extra questions for each section to make sure they've got them right.
- SS in new pairs, A and B. Tell A to close his / her book and answer B's questions, including B's four new ones.

Tell **B** to make follow-up questions if they can, as in the example (even if it's only *Why?*). Encourage SS to ask the questions in random order within each section.

- When they finish, get them to swap roles.
- Feedback. Ask each pair to tell you something new they learned about their partner.

■ ⏺8⏺ ♫ *Nothing compares 2U*

- The words to this song are on P **Nothing compares 2U** *p.204* (see **Extras**). If you can't make photocopies, exploit the song as follows:
- Write these lines from the song on the board:

a	I went to the doctor's
b	Since you took your love away
c	All the flowers that you planted
d	Like a bird without a song
e	I can see whoever I choose
f	I could put my arm around every boy I see

- ⏺8⏺ SS listen to the song and number the lines in the order they hear them, 1 to 6. Play the tape as often as necessary. Check answers.

1 b　**2** e　**3** d　**4** f　**5** a　**6** c

Lesson notes

This lesson revises all the tenses and question forms SS have learnt during the course through the context of an interview which the controversial Irish singer, Sinead O'Connor, gave to *English File*. The lesson ends with her most famous song, *Nothing Compares 2U* (Written by Prince in 1987).

Extras

Nothing compares 2 U $\boxed{P}$ *p. 204* A song by Sinead O'Connor. Instructions *p. 142*.

■ Learner-training

⚠ If you're going to give SS the **End-of-Book test**, it is important to tell them exactly what they need to revise. Tell them to revise the following:
- **Word bank** and **Ⓥ** boxes
- **Grammar files** and **Grammar checks**
- **Read and writes** for writing models
- 🗀 **Travel phrasebook** and 📓 **Classroom language**
- 📓 **English sounds** chart

■ Homework

SS complete the revision crossword **WB 9A / B** *p58*.

Writing: Questionnaire SS write five paragraphs about themselves, headed 'Profile', 'Tastes', 'Habits', 'Personality', and 'Future', based on their answers to the questionnaire. OR SS can write a profile of their teacher, or of someone else they have interviewed with the questionnaire.

Teacher's Book

End-of-book test *p. 217* A two-page exit test for you and your SS to see what progress they've made. Do this next lesson or after 🗀 **9**. Instructions *p. 211*, key *p. 219*.

9 🧳 *Going home*

REVISION

Lesson aims

Revision	Travel with English 1 to 8
	All travel functions and phrases
Skills	Fluency practice

Lesson plan

■ Warmer: Pieter

- Books closed. Ask *What can you remember about Pieter? Which five countries has he visited? What happened to him each time?* Tell SS to try to remember first, then check in their books.

> **1** Britain (arrived, lost his suitcase, changed money, went into the centre of London)
> **2** Sweden (checked into a hotel, met some friends in a restaurant)
> **3** USA (went sightseeing and got lost, went shopping)
> **4** Brazil (made phone calls)
> **5** Thailand (went to the doctor).

- Feedback answers.

1 Presentation: Checking out

a
- Focus on the photo. Ask *Where is Pieter today?* (in a hotel, at Reception) *What do you think he's doing?* (checking out) *What does he have to do before he leaves the hotel?* (have breakfast / a shower, pack, pay his bill, call a taxi, etc.).

b
- ▸ 9 ◂ In pairs, SS listen to Pieter checking out and mark sentences 1 to 6 true (T) or false (F).
- SS listen again to check, then compare in pairs.
- Check answers. Get SS to correct the false sentences.

> **1** F **2** T **3** T **4** F **5** F **6** F
> Tapescript **SB Listening** *p. 131*

- Ask *Have you, or anyone your know, ever nearly missed a plane or train / left your passport at home?*

2 Vocabulary: Travel phrasebook 9

- SS turn to 🧳 *p. 133* and translate the phrases.

Tip As preparation for **ex. 5**, get SS to test each other again on the **Travel phrasebook**.

- A says the phrase in L1, B says it in English.
- A describes a situation when you need to say the phrase and B supplies it, e.g.
  - A *It's what you say when you want to find the bank.*
  - B *Could you tell me the way to the bank?*

3 Revision: The Travel with English game

a
- Focus on the photos. Ask *What situations do they represent? What was Pieter doing in each place?*

> **1** checking in **2** at the lost luggage office
> **3** buying a train ticket **4** getting a taxi
> **5** checking into a hotel **6** having a meal in a
> restaurant **7** lost in the street **8** buying food
> **9** buying jeans **10** talking on the phone
> **11** seeing a doctor **12** at airport departures

b
- SS in small groups. Explain the rules of the game.
- SS use a coin to move round the board. Make sure SS know *heads* and *tails*. If they
- throw heads they move two squares
- tails they move one square.
- When SS land on a square, they must say a phrase appropriate for the traveller in that situation, e.g. on the first square they could say *Could I have a window seat? / Which gate is it?* etc.
- the rest of the group decide if what the student says is correct and appropriate. They can use the **Travel Phrasebook** to check. If SS disagree they can ask you to arbitrate. Decide how strict you want to be about correct pronunciation.
- If a student makes a correct sentence, they stay where they are on the board. If their sentence is incorrect/inappropriate they move back one square.
- No student can repeat a phrase that another has said previously. It must always be a different phrase.
- The first student to arrive home is the winner.

Tip If a group finish quickly they can repeat the game, but tell them they can't repeat any of the phrases used in the first round.

Lesson notes

This last **Travel with English** lesson includes a new situation (checking out of a hotel) and revises checking in for a flight home which takes SS full circle from **Travel with English 1**. The rest of the lesson is a game to revise all the main **Travel with English** and **Travel phrasebook** language, and promote oral fluency and confidence.

Extras

The describing game 🎲 *p. 208* Play the game with the following words:

A gate   return ticket   double room   bill   traffic lights   size   reverse charge call   medicine

B trolley   platform   lift   menu   map   changing room   message   flu

■ Learner-training

Give SS advice about what they can do to keep up their English after the course, e.g. revise **Vocabulary** and **Grammar files**, **Word banks** and their own lists, read *Easy Readers*, etc. Remind SS to take their **Travel phrasebook** with them if they're travelling abroad after the course.

■ Homework

SS do **WB 9**🛄 *p. 59*.

Are you a good citizen?

What would you do if you saw two people fighting?

Lesson aims

Grammar	Preview: Second conditional
Revision	Past simple
Pronunciation	Sentence stress, silent *l*
Optional materials	A lottery ticket (Books-closed presentation)

Lesson plan

■ Warmer: ℝ *would*

- Write these questions and responses on the board for SS to match:

  1 Would you like a cup of tea?
  2 Would you like to go out tonight?
  3 Would you like to be a millionaire?
  4 Would you like to travel more?
  a Sorry, I'm busy. How about tomorrow?
  b Yes, I've always wanted to go to Africa.
  c Yes, please. I'd love one.
  d No, I wouldn't, but I'd like to be richer.

- Check answers.

  1 c 2 a 3 d 4 b

- Remind SS that *'d* is the contraction of *would*, that the negative form is *wouldn't*. Drill pronunciation /wʊd/, /ˈwʊdnt/ (the *l* is not pronounced).

■ Presentation: Second conditional

- Focus on the lesson title. Check SS understand *citizen*. Ask *What is a good citizen?* Elicit answers from individual SS. Allow the use of L1 if necessary.
- Focus on the picture of the two men fighting (question 1). Say *Imagine you were walking along the street and you saw this happening. What would you do?*
- SS read question 1 and circle the answer which is nearest to their own.
  ⚠ SS may be confused by the past tense *saw*. Make sure they are clear that this is an imaginary situation in the present or future.
- Get SS to compare with a partner and the other SS near them.
- Feedback answers.
- Ask SS if their answer would be the same if it were a) two women, or b) a man and a woman fighting.

■ GRAMMAR FOCUS
Second conditional

a • SS highlight all the verb forms in question 1. Make sure they've highlighted all seven, including the auxiliary *would / 'd / wouldn't*.

  would do   were   saw   'd try to stop   wouldn't do
  'd walk   'd call

b • Focus on the grammar chart. Tell SS to look carefully at the verb forms there too, then complete the rule below.
- Check answers.

  if + past simple tense, **would / wouldn't** + infinitive

c • Tell SS that we use the second conditional to talk about an imaginary situation. Read them the example. Emphasize that these situations are imaginary / hypothetical.
- Highlight that:
  – the *if*-phrase can come first or second. Reverse both the example sentences from **c** to show *if* in different positions.
  – *would / wouldn't* never goes with the *if*-phrase **NOT** *If I would …*
  – with the verb *be* you can say *If I was (rich) …* **OR** *If I were (rich) …*
  ⚠ Although we use the past tense form in the second conditional we are not talking about the past but about the imaginary present or future. Ask SS to translate the two examples from **c** and to contrast them with the tenses they use in their L1.

  Tip Since this is just a preview of what we consider a third year structure, we suggest you try to avoid contrasting the first and second conditionals at this stage. If SS ask what the difference is, tell them that the first conditional is a <u>real</u> possibility. The second conditional is <u>improbable</u> / purely *imaginary*: *If I had more free time I'd learn another language* (= but I haven't got much free time so I won't learn one).

PRACTICE

a • SS do the rest of the questionnaire individually. Use the pictures to make sure they understand the questions. You do it too.
- SS work out their scores and compare their answers and score with a partner.
- Tell the class your score. Feedback who got the highest and lowest scores. Explain / elicit the meaning of <u>model</u>, <u>civilized</u>, <u>community</u>. Ask *Have you been in any of these situations? What did you do?*
- Get SS to cover the questions and remember the question for each picture.

b • SS complete the gapped phrases with the verbs in brackets, as in the example. Tell them to use contractions whenever they can, e.g. *I'd call*. Check answers.

  2 'd help, had   **3** spoke, 'd get   **4** 'd go, was
  5 was (or were), 'd learn

c • SS match the correct endings to the conditional sentences 1 to 5 in **b**. This exercise helps reinforce the concept of imaginary situations.

- Check answers.

> 4 ... but we're working on Friday.
> 5 ... but I'm much too old now.
> 2 ... but I can't. I'm too busy.
> 3 ... but she's never tried to learn.

■ PRONUNCIATION
Sentence stress

a • [°10°] SS listen and write the six sentences. Pause the tape after each sentence to give them time to write.
- SS check answers and spelling quickly in pairs. Don't confirm yet.

b • SS underline the stressed words, then listen again and check.
- Elicit the answers onto the board.

> <u>What</u> would you <u>do</u> if you <u>won</u> a <u>lot</u> of <u>money</u>?
> I'd <u>spend</u> it.
> <u>Would</u> you <u>spend</u> it <u>all</u>?
> <u>Yes</u>, I <u>would</u>. I <u>wouldn't</u> save <u>any</u>.
> <u>Wouldn't</u> you <u>put</u> some in the <u>bank</u>?
> <u>No</u>, I <u>wouldn't</u>.

- Highlight that *would*, *could*, and *should* all have the silent letter *l*.

2 Practice: Speaking
- SS in pairs, A and B, turn to ►◄ **What would you do ...?** A *p. 122* B *p. 125*, read the instructions and look at the example.
- Show SS that they have to put the verb in brackets in the past tense. Demonstrate with A's first question as the example on the board:

> *won*
> What would you do if you (~~win~~) first prize in the lottery?

- Pre-teach *luxury* /ˈlʌkʃəriː/ and *millionaire*. Ask individual SS the question. Encourage them to use contractions and ask *What about you?*
- SS ask and answer their five questions. Encourage them to ask *What about you?* after each answer. Monitor and help as necessary. Fast finishers can try to make more questions of their own.
- Feedback any interesting answers with the class. Ask individual SS what they would do in each situation.

3 Personalization: Talk about your dreams
- Tell SS they're going to talk about their dreams. Focus on the speech bubbles and example. Give a few examples yourself, e.g. *If I weren't here today, I'd be at the beach.*
- Elicit a few examples from individual SS. Encourage them to use contractions wherever they can.
- SS in small groups. Each student makes a conditional sentence from the prompts. Other SS in the group ask follow-up questions with *would you*, e.g.
  > A *If I had more free time, I'd learn another language.*
  > B *Which language would you learn?*
- Feedback with the whole class, eliciting sentences from individual SS.

Lesson notes

The second conditional is not included in the syllabus of *English File 2*, but this optional lesson gives teachers the chance to preview the structure if they wish. SS talk about imaginary situations in the context of a magazine questionnaire to find out whether SS are model citizens.

Second conditional SS will be surprised to find the past tense used to express the future. SS may put *would* in the *if*-phrase, e.g. ~~*If I would be rich ...*~~

If I were Although grammar books often teach *If I were ...* as the first person second conditional, many native speakers nowadays use *If I was ...* The only place where native speakers always use *were* is in the expression *If I were you ...*

⚠ There is no **Grammar file** for the second conditional, and it is not included in the **End-of-book** test.

Books-closed presentation

- Buy an inexpensive lottery ticket before class.
- Tell SS that last night you dreamt the winning numbers for the national lottery. Tell them that you're going to tell the numbers to one pair of students, those with the best plans for how to spend the money.
- In pairs, SS note three things they'd do, with verbs in the infinitive, e.g. buy a house, go round the world, etc.
- Ask *Do you really think that you're going to win the lottery?* Establish that it's only an imaginary / hypothetical situation.
- Ask one pair for their plans Elicit *If I **won** the lottery I'd ...* Write one example sentence on the board. Highlight the verb forms.
- Feedback the rest of the class's plans, getting them to use second conditionals. Decide whose plans you think are the most imaginative. Give the ticket to the winning pair. Then start **ex. 1**.

■ Learner-training
Tell SS when they're revising vocabulary, apart from revising the **Word banks**, to also look back through the lessons at the ⓥ boxes.

■ Homework
SS do **WB 9C** *p. 60*. Make sure SS have also learnt the **Grammar words to learn** and done the **Contractions file WB** *p. 87*.

Photocopiable activities

Contents

Important Please note that for copyright reasons, Oxford University Press cannot authorize the photocopying of any of the song lyrics in this section. Where activities contain song lyrics (activities 15, 22, 33, 51, 59, and 62), the lyrics themselves are **not photocopiable**.

ℙ Instructions

Tips for using photocopiable activities

- We have suggested the ideal numbers of copies for each activity. You can often manage with fewer. e.g. one copy per pair instead of each, or have two **A**s and two **B**s using one copy in pairwork activities.

- SS should store activities with hole-punch marks in their files. SS may want to have a sheet each in these cases, even if the activity requires one between a pair / group. Card sets are best stored in envelopes so they can be re-used.

- Cut-up activities can also work using the sheet complete, e.g. with question prompts, one student asks the group for one minute, then passes the sheet on.

- If a class doesn't divide equally into pairs / groups, either:
  - take part yourself.
  - two SS share one role.
  - the extra student can monitor, help, and correct.

- Stop and re-start an activity if SS obviously don't understand what to do. Use SS' L1 (if you can) to repair an activity half-way through should things break down.

- If some SS finish early, they can:
  - swap roles and do it again.
  - do it again but better (some SS tend to treat pairwork activities as a race rather than language practice).
  - write some of the sentences.
  - just relax for a minute while the others finish.

- With some activities you can add your own examples of **locally famous** names and places to make them more relevant to your SS.

1	Why are you learning English?	Introduction

A needs-analysis form. SS fill it in for themselves and compare with other SS. Copy one form per student.

> **LANGUAGE**
> *I want / need to learn English*   *for* + noun
> *I find (listening) difficult in English*   *because …*

- Quickly go through all the questions and answers. Elicit / teach the meanings of any new words.

- SS answer the questions. Monitor and help them with the written answers.

- In pairs or threes, SS compare their answers.

- Feedback each question in turn
  1 Find out the various / most common reasons for learning English.
  2 Ask *Who put 3?* for each sentence. Is there anything else they need or want to do?
  3 Ask *Who put 3 (very difficult)?* for each sentence. Is there anything else they find difficult?

Tip Collect the forms to analyse SS' answers in detail. This information can be very useful when trying to decide which areas / skills to emphasize during the course.

2	No article	Introduction

Word and picture pairwork prompts to revise the omission of the definite article. Copy one sheet per student.

> **LANGUAGE**
> Singular and plural nouns with / without *the*
> *Which do you prefer, cats or dogs?*   *I prefer cats to dogs.*
> *I don't like cats or dogs.*   *I like both.*

- Give each student a copy (or one per pair). Focus on rule 1 and the examples. Ask individual SS questions with the prompts, e.g. *Which do you prefer, (watching TV or listening to music)? Why?* Make sure they don't use *the*.

- Get SS to ask you some questions with the picture prompts. *Which do you prefer, (trains or buses)? Why?*

- In pairs, SS ask and answer. Monitor and help. Make sure **A** asks *Why?* each time, and **B** answers *Because …*

  Tip Get SS to improvise more questions.

- Focus on rule 2. Highlight that *school / home / work / bed* are a special group where the article is not used. Get SS to ask you a few questions, then continue in pairs.

- Repeat the procedure with rule 3. Drill pronunciation of any difficult words e.g. gui*tar* /gɪtˈɑː/, *violin* /vaɪəˈlɪn/, and *poker* /ˈpəʊkə/.

- Add a few other locally common games and instruments, e.g. *the recorder, bridge*, etc.

3	Question words	1	A

A pairwork activity to revise question words and personal information questions. Copy one half sheet per student.

> **LANGUAGE**
> Question words   Mixed tense questions and answers
> *Really?*

- Give each student a copy (or one per pair). Focus on the question words. SS use them to complete the questions. Do the first example, showing them that they should cross out each question word as they use it (~~Where~~).

- Check answers. Drill to encourage them to ask the questions quickly with correct stress (i.e. stressing the important words), and using weak forms for *do you, are you*, etc.

> **2** Who   **3** What kind   **4** What time   **5** Why
> **6** When   **7** How often   **8** Which   **9** How many
> **10** How much   **11** What   **12** What

- SS in pairs, **A** and **B**. **A** puts his / her sheet face down and **B** asks all the questions. Then they swap roles and **A** asks the questions in a different order.

  Tip Encourage SS to react to their partner's answers with *Really?* etc. and ask follow-up questions where they can. This way the activity becomes a series of mini-conversations.

- Ask each student to feedback with one interesting fact about their partner, e.g. *Marcos doesn't drink beer or wine.*

4 | Find your way round *English File*   **1 A**

A reading activity to help SS get to know the **Student's Book** and **Workbook**. Copy one set of questions per pair (or one set per student if setting it for homework).

- In pairs, SS read questions 1 to 12 about the **Student's Book** and look through the book to find the answers. Set a time limit, e.g. eight minutes, but give SS longer if necessary so they can get to know the book.
- With the class, check answers, and highlight and explain the different sections of the book.
- Repeat the procedure with the questions 13 to 20 about the **Workbook**, with another time limit of, e.g. five minutes.

Tip Encourage SS to keep their Workbooks in a ring file together with their lesson notes and photocopies (see **WB** *p. 2*).

> **Student's Book**
> **1** 9   **2** 2 to 7   **3** 9
> **4** no (after Files 1 to 8 but not after File 9)   **5** 9
> **6** listening, reading, speaking   **7** 6   **8** 126 to 131
> **9** 132–3   **10** 11   **11** 141   **12** 143
>
> **Workbook**
> **13** Vocabulary review   **14** i–viii   **15** 8   **16** 70–80
> **17** 25   **18** the Sound bank, sounds and spelling
> **19** 4   **20** 87

5 | How often do you …?   **1 B**

A pairwork activity. Words and pictures to prompt questions and answers with *How often* + adverbs / expressions of frequency. Copy one sheet per pair and cut into **A** and **B**.

> **LANGUAGE**
> *How often do you* (go to church)?   *Every day | week*
> (*About*) *once | twice | three times a day | week*
> *hardly ever | never   What about you?   It depends*

- Ask individual SS *How often do you* (*come to class, go to the cinema*)? Elicit possible answers, e.g. *once a week, hardly ever*, etc. Drill pronunciation of the question.
- SS in pairs, **A** and **B**. Give out the copies. Get them to focus on the expressions of frequency in the box.
- Get one pair to demonstrate the activity first like this:
  - **A** *How often do you buy flowers?*
  - **B** *Not very often. About once a year. For my mother's birthday. What about you?*
- SS take turns to ask and answer.

Tip Encourage SS to react to their partner's answers with *Really?* etc. and ask follow-up questions where they can, e.g. *Why (not)?*

6 | Are you stressed?   **1 C**

A questionnaire to practise past tense *Did you …?* questions and to measure SS stress levels. Copy one sheet per student.

> **LANGUAGE**
> Regular and irregular past tense forms
> *Did you* (sleep well)? *Yes I did. | No I didn't.*

- Give each student a copy and tell them to fold back the scoring system so they can't read it yet.
- Read the introductory questions and then go through the survey questions, checking that SS know the vocabulary and eliciting the infinitive form for each verb. Tell SS that the questionnaire refers to 'yesterday'.

Tip These questions should be asked about a working day, i.e. a weekday, so try not to do the activity on a Monday!

- Go through the first three or four questions with the SS so that they get used to changing the past tense form (e.g. *slept*) to the infinitive in the question. (The verbs they need to change are in italics.) Elicit the short answers *Yes, (I did). | No, (I didn't)*.
- **1** In pairs, SS interview each other and tick or cross the boxes. Get **A** to do the interview first, and then swap.
- **2** At the end of the interviews SS calculate their partner's score.
- **3** Then they tell each other what the score means.
- Feedback and ask *Who is very stressed?*

Tip Encourage SS to ask follow-up questions e.g.
  - **A** *Did you get angry?*
  - **B** *Yes, I did.*
  - **A** *Why? | Who with?*

- If you have time, at the end you could get the class to interview you and note down your total points.

7 | Find somebody who …   **1 D**

A class mingle activity. SS find somebody in the class who has done each thing and ask *What's it like?* Copy one grid per student.

> **LANGUAGE**
> *Have you been skiing?   Yes, I have. | No, I haven't.*
> *What's it like?*

- Before copying, complete 9 and 10 with locally relevant questions, e.g. (*Find somebody who*) *has been to* (a popular local place), *seen* (a current film), *done* (a dangerous sport), or something fun like *milked a cow, ridden a camel*, etc.
- Give out the copies. SS complete the prompts with past participles. Check answers.

> **2** tried (or eaten)   **3** been to   **4** seen   **5** played
> **6** read   **7** had   **8** heard

- Explain *Find somebody who* … Elicit questions 1 to 10, e.g. *Have you tried Indian food?*
- Demonstrate the activity. Write on the board a question not in the list, e.g. *Have you drunk coconut milk?* Ask individual SS until somebody answers *Yes, I have.* Write their name on the board next to the question. Then ask *What's it like?* Write up their answer next to the name, e.g. *lovely.*

- Tell all SS to stand up and move around asking questions to find somebody in the class for each of the things on the list (preferably a different student for each question). When they find somebody who answers *Yes* they must ask *What's it like?* and note their name and answer.
- When one student has completed their list, stop the activity.
- Feedback. Ask *Who has been skiing?* etc. Ask what SS think of it. You may need to teach the form *Nobody (in the class) has …*

| 8 | At the airport | 1 | 🧳 |

A pairwork information gap activity. Orally, SS have to find ten differences between two similar pictures of an airport.

> **LANGUAGE**
> Present continuous: *They're checking in / wearing, kissing,* etc.   *There is / are*
> Airport signs / facilities: *departures / arrivals board, check in / information desk, passport control, gate*
> Locations: *in the corner, in front / behind, on the left / right*
> Numbers, alphabet, time

- Revise describing people by asking SS to describe what you're wearing / doing.
- SS in pairs. Give out copies and sit **A** and **B** so they can't see each other's picture. Pre-teach all the words by asking *What can you see (on the left / in the corner,* etc.)? Avoid giving away any of the differences.
- Explain the activity. SS describe their pictures to find ten differences between the two pictures, but only look at their own copy.
- Demonstrate how to find differences by playing the parts of both **A** and **B**, e.g. **A** *In my picture, the next plane is from Athens. It arrives at 14.35.* **B** *In my picture, it says that it arrives at 14.25. And it's delayed,* etc.
- In pairs, SS find and circle the ten differences.

  Tip Fast finishers can compare their pictures and write down some of the differences.

- Finally all SS compare their pictures. Elicit the ten differences.

1 In B the Paris check-in is for Athens.
2 In B the couple are not kissing. They are just talking.
3 In B the arrivals board says Flight BA 434 arrives at 14.25.
4 In B the departures board says Flight AE602.
5 In B the departures board says Flight AE602 is boarding at Gate 13.
6 In B the toilet sign is for telephones.
7 In B the woman traveller is looking at the sign not at her watch.
8 In B the woman going to Rome has two big cases.
9 In B a woman is working at the Paris/Athens check-in not a man.
10 In B the female tourist has a box on her trolley.

| 9 | Yesterday and tomorrow | 1 | Revision |

Picture prompts to give SS practice in talking about what they did / didn't do yesterday and what they are / aren't going to do tomorrow. Copy one page per student (or pair of SS).

> **LANGUAGE**
> *Yesterday I got up late. I didn't have breakfast.* etc.
> *Tomorrow I'm going to go shopping. I'm not going to have lunch at home.*
> *What / How about you?*

- Give out the sheet and elicit the verbs.

1	get up early	11	meet a friend
2	have breakfast	12	clean the house
3	buy a newspaper	13	wash your hair
4	have lunch at home	14	read a book
5	go shopping	15	listen to music
6	watch TV	16	do sport
7	study English	17	cook the dinner
8	see a film	18	go swimming
9	have a bath	19	speak English
10	go for a walk	20	go to bed late

- SS in pairs, **A** and **B**. **A** goes through the pictures and tells **B** what he / she did / didn't do yesterday. **B** listens and asks questions, e.g.
  A *I bought a magazine.*
  B *Which magazine did you buy?*
- They swap roles and repeat the procedure.
- Tell them to look at the sheet together and say which of the things they're going to do tomorrow, e.g.
  A *I'm going to see a film tomorrow. What about you?*
  B *I'm not. I'm going to go to work.*

  Tell SS they don't need to talk about all the pictures, only those which they are going to do.

  Tip You can also use this to drill questions. Cut up the pictures and put them in an envelope. SS pick a card and ask *Did you have a bath yesterday?* or *Are you going to have a bath tomorrow?* They can also change time phrases, e.g. *next / last weekend.*

| 10 | Have you ever …? | 2 | A |

A class mingle activity to contrast the present perfect and past simple tenses. SS practise with question prompts. Copy and cut up one sheet per class. (If you have more than fourteen SS, give some cards to pairs of SS or invent some more questions and write them on pieces of paper.)

> **LANGUAGE**
> *Have you ever …?* + past participles
> *Yes, I have. / No, I haven't.*
> Past and present tense follow-up questions
> Past tense ⊞ and ⊟ forms.

- Give a card to each student and tell them to memorize the questions. Check they all understand their questions.

- Tell SS they are going to do a class survey with their question. They have to ask every student their question. When a student answers *Yes, I have.* they must ask the follow-up questions. They don't have to write the answers, but should try to remember to report back at the end.
- SS mingle and ask the questions. Monitor and help.

Tip If you have an uneven number of SS, join in yourself with a question so that SS always have someone to talk to.

- Feedback. Get SS to sit down, then ask each one *What was your question? How many people said yes? Were there any interesting answers?*

11 | What do they have to do? 2 | B

A pairwork activity. SS describe jobs with *He / She has to …* Copy one sheet per pair (or each).

> **LANGUAGE**
> *He / She has to / doesn't have to (wear a uniform).*
> Vocabulary: *serve people, practise a lot*, etc.

- Write on the board *What does a (bus-driver) have to do?* Elicit answers e.g. *He / She has to drive a bus / wear a uniform / concentrate all day / work long hours / take money / give out tickets / talk to the public*, etc. Elicit some negative answers e.g. *He doesn't have to speak languages.*
- Ask *What doesn't a bus-driver have to do?* (work in an office / speak languages, etc.).
- Give out the copies to SS in pairs. Elicit and drill the twenty jobs. Make sure they use *a / an* for all the jobs. Write any new jobs on the board with the stress marked.

1 photographer	8 footballer	15 taxi-driver
2 waiter	9 chef	16 police officer
3 interpreter	10 nurse	17 actor
4 pilot	11 teacher	18 model
5 pianist ·	12 housewife	19 bank manager
6 student	13 flight attendant	20 journalist
7 secretary	14 shop assistant	

In pairs, **A** secretly chooses a picture and makes sentences about the job with *has to / doesn't have to* e.g. *He has to wear uniform.* **B** guesses the job. They swap roles.

12 | Find twelve differences 2 | C

A pairwork information gap activity to revise descriptions. Copy one sheet per pair and cut into **A** and **B**.

> **LANGUAGE**
> *She's got long hair / hasn't got any pockets on her jacket.*
> *He's wearing / carrying …*   Clothes and jewellery

- Revise describing people by asking SS to describe what you or other SS are wearing. Remind SS of the difference between *wear* and *carry*.
- SS in pairs. Give out copies and sit **A** and **B** so they can't see each other's pictures. Explain the activity. SS describe the six models and try to find two differences for each one by looking only at their own pictures.

- Demonstrate how to find differences by playing the parts of both **A** and **B**, e.g. **A** *In my picture, the first model's wearing a long skirt.* **B** *Yes, in my picture too. And she's carrying three roses.* etc.
- In pairs, SS find and circle the differences. Tell them that they have to find twelve differences (two in each picture).

Tip Fast finishers can compare their pictures and write some of the differences.

- Finally all SS compare their pictures. Elicit the differences.

> 1 In B the woman's got straight hair and hasn't got any pockets on her jacket.
> 2 In B the woman's got a longer skirt and hasn't got any earrings.
> 3 In B the man's got normal glasses (not sunglasses) and black socks.
> 4 In B the man's got normal lace-up shoes and a T-shirt.
> 5 In B the man hasn't got a beard or a scarf.
> 6 In B the woman's got short hair and hasn't got a hat or a bag.

13 | What's the word? 2 | D

A group card game. SS practise giving definitions. Copy and cut up one set of cards per group.

> **LANGUAGE**
> *It's a verb / adjective …*   *It's a word / expression …*
> *It's the opposite of …*   *It's a kind of …*
> *It's made of …*   *It's a thing …*
> *It's like a …*   *It's something …*

- SS in small groups. Give each group a set of cards face down or in an envelope.
- Demonstrate. Pull out a picture and describe the word in as many ways as you can using the phrases from **LANGUAGE** until SS guess it. Insist they say the exact form of the word on the card, and use correct stress and pronunciation before revealing the picture.
- SS play in groups, taking turns to take a card and describe the word and picture on it. SS mustn't let anyone else see the picture or use the word on the card itself.
- The activity works better if you don't make this competitive.

Tip Groups who finish first can continue thinking of their own words.

14 | From London to Amsterdam 2 | 👜

A pairwork information gap activity. SS revise travel information questions. Copy one sheet per pair and cut into **A** and **B**.

> **LANGUAGE**
> *What time does the (train) leave (Victoria) /*
> *get to Waterloo?*   *It leaves / gets to … at (6.10).*
> *How much is a single / return ticket?*

- Ask *What do you know about Amsterdam? Have you ever been there? Would you like to go?* etc.

- Ask *How can you get there from London?* Elicit *by plane, car / bus and ferry, through the Channel Tunnel.*

- SS in pairs. Give out copies to **A** and **B**. SS sit so that they can't see each other's information.

- Elicit / explain the time difference between Britain and Europe. (Europe is an hour ahead, which is why the flight and train crossing appear long.)

- Tell SS they have to ask questions to complete their missing information. Rehearse and drill the questions in **LANGUAGE**.

- Drill the place names, and tell SS to use digital time e.g. *10.30* (= ten thirty), *12.15* (= twelve fifteen).

- Demonstrate the activity. Take the part of **A**. Ask **B** the first two questions on the **A**-sheet. Then get **B** to ask the first two questions on the **B**-sheet.

- **A** and **B** take turns to ask and answer. When they have completed their information, get them to compare brochures. Ask *Which way would you prefer to travel? Why?*

  ⚠ The single and return flights cost the same (apart from the additional airport tax for the return) because they are the same ticket.

15 | *You don't have to say you love me* | 2 | ◁▷

🔊 **20** A listening activity. SS listen and correct the words of a song by Dusty Springfield.

- **1** Play the first verse of the song. Ask *Do you know / like it? Who's the singer? Do you know anything about her?*

- Show the song text on OHT / the board. Explain the task using the first line as an example. SS listen and note the words in the song text that are different from those on tape.

- Play the song, pausing after each verse for SS to compare their words in pairs.

- **2** Play the song again. This time SS correct the wrong words and write the correct word. Re-play any lines that SS have problems with.

Verse 1	2 <u>never</u> = always 4 <u>again</u> = away
Verse 2	5 <u>know</u> = see 7 <u>go to</u> = follow
	8 <u>back</u> = home
Chorus	10 <u>heart</u> = hand 11 <u>play</u> = stay
	15 <u>hate</u> = love 16 <u>up</u> = down
Verse 3	17 <u>photograph</u> = memory 18 <u>bad</u> = dead
	20 say = feel

- Go through the song, checking meaning and teaching new vocabulary. Use the picture and **Glossary** (and SS' L1 if you can / want to) to help you.

- **3** Ask *What's the song about?* SS read the three options and choose.

c

- SS read the biography of Dusty Springfield. If your SS like singing they can sing with the tape.

16 | Interview for a job | 2 | Revision

A pairwork roleplay. Copy one sheet per pair and cut into **A** and **B**.

> **LANGUAGE**
> General revision of Files 1 and 2
> accommo<u>da</u>tion, <u>can</u>didate

- SS in pairs. Give out the copies to **A** and **B**. Focus on the advert and explain that SS are going to roleplay a job interview. Make sure SS understand what a 'summer camp' is (= a holiday camp for children, with staff employed to look after and entertain them).

- SS read their instructions 1–3. Check they understand.

- Give **A**s and **B**s three minutes to memorize their questions. **A**s should also try to memorize the information in **Conditions**.

- When they're ready SS roleplay in pairs. SS should try to ask as many of the questions as they can from memory. Remind SS to ask follow-up questions when they can.

- Monitor, but don't interrupt interviews. Make a note of any common errors and deal with them later.

- When the interviews are finished, tell the managers to decide if they are going to offer the candidates the job. If they do, tell the candidates to decide if they want the job.

- Feedback. How many candidates were offered the job? How many accepted? Why (not)?

17 | Grammar auction | 3 | A

A game where SS have to bid to buy correct sentences. Copy one list per pair.

> **LANGUAGE**
> General revision

- SS in pairs. Give each pair the list of twenty sentences. Explain that they have £1,000 to spend and have to try to 'buy' the correct sentences in an auction. Some of the sentences are correct, some incorrect. If they think a sentence is correct, they can bid to buy it. They then record the price they have paid for each sentence on the forms.

- Bids starts at £50, the second bid is £100, then £150, etc.

- The pair that buy the most correct sentences with their £1,000 are the winners. So, if one pair spends all their money on one sentence they are unlikely to win.

- To demonstrate, write example sentences on the board, e.g. *Whose is that sweater black? I live in my parent's flat.* Invite bids. Make it more fun by using typical language of an auctioneer, e.g. *How much am I offered for this sentence? Going, going, gone to the pair in the corner.* etc. If nobody bids for a sentence (because they know it's wrong), quickly elicit the error and move on to the next one.

- Feedback, going through sentences, confirming if they are right or wrong. Who bought the most correct sentences?
  Adapted from Grammar games, Mario Rinvolucri, OUP 1984.

| 2 ~~gone~~ been   4 ~~have~~ has   7   husband's sister |
| 10 ~~which~~ who   11 ~~never~~ ever   13 ~~'ve~~ have |
| 15 ~~the~~   16   theirs   18 ~~to~~   19   does the train leave? |

| 18 | Where are you going on holiday? | 3 | B |

A class mingle activity. SS choose from a variety of holiday options then try to find somebody who's made exactly the same choice. Make one copy per student.

> **LANGUAGE**
> Present continuous (future)   Travel verbs
> Holiday facilities

- **1** Give each student a copy. Focus on the photos. Ask *What can you see?* (tropical beach, palm trees, temples, etc.).
- SS read the adverts. Elicit / teach *island*, *tropical*, *water sports*, *luxury*, *Dep.* (= Departure), *accommodation*, *double-decker bus*, *campsite*.
- SS read the five questions and individually make their choices.

  Tip Highlight all the options: the choice of destination, departure dates, airlines, and accommodation.

- **2** Demonstrate what they have to do, following the example. Ask a student the five questions from **1** to see if their chosen holiday details are the same as yours. As soon as you get a different answer, move on to another student.
- SS do the same, first with the SS next to them, then by standing up and moving around the class. Make sure SS use the present continuous, *by* + transport, *on* + date, *at* + hotel name.
- If SS quickly find somebody with exactly the same holiday details, tell them to find as many other people as they can.
- Feedback. Ask *Who found a partner? Which was the most popular holiday?*

| 19 | How long does it take? | 3 | C |

A pairwork information gap activity about journey times. Copy one sheet per pair and cut into **A** and **B**.

> **LANGUAGE**
> *How long does it take to get to …?   It takes …*

- Tell SS to imagine they're in London on holiday for ten days. Ask them what other cities in Britain and Ireland they'd like to visit and why.
- **1** Give out the copies to **A** and **B**. SS sit so that they can't see each other's information. Focus on the map and the place names. Drill pronunciation, especially Edinburgh /ˈedɪnbrə/, and Brighton /ˈbraɪtn/. Find out if SS know anything about the places or have visited them.
- Focus on the symbols and elicit that they represent *by train*, *coach*, and *plane*. Make sure they know that all the journey times are from London. Elicit the meaning of *ferry crossing*.
- **2** Elicit **A**'s first question *How long does it take to get to Bath by train?* and **B**'s *How long does it take to get to Bath by coach?* SS continue in pairs.

  Tip Tell SS to ask questions in *any* order, to make their partner listen.

- When SS have finished, get them to decide where they would like to visit and how they would get there.

| 20 | How Sally met Harry | 3 | D |

A pairwork split reading. Copy one sheet per pair and cut into **A** and **B**.

> **LANGUAGE**
> Past simple and past continuous

- In pairs, give out the copies to **A** and **B**. Tell them to read their instructions. Check that they know what to do.
- **1** Give SS two minutes to read and remember. (**A** reads Part 1 and **B** Part 2.)
- Elicit / pre-teach *disc jockey* (= DJ), *accident*, *hit*, and *strange*.
- **B** asks **A** *How did Sally and Harry meet?* **A** answers, and then asks *What happened next?* Monitor, encouraging SS to answer from memory and not to read out their answers.
- **2** SS repeat with parts 3 and 4 of the story.
- **3** In pairs, they try to work out exactly how Harry died.
- Feedback. Sally hit him when he was crossing the road but she didn't stop. Ask *Do you like the story? Why (not)?*

| 21 | Hotel check-in | 3 | |

Role-cards for pairwork. **A** and **B** are a traveller and a receptionist. Copy one sheet per pair and cut into **A** and **B**.

> **LANGUAGE**
> **1** *How much is a (single) room? Can I pay by credit card? Is there a (TV)? What time's breakfast?*
> **2** *My TV doesn't work. My room's too noisy.*

- Elicit / revise the **LANGUAGE** for both situations. Ask *What do you say if you want to pay by credit card?* etc.

  Tip Alternatively use a 'deep-end' approach. Let SS do it once, monitor, then correct the mistakes that you heard before they swap roles and do it again 'perfectly', having learnt from their mistakes.

- SS in pairs, **A** and **B**. Give out the role-cards. Give SS time to read them and answer any questions. Tell them to role-play both situations, i.e. when **A** has finished checking in (**1**), he / she phones immediately with the problem (**2**).
- In pairs, **B** begins both conversations of the roleplay, with *Good evening, can I help you?* in the first and *Hello, Reception, can I help you?* in the second. Get one pair to demonstrate.
- If time, get SS to swap roles, but tell **B** to choose a different problem or put other problems on the board for SS who finish first, e.g. *The pool is empty. The car park is full.* etc.

| 22 | *Don't you want me baby?* | 3 | ◁▷ |

⌐20⌐ A listening / reading activity based on a song by The Human League.

- Play the first verse of the song. Ask *Do you know this song? Do you know who it is by? What year is it from?*
- Show the song text on OHT / the board. Explain the task. Elicit that she's a waitress and he's a manager, and that he's making her a star.

- **1** In pairs, SS read and answer the clues. They complete the song from the clues. Monitor and help with spelling if necessary, but don't tell them the answers yet.
- **2** Play the song for SS to check their answers.

1 waitress	**2** new	**3** feet	**4** forget	**5** hear
6 late	**7** sorry	**8** waitress	**9** true	**10** better
11 years	**12** love			

- Play the song again. Tell SS to listen and read it with the **Glossary**.
- Ask *What's the song about?* (a woman was working in a bar when she met a man – he helped her to become famous but then she left him – he wants her to come back but she wants to be independent).
- Tell SS to read about *The Human League* and the origin of the song. If they like singing they can sing with the tape.

23 | Revision conversations | 3 | Revision

Question cards in topic groups for speaking practice of all known tenses. Copy and cut up one set of cards per pair.

> **LANGUAGE**
> Questions and answers: past, present, and future
> Personal information

- Tell SS the object of the activity is to ask and answer as many questions as they can to revise **Files 1–3**. Demonstrate by taking a card and asking one student the questions, plus any others which naturally arise from his / her answers.
- SS in pairs. Give each pair a set face down. Give a time limit, e.g. 10 to 15 minutes. SS take turns to take a card and ask their partner the questions. Encourage SS to ask follow-up questions. Monitor, help, and correct.

> **Tip** If you don't want to make cards, copy one sheet per student. **B** puts his sheet face down. **A** chooses a group and asks **B** the questions. They swap roles. You can also use this activity as the basis of an oral test (see *p. 212*). You could even give the sheet to SS the lesson before you intend to use it in class to encourage them to revise!

24 | *Easy Reader* reviews | 3 | 🔍

Book review forms. SS can complete these after reading *Easy Readers*. Copy one form per student.

> **LANGUAGE**
> Types of book   Writing a brief description of the story
> (present tense)   Adjectives of opinion

> **Tip** If you're going to encourage regular reading and reviewing, make spare copies and keep them with your register to give out when necessary.

- Give each student a form and go through it with them. Highlight that they should answer *What's it about?* in the present tense.
- Tell SS to complete the form after they've finished their first reader.

- Collect the forms in and remind SS regularly of them. Keep a record of the books SS have read (see **Activity 25** below). You could set reading and reviewing (e.g. three books) as part of their evaluation.

> **Tip** When you've got several completed forms, find five minutes at the beginning / end of a class to pass them round for SS to read each other's opinions of the books they've read. Get SS to recommend books to each other.

25 | *English File* reading chart | 3 | 🔍

A chart to use with *Easy Readers*. SS record their progress and opinions. If you have more than eight SS, copy the chart twice.

- Put the chart on the classroom wall. Explain to the class that it's for them to write their names, the title of the readers they've read, and an opinion in the boxes (from 1 to 3) to guide other SS.
- Set SS a realistic goal, e.g. to read three readers a term, etc. Monitor regularly and use it in combination with **Activity 24** above.

> **Tip** Write each class name clearly at the top. If you don't always have the same classroom, keep the chart with your register and pass it round once a fortnight for SS to add to.

26 | Compare the pairs | 4 | A

A pair or team game. SS race to write comparative sentences. Copy and cut up one set of cards for each pair (or group).

> **LANGUAGE**
> Comparative adjectives, *as … as*
> *is better… / is worse than …*
> *Travelling by car isn't as fast as travelling by plane.*

- SS in pairs or threes / fours.
- Shuffle the cards and give each pair / group a set, face down.
- SS take a card and write two different sentences comparing the things on the card, one with a comparative and one with *as … as*. They must use a different adjective in each sentence.
- When they've finished, one student from the pair / group shows you their card and sentences. If they are correct, they continue with another card. If not, they have to go back and correct or change the sentences.

> **Tip** Help SS to correct sentences by telling them if the mistake is spelling, grammar, or vocabulary. They can do this activity again later in the course for revision.

- The first pair / group to finish the cards is the winner.

27 | If … | 4 | B

A board game. SS move round the board making conditional sentences. Copy one game board per group.

> **LANGUAGE**
> First conditional: *If you go to bed late, you'll be tired tomorrow morning.*

- SS in threes / fours. They need markers (e.g. paper clips, bits of paper, or small coins) and a coin to toss.

- Each player puts his marker on the 'start' square. (As it's an advantage to start ,the order of starting can be decided by the order of SS' birthdays.)
- S1 tosses the coin. *Heads* = move two squares,
  Tails = move one square.
- S1 now has to make a correct conditional sentence by completing the sentence stem on the square where he / she lands. The rest of the group have to decide if the sentence is correct and makes sense. Be the final judge in case of dispute.
- If the sentence is wrong, S1 moves back a square. If it is correct, he / she stays on the square.
- If another student lands on the same square they can't repeat S1's sentence.
- The first student to reach the end of the board is the winner.

28 | Odysseus and the Cyclops | 4 | C

A read-and-order story with pictures for re-telling. Copy one sheet per student (or pair).

> **LANGUAGE**
> Past simple

- Before giving out the sheets ask *What do you remember about Odysseus from* **File 3C**? Ask *Can you remember any of the places he went to on his way home?* Now tell SS to read the story of what happened on the Cyclops island.
- 1 Hand out the sheets. In pairs, SS read the story and number the paragraphs in order. Tell them to use the pictures to help them (they're in the right order).
- 2 SS complete the **Glossary**.
- Check answers.

Tip If time, get SS to cover the text and use the pictures to re-tell the story in their own words.

> 1 D 2 H 3 C 4 F 5 A 6 E 7 G 8 B
> **Glossary** exhausted sheep giant cave
> blind (*v.*) blind (*adj.*) hid

29 | Do you agree? | 4 | D

A group activity in which SS give their opinions about entertainment. Copy and cut up one sheet per group.

Tip If teaching in the UK, use only **The cinema** and **Music** and not **TV and radio** as they may not know enough to agree and disagree with each other. Depending on where you are teaching, tell the SS to either talk about international actors / singers / films, etc. or limit their discussion to their own country (good for mono-lingual classes).

> **LANGUAGE**
> Superlative adjectives: *the funniest, the most intelligent*, etc.
> Agreeing / disagreeing: *Presenter, newsreader* etc.

- SS in groups of three.
- Demonstrate the activity first. Tell SS *I think the best programme on TV is ...* Elicit agreement / disagreement (*I agree / I think so too*, etc.). If SS disagree, ask *Which programme do you think is the best?*

- Give out a different section to each student in the group. Elicit / teach *programme, comedy, stupid, presenter, newsreader, radio station, disc jockey, soundtrack, decade.* SS complete the sentences.
- S1 reads out his / her first sentence. S2 and S3 agree or disagree and give their opinions.
- Monitor, and join in agreeing / disagreeing with SS.
- Get feedback on any major agreements / disagreements.

30 | Going out for dinner | 4 |

A facsimile menu to use for an extended role-play. Copy two menus and one role-card per group.

> **LANGUAGE**
> *What would you like ...? I'll have ...   Can I have ...?*

- Revise the phrases from 4 . Ask *What does the waiter say?* (*Are you ready to order? What would you like?* etc.)
- SS in threes / fours. One from each group is the waiter.

Tip If possible, arrange the chairs in 'tables'. Give the waiters two menus each (one to give the customers and one to use to calculate the bill), and some paper and a pencil to take the orders. The other SS go out of the class in their groups.

- Each group comes into the class and asks their waiter for a table, and a menu. Check they understand the menu. Give definitions to explain *avocado, cocktail, vanilla, soft drinks, rosé, VAT* (= Value Added Tax).
- While the customers are reading the menu to decide what they want, give the waiters their rolecards to read. Then the waiters take the orders and bring the meals.

Tip Encourage SS to complain if there are any problems when they receive their meals.

- When they have ordered all courses, drinks, etc. the customers should ask for the bill. Get the waiters to add up the bill (using their menu). At the same time the customers work out what they think the bill should be.
- The waiter gives the customers the bill. If the customers think it is wrong they should say so.
- Feedback. Ask for marks out of ten for the waiters.

31 | Talk for a minute | 4 | Revision

A board game to prompt free speaking.

> **LANGUAGE**
> Revision of language from **Files 1 to 4**.

- SS in fours. They need markers (e.g. paper clips, bits of paper, or small coins) and a coin.
- Each player puts his marker on a different start square. As it's an advantage to start first, tell SS to start, e.g. in the alphabetical order of their names or surnames, or draw lots.
- S1 tosses the coin. *Heads* = move two squares,
  Tails = move one square.
- He / she has to try to talk for at least a minute about the topic on the square.

Tip Tell SS not to be too strict about the time limit. What's important is to say as much as they can on each topic.

- Other SS should listen and help, or ask more questions. Emphasize that it doesn't matter if SS make mistakes – the important thing is to keep talking.
- SS take turns tossing the coin and talking for a minute.
- Monitor and note the kinds of mistakes SS are making, but don't interrupt and correct.
- If SS land on 'Have another go' they toss the coin and move forward one or two squares.
- The winner is the first person to do a complete circuit of the board and return to their own 'Finish' square.

32 | Who's going to get promotion? | 5 A

A pairwork information gap activity. Copy one sheet per pair and cut into A and B.

> **LANGUAGE**
> *How long has he / she …?*
> *He's / She's worked there for / since …*

- SS in pairs, facing each other. SS read the introduction. Elicit / teach *employees* and *promote* / *get promotion*.
- 1 SS read their instructions. They have to ask their partner questions to complete the missing information.
- Demonstrate. Ask As *What's your first question?* and get the Bs to answer them. Ask Bs *What's your first question?* and get the As to answer them. Make sure SS know they have to answer the *How long …?* questions with *for* or *since*, according to the information they have. They may also need to spell the jobs.
- 2 When they've both completed their charts get them to work out who's going to get promoted. (This will depend on what the year is when you do this activity.)

33 | *I want to break free* | 5 B

∘ 6 ∘ A listening / reading activity based on a song by Queen.

- Play a few seconds of the song and ask *Who's it by? What's it called?* Elicit anything SS know about Queen and their music.
- Read the biographical information about the group. Help with vocabulary.
- Focus on the picture. Elicit that it represents *break free*.
- 1 Show the song text on OHT / the board. Focus on the jumbled words. In pairs, SS re-order the letters to make words, following the example. Don't write them until they've listened and checked.
- 2 Play the song once. SS listen and check. Check answers.

> need   love   time   true   sure   want   life   side   live

- 3 Play the song again. SS listen and read.
- Focus on the sentences. SS mark them (T) or (F).
- Check answers.

> They're all true.

- If your SS like singing they can sing with the tape.
  Thanks to Michael O'Brien for the idea of using conundrums with songs.

34 | An Indian legend | 5 B

A reading and predicting activity. Copy one sheet per student (or pair).

> **LANGUAGE**
> Verbs + *to* + infinitive: *wanted to, decided to*
> Past (simple and continuous)

- Give each student a copy. Make sure they have a piece of paper to cover the story before they start reading.
- SS cover all the text and focus on picture. Ask *What can you see?* and elicit / teach <u>Indian</u>, <u>legend</u> (= old story), <u>canoe</u> /kəˈnuː/, *lake*, (*full*) *moon*, <u>forest</u>.
- SS uncover and read only the first paragraph, up to the question *What was he hoping to do?*
- Focus on the question and elicit several suggestions (someone will almost certainly get the answer right). SS then uncover and read the next paragraph to see if they were right.
- Read the paragraph together as far as *Who did he see?* Elicit SS' suggestions before uncovering to see if they were right.
- Continue, getting SS to read and predict the whole story. When you come to *What name did they give to the lake?* get as many suggestions as possible (e.g. Lake Black Eagle, Lake Nakoma, Lake Love, Lake Death). Then tell SS that, according to the legend, it was named *Lake Stupid*!

Tip If time, SS can take turns to re-tell the story from memory while their partner listens, helps and prompts.

35 | Finish the sentences | 5 C

A group activity. SS race to complete sentences. Copy and cut up one sheet per group.

> **LANGUAGE**
> *so, because*   Past and present tenses

- SS in small groups (four or five). Give each group a set of cards, either face down or in an envelope.
- Each group picks up a card, thinks of a way to correctly finish the sentence and completes it. As soon as they've done so they give the card to the teacher who checks if it is correct. If it's correct, add one point to that group's score. If it isn't they must rewrite the sentence.
- Set a time limit (e.g. eight minutes). When the time is up the group who has given you most correct sentences wins.

Tip You could do this as a competition between pairs. Give one sheet to each pair. The pair who makes the most sentences within a time limit wins.

36 | Hollywood quiz | 5 | D

A team quiz about American cinema. Copy one sheet per pair and cut into **A** and **B**.

> **LANGUAGE**
> Past simple subject / object questions: *Who directed Psycho? / When did Hitchcock die?*

- Divide the class into two teams, **A** and **B**. Give each student a copy of his / her question sheet.

  Tip With a large class, you could have two **A** teams and two **B** teams.

- In pairs, SS write the questions.
- One student from team **A** asks question 1, without giving the three options for the answer (the option in **bold** is the correct answer).
  - If team **B** can answer the question correctly, they get two points.
  - If not, team **A** now gives them the three options. If they choose the right answer they get one point.

  ⚠ Help SS with correct pronunciation, but don't worry too much about the proper names.
- A student from team **B** now asks their first question.
- Keep the scores to find the winner.

  Tip You could get SS to ask more questions at the end or write one each for homework to play again next lesson.

37 | Could you tell me the way to …? | 5 | 🧳

A pairwork information gap activity to practise asking for and giving directions. Copy one sheet per pair and cut into **A** and **B**.

> **LANGUAGE**
> *Excuse me, …   Could you tell me the way to …?*
> *Take the first turning on the right.* etc.

- Quickly revise the language of giving directions in **Travel phrasebook 5** (**SB** *p. 133*).
- SS in pairs, **A** and **B**, facing each other. Give out the copies, and give SS time to read their instructions and look at their map.
- Both have different places missing from their maps.
- Explain to SS that the five shaded buildings are marked on both maps, so they can use them as points of reference. SS give directions from the point of view of the two people on the map.
- **A** begins, and asks **B** the way to the first place on his / her list. **B** directs **A**, and when **A** thinks he / she has found the building he / she labels it. **B** now asks **A** for directions. Monitor, help and correct. Make sure the student asking always begins *Excuse me. Could you tell me the way to …?*
- When they finish, SS compare maps to check they have all the places labelled correctly.

38 | Eva Perón – *Evita* | 5 | ◁▷

A gapped reading activity based on a biography of Eva Perón. Copy one sheet per student (or pair).

⚠ Don't forget to take the **Teacher's Book** to class for the answers!

> **LANGUAGE**
> Past simple questions.
> Biography expressions: *be born, get married,* etc.

- Before giving out the copies, elicit anything SS know about Eva Perón.
- SS in pairs / small groups. Give them each a copy.
- **1** Read the biography with the class, ignoring the gaps, and elicit / explain *officer, army, mistress, popularity, worker, treated, Foundation, Vice, cancer, funeral, ambition, exhibition, equivalent.*
- **2** In pairs, SS focus on the gaps and complete the questions they need to ask to get the missing information (1 to 10). Monitor to see what errors they're making but don't correct yet.
- **3** When they've finished, pairs take turns to ask you the questions.

  Tip To make the rest of the class listen carefully, ask *Is that question right?* Elicit any alternatives each time before you write it on the board. Then give the correct answer for them to write in.
- Pairs should award themselves a mark for each correct question. Check who has the highest mark at the end.

> **Questions and answers**
> 1 When **was** Eva **born**? **May 7th 1919**
> 2 **Where did** Magaldi **take** her?   **Buenos Aires**
> 3 **When did she meet** Juan Perón?   **1943**
> 4 How **old was** Perón?   **48**
> 5 **When did** Perón **become** President?   **1946**
> 6 **Where did** Eva **go** in 1947?   **Europe**
> 7 How **many hours did** she **work** a day?   **14 or 15**
> 8 Why **didn't she** become Vice President?   **She fell ill.**
> 9 **When did** she **die**?   **26th July 1951**
> 10 How **many suits** and dresses **did** she **have**? **400**

Tip If time at the end, SS can turn over their copies and remember all they can about her orally.

39 | *May and June* | 5 | Revision

An adaptation of a short story by Ruth Rendell for SS to read in paragraphs. Copy one sheet per student.

> **LANGUAGE**
> Past simple and present perfect

- Elicit what SS remember about Ruth Rendell.
- Give each student a copy. Make sure they have a piece of paper to cover the story before they start reading.
- SS uncover and read only paragraph 1. Ask (or write on the board) *What do you know about May, June, and Walter?* Elicit answers. Tell SS not to look at the text and answer from memory. Then ask *What's going to happen next?*

- Do the same with the other paragraphs, uncovering and reading them one by one, then asking the following questions after each (plus *What's going to happen next?*):
  1 Why didn't May get married?
  2 Why did she read June's letters?
  3 What happened when May's parents died? What happened when Walter died?
  4 Why was May happy for the first time?
  5 What happened one night? What did May do? What did June do?
  6 What exactly do you think happened next?

- Deal with any vocabulary problems after each paragraph.

- At the end, get the class to react to the story, e.g. *Were you surprised by the ending? Can you understand May?* etc.

40 | Free-time activities | 6 A

A pairwork activity. SS use picture prompts to talk about free-time activities. Copy one sheet per student.

> **LANGUAGE**
> Gerunds: *I enjoy reading novels.   I don't like gardening. Doing exercise is boring.*

- Give a copy of the pictures to each student. Elicit what the first activity is (collecting stamps). In pairs, they list the names of the other activities, 1 to 20. Tell SS to use a verb in the gerund and to leave any they're not sure of.

  Tip Tell SS not to write on the page but on a sheet of paper so they have to remember the names later.

- Check answers. Drill pronunciation, especially *climbing* /klaɪmɪŋ/. Teach *DIY*.

1 collecting stamps	11 doing DIY (= Do It Yourself)
2 taking photos	12 listening to music
3 climbing	13 reading
4 walking	14 painting
5 shopping	15 going to the theatre
6 gardening	16 watching TV
7 fishing	17 travelling
8 doing sport	18 doing nothing
9 going to art galleries	19 dancing
10 cooking	20 playing cards

- In pairs, SS talk about the activities. Encourage them to say if they *like / love / hate / don't mind* each activity and why. Tell SS to say *I never go fishing.* or *I've never climbed (but I'd like to).* for activities they haven't experienced.

- Demonstrate by talking about some of them. Elicit a few questions from the class with some prompts on the board, e.g. *Why? When? How often? Who / with? How long have you been …? When was the last time?* etc.

- Set a time limit and SS begin talking. Encourage SS to ask follow-up questions whenever they can.

- When SS have finished or your time limit is up, get them to write down their three favourite activities and their least favourite.

- Feedback, to find out which activities are the most / least popular in the class.

41 | Are you a good matchmaker? | 6 B

A pairwork information gap activity. SS complete information about a friend. Copy and give one form to each student.

> **LANGUAGE**
> *What's he / she like?   What does he do?* etc.   Star signs

- Elicit / teach the meaning of <u>matchmaker</u> (someone who brings people together romantically, often by introducing them).

- **1** Tell SS to think of one of their friends who's single, and would like to meet a partner. If they can't think of anyone, they can write about any person they know well who would like a new partner. They fill in the form for him / her.
  ⚠ Try to make sure there's a mix of men and women by telling half the class to fill in the form for a man and the other half for a woman.

- Go through the form and elicit the questions SS need to ask to find out about other students' friends.

  What's his / her name?
  How old is he / she?
  What does he / she do?
  Does he / she smoke?
  Is he / she interested in politics? etc.
  What does he / she look like
  What does she do in her free time?
  What's she like?

- **2** Set a time limit, e.g. ten minutes. SS try to find a 'partner' for their friend by interviewing other SS about their person to decide if they think the two people would be a good match.

  Tip Encourage SS to 'market' their friend, but they should be honest about any defects or possible incompatibilities!

- Get SS to interview as many people as possible and then decide on the best match for their friend.

- Get feedback to see how many SS have found a good match for their friend.

42 | Food, food, food! | 6 C

A pairwork activity. SS ask and answer questions about food and cooking. Copy one sheet per student.

> **LANGUAGE**
> Quantifier: (*not*) *much / many, a little,* etc.
> Food and cooking vocabulary

- Give out a copy each and tell the class to interview you. Individual SS ask you the questions. Drill pronunciation problems, e.g. *foreign* /fɒrən/, *vegetarian, speciality*. Illustrate a range of language in your answers, especially to question 8, e.g. *quite / not a lot, just a bit, too much,* etc.

- SS in pairs. **A** asks **B** question 1. **B** answers and says *What about you?* Then **B** asks question 2.

  Alternatively **A** could ask **B** all the questions first (**B** mustn't look at the questions) then swap, with **B** asking **A** the questions in a different order.

- Feedback to find out any interesting findings, e.g. who has the healthiest diet, what people's specialities are, etc.

43 | Talk about television | 6 | D

A pairwork activity about television. Copy one sheet per student.

> **LANGUAGE**
> *There's / there are too much / many, not enough*
> Types of TV programme: *soap operas, documentaries,* etc.

- Give out a copy each and focus on the TV screens. Ask *What kind of programmes do you think they are?* List them on the board with the stress marked (a docu<u>men</u>tary, a car<u>toon</u>, a quiz <u>pro</u>gramme, a soap <u>op</u>era). Elicit examples of soap operas.
- Quickly go through questions 1 to 7 to make sure SS understand them. Check the SS know the meaning and pronunciation of all the programme types in question 7.
- Ask *For which of the items in question 7 do we say 'There's too much …' and 'There's not enough …?'* (i.e. if they're uncountable: *music, violence,* and *sport*). Tell SS to mark them 'U' so they remember.
- SS in pairs. A asks B questions 1 to 5. Then they swap and B asks A the same five questions. Make sure neither listener can see the paper when they're being interviewed.

  Tip For SS in the UK who haven't been there long, get them to talk about the TV in their countries.

- SS answer questions 6 and 7 together in pairs, taking turns to make sentences about each topic, followed by *What about you?* Monitor, help, and correct as necessary.
- Feedback any interesting answers, especially to question 6.
- SS could write up their opinions of TV in their country as a composition for homework.

44 | I'd like my money back! | 6 | 🧳

Two roleplays to practise complaining in a shop. Copy and cut one sheet per pair and cut into A and B.

> **LANGUAGE**
> *The … doesn't work. The zip's broken.*
> *Could I change it / them? Could I have my money back?*

- Tell SS that they're going to do two roleplays, one as a customer and one as a shop assistant. They should read their instructions for **Roleplay 1** only. A is the customer first and B the shop assistant.
- Check that SS understand their instructions. Elicit that the shop assistant starts the conversation with *Can I help you?* Elicit other phrases the customer needs, e.g. *The flash doesn't work. Could I have my money back, please?* etc. Tell them that they must continue the conversation until the customer is satisfied. Tell them that this is a fluency activity and not to worry about their mistakes.
- Monitor and help as necessary. Feedback any common mistakes before doing **Roleplay 2**.
- When SS have finished the first roleplay tell them to stop and read their instructions for **Roleplay 2**. Now A is the assistant and B the customer.
- Do **Roleplay 2**.
- Feedback. Ask *Were the customers satisfied? What did the shop assistants offer?*

45 | Too much football | 6 | Revision

An error correction exercise to revise **File 6**. Copy one sheet per student.

> **LANGUAGE**
> *too much / many, not enough   like + -ing,* quantifiers

- Ask *Do you watch sport on TV? What's your favourite programme / channel? Do you know the names of the main British TV channels?* (BBC1, BBC 2, ITV, and Channel 4).
- Check answers.
- **1** Give out copies. Tell SS to read it quickly (e.g. in a minute) and answer the questions in **1**. If they ask, tell them not to worry about mistakes in the letter at this stage.

> **1 To** the Programme controller at the BBC
>   **From** Angela Pera
> **2** too much football on TV

- **2** In pairs, SS read the letter again and underline and correct one mistake in each line, 1 to 10, as in the example.

  Tip You could ask SS to categorize the mistakes as spelling, grammar, punctuation, or word order.

- Check answers.

> 2 **doing** sport   3 **go** jogging   4 mind **watching**
> 5 too **much** football   6 too **many** programmes
> 7 **many / a lot of** people   8 isn't **enough basketball**
> 9 **much** tennis   10 **too** boring

- If you haven't been using the **Workbook**, take this opportunity to focus on stylistic features of formal letters in English (see **Read and write 2** *p. 62*).

46 | I haven't done it yet | 7 | A

A pairwork activity. SS make questions and answers with *just, yet* and *already*. Copy one sheet per pair and cut into A and B.

> **LANGUAGE**
> Present perfect + *yet / just / already*

- Demonstrate the activity before you give out the copies. Write on the board:

  > No thanks / just / have

- Ask *Would you like a Coke?* Tell SS to answer using the words on the board. (*No thanks, I've just had one.*)
- Rub out *just* and write:

  > No thanks / already / see

Ask *Would you like to see* (a film on locally) *tonight?* Elicit the phrase (*No thanks, I've already seen it.*).

- Tell SS to answer their partners' questions with the word prompts on their card in the same way. Give out copies to A and B, and give them a minute to look at their prompts.
- Get a good pair of SS to demonstrate the first two sentences to the rest of the class.
- A and B ask and answer questions alternately.

  ⚠️ Monitor for correct use of pronouns e.g. *I've just had one. / I've already seen it.*

| **47** | I went to the supermarket to … | **7** | **B** |

A board game. SS make sentences about places with *to* + infinitive. Copy one sheet per group.

> **LANGUAGE**
> *to* + infinitive   Shops / places in town

- SS in threes or fours. They need markers (paper clips, bits of paper, or small coins) and a coin. Give out the boards.
- Demonstrate the game first. Write an example sentence on the board, e.g. *I went to the bus station to …* Elicit all the different endings SS can think of, e.g. *get a bus, meet my friend, change my ticket*, etc.
- Each player puts his marker on the 'Start' square. As it's an advantage to start, the order of starting can be decided, e.g. by the number of their address, the lowest going first.
- S1 tosses the coin. *Heads* = move two squares,
                        Tails = move one square.
- S1 moves his marker. He / she then says *I went to the* (the place on the square on which he / she lands) *to …* The rest of the group listen and decide if the sentence is correct and / or makes sense. Be the final judge if there are disputes.
- If the sentence is wrong, S1 moves back a square. If it is correct, he / she stays on the square.
- SS take turns tossing the coin and making sentences. If SS land on the same square, they mustn't repeat S1's sentence.
- The first student to reach 'Home' is the winner.

| **48** | I need some advice | **7** | **C** |

A group activity to practise giving advice. Copy and cut up one sheet per group.

> **LANGUAGE**
> *I (don't) think you should …   You shouldn't …*
> *Why don't you …?   What about* (verb + *-ing*)

- SS in groups of four or five. Put a set of cards face down or in envelopes, and give one to each group.
- S1 takes out a card and reads out his / her situation. Each S in the group has to give a different piece of advice. S1 gives the card to the person who has given the best advice. Now S2 takes a card and the other SS offer advice. The SS giving the best advice receive the card.
- When all the cards are finished, the person with the most cards is the winner.
- Demonstrate yourself first. Pull out a card, dramatically read out your situation and elicit suggestions. Invent excuses for not accepting the first few pieces of advice, however good, before finally accepting a suggestion with *That's a good idea. I'll do that.* Make sure SS use all the forms in the **LANGUAGE** box.
- If time, get feedback, asking SS what was the best advice for each situation.

| **49** | Find somebody who … | **7** | **D** |

A class mingle activity to practise asking questions and understanding phrasal verbs. Copy one sheet per student.

> **LANGUAGE**
> Phrasal verbs   Mixed tenses   Question formation

- Give out the grids. Elicit the ten questions SS need to ask, e.g. *Did you wake up late this morning?* Tell SS to find and write the name of a different student for each question.
- Demonstrate the activity by using the first question.
- When they find somebody who says *Yes*, they must ask a follow-up question and note some extra details. Elicit some possible follow-up questions, e.g. *What time did you wake up? Did you get to work late? What kind of flat would you like?* etc.
- Get feedback to find out which SS have done what and any interesting answers that emerged.

| **50** | What's the problem? | **7** | |

A group mime game to revise key travel language. Copy and cut up one sheet per group.

> **LANGUAGE**
> Hotel language   Requests: *Could you / Could I have …?*

- SS in groups of three or four (or with a small class divide them into two equal teams). Put a set of cards face down or in envelopes, and give one to each group.
- S1 takes out a card and mimes his / her problem. The other SS in the group have to call out suggestions to guess the exact words on the card. As soon as they guess it, S2 takes another card, then S3 and so on. The first team or group to guess all the cards correctly is the winner.
- Demonstrate yourself first. Say *Imagine you are at a hotel reception in a country where you can't speak the language. You've got a problem and have to communicate it to the hotel receptionist by mime.* Pull out a card and mime the phrase, e.g. *Where's the lift?* You can draw on the board (e.g. a question mark or a lift), make noises (e.g. of a lift going up and down), but you cannot speak. Elicit guesses from SS, pointing / nodding at SS who provide accurate / close guesses until you guide them to the exact words.
- SS do the same. Monitor and help as necessary, making sure no one starts talking or accepts an approximate guess.

| **51** | *Message in a bottle* | **7** | |

◦ **16** ◦ A listening activity based on a song by The Police.

- **1** Focus on the picture. In pairs, SS match five of the words, following the example.
- **2** SS match the remaining words to the definitions. Check answers and drill pronunciation.

> **1** b shore   c island   d sea   e note
> **2** 1 despair   2 lonely   3 mend   4 rescue

- **3** Show the song text on OHT / the board. SS listen to the song and complete it with the words from the first activity. Play it at least twice for them to check. Check answers.

> **2** island   **3** sea   **4** lonely   **5** rescue   **6** despair
> **7** note   **8** mend   **9** shore   **10** castaways

- Ask *What's the song about?* Tell SS to read it carefully, using the **Glossary** (it's about people who are lonely – the island is a metaphor for loneliness – the 'hundred million bottles' are from other lonely people in the world and the singer realises he is not alone).

- Tell SS to read the biographical information about the group. Help with vocabulary.

- If your SS like singing they can sing with the tape.

52	*get* questionnaire	7	Revision

A pairwork activity to revise different meanings of the verb *get*. SS ask and answer questions. Copy one sheet per pair.

> **LANGUAGE**
> Phrases with the verb *get*   Mixed tenses

- SS in pairs. Give out a copy to each pair and quickly go through the questions to make sure SS understand them.

- **A** asks **B** question 1. **B** answers and says *What about you?* Then **B** asks question 2. Encourage both SS to ask follow-up questions too.

  Tip Alternatively **A** could ask **B** all the questions first (**B** mustn't look at the questions) then swap, with **B** asking **A** the questions in a different order.

- Get feedback to find out any interesting findings, e.g. who gets up the earliest / latest, takes the longest / shortest to get ready, etc.

- If time, ask SS to list the additional meanings of *get* in the **Word bank** (SB *p. 134*)

  Tip An alternative way to do this activity is to cut up and give each student only one or two of the questions. They survey the class, asking everybody else their question(s), then report back with an overview of class habits.

53	Do you? So do I.	8	A

Speaking prompts. Copy one sheet per pair. Cut into **A** and **B**.

> **LANGUAGE**
> Echo questions: *Don't you? Can you? Can't you? Haven't you?*
> Agreeing / disagreeing: *So (do) I. / Neither (do) I. I do. / I don't.*
> General tense and vocabulary revision
> Star signs

- SS in pairs, preferably face to face. Give **A** and **B** their prompt sheet. They shouldn't look at each other's.

- Demonstrate the activity by choosing a topic and making a true sentence to tell the class e.g. *I can't ski.*

- Get individual SS to respond first with an echo question, then agree or disagree:
  T   *I can't ski.*
  S   *Can't you? Neither can I. / I can.*

- Choose another topic and demonstrate again:
  T   *I'd like to go to India.*
  S   *Would you? So would I. / I wouldn't.*

- Go through the topics. Make sure they are clear that each sentence must begin with *I*, e.g. 'Tell **A** what star sign you are.' = *I'm* (*Pisces*). Drill the star signs.

- SS work in pairs, taking turns to make a sentence / respond. When SS finish they swap role sheets. Fast finishers can invent more examples of their own i.e. any sentence beginning with *I* ….

  Tip SS will find this activity challenging. Give more practice by changing pairs and repeating the activity.

54	Talk about … the cinema	8	A

A pair or groupwork questionnaire to prompt conversation about the cinema. Copy one questionnaire per student.

> **LANGUAGE**
> Talking about the cinema   *dubbed, subtitles*

- Focus on the pictures. Ask *What / Who can you see?* etc.

- Go through questions 1 to 9 and make sure SS understand them. Check vocabulary.

  Tip Get SS to ask you the questions to check pronunciation. Your answers will also help to get them thinking.

- SS in pairs or small groups. **A** asks **B** the first question. **B** answers and says *What about you?* Then **B** asks **A** the second question, etc. (If SS are in groups, SS take turns to ask the others a question.)

- Get feedback from the whole class to find out, e.g. the best / worst film of the year, the class record for the number of times a film has been seen, etc.

55	Offers	8	B

A pairwork information gap to revise offers *I'll … / Shall I…?* Copy one sheet per pair and cut into **A** and **B**.

> **LANGUAGE**
> *I'll … / Shall I …?*

- SS in pairs. Give out copies to **A** and **B**. Make sure they can't see each other's sheet.

- 1 Demonstrate. Take the part of **A**. Focus on **Your problems** and say *It's very hot in here.* Now take the part of **B** and pretend to look for the correct response in **Your offers**, then say *Shall I open the window?* Take the part of **A** again and mime writing in the sentence.

- The **A**s say their sentences in **Your problems** to the **B**s. The **B**s find the correct response in **Your offers** and answer. The **A**s write in the response.

- Get **A** and **B** to do the first situation as an example and then check that everyone knows what they have to do.

- 2 When the **A**s have completed all of **B**'s offers, check answers. Then SS swap roles and **B** reads out their situations to **A**, etc.

  Tip When all the sentences are completed, get SS to cover the right hand column of both sheets and look only at the twelve problems. Can they remember all the offers?

56 *will* or *going to*?   8 B

A discrimination exercise. Copy one sheet per pair and cut into **A** and **B**.

> **LANGUAGE**
> Future forms. discriminating between *will* and *going to*

- Write on the board:

	will / won't	going to
1	First conditional	
2		
3		
4		
5		

- Elicit onto the board the other uses of *will* (2 offers, 3 promises, 4 unplanned decisions, 5 predictions / opinions) and the use of *going to* (plans). Invent example sentences if SS can't remember them all.

  ⚠ If SS remember the use of *going to* for predictions from evidence (**G◄◄ 7** p. 4) you can write it up too. It is not revised in this exercise.

- Give out the copies. Tell SS in pairs first to decide what is happening in each sentence for e.g. an unplanned decision, first conditional, plans. SS then complete the sentences with *will* or *going to*.

- Check answers.

> 1 I**'ll have** an orange juice please.
> (unplanned decision)
> 2 … he's **going to stay** with a friend in Italy, and then he**'s going to go** to France. (plans)
> 3 A What **will** you **do** if she doesn't phone?
> (first conditional)
>   B I**'ll** write to her. (unplanned decision)

> 4 A Fine. I**'ll take** it. (unplanned decision)
> 5 A What **are you going to do** tonight? (plans)
>   B … I**'ll** probably **go** to the cinema. (first conditional)
> 6 … we **'re going to have** dinner at that new Italian restaurant. (plans)
> 7 … I**'ll make** you a cup of tea. (offer)
> 8 A Who do you think **will win** the World Cup?
>   B I don't know, but England **won't win** it.
>   A I think Brazil **will win** it again. (predictions / opinions)
> 9 I **won't forget.** (promise)
> 10 A Which train **are** you **going to catch**? (plan)
>   B I**'ll be** home … (conditional)

57 Passive quiz   8 D

A quiz about unusual facts. Copy one sheet per pair /group.

> **LANGUAGE**
> Present and past passive

Tip You could cut this in half to do questions I to 7 after **File 8C** (the present passive) and 8 to 14 after **File 8D** (the past passive).

- SS in pairs or threes / fours. Give out copies. Set a time limit, e.g. five minutes for SS to read and complete the questions and choose the right answers. Monitor and help with vocabulary where necessary, but don't tell SS the answers. If they don't know, they should guess.

- Get feedback, and tell SS the right answers. Ask *Which surprised you the most?*

- Check the scores to see which pair / group is the winner.

2	are drunk	c	9 was bought	c
3	are stolen	a	10 was invented	c
4	is used	b	11 was first played	c
5	are killed	b	12 were worn	c
6	is read	a	13 was used	c
7	are born	b	14 was made	c
8	was designed	c		

58 *Travel with English* revision   8

A pairwork information gap activity. Copy one sheet per pair and cut into **A** and **B**.

> **LANGUAGE**
> Revision of travel phrases
> Present continuous: *There's a man standing in a shop carrying a pair of jeans.*   Places

- Revise describing people / the present continuous by asking SS to describe you / what you're wearing / where you're standing.

- Give out copies and sit **A** and **B** so they can't see each other's pictures. Give SS a minute to read their instructions and look at their lists of phrases.

- Explain the activity. **A** describes what's happening in each of the four cartoons. **B** can ask questions for clarification and when they're sure, choose the correct answer from their list and tell **A**, who writes it in. Then they swap roles.

- Monitor, correcting mistakes.

- Finally, SS look at each other's pictures to see if they were as they imagined.

1 k	2 l	3 m	4 p	5 f	6 e	7 g	8 d

59 *Imagine*   8 ◁▷

▸15◂ A listening / reading activity.

- Ask *What do you know about John Lennon? What's his most famous song?* SS read the paragraph about his life. Ask a few comprehension questions e.g. *How did he die?*

- **1** SS match the opposites, drawing a line between them as in the example.

- Check answers.

war / peace	today / tomorrow	below / above
live / die	easy / hard	

- **2** Show the song text on OHT / the board. SS read the song with the **Glossary** and complete it with words from the box. Tell them to use rhyme to help them. Feedback but don't tell them the answers.

- Play the song once for them to check.

> **1** sky **2** today **3** kill **4** peace **5** dreamer
> **6** world **7** hunger **8** man

- Play the song again for SS to listen and read.
- **3** In pairs, they complete the missing words in the text about John Lennon's ideal world.

> religion   countries   wars   possessions   eat   peace

⚠ There are two grammatical inaccuracies in the song: *there's no countries* instead of *there are* and *no religion **too*** instead of *no religion **either***. If SS ask, say it's poetic licence!

- Check answers. Ask *Do you think his dreams will ever happen?*
- If your SS like singing they can sing with the tape.

60 | Revision questions   8 | Revision

Free oral practice. Prompts to revise the main tenses taught in *English File 2*. Copy and cut up one set of cards per pair.

> **LANGUAGE**
> Question and answer: all tenses

- SS in pairs. Give them a set of cards in an envelope (or placed face down in a pile between the two SS).
- Tell SS the object of the activity is to ask questions to revise the tenses they've learnt in the book and to have mini-conversations to improve their oral fluency. Tell SS that they should try to continue the conversation whenever possible by
  – asking a follow-up question.
  – agreeing / disagreeing with their partner.
  – returning the question with *What / How about you?*
- SS in pairs. Each pair has a set of cards. Set a time limit, e.g. ten minutes. SS take turns to take a card and ask their partner the questions. Monitor, help, and correct.

Tip See Tip at the end of activity 23 p.133

61 | Tell us about …   9 | A

Speaking topics to revise the main tenses taught in *English File 2*. These aim to give SS fluency practice speaking continuously for a few minutes rather than just answering questions. Copy and cut up one set of cards per group of four / five.

> **LANGUAGE**
> Revision of Files 1 to 8

- Give one set of cards (in an envelope or face down) to each group.
- Explain that they have to pick a topic and then talk for a minute. While one student is talking the others should listen and then ask questions or join in with their opinions. One member of each group should time the speaker and signal when the minute is up.

Tip If your SS are enjoying speaking, you could increase or even abolish the time limit.

- Monitor and note down any repeated errors to correct with the whole class at the end.

Tip If you don't want to cut up cards, copy one sheet per group. Give it to S1 who chooses a topic and speaks, then passes the paper to S2, etc.

62 | *Nothing compares 2 U*   9 | B

∘ 8 ∘ A listening activity based on a song by Sinead O'Connor.

> **LANGUAGE**
> Question and answer: all tenses

- Play the chorus of the song. Ask *Do you know / like it? Who's it by? What do you think it's about?*
- **1** Show the song text on OHT / the board. SS read the words with the **Glossary** and complete verses 1 and 2 with the two sets of verbs. They compare with a partner but don't tell them the answers yet.
- **2** Play the song once for SS to listen and check.
- Check answers.

> **l.3** go out, sleep **l.6** do **l.7** see, choose **l.8** eat
> **l.14** stop **l.15** Tell **l.16** put, see **l.18** guess, guess

- **3** Ask SS which line(s) from each verse they can see in each picture.
- Play the song again for SS to listen while they read the six sentences and decide if they are true or false.
- Check answers.

> **1** F **2** T **3** T **4** F **5** F **6** F

- If your SS like singing, rehearse the song line by line and sing with the tape. If not, just play it again for SS to listen to.

Student profile

First name _____ Surname _____

1 Tick ✓ or cross ✗ and complete the sentences.

Why are you learning English?

☐ For my job.
☐ For travelling.
☐ For my studies.
☐ Because I like it.

Any other reason? _____
_____
_____
My main reason is _____
_____ .

2 Number the sentences 1 to 3.
1 = not important
2 = quite important
3 = very important

What do you need / want to do in English?

1 I want to speak English well. ☐
2 I want to improve my pronunciation. ☐
3 I need to speak English at work / school. ☐
4 I need to use English on the phone. ☐
5 I need to speak English when I travel. ☐
6 I want to understand songs and films in English. ☐
7 I want to study in the UK or the USA. ☐
8 I need to get a qualification in English. ☐
9 I need to read textbooks in English. ☐
10 I want to read magazines and books in English. ☐
11 I need to write well. ☐
     Anything else? _____

3 Number 1 to 3.
1 = OK
2 = quite difficult
3 = very difficult

What do you find difficult?

☐ English pronunciation
☐ English spelling
☐ English grammar
☐ Speaking
☐ Reading
☐ Writing

☐ Understanding cassettes / TV
☐ Understanding the teacher
☐ Remembering words
Anything else? _____
_____
_____

143

1 Don't use *the* to speak generally about things.

2 Don't use *the* for meals or special places.

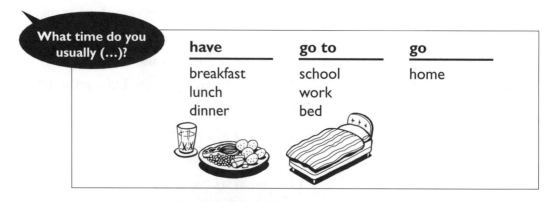

have	go to	go
breakfast	school	home
lunch	work	
dinner	bed	

3 Don't use *the* for sports or games. (but use *the* for musical instruments).

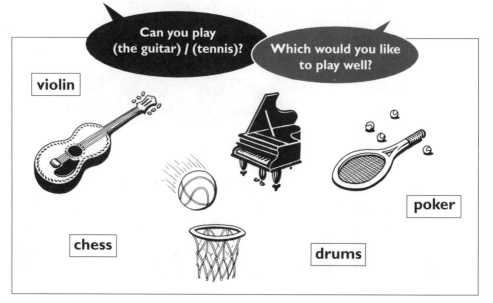

1 Complete with the question words.

How often	What	What time	~~Where~~	When	How much
How many	Which	What kind	Why	Who	What

1 *Where* do you live?
2 _____ do you live with?
3 _____ _____ of music do you like?
4 _____ _____ do you usually get up in the morning?
5 _____ are you learning English?
6 _____ did you start learning English?
7 _____ _____ do you go to the cinema?
8 _____ do you prefer: beer or wine?
9 _____ _____ brothers and sisters have you got?
10 _____ _____ tea and coffee do you drink a day?
11 _____ did you do last night?
12 _____ are you going to do after the class?

2 Interview a partner. Ask the questions in a **different** order.
Ask follow-up questions.

---

1 Complete with the question words.

How often	What	What time	~~Where~~	When	How much
How many	Which	What kind	Why	Who	What

1 *Where* do you live?
2 _____ do you live with?
3 _____ _____ of music do you like?
4 _____ _____ do you usually get up in the morning?
5 _____ are you learning English?
6 _____ did you start learning English?
7 _____ _____ do you go to the cinema?
8 _____ do you prefer: beer or wine?
9 _____ _____ brothers and sisters have you got?
10 _____ _____ tea and coffee do you drink a day?
11 _____ did you do last night?
12 _____ are you going to do after the class?

2 Interview a partner. Ask the questions in a **different** order.
Ask follow-up questions.

Student's Book

1 Where's the **Progress chart**?
On pages 8 and _____ .

2 What pages are the Level 1 **Grammar review** **G◄◄** on?
Pages _____ to _____ .

3 How many Files are there? _____

4 Are there **Vocabulary V** and **Grammar files G** at the end of every file? _____

5 How many **Travel with English** lessons are there? _____

6 What are the four **Focus on …** lessons about?
Pronunciation, _____, _____, and _____ .

7 How many pages of **Communication** activities **►◄** are there? _____

8 What pages are the **Listening** scripts on?
Pages _____ to _____ .

9 What pages are the **Travel phrasebook** on?
Pages _____ to _____ .

10 How many different **Wordbanks** are there? _____

11 Where's the list of irregular verbs?
On page _____ .

12 Where's the **Classroom language**?
On page _____ .

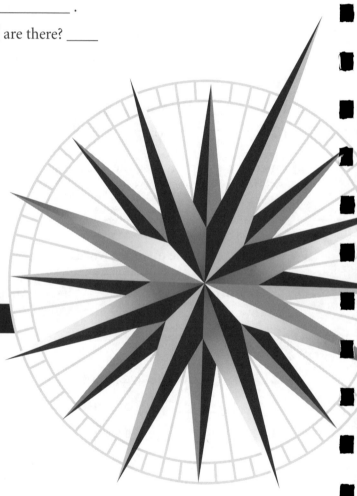

Workbook

13 Which sections are on pages 3 to 6?
Level 1 Grammar check and _____ .

14 Where's the **key**? *On pages _____ to _____ .*

15 How many **Read and write** lessons are there? _____

16 What pages are the **Listen and speak** scripts on?
On pages _____ to _____ .

17 Find **Grammar check 1**. When you do it, what page in the Student's Book do you also look at?
Page _____ .

18 What's on page 81? _____
What does it help you with? _____

19 How many **Quicktests** are there? _____

20 Where's the list of **Grammar words to learn**?
On page _____ .

A Ask and answer questions.
Ask follow-up questions too.

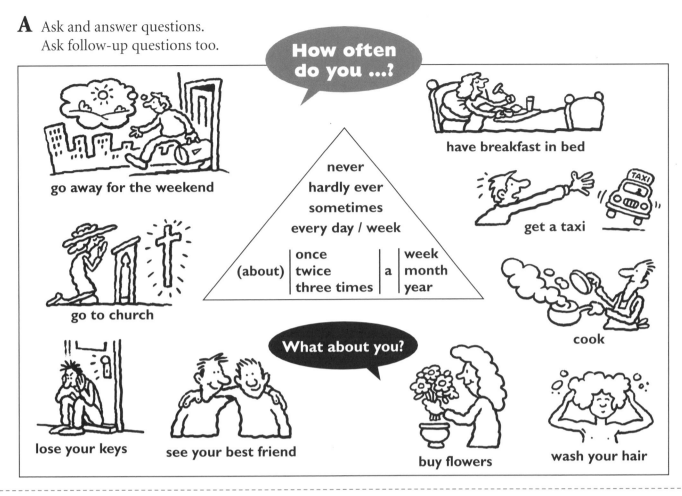

B Ask and answer questions.
Ask follow-up questions too.

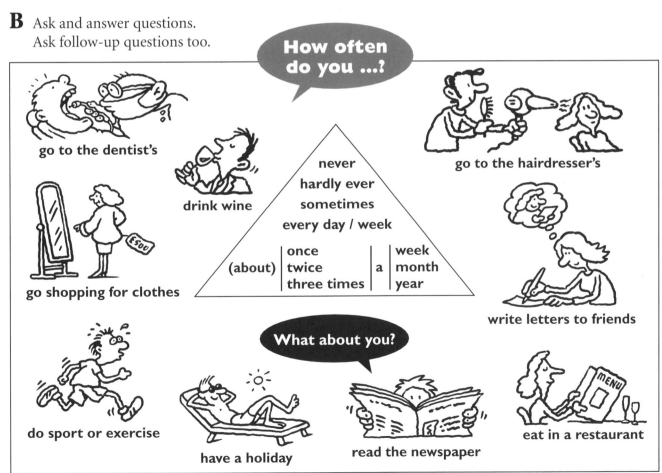

Are you STRESSED?

• Do you find it difficult to relax? • Do you worry a lot? • Do you sleep badly? • Do you never have enough time for everything? • When was the last time you sang in the bath? • Are you stressed?

1 Ask your partner about **yesterday**. Tick ✓ or cross ✗.
Did you sleep well yesterday?

Part 1

- [ ] *slept* well
- [ ] *had* a good breakfast
- [ ] *had* a long, hot shower or bath
- [ ] *listened* to music
- [ ] *read* a magazine or book
- [ ] *went* for a walk
- [ ] *did* sport or exercise
- [ ] *had* a massage or a sauna
- [ ] *went* out with a friend / friends
- [ ] *watched* TV
- [ ] *relaxed* after dinner
- [ ] *went* to bed early

Part 2

- [ ] *woke* up late
- [ ] *drove* a car or motorbike
- [ ] *got* to work / school late
- [ ] *phoned* more than five people
- [ ] *got* angry
- [ ] *felt* worried
- [ ] *forgot* something important
- [ ] *smoked* more than two cigarettes
- [ ] *slept* less than seven hours
- [ ] *worked* or studied more than eight hours
- [ ] *had* more than two cups of coffee
- [ ] *had* a meal standing up

······ FOLD ······

2 Calculate your partner's score:

In Part 1 each ✓ = +1 point.
In Part 2 each ✓ = −1 point.

Part 1 = _____ points
Part 2 = _____ points
Total = _____ points

3 Tell your partner how stressed he / she is.

−7 to −12 You're **very** stressed. Change your life style **quickly**! **−6 to −1** Be careful! You're quite stressed. Life's short. Try to work less, to relax more, and to decide what's really important.	**0 to 5** You're quite busy and a little stressed at the moment. Learn to relax more and enjoy a long and happy life. **6 to 12** Congratulations! You're **very** lucky! You have a **very** stress-free life. Are you on holiday?

Find somebody who has ...	Student's name	What's it like?
1 *been skiing*		
2 _____ Indian food		
3 _____ London		
4 _____ *Evita*		
5 _____ squash		
6 _____ *Asterix in Britain*		
7 _____ a sauna		
8 _____ Ravel's *Bolero*		
9 _____		
10 _____		
Find somebody who has ...	Student's name	What's it like?

A

Describe your picture to **B**. Find ten differences between the pictures.

B

Describe your picture to **A**. Find ten differences between the pictures.

1. early
2.
3.
4. lunch at home
5.
6.
7.
8.
9.
10. walk
11. a friend
12.
13.
14.
15.
16. sport
17. dinner
18.
19. Hello! How are you?
20. late

2 **A**

1 **Have you ever been on TV or in the newspapers?**

When was it?

What did you do?

8 **Have you ever found any money in the street?**

How much did you find?

What did you do?

2 **Have you ever forgotten a very important date?**

What date was it?

What happened?

9 **Have you ever cried during a film?**

Which film was it?

What happened at the end of the film?

3 **Have you ever played a musical instrument?**

What was it?

Do you still play it?

10 **Have you ever spoken or sung in public?**

What did you speak / sing about?

Did you enjoy it?

4 **Have you ever played a team sport?**

Which sport did you play?

Do you still play it?

11 **Have you ever studied another language apart from English?**

Which language did you study?

Can you speak it well? Why (not)?

5 **Have you ever travelled by boat?**

When was the last time?

Where did you go?

12 **Have you ever done a dangerous sport?**

Which sport was it?

Did you enjoy it?

6 **Have you ever won a competition?**

What competition was it?

What was the prize?

13 **Have you ever asked a famous person for their autograph?**

Who was it?

Did they give it to you?

7 **Have you ever called the police?**

Why did you call them?

What happened?

14 **Have you ever had dancing lessons?**

What kind of dancing did you learn?

When?

Were you good at it?

2 **C**

A

1   **2**   **3**   **4**   **5**   **6**

B

1   **2**   **3**   **4**   **5**   **6**

have a <u>shower</u>	go on <u>h</u>oliday	a <u>river</u>
rel<u>ax</u>	<u>thirsty</u>	a <u>ticket</u>
<u>sun</u>bathe	a <u>park</u>	a <u>boarding</u> pass
a horse	jeans	an <u>or</u>chestra
go <u>shopping</u>	a <u>market</u>	chess
a cat	a <u>track</u> suit	squash
do the <u>washing</u>-up	a hotel	a <u>taxi</u> driver
stressed	a <u>living</u> room	a <u>secretary</u>

A Ask **B** questions to complete the travel information.
What time does the train leave London?
How much is a single / return ticket?

B ravel
Bargain

𝒲ould you like to spend a
long weekend in Amsterdam?
ℋere are our low price choices.

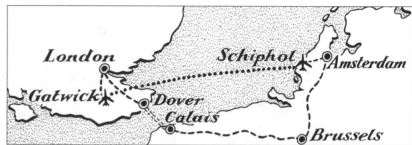

by train (Eurostar)

Single £87.50   Return £ _____

	Depart London (Waterloo)	_____
	Arrive Brussels (Midi)	11.10
	Depart Brussels (Midi)	12.10
	Arrive Amsterdam (Central)	_____

by train and plane

Single £ _____   Return £128.05

	Depart London (Victoria)	06.00
	Arrive Gatwick Airport	_____
	Depart Gatwick Airport	07.55
	Arrive Amsterdam (Schiphol)	_____
	Depart Amsterdam (Schiphol)	_____
	Arrive Amsterdam (Central)	11.05

B Ask **A** questions to complete the travel information.
What time does the train get to / leave Brussels?
How much is a single / return ticket?

B ravel
Bargain

𝒲ould you like to spend a
long weekend in Amsterdam?
ℋere are our low price choices.

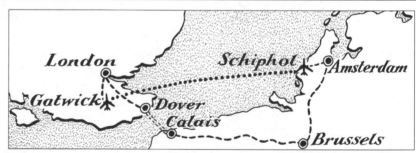

by train (Eurostar)

Single £ _____   Return £175.00

	Depart London (Waterloo)	06.53
	Arrive Brussels (Midi)	_____
	Depart Brussels (Midi)	_____
	Arrive Amsterdam (Central)	15.08

by train and plane

Single £99.90   Return £ _____

	Depart London (Victoria)	_____
	Arrive Gatwick Airport	06.35
	Depart Gatwick Airport	_____
	Arrive Amsterdam (Schiphol)	10.15
	Depart Amsterdam (Schiphol)	10.45
	Arrive Amsterdam (Central)	_____

You don't have to say you love me 1966

1 **File 2** ·20· Listen and note the words that are wrong.

2 Listen again. Correct the wrong words.

3 What's the song about?

   a A couple who have separated. She's happy that he's gone and enjoys being alone.

   b A couple who separated. He came back and now they're happy again.

   c A couple who have separated. She begged him to come home, but he said no and now she feels terrible.

When I said I <u>wanted</u> you	*needed*
2 You said you would never stay	_____
It wasn't me who changed but you	
4 And now you've gone again	_____
Don't you know that now you've gone	_____
6 And I'm left here on my own	
That I have to go to you	_____
8 And beg you to come back	_____
Chorus	
You don't have to say you love me	
10 Just be close at heart	_____
You don't have to play forever	_____
12 I will understand	
Believe me	
14 Believe me	
I can't help but hate you	_____
16 But believe me, I'll never tie you up	_____
Left alone with just a photograph	_____
18 Life seems bad and so unreal	_____
All that's left is loneliness	
20 There's nothing left to say	_____
Chorus	

Dusty Springfield (1939–)

DUSTY SPRINGFIELD

has often been called the best British female soul singer ever. Real name Mary O'Brien, she was born on 16th April 1939 in London. She had 14 British hits between 1963–68, including *I only want to be with you* and *I just don't know what to do with myself*. In 1987 she had a hit with *What have I done to deserve this?* with the Pet Shop Boys. *You don't have to say you love me* was her most popular song, selling over a million copies.

Glossary

on my own = alone
beg = ask
close /kləus/ (at hand) = near to me
forever = until the end of our lives
I can't help but = the only thing I can do is
tie you down = stop you from being free
unreal = not real
loneliness = the feeling of being very alone

157

A

Summer camps in Britain

Can you speak English?

Would you like to work in a summer camp?

For an interview write to this address:

Summer Camps in Britain
Sandalwood Park
Essex EX5 2DU

The manager

You're interviewing candidates for a job as a summer camp assistant.

Interview the candidate (**Student B**).

You start: *Good morning, please sit down.*

1 Find out **B**'s name, address, nationality, and age.

Find out what qualifications **B** has. Ask:

Can you …?   *drive*
              swim
              speak English quite well
              cook
              play a musical instrument

Have you …?   *(work) with children before*
              (be) abroad before

Do you …?   *smoke*
              like sports and games
              like meeting people

Ask **B** Why do you want the job?

2 Ask **B** Do you have any questions?
Answer **B**'s questions about conditions.

Conditions
- £550 a month for 55 hours a week
- weekends are free, but some evenings you have to work until 10.00 p.m.
- a free uniform
- free meals and accommodation

3 Decide if you are going to offer **B** the job.

B

Summer camps in Britain

Can you speak English?

Would you like to work in a summer camp?

For an interview write to this address:

Summer Camps in Britain
Sandalwood Park
Essex EX5 2DU

The candidate

You're going to an interview for a job as a summer camp assistant in Britain. **A** starts.

1 Answer the manager's questions (**Student A**).

2 Ask some questions. You want to know:

Do I have to …?
   pay for meals and accommodation
   wear a uniform
   work at weekends (you don't want to)

How many hours do I have to work?

How much is the salary?

3 If the manager offers you the job, decide if you want to accept it.

3 **A**

Grammar auction

Names _____   Total money
_____   **£1,000**

Sentences	Price
1 A chair is a thing which you sit on.	_____
2 Have you ever gone to Rome?	_____
3 How often do you go to the hairdresser's?	_____
4 How many children have your brother got?	_____
5 I've seen that film three times.	_____
6 A market is a place where you can buy food.	_____
7 Mary is my sister's husband.	_____
8 'Are there your keys?' 'No, they're hers.'	_____
9 She doesn't have to wear a uniform.	_____
10 A photographer is a person which takes photos.	_____
11 They hardly never go to the theatre, only once a year.	_____
12 'Whose is this book?' 'It's Peter's.'	_____
13 They've to get up early tomorrow.	_____
14 Yesterday morning I went jogging in the park.	_____
15 It's the David's car.	_____
16 This isn't mine, it's their.	_____
17 Do banks open on Sundays?	_____
18 The Amish can't to drive cars, only tractors.	_____
19 What time does leave the train?	_____
20 The end of the film was very sad.	_____

MAURITIUS

Spend 10 or 15 days on this fantastic island in the Indian Ocean with tropical beaches, sun, water sports, luxury hotels, etc. An unforgettable experience.

Prices from £499
Fly Air France or British Airways
Dep. dates 9 Nov. or 22 Dec.
Hotels The Blue Lagoon★★★ or Tropical Paradise★★

KATHMANDU

Take the best and most exciting journey of your life by double-decker bus through beautiful Turkey, Jordan, Iran, Pakistan, India, and Nepal.

7 weeks from £999
11 weeks from £1,599

Dep. dates 15 Nov. or 2 Dec.
Accommodation On local campsites. (Hotels can be booked if you prefer.)

BUS Co.

1 Read the adverts and choose a holiday. Decide: Where are you going?

_____

How are you getting there?

_____

When are you leaving?

_____

How long are you staying?

_____

Where are you staying?

_____

2 Find a partner to travel with.

A *Where are you going?*
B *To Mauritius.*
A *How are you getting there?*
B *I'm flying with Air France.*
A *I'm flying with British Airways, so we can't go together.*

MAURITIUS

Spend 10 or 15 days on this fantastic island in the Indian Ocean with tropical beaches, sun, water sports, luxury hotels, etc. An unforgettable experience.

Prices from £499
Fly Air France or British Airways
Dep. dates 9 Nov. or 22 Dec.
Hotels The Blue Lagoon★★★ or Tropical Paradise★★

KATHMANDU

Take the best and most exciting journey of your life by double-decker bus through beautiful Turkey, Jordan, Iran, Pakistan, India, and Nepal.

7 weeks from £999
11 weeks from £1,599

Dep. dates 15 Nov. or 2 Dec.
Accommodation On local campsites. (Hotels can be booked if you prefer.)

BUS Co.

1 Read the adverts and choose a holiday. Decide: Where are you going?

_____

How are you getting there?

_____

When are you leaving?

_____

How long are you staying?

_____

Where are you staying?

_____

2 Find a partner to travel with.

A *Where are you going?*
B *To Mauritius.*
A *How are you getting there?*
B *I'm flying with Air France.*
A *I'm flying with British Airways, so we can't go together.*

A

How long does it take to get from London to other famous tourist towns:

- by train?
- by coach?
- by plane?

1 Ask **B** questions to complete the information. *How long does it take to get to Bath by train?*

2 Answer **B**'s questions. *It takes …*

	Bath	Cambridge	Brighton	Oxford	Edinburgh	Dublin*
train	_____	1 hr	_____	48 mins	_____	9 hrs
coach	3 hrs 5 mins	_____	1 hr 45 mins	_____	7 hrs 45 mins	_____
plane	×	×	×	×	1 hr 50 mins	_____

* Travel times to Dublin by coach and train include ferry crossings.

B

How long does it take to get from London to other famous tourist towns:

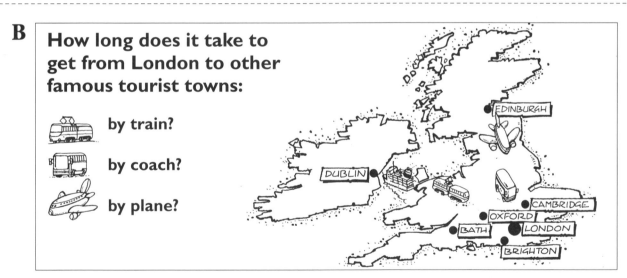

- by train?
- by coach?
- by plane?

1 Ask **A** questions to complete the information. *How long does it take to get to Bath by coach?*

2 Answer **A**'s questions. *It takes …*

	Bath	Cambridge	Brighton	Oxford	Edinburgh	Dublin*
train	75 mins	_____	51 mins	_____	4 hrs 6 mins	_____
coach	_____	2 hrs	_____	90 mins	_____	12 hrs
plane	×	×	×	×	_____	1 hr 10 mins

* Travel times to Dublin by coach and train include ferry crossings.

A

1 Read and remember **Part 1** of the story. Tell **B** what happened.

2 Read and remember **Part 3**. Tell **B** what happened.

3 Now answer this question with **B**. *How did Harry die?*

Part 1

Sally met Harry on the night of her twenty-first birthday. She was at a disco with some friends and Harry was the disc-jockey. She was wearing a new red dress. She and her friends were dancing but they didn't like the music. Sally went to the disc-jockey and said, 'This music is awful! Could you play something else, please?' Five minutes later he said, 'This next record is for a very beautiful girl in red.' The record was *The Lady in Red* and she knew the record was for her!

When the disco closed Harry said, 'Can I see you again?' and she gave him her phone number.

Part 3

The accident happened exactly a year later. It was a Wednesday evening in winter. Harry arrived home from work and he parked his car opposite his house. It was dark and it was raining. He was crossing the road and he was wearing a dark coat. A car was coming along the road very quickly. The driver didn't see Harry and hit him. But the driver didn't stop. Later people asked 'Why didn't the driver stop and help?' They took Harry to hospital, but it was too late. When they arrived he was already dead.

B

1 Read and remember **Part 2** of the story. Tell **A** what happened.

2 Read and remember **Part 4**. Tell **A** what happened.

3 Now answer this question with **A**. *How did Harry die?*

Part 2

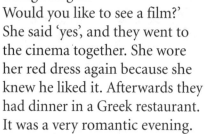

The next day, Harry phoned Sally and asked, 'What are you doing tonight? Would you like to see a film?' She said 'yes', and they went to the cinema together. She wore her red dress again because she knew he liked it. Afterwards they had dinner in a Greek restaurant. It was a very romantic evening.

After that they saw each other every day and soon they fell in love. It was strange because Harry and Sally were completely different. Harry liked rock music and fast cars, but Sally hated them. She loved opera and going to the theatre. But they were in love and that was enough.

Part 4

Exactly a year later Sally drove to her friend Karen's house to see a film. It was a Wednesday evening, and they were going to watch a film on TV. Karen lived near Harry, and Sally drove along the street where he lived, past his house. She didn't have time to stop and say hello because she was late and it was raining. But she quickly looked up at his bedroom window to see if his light was on. It wasn't. She only looked for a moment! She just wanted to see if he was at home!

A

1 You've just arrived at the Astoria Hotel.
B is the receptionist. **B starts**.

  a Ask: *How much / room?*
         pay / credit card?
         TV in the room?

  b Book a room for five nights.

  c Ask: *What time / breakfast?*
         Where / dining room?
         Where / swimming pool?

2 Now you're in your room but there's a problem.
Choose one problem and phone reception. **B starts**.

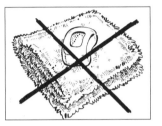   

B

1 You're a receptionist at
the Astoria Hotel.
A has just arrived.
You start: *Good evening,
can I help you?*

  a Answer **A**'s questions.
    Use the Astoria Hotel
    information.

  b If **A** wants a room:
    • Write down **A**'s name and
      nationality.
    • Ask to see his / her passport.
    • Give **A** a room number.

  c Answer any more questions.

2 **A** is now in his / her room but
phones you with a problem.
Listen and try to help.
You start: *Hello, reception.
Can I help you?*

STORIA HOTEL

Prices

Single room with bathroom	$60
Double room with bathroom	$90
Single room without bathroom	$40
Double room without bathroom	$70

We accept Visa and American Express credit cards.
All rooms have a colour TV and a mini-bar.

Meals

Breakfast	7.30–10.30 a.m.
Lunch	1.30–3.00 p.m.
Dinner	8.00–9.30 p.m.

4	Pool, gym and sun terrace	I Dining room
3	Bedrooms	G Reception
2	Bedrooms	B Car park

4

3

2

I

G

B

Don't you want me baby? *1981*

You were working as a ¹_____ in a cocktail bar

2 When I met you

I picked you out, I shook you up, and turned you around

4 Turned you into someone ²_____

Now five years later on you've got the world at your ³_____

6 Success has been so easy for you

But don't ⁴_____ it's me who put you where you are now

8 And I can put you back down too

Don't, don't you want me?

10 You know I can't believe it when I ⁵_____ that you won't see me

Don't, don't you want me?

12 You know I don't believe you when you say that you don't need me

It's much too ⁶_____ to find

14 You think you've changed your mind

You'd better change it back or we will both be ⁷_____

16 Don't you want me baby?
Don't you want me?

18 Don't you want me baby?
Don't you want me?

20 I was working as a ⁸_____ in a cocktail bar,

That much is ⁹_____

22 But even then I knew I'd find a much ¹⁰_____ place

Either with or without you

24 The five ¹¹_____ we have had have been such good times

I still ¹²_____ you

26 But now I think it's time I lived my life on my own
I guess it's just what I must do

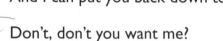

1 File 3 [20] Read Clues 1 to 12 for the missing words. Complete the song.

2 Listen and check.

Clues

1 A woman who serves food.
2 The opposite of *old*.
3 The plural of *foot*.
4 The opposite of *remember*.
5 It's a verb which rhymes with *beer*.
6 The class starts at 10.00. If you arrive at 10.15 you're _____.
7 You say this if you do something wrong.
8 The same as Clue 1.
9 The opposite of *false*.
10 *big / bigger, good /* _____.
11 There are seven hundred and thirty days in two _____.
12 The opposite of *hate*.

THE HUMAN LEAGUE

The Human League (1977–)

Singer / song-writer Phil Oakey formed the Human League in 1977. When two male band members left, Oakey replaced them with two teenage girls he saw dancing in a Sheffield club where they were working as cocktail waitresses. He's now married to one of them. The Human League are still making hit records today. *Don't you want me baby?* is their most famous song. It was the biggest-selling single of 1981.

Glossary

turn into = change
success = getting to the top of your profession
change your mind = decide to do something different
you'd better = you have to
I guess (US) = I think

365
365
0

Home

Do you live in a house or a flat?

Is it yours? What's it like?

How many rooms are there?

Is there a (garage, etc.)?

What's your bedroom like?

Have you got a (TV, etc.)? Where is it?

Family

Who do you live with?

Have you got a large family?

What does your (sister, etc.) do?

Describe one of the people in your family.

Have you got any pets?

Routine

What time do you usually get up?

Do you always have the same thing for breakfast?

How do you get to work / school?
How long does it take?

What do you usually do in the morning / afternoon?

Are you often very busy or tired? Why?

How many hours do you usually sleep?

Lifestyle

Do you smoke?

Do you do much exercise?

How do you relax?

Do you watch a lot of TV?

How often do you go shopping?

Do you go out much during the week?

What do you usually do at the weekend?

How often do you go away?

Now and usually

What's the weather like today?

What are you wearing today?

How often do you buy new clothes?

Are you reading a book at the moment?

What kind of books do you usually read?

Why exactly are you studying English?

What do you think your (best friend / sister, etc.) is doing at the moment?

The future

Where are you going (to go) after class today?

What are you doing tonight?

Are you going (to go) anywhere at the weekend?

Are you going to have a holiday soon? When? Where?

Are you going to change your job / school next year?

Are you going to study anything new next year?

The past (1)

What was the weather like yesterday?

What time did you go to bed last night?

What did you have for lunch?

What did you do last night?

What was the last film you saw at the cinema?

Where did you go for your last holiday? What was it like?

The past (2)

Where were you at 7.00 yesterday evening?

What were you doing?

Were you sleeping at midnight last night?

What was happening today when you arrived in class?

What were you doing exactly a year ago?

What were you wearing yesterday morning?

Experiences

How many times have you been abroad?

Have you been out for a meal this month?

Have you seen (NAME OF A FILM)?

Have you ever read an Agatha Christie book?

Have you been to (NAME OF CITY)?

Have you bought a lottery ticket this month?

Have you done any sport or exercise this week?

Permission and obligation

Can you smoke in your house / flat? Can you have pets?

Is there anything that you **can't** do?

What do you have to do in your job / at school?

Do you ever have to wear special clothes?

Do you have to work or study at weekends?

Do you have to cook / clean a lot?

Easy Reader review

Answer the questions, tick the boxes, ✓ and write your name.

1 What's the title? _____

2 Who's it by? _____

3 It's …
- ☐ a love story
- ☐ science fiction
- ☐ non-fiction
- ☐ a biography
- ☐ a thriller
- ☐ an adventure
- ☐ a mystery
- ☐ a detective story
- ☐ an autobiography
- ☐ a historical book

4 What's it about? _____
_____
_____
_____
_____
_____
_____

5 What's it like? _____
_____

6 I recommend it. ☐   I don't recommend it. ☐

Reviewer's name _____   Date _____

- -

Easy Reader review

Answer the questions, tick the boxes, ✓ and write your name.

1 What's the title? _____

2 Who's it by? _____

3 It's …
- ☐ a love story
- ☐ science fiction
- ☐ non-fiction
- ☐ a biography
- ☐ a thriller
- ☐ an adventure
- ☐ a mystery
- ☐ a detective story
- ☐ an autobiography
- ☐ a historical book

4 What's it about? _____
_____
_____
_____
_____
_____
_____

5 What's it like? _____
_____

6 I recommend it. ☐   I don't recommend it. ☐

Reviewer's name _____   Date _____

English File reading chart

Class name _____

Write the titles of the books you have read. Give your opinion. Very good 3   Quite good 2   Boring 1

Name	Book 1	Book 2	Book 3	Book 4

1 travelling by plane / travelling by car

2 men / women

3 living in the city / living in the country

4 English clothes / Italian clothes

5 Sean Connery / Hugh Grant

6 a teacher / a waiter

7 Spain / Germany

8 football / motor racing

9 the Americans / the British

10 Madonna / Barbara Streisand

Finish

You'll find the love of your life if you ...

If you go to bed late, you ...

If I win the lottery, I ...

He won't pass his driving test if he ...

If you don't do your homework, the teacher ...

I'll be really happy if you ...

If they don't hurry up, they ...

I'll make lunch if you ...

If the weather's good tomorrow, we ...

You'll learn English quickly if you ...

If we go by plane, it ...

If they get married, they ...

I'll write to you if ...

It'll take two hours to get there if we ...

Start

You'll feel better if you ...

If he doesn't have time to do it today, he ...

ꙮ ODYSSEUS AND THE CYCLOPS ꙮ

1 Read the story. Number the paragraphs 1 to 8. Check with the pictures.

A ☐ 'My name's Nobody,' Odysseus answered. 'And now my men and I are going to leave the island.'

'No you're not,' shouted the giant. 'I'm not going to open the door of the cave. You're going to stay here and I'm going to eat you tomorrow.'

B ☐ But his brothers answered, 'Polyphemus, you're mad. If nobody has blinded you and nobody is escaping, what's the problem?' They went back to what they were doing. And so Odysseus and his men escaped.

C ☐ Odysseus thought of a plan to save them. While the giant was sleeping, he found a big piece of wood and put it in the fire. When the wood was hot he used it to hit the giant in his eye, and he blinded him.

D ☐ When Odysseus and his men were travelling home to Ithaca, they landed on an island which looked uninhabited. They were exhausted and they didn't have anything to eat. After looking all over the island for food, they finally found some sheep, so they killed one and ate it.

E ☐ But Odysseus had another brilliant idea. The giant's sheep were with them in the cave. The next morning, when the giant opened the door of the cave for his sheep to go outside, Odysseus and his men each hid under a sheep. Although the giant counted his sheep as they went out, he didn't see them.

F ☐ The giant woke up and shouted, 'I'm blind! I can't see anything! Who has done this to me? What's your name?'

G ☐ When they were all outside, Odysseus shouted, 'Goodbye, Polyphemus! We're free, and now we're going to leave the island.'

'Oh no you aren't,' the giant shouted angrily. He called his brothers: 'Help me! Nobody has blinded me. Nobody is escaping. Catch him!'

H ☐ But while they were eating, a terrible giant with one eye called Polyphemus attacked them. He was one of the Cyclops who lived on the island with his brothers, and the sheep were his. He put Odysseus and his men in his cave. He planned to eat them later.

2 Complete the glossary.

Glossary

uninhabited	(adj.)	= empty, without people
_____	(adj.)	= very tired
_____	(n.)	= farm animals which are usually white
_____	(n.)	= a very, very large person
_____	(n.)	= a large hole in the side of a hill or mountain
_____	(v.)	= to stop somebody from seeing
_____	(adj.)	= can't see
_____	(v.)	= past tense of hide

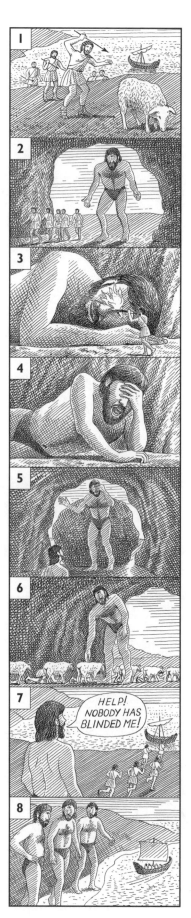

TV and RADIO

Do you agree?

1 The _____ (*bad*) TV programme at the moment is …
2 The _____ (*funny*) comedy on TV is …
3 The _____ (*stupid*) presenter on TV is …
4 The _____ (*good*) newsreader is …
5 The _____ (*interesting*) programme is …
6 The _____ (*good*) radio station for pop music is …
7 The _____ (*bad*) disc jockey on the radio is …
8 The _____ (*popular*) radio station is …

THE CINEMA

Do you agree?

1 The _____ (*bad*) film I've ever seen is …
2 The _____ (*good*) film I've seen this year is …
3 The _____ (*sad*) film I've ever seen is …
4 The _____ (*beautiful*) film soundtrack I've ever heard is …
5 The _____ (*exciting*) film I've ever seen is …
6 The _____ (*attractive*) actor or actress is …
7 The _____ (*good*) young actor or actress is …
8 The _____ (*interesting*) film director is …

MUSIC

Do you agree?

1 The _____ (*good*) female singer is …
2 The _____ (*good*) male singer is …
3 The _____ (*bad*) pop group are …
4 The _____ (*famous*) musician is …
5 The _____ (*relaxing*) music is …
6 The _____ (*exciting*) dance music is …
7 The _____ (*interesting*) decade for pop music is / was …
8 The _____ (*great*) pop group in the world is / was …

Menu

Starters

Avocado with prawns £7.95
French onion soup £5.50
Grapefruit cocktail £4.75
Grilled mushrooms £5.95

Main Courses

Vegetarian lasagne £8.50
Grilled chicken with lemon sauce £8.95
Roast beef £10.30
Lamb chops with garlic mayonnaise £9.25
Fresh salmon £11.00

Vegetables £2.50 each

Garden peas   Cabbage   Carrots   Spinach
Green beans   Potatoes (boiled or fried)

Desserts

Baked apples £4.35
Chocolate cake with vanilla ice-cream £4.50
Pears in red wine £3.20
Strawberries and cream £4.75

Drinks

Wine (red, white, rosé)   Soft drinks £1.50
French £9.00   Mineral water £1.00
Italian £8.00   Fruit juice £1.50
Spanish £8.00   Beer £2.50

Coffee £1.50

VAT AND SERVICE CHARGE INCLUDED

Menu

Starters

Avocado with prawns £7.95
French onion soup £5.50
Grapefruit cocktail £4.75
Grilled mushrooms £5.95

Main Courses

Vegetarian lasagne £8.50
Grilled chicken with lemon sauce £8.95
Roast beef £10.30
Lamb chops with garlic mayonnaise £9.25
Fresh salmon £11.00

Vegetables £2.50 each

Garden peas   Cabbage   Carrots   Spinach
Green beans   Potatoes (boiled or fried)

Desserts

Baked apples £4.35
Chocolate cake with vanilla ice-cream £4.50
Pears in red wine £3.20
Strawberries and cream £4.75

Drinks

Wine (red, white, rosé)   Soft drinks £1.50
French £9.00   Mineral water £1.00
Italian £8.00   Fruit juice £1.50
Spanish £8.00   Beer £2.50

Coffee £1.50

VAT AND SERVICE CHARGE INCLUDED

Waiter: role-card

Take the customers' orders. Remember:

- There are a lot of grilled mushrooms and lamb chops, so recommend them!
- There's only enough salmon for **one** person.
- The avocados and strawberries are finished.
- There's only **one** piece of chocolate cake.

Be polite! You aren't very good at mathematics. Make a small mistake in the bill.

Waiter: role-card

Take the customers' orders. Remember:

- There are a lot of grilled mushrooms and lamb chops, so recommend them!
- There's only enough salmon for **one** person.
- The avocados and strawberries are finished.
- There's only **one** piece of chocolate cake.

Be polite! You aren't very good at mathematics. Make a small mistake in the bill.

photocopiable 4 ◁▷

Have another go!

START

Your teacher

Last summer

Your typical day

A restaurant you like

You

FINISH

Have another go!

START

FINISH

Your home

If you become rich and famous

Your best friend

What you eat and drink

Your plans for tonight

Talk for a minute about ...

Yesterday

Compare the English and the people from your country

Compare yourself with somebody in your family

How you relax

Compare two cities you know

FINISH

START

Have another go!

FINISH

The best holiday you've ever had

Last weekend

Your typical weekend

The weather in your country

A country you'd like to visit

START

Have another go!

A Nasard Computers are going to promote two employees. They're going to promote the two people who have worked there for the longest time.

1 Ask and answer questions with **B** to complete the chart. Use *for* or *since* in your answer. Spell the jobs if necessary.

Ask: *What does Kate do?*
How long has Jim worked for the company?

Nasard Computers

Name	Kate	Jim	Leila	Peter	Sylvia	Hari	Jane	Joe
with the company for / since	June 1995		2 years	April 1996			18 months	
Job		technician		economist		electrician		accountant

2 Which two employees are going to get promotion?

B Nasard Computers are going to promote two employees. They're going to promote the two people who have worked there for the longest time.

1 Ask and answer questions with **A** to complete the chart. Use *for* or *since* in your answer. Spell the jobs if necessary.

Ask: *How long has Kate worked for the company?*
What does Jim do?

Nasard Computers

Name	Kate	Jim	Leila	Peter	Sylvia	Hari	Jane	Joe
with the company for / since		3 years			August 1996	4 years		July 1994
Job	secretary		receptionist		manager		psychologist	

2 Which two employees are going to get promotion?

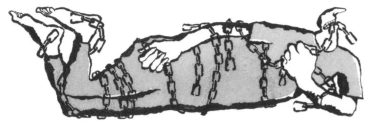

I want to break free *1984*

I want to break free
2 I want to break free
I want to break free from your *lies* | `sile`
4 You're so self-satisfied, I don't _____ you, | `dene`
I've got to break free
6 God knows, God knows I want to break free

I've fallen in _____ | `elov`
8 I've fallen in love for the first time
And this _____ I know it's for real | `imte`
10 I've fallen in love
God knows, God knows I've fallen in love

12 It's strange but it's _____ | `ruet`
I can't get over the way you love me like you do
14 But I have to be _____ | `reus`
When I walk out that door
16 Oh how I want to be free, baby
Oh how I _____ to be free | `anwt`
18 Oh how I want to be free

But _____ still goes on | `fiel`
20 I can't get used to living without, living without
living without you, by my _____ | `edis`
22 I don't want to _____ alone, hey | `ivel`
God knows, got to make it on my own
24 So baby can't you see?
I've got to break free

26 I've got to break free
I want to break free, yeah
28 I want, I want, I want, I want to break free

1 File 5 ⟨·6·⟩ Rearrange the letters
to make words (e.g. `sile` = *lies*).

2 Complete the song.
Listen and check.

3 Read the song. True or false?
  1 He's trying to leave his partner.
  2 He's fallen in love with
    somebody else.
  3 He wants to live alone but he
    finds it difficult.

Queen (1972–)

QUEEN

Queen, formed in 1972, were one
of the biggest bands of the seventies
and the eighties. The musicians were
highly intelligent: Freddie Mercury
(vocals) was an art school graduate,
Brian May (guitar) had a degree in
physics, Brian Taylor (drums) trained
to be a dentist and John Deacon
(bass) had a degree in electronics.
I want to break free was the first single
from the 1984 album *The Works*.
Sadly, Freddie Mercury died of AIDS
on 24th November 1991. Perhaps
Queen's most unforgettable
performance was at Live Aid, the
concert for Ethiopia, in 1985.

Glossary
a lie (*n.*) = the opposite of the truth
self-satisfied (*adj.*) = happy with yourself
I can't get over = I still find it surprising
get used to (*v.*) = become accustomed to
  something
go on (*v.*) = continue

175

photocopiable **5** **B**

AN INDIAN LEGEND

Many years ago in the USA, two Indian tribes (the blue tribe and the red tribe) were living on the opposite sides of a beautiful but dangerous lake. The blue tribe hated the red tribe and the red tribe hated the blue tribe. They were always at war. One day, Black Eagle, a tall young Indian from the blue tribe crossed the lake in his canoe and went into the forest. He was hoping …

What was he hoping to do?

He was hoping to kill some Indians from the red tribe. He was walking slowly and carefully through the forest when suddenly he saw somebody.

Who did he see?

He saw an Indian girl from the red tribe. She was washing some clothes in the lake. Black Eagle wanted to kill her but he couldn't because …

Why couldn't he kill her?

He couldn't kill her because she was really beautiful. The girl's name was Nakoma. At first she was afraid, but they talked and laughed and walked in the forest, and soon they …

What happened?

They fell in love. That night they went back to their tribes but before they said good-bye, Black Eagle made a promise to Nakoma …

What did he promise to do?

He promised to go back and see her again. They planned to meet every full moon. So Black Eagle hid his canoe near the lake and, every month, he crossed the lake to be with Nakoma. They were madly in love. But one night when he looked for his canoe …

What happened?

It wasn't there. Black Eagle looked everywhere but he couldn't find it. So, he decided …

What did he decide to do?

He decided to swim across the lake. The lake was wide and the water was freezing but Black Eagle was young and strong. He swam quickly and soon he could see Nakoma waiting for him on the other side but he was getting tired. He began to swim more slowly, until finally …

What happened?

Finally, he disappeared into the lake and drowned. Nakoma couldn't do anything to save him. But she never forgot the boy who died for her, and she promised never to fall in love again. And the legend is that the Indians named the lake in memory of the poor Indian boy.

What name did the Indians give to the lake?

It was really sunny so …

I lost my keys so …

The bank was closed because …

He had a headache so …

She didn't buy the dress because …

I live with my parents because …

I didn't phone you because …

He got up in the middle of the night because …

I can't drive so …

I don't want to go out with him because …

It was raining so …

The beach was really crowded because …

The hotel was full so …

He's going to Brazil because …

I'm from Italy so …

I called the police because …

We missed the last bus so …

I had to get up early because …

She didn't love her husband so …

She doesn't have to work because …

Hollywood quiz

A

Write the questions. Then ask B.

I Who (sing) in the rain in 1952?
Who sang in the rain in 1952?
a Bing Crosby   **b** John Travolta   **c Gene Kelly**

2 How (die) James Dean?

_____?

a he committed suicide   **b in a car crash**
c of drugs and alcohol

3 How many times Christopher Reeve (play) *Superman*?

_____?

a twice   **b** three times   **c four times**

4 Who (win) the 1995 Oscar for Best Actor in *Forrest Gump*?

_____?

a Tom Hanks   **b** Tom Jones   **c** Tom Cruise

5 Who (direct) the three *Godfather* films in 1971, 1974, and 1989?

_____?

a Martin Scorsese   **b** Quentin Tarrantino
c Francis Ford Coppola

6 Who (say) 'Phone home' in a Stephen Spielberg film?

_____?

a A dinosaur   **b ET**   **c** Peter Pan

7 Who (play) the boxer in four *Rocky* films from 1976 to 1985?

_____?

a Robert de Niro   **b** Al Pacino
c Sylvester Stallone

8 How many Oscars (win) Walt Disney?

_____?

a 10   **b 20**   **c** 30

Hollywood quiz

B

Write the questions. Then ask A.

I Who (play) Scarlett O'Hara in *Gone with the Wind*?
Who played Scarlett O'Hara in 'Gone with the Wind'?
a Vivien Leigh   **b** Elizabeth Taylor
c Meryl Streep

2 How many films (make) Marilyn Monroe?

_____?

a 20   **b 30**   **c** 40

3 Who (star) in *Braveheart*?

_____?

a Kevin Costner   **b Mel Gibson**
c Sean Connery

4 Who (sing) *Philadelphia* in the film of the same name?

_____?

a Bruce Springsteen   **b** Bob Dylan   **c** Sting

5 Who (catch) the plane at the end of *Casablanca* in 1942?

_____?

a Bette Davis   **b** Katherine Hepburn
c Ingrid Bergman

6 Who (write) and (direct) *Annie Hall* in 1977?

_____?

a Woody Allen   **b** Diane Keaton
c Kevin Costner

7 When (die) Charlie Chaplin?

_____?

a 1967   **b 1977**   **c** 1987

8 Which detective (play) Humphrey Bogart?

_____?

a Poirot   **b** Clouseau   **c Marlow**

A

1 **a** Ask **B** the way to:
- the post office
- the bookshop
- the station
- the chemist's
- the shoe shop
- the Tower Hotel
- the gift shop
- the hospital
- the National Art Gallery

b Mark them on your map.

2 Give **B** directions.

B

1 Give **A** directions.

2 **a** Ask **A** the way to:
- the car park
- the bank
- the Oasis Hotel
- the Science Museum
- the bus station
- the market
- the police station
- the swimming pool
- the library

b Mark them on your map.

Eva Perón – *Evita*

Eva Perón was born in Argentina on [1] _____. She was a beautiful child and she dreamed of becoming famous but her life was difficult because her family were poor.

When she was fifteen years old, she met Agustin Magaldi, a singer who worked at a local nightclub. He took her to [2] _____ _____ where she tried to become an actress. Then in [3] _____ she met Juan Perón, an officer in the army. He was [4] _____ years old and she was 24. She became his mistress and he helped her to become a famous radio actress. They got married in 1945. Eva's popularity with the poor workers of Argentina helped her husband, and he became President of Argentina in [5] _____.

In 1947 she went to [6] _____ where she was treated like a pop star. In the same year she formed the *Eva Perón Foundation* and worked [7] _____ hours a day, travelling around the country and giving money to poor people. They loved 'Evita' and she spent much of her life working for them and for women in Argentina.

But Eva's dream of being Vice President of Argentina did not come true because [8] _____ _____ _____ .

She died of cancer on [9] _____. She was only 33 years old. Life in Buenos Aires stopped for the funeral of the woman they called 'Santa Evita'.

Millions of people loved Eva Perón but her enemies said she used the poor for her own ambitions. Two years after her death, the new government organized an exhibition of her clothes and jewellery. She had [10] _____ suits and dresses and some of her coats cost the equivalent of 300 years' salary for a poor worker.

1 Read the biography of Eva Perón.

2 Write the questions to find the missing information.

1 When _____ Eva _____?

2 _____ _____ Magaldi _____ her?

3 _____ _____ _____ _____ Juan Perón?

4 How _____ _____ Perón?

5 _____ _____ Perón _____ President?

6 _____ _____ Eva _____ in 1947?

7 How _____ _____ _____ she _____ a day?

8 Why _____ _____ become Vice President?

9 _____ _____ she _____?

10 How _____ _____ and dresses _____ she _____?

3 Ask your teacher and complete the text.

May and June by Ruth Rendell

1   **Mr and Mrs Thrace had two daughters, called May** and June because of the months when they were born.

May was the oldest. She was changeable like the month, sometimes warm, sometimes cold. She wasn't pretty or clever, although June was. When May was twenty she met a rich, attractive lawyer called Walter and she fell passionately in love with him. He asked her to marry him, and of course she accepted. June was away from home studying to be a teacher when May and Walter got engaged, so Walter never met her. But a month before the wedding June came home for the summer holidays, and Walter immediately fell in love with her.

May

2   **May couldn't accept it. She became violent and tried** to attack June, but there was nothing she could do. Walter and June got married and went to live in a big house in the country. May never married or left her parents' home, and she never forgave her sister.

'She stole my husband,' she said to her mother.

'He wasn't your husband, May,' her mother replied.

When June and Walter came to visit, May always went out, but she knew about them because she always read June's letters to her mother. She knew that they had a big house, that they collected furniture and pictures, and that they didn't have any children. She knew where they went for their holidays and who their friends were. But she could never discover if Walter loved June or not. She thought that perhaps he was sorry that he had married June and not her. This thought was the only thing that made her happy.

3   **May lived at home until her parents died. Mrs** Thrace died in March, and her husband six months later. At her father's funeral May saw Walter and June again. Walter was still good-looking and May wanted to die when she saw him. 'Please come and speak to your sister,' he said to her. But May refused.

Some years later Walter died. June asked May to come to the funeral and at last the sisters met again. June came up to May and asked her to forget about the past. 'Now you know what it's like to lose him,' May said.

Two days later May got a letter from June. June asked her to come and live with her now that they were both alone. 'Now that you've retired and haven't got very much money, I'd like to share my beautiful house with you,' she wrote. 'Perhaps this way I can give you something in return for what I took away from you.'

4   **May decided to accept. She thought it was right.** She went to live with her sister. She asked June to talk about her marriage, about her life with Walter. But June didn't want to talk. May looked in the house for letters or presents from Walter, jewellery or pictures. She couldn't find anything. Even June's wedding ring wasn't as beautiful as the engagement ring Walter gave May all those years ago. 'He never really loved her,' she thought. 'All these years he loved me.' For the first time in years May was happy.

5   **One night May** woke up and heard a noise. 'A burglar,' she thought. She put on her dressing gown and went to June's room. The bed was empty. She looked out of the window and saw a car parked outside the house, and a light in the living-room window. Then she heard a cry and saw a man running out of the house covered in blood. He got into the car and drove away.

June

May went into the living room. June was standing next to her desk, the desk which she always kept locked. It was open now, and the contents were all over the room. There was broken glass on the floor, and a gun. May went up to her.

'Are you all right?'

'Yes, I'm fine. I threw a bottle at him and he ran away. He pointed a gun at me but I wasn't afraid. He only took a few pieces of silver.'

6   **Suddenly May saw a letter which was open in the** desk. It was a letter to June from Walter, the last one he wrote to her when he was dying.

> *My darling love, I want to tell you how happy I have been all these years with you. If I die, I want you to know that you are the only woman I have ever loved.*

'Could you call the police, please May?' asked June.

'Yes,' said May. She picked up the gun.

7   **The police arrived fifteen minutes later. They brought** a doctor with them, but June was already dead.

'Don't worry, Miss Thrace, we'll catch the person who did this,' said the inspector. 'But it's a pity you touched the gun. I suppose you weren't thinking.'

'That's right,' said May. 'It was the shock. I haven't had a shock like that since I was a girl.'

1 Fill in the form for a friend or relative.

Have you got a friend or relative who's looking for a partner?

Name

Age

Job

Smoker yes ☐ no ☐

Interested in
- ☐ politics
- ☐ sport
- ☐ cinema
- ☐ music

Anything else?

Appearance

Favourite free time activities

Personality

good qualities
- ☐ generous
- ☐ unselfish
- ☐ extrovert
- ☐ tidy
- ☐ friendly

Anything else?

bad qualities
- ☐ mean
- ☐ selfish
- ☐ shy
- ☐ untidy
- ☐ unfriendly

Anything else?

Any other information

2 Interview other students to find a 'good match' for your friend.

---

1 Fill in the form for a friend or relative.

Have you got a friend or relative who's looking for a partner?

Name

Age

Job

Smoker yes ☐ no ☐

Interested in
- ☐ politics
- ☐ sport
- ☐ cinema
- ☐ music

Anything else?

Appearance

Favourite free time activities

Personality

good qualities
- ☐ generous
- ☐ unselfish
- ☐ extrovert
- ☐ tidy
- ☐ friendly

Anything else?

bad qualities
- ☐ mean
- ☐ selfish
- ☐ shy
- ☐ untidy
- ☐ unfriendly

Anything else?

Any other information

2 Interview other students to find a 'good match' for your friend.

Food, food, food!

Interview your partner.

Your tastes

1 How important is food in your life?
  Tick the box ✓.

  ☐ really important
  ☐ very important
  ☐ quite important
  ☐ not very important

2 Look at the picture.
  Do you like all the food?
  Which one(s) don't you like?

3 Have you tried …? Tick the boxes ✓.

  ☐ Indian food
  ☐ Chinese food
  ☐ Japanese food
  ☐ Italian food
  ☐ English food

  Which did you like best?

4 What other kinds of foreign food have you tried?

5 Are you or could you be a vegetarian?

6 Is there any food you hate?

Your diet

7 Are you careful about what you eat or drink?
  Is there anything you try not to eat or drink too often?

8

How much	meat fruit fried food fish pasta chocolate fast food	do you eat?
How many	fresh vegetables biscuits or cakes chips or crisps sweets eggs	do you eat?
How much	water coffee milk alcohol	do you drink?

9 Do you think your diet is healthy? Why (not)?

Your meals

10 Do you usually have breakfast?
   What do you usually have?

11 What's your favourite meal of the day? Why?

12 How often do you cook? What's your speciality?

Talk about television

1   Have you got a TV? How many?
    Where exactly is it / are they?
    Do you know anybody who **hasn't** got a TV?

2   How many different TV channels have you got?
    Which one / ones do you watch the most?

3   How much TV do you watch during the week / at the weekend?

4   Who watches the most TV in your family?

5   What do you think of the TV in this country? Tick the box ✓.

    excellent ☐   good ☐   OK ☐   not very good ☐   awful ☐

6   What's your favourite programme on TV? What's your least favourite?
    Are there any adverts you like / don't like?

7   Talk to your partner about the following:

    adverts   news programmes   old films
    quiz programmes   cartoons   documentaries
    comedy shows   violence   sport
    soap operas   music (what kind?)   children's programmes
    Anything else?

I think	*there's* *there are*	*too much* *too many* *not enough*

A

Roleplay 1
You're a customer.

You bought a camera last week because you wanted to take photos at your brother's wedding. But when you tried it, the flash didn't work. You changed the batteries but it still didn't work. Take it back to the shop. You've got the receipt. **You want your money back.**

B starts: *Can I help you?*

You say: *Yes, I bought this camera last week …*

Roleplay 2
You're a shop assistant.

B has a problem with a suit he/she bought at your shop. Find out:

• what the problem is

• when **B** bought it

• if **B** has the receipt

Offer to change it.
You don't want to give **B** the money back.

You start: *Can I help you?*

B

Roleplay 1
You're a shop assistant.

A has a problem with a camera he/she bought at your shop. Find out:

• what the problem is

• when **A** bought it

• if **A** has the receipt

You're a bit nervous because it's your first day at work. Be as friendly as possible. Offer to change it. You don't want to give **A** the money back.

You start: *Can I help you?*

Roleplay 2
You're a customer.

You bought a suit yesterday but when you got home, the zip broke on the trousers. It was very expensive. You wanted to wear it to an important interview this morning but you couldn't. Take it back to the shop. You've got the receipt and you're quite angry. **You want your money back.**

A starts: *Can I help you?*

You say: *Yes, I bought this suit yesterday …*

12 Church Street
Manchester
MC12 6DP
8 March, 1997

BBC TV
Programme Controller
Portland Place
London W1

Dear Sir / Madam,

I am an Italian student living in Manchester and I am <u>writting</u>
to complain about your sports programmes. I love do sport
and I make jogging every morning and play tennis at
weekends. I also like watching sport on TV and I don't
mind to watch football sometimes, but not every day!
There's too many football on the BBC and too
much programmes about football, too. I think you've
forgotten that much people don't like football and
prefer other sports. For example, there isn't basketball enough
and there isn't any volleyball. There also isn't many tennis,
which is a very popular sport. So please, could we have less
football. It's too much boring! I look forward to hearing
from you.

Yours faithfully,

Angela Pera
Angela Pera

1 *writing*
2 _____
3 _____

4 _____
5 _____
6 _____
7 _____
8 _____
9 _____

10 _____

1 Read the letter and answer the questions.

1 Who's it to? Who's it from? _____

2 What's it about? _____

2 Find and underline mistakes (1 to 10) and correct them.

187

A Ask / say **1**, **3**, **5**, **7**, **9**, **11**, and **13** for **B** to answer.

1 Can I borrow your ?

2 No thanks JUST (*have*) one.

3 Did you buy any ?

4 Thanks JUST (*wash*) it.

5 I like your .

6 No (*not start*) it YET.

7 Don't forget to buy the .

8 JUST (*have*) some good news.

9 Are you hungry?

10 Sorry (*not be*) to the bank YET.

11 Do you want an ?

12 Yes ALREADY (*do*) it.

13 You look tired .

14 No thanks ALREADY (*see*) it.

B Ask / say **2**, **4**, **6**, **8**, **10**, **12**, and **14** for **A** to answer.

1 Sorry (*not finish*) it YET.

2 Would you like a ?

3 No (*not be*) to the supermarket YET.

4 Your looks nice.

5 Thanks JUST (*buy*) them.

6 Have you finished your ?

7 ALREADY (*get*) them.

8 You look .

9 No JUST (*have*) a .

10 Can you lend me some ?

11 No thanks ALREADY (*have one*).

12 Have you booked the ?

13 Yes JUST (*get up*).

14 Would you like to see ?

I want to be famous.

I want to be famous.

I forgot my best friend's birthday yesterday.

I forgot my best friend's birthday yesterday.

I want to learn to dance the tango.

I want to learn to dance the tango.

My sister wants to leave her boyfriend and she doesn't know how to tell him.

My sister wants to leave her boyfriend and she doesn't know how to tell him.

I'd like to learn another foreign language.

I'd like to learn another foreign language.

I'd like to buy a pet but I live in a flat.

I'd like to buy a pet but I live in a flat.

I was looking after my friend's cat and now I can't find it.

I was looking after my friend's cat and now I can't find it.

I want to do something new and different in my free time.

I want to do something new and different in my free time.

I want to have a really romantic evening.

I want to have a really romantic evening.

I've got an important exam tomorrow but I haven't studied anything.

I've got an important exam tomorrow but I haven't studied anything.

I want to improve my English pronunciation.

I want to improve my English pronunciation.

I'm planning to buy a new car.

I'm planning to buy a new car.

I'd like to see a really good film.

I'd like to see a really good film.

I've fallen in love with my best friend's girl / boyfriend.

I've fallen in love with my best friend's girl / boyfriend.

Find somebody who	Name	More information
1 woke up late this morning.		
2 is looking for a new flat.		
3 has taken something back to a shop recently.		
4 puts on sun cream in the winter.		
5 is going to look after children at the weekend.		
6 has looked up a word in English today.		
7 hates trying on clothes in shops.		
8 gets on badly with his / her boss or teacher.		
9 turns on the radio when he / she wakes up.		
10 has filled in a form today.		

Where's the lift?	Could I have a sandwich for room 109?
A single room with a bath, please.	I can't open the window.
Can I change $500, please?	The phone in my room doesn't work.
Have you got a map?	I've lost my key.
The lift doesn't work.	Could you help me with my cases?
Where's the dining-room?	Could you call me up at seven o'clock tomorrow morning?
Is there a gym near here?	Could I have a double room for two nights?
The TV doesn't work.	Could you tell me the way to the swimming pool?
I need to see a doctor.	I'd like to change my room. It's too noisy.
There aren't any towels.	Could I have my bill, please?
There isn't any hot water.	Could you call me a taxi to take me to the airport?

1 **File 7** ·16· Label the picture with five of the words.

~~castaway~~ note island
despair (*n.*) sea lonely (*adj.*)
mend (*v.*) shore rescue (*v.*)

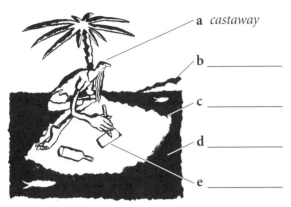

a *castaway*
b _____
c _____
d _____
e _____

2 Match the other words to the definitions.

1 the feeling when you have no hope

_____

2 alone and sad _____

3 another way of saying *repair* _____

4 help somebody who is in danger

_____

The Police (1977–1985)

THE POLICE

formed in 1977 were Sting (real name Gordon Sumner), Andy Summers (guitar), and Stewart Copeland (drums). BBC radio didn't play their first singles because they were about prostitution, *Roxanne* and teenage suicide, *Can't stand Losing You*. *Message in a Bottle* was No.1 all around Europe in 1979. The group separated in 1985. As a solo artist Sting has sold more than 50 million records.

3 Listen and complete with the words.

Message in a bottle 1977

Just a ¹castaway
2 An ²_____ lost at ³_____
Another ⁴_____ day
4 No one here but me
More loneliness
6 Than any man could bear
⁵_____ me before I fall into ⁶_____

Chorus
8 I'll send an SOS to the world
I'll send an SOS to the world
10 I hope that someone gets my
I hope that someone gets my
12 I hope that someone gets my
Message in a bottle

14 A year has passed since I wrote my ⁷_____
But I should have known this right from the start
16 Only hope can keep me together
Love can ⁸_____ your life
18 But love can break your heart

Chorus

Walked out this morning
20 Don't believe what I saw
A hundred billion bottles
22 Washed up on the ⁹_____
Seems I'm not alone in being alone
24 A hundred billion ¹⁰_____ s
Looking for a home

Chorus

26 Sending out an SOS
Sending out an SOS, etc.

Glossary
loneliness = the noun from lonely
bear = accept without complaining
SOS = (**S**ave **O**ur **S**ouls) a message asking for help

193

1 What time do you usually **get up** during the week? Do you ever **get to** school / work late? When was the last time?

2 How long does it take you to **get ready** to leave in the morning? What exactly do you do after you **get up**, and in what order?

3 How long does it take you to **get to** work / school?

4 When was the last time you **got lost**? Where? What happened?

5 What makes you **get angry**? When was the last time you got really angry? Why?

6 Are you afraid of **getting old**? Why (not)?

7 Do you think housewives should **get a salary**? Who should pay it?

8 When was the last time you **got a letter**? Who was it from? What was it about?

9 Who do you **get on** best **with** in your family? Is there anybody in your family you **don't get on** with very well?

10 Have you ever **got drunk**? When was the last time? What happened?

11 What do you think is the best age **to get married**? Do you think men should be older than women? Why do you think people usually **get married**?

12 Which problems in your country are **getting better**? Which are **getting worse**?

1 What time do you usually **get up** during the week? Do you ever **get to** school / work late? When was the last time?

2 How long does it take you to **get ready** to leave in the morning? What exactly do you do after you **get up**, and in what order?

3 How long does it take you to **get to** work / school?

4 When was the last time you **got lost**? Where? What happened?

5 What makes you **get angry**? When was the last time you got really angry? Why?

6 Are you afraid of **getting old**? Why (not)?

7 Do you think housewives should **get a salary**? Who should pay it?

8 When was the last time you **got a letter**? Who was it from? What was it about?

9 Who do you **get on** best **with** in your family? Is there anybody in your family you **don't get on** with very well?

10 Have you ever **got drunk**? When was the last time? What happened?

11 What do you think is the best age **to get married**? Do you think men should be older than women? Why do you think people usually **get married**?

12 Which problems in your country are **getting better**? Which are **getting worse**?

A

Tell B about ...

a sport you can't play

a country you'd like to go to

where you were born

a famous book you haven't read

a kind of food you love

a place you went to last summer

a kind of music you don't like

a job in the house you hate doing

something you didn't do yesterday

something you're going to do next weekend

B

Tell A about ...

a kind of music you like

something you did last night

something you're going to do tonight

a language you can't speak

a new film you'd like to see

a sport or game you can play

a famous film you haven't seen

what star sign you are

a drink you don't like

a foreign country or city you've been to

A

Tell B about ...

a sport you can't play

a country you'd like to go to

where you were born

a famous book you haven't read

a kind of food you love

a place you went to last summer

a kind of music you don't like

a job in the house you hate doing

something you didn't do yesterday

something you're going to do next weekend

B

Tell A about ...

a kind of music you like

something you did last night

something you're going to do tonight

a language you can't speak

a new film you'd like to see

a sport or game you can play

a famous film you haven't seen

what star sign you are

a drink you don't like

a foreign country or city you've been to

THE CINEMA

1 **How often do you …?**
go to the cinema
watch films on TV
watch films on video

2 **What kind of films do / don't you like?**

☐ westerns   ☐ science fiction

☐ love stories   ☐ thrillers

☐ detective films   ☐ musicals

☐ action films   ☐ comedies

☐ violent films   ☐ cartoons

3 **What was the last film you saw?**
What kind of film was it?
Who was in it?
What was it about?
What was it like?

4 **What's the best film you've seen this year?**

5 **What's the worst film you've seen this year?**

6 **Who's your favourite actor / actress?**

7 **What's your favourite film of all time?**
How many times have you seen it?

8 **Do you prefer seeing foreign films with subtitles or dubbed?**

9 **Have you ever …?**
been in a film
met a film actor / actress

A

1 Say the first sentence from **Your problems**. Listen to **B**'s offers.
If you both think it's correct, write it next to the sentence.
Don't look at **B**'s sentences.

Your problems	B's offer
It's very hot in here.	*Shall I open the window?*
I can't do my homework.	
It's very dark here.	
I'm thirsty.	
There isn't any milk.	
The phone's ringing.	

2 Now listen to **B**'s sentence.
Answer **B** choosing the right
sentence from **Your offers**.

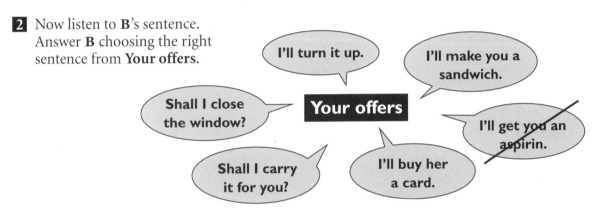

I'll turn it up.

I'll make you a sandwich.

Shall I close the window?

Your offers

I'll get you an aspirin.

Shall I carry it for you?

I'll buy her a card.

B

1 Listen to **A**'s problems.
Answer **A** choosing the
right sentence from **Your offers**.

2 Say the first sentence
from **Your problems**.
Listen to **A**'s offer.
If you both think it's correct
write it next to the sentence.
Don't look at **A**'s sentences.

I'll help you.

I'll answer it.

Shall I turn on the light?

Your offers

I'll go to the supermarket.

Shall I open the window?

I'll make some coffee.

Your problems	A's offer
I've got a terrible headache.	*I'll get you an aspirin.*
I can't hear the TV.	
I'm very hungry.	
It's very cold in here.	
This case is very heavy.	
It's Jane's birthday tomorrow.	

will or *going to*?

Complete with *will* or *going to* + verb. Use contractions.

I **A** Would you like fruit juice or mineral water?

  B I _____ an orange juice please. (*have*)

2 **A** What are Mike's plans for the summer?

  B Well, first he _____ with a friend in Italy (*stay*), and then he _____ to France. (*go*)

3 **A** What _____ you _____ if she doesn't phone? (*do*)

  B I _____ to her. I haven't got her phone number. (*write*)

4 **A** How much is this sweater?

  B £24.99.

  A Fine. I _____ it. (*take*)

5 **A** What _____ tonight? (*do*)

  B Well, if I finish work early I _____ probably _____ to the cinema. (*go*)

6 **A** Have you decided what to do on Saturday night?

  B Yes, we've got tickets for the theatre and after that we _____ dinner at that new Italian restaurant. (*have*)

7 **A** I've had a terrible day today.

  B Sit down, I _____ you a cup of tea. (*make*)

8 **A** Who do you think _____ the World Cup? (*win*)

  B I don't know, but England _____ it. (*not win*)

  A I think Brazil _____ it again. (*win*)

9 **A** Please remember to turn off the lights before you leave.

  B Don't worry, I promise I _____ . (*not forget*)

10 **A** Which train _____ you _____ ? (*catch*)

  B The 5.30 train. If it arrives on time, I _____ home at 7.00. (*be*)

Complete the sentences. Circle the correct answer **a, b,** or **c.**

Present

1 The country in the world which is *visited* (visit) by the highest number of tourists is ⓐ France **b** the USA **c** Spain.

2 **a** 10 million **b** 50 million **c** 110 million bottles of Coca Cola _____ (*drink*) every day.

3 The most common objects which _____ (*steal*) from hotels are **a** towels **b** ashtrays **c** blankets.

4 The noun which _____ (*use*) most frequently in conversation is **a** money **b** time **c** work.

5 2,000 African elephants _____ (*kill*)
a every year **b** every month **c** every week.

6 The New York Times _____ (*read*) every day by
a 1,400,000 **b** 5,400,000 **c** 10,400,000 people.

7 In the world 11,000 babies _____ (*be born*)
a every second **b** every hour **c** every day.

Past

8 The Italian flag _____ (*design*) by
a Garibaldi **b** Mussolini **c** Napoleon.

9 The *Mona Lisa* _____ (*buy*) by King Francis I of France to decorate his **a** bedroom **b** living room **c** bathroom.

10 Chess _____ (*invent*) by
a the Egyptians **b** the Indians **c** the Chinese 1,500 years ago.

11 Football _____ first _____ (*play*) by
a the Romans **b** the Greeks **c** the English.

12 The first Levi Jeans _____ (*wear*) by
a cowboys **b** farmers **c** miners.

13 The first credit card _____ (*use*) in
a 1950 **b** 1960 **c** 1970.

14 The Jazz Singer, the first film with sound,
_____ (*make*) in **a** 1905 **b** 1919 **c** 1927.

A

Certainly, sir. What time?

Can I speak to Martin, please?

a **Can I try them on?**
b **Could I have the bill, please?**
c **I've got a sore throat.**
d **My shoulder hurts.**
e **Rare, medium, or well-done?**
f **Single or return?**
g **What size are you?**
h **Which platform is it?**

1 Describe your cartoons to **B**. **B** will tell you the missing phrases. Write them in the speech bubbles.

2 Listen to **B** describe four cartoons. Choose the missing phrase from the phrases on the right and tell **B**.

B

Oxford, please?

I'll have the steak.

What is the matter?.

i **Can I leave a message?**
j **Could I have a sandwich, please?**
k **Could I have a window seat?**
l **Could you wake me tomorrow morning, please?**
m **Does this bus go to Piccadilly?**
n **Is there a post office near here?**
o **One of my cases hasn't arrived.**
p **Who's calling?**

1 Listen to **A** describe four cartoons. Choose the missing phrase from the phrases on the right and tell **A**.

2 Describe your cartoons to **A**. **A** will tell you the missing phrases. Write them in the speech bubbles.

Imagine *1975*

Imagine there's no heaven

2 It's easy if you try

No hell below us

4 Above us only ¹_____

Imagine all the people

6 Living for ²_____

Imagine there's no countries

8 It isn't hard to do

Nothing to ³_____ or die for

10 And no religion too

Imagine all the people

12 Living life in ⁴_____

Chorus

You may say I'm a ⁵_____

14 But I'm not the only one

I hope some day you'll join us

16 And the ⁶_____ will live as one

Imagine no possessions

18 I wonder if you can

No need for greed or ⁷_____

20 A brotherhood of ⁸_____

Imagine all the people

22 Sharing all the world

Glossary

heaven = where God lives
hell = the opposite of heaven
religion = e.g. Christian, Hindu, etc.
join = come together with
a dreamer = somebody who isn't realistic
as one = united
possessions = things that you have or own
wonder = ask yourself questions
greed = wanting more food or money than you need
hunger = the noun from hungry
a brotherhood = a feeling of great friendship
sharing = to divide something between several people

1 **File 8** ⊡15⊡ Match the opposites.

heaven — above
war — die
today — hell
below — peace
live — hard
easy — tomorrow

2 Read the song with the **Glossary**. Complete with words from the box. Listen and check.

dreamer	kill	peace	man
hunger	today	world	sky

3 Complete with **one** word in each gap.

In John Lennon's ideal world nobody believes in r_____n. There are no c_____s and so there aren't any w_____s. Nobody has any p_____s and everybody has enough to e__t. Everybody lives in p_____e.

4 Do you think any of his dreams will ever happen?

John Lennon (1940 – 1980)

JOHN LENNON

was born in Liverpool in 1940. After The Beatles broke up in 1970, he became famous for his anti-war campaigning. He was shot dead by a fan outside his flat in New York on 8th December 1980. On 9th October 1990, *Imagine* was played simultaneously in 130 countries to commemorate Lennon's fiftieth birthday. After John's death, Yoko Ono bought an area of Central Park and called it *Strawberry Fields* in memory of her husband.

8 ◁▷

1 Have you ever …?

(*be*) to a Karaoke bar

(*meet*) an English or American person

(*get*) a very romantic present

(*sleep*) all night on a beach

2 How long have you …?

(*be*) in this class

(*have*) the shoes you're wearing

(*live*) in this town / city

(*know*) your best friend

3 What are you doing …?

after class

this evening

tomorrow morning

next weekend

4 What will you do if …?

you wake up late tomorrow

you pass the exam at the end of the course

you go out of the school today and
    it's raining

there's no food in the fridge when you
    get home

5 What were you doing …?

two hours ago

at 8.00 last night

at 11.00 yesterday morning

exactly a year ago

6 What do you think is …?

the best restaurant in this town / city

the worst programme on TV at the moment

the most interesting newspaper or
    magazine to read

the cheapest place to buy nice clothes

7 How often do you …?

come to English classes

study English outside class

listen to English

revise vocabulary

8 When was the last time you …?

(*have*) a really good holiday

(*buy*) a new CD

(*do*) sport or exercise

(*go*) to a wedding

9 Would you like to …?

go to another continent

be very famous

know your future

spend a day with a famous person

10 Which do you prefer? Why?

the summer / the winter

the north / south of your country

Saturday / Sunday

travelling by plane / by train

11 What do you love or hate doing …?

when you're at home

when you're on holiday

at work / school

when you go out

12 Do you think …?

cars should be banned in cities

smoking should be illegal

women with children shouldn't work

all countries should use the same money

what you eat and drink	what you eat and drink
your last holiday	your last holiday
your favourite person in your family	your favourite person in your family
the weather in this country	the weather in this country
a city you like	a city you like
problems in your city	problems in your city
a recent film you liked / didn't like	a recent film you liked / didn't like
your plans for the future	your plans for the future
the most interesting building you've visited	the most interesting building you've visited
what you like / don't like doing in the house	what you like / don't like doing in the house
the people in two different regions of your country	the people in two different regions of your country
your favourite day of the week	your favourite day of the week
the room where you work / study	the room where you work / study
a teacher you remember	a teacher you remember

1 File 9 ⏺8⏺ Read the song with the **Glossary**. Complete with the verbs in the box.

2 Listen and check.

3 True or false? *T* or *F*.

1 Her boyfriend left her a week ago.

2 She can see and meet anybody she wants to.

3 She feels sad and lonely.

4 She thinks she should get another boyfriend.

5 She thinks her doctor's advice is good.

6 She doesn't want to see her boyfriend again.

Nothing compares 2 U *1990*

It's been seven hours and fifteen days
2 Since you took your love away
I _____ every night and _____ all day
4 Since you took your love away
Since you've been gone
6 I can _____ whatever I want
I can _____ whoever I _____
8 I can _____ my dinner in a fancy restaurant
But nothing, I said nothing can take away these blues
10 'Cause nothing compares
Nothing compares 2 U

| choose | do | eat | go out | see | sleep |

12 It's been so lonely without you here
Like a bird without a song
14 Nothing can _____ these lonely tears from falling
_____ me baby, where did I go wrong?
16 I could _____ my arms around every
boy I _____
But they'd only remind me of you
18 I went to the doctor's and _____ what he told me
_____ what he told me
He said girl you'd better try to have fun no
matter what you do
20 But he's a fool

'Cause nothing compares
22 Nothing compares 2 U

| guess (×2) | put | see | stop | tell |

All the flowers that you planted boy, in the backyard
24 All died when you went away
I know that living with you baby was sometimes hard
26 But I'm willing to give it another try
'Cause nothing compares
28 Nothing compares 2 U
Nothing compares
30 Nothing compares 2 U

Glossary

2 U = to you
whatever = what
whoever = who
fancy = elegant, smart
blues = sadness / depression
lonely = sad and alone
tears = when you cry they
come out of your eyes
remind = make you remember
you'd better = you should
no matter = it doesn't matter
a fool = a stupid person
backyard = (US) garden
willing = ready
give it another try = try again

Note *Nothing compares 2 U* was written by the American singer / songwriter Prince.

1 A

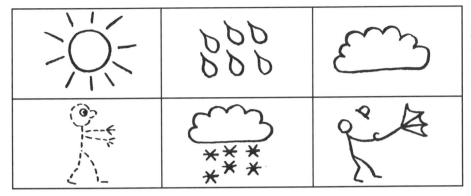

It's sunny.
It's raining.
It's cloudy.

It's foggy.
It's snowing.
It's windy.

1 C

What was the hotel like?
What was the food like?

What was the weather like?
What were the people like?

1 D

Have you been to London?
Have you been to McDonald's?
Have you tried Chinese food?

Have you met a famous person?
Have you seen (name of film)?
Have you heard *Bolero*?

2 A

Have you ever been to Africa?
Have you ever driven a tractor?
Have you ever drunk *Guinness*?

Have you ever done yoga?
Have you ever worked in a restaurant?
Have you ever spoken English on
the phone?

2 B

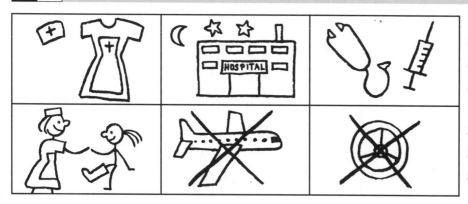

She has to wear a uniform.
She has to work at night.
She has to use special equipment.

She has to look after children.
She doesn't have to travel.
She doesn't have to drive.

2 C

You can smoke.
You can pay by credit card.
You can't park here.

You can't walk on the grass.
You can't turn left.
You can't take photos.

3 B

She's playing tennis at 7.00.
She's going to the hairdresser's at 9.15.
She's meeting her manager at 10.30.

She's recording a song at 11.45.
She's having lunch with her boyfriend at 2.00.
After that they're flying to Mexico.

3 D

At seven o'clock he was sleeping.
At a quarter past eight he was jogging.
At nine o'clock he was having breakfast.

At half past eleven he was working.
At four o'clock he was watching TV.
At a quarter past ten he was playing the saxophone.

4 D

The highest mountain in the world

The longest river in the world

The biggest country in Europe

The tallest animal in the world

The most expensive car in the world

6 D

There are too many cars.

There are too many people.

There are too many factories.

There's too much pollution.

There's too much rubbish.

There's too much unemployment.

7 B

I went to the post office to buy some stamps.

I went to the travel agent's to book a ticket.

I went to the bank to get some money.

I went to the market to buy some fruit.

I went to the cinema to see a film.

I went to the library to borrow a book.

Games bank

A resource bank of easy-to-play games to practise and revise structures and vocabulary. See the **Games bank** in *English File 1* **Teacher's Book** for more ideas.

Alibi

Aim	To revise past simple / past continuous tenses

- Prepare small pieces of paper for each student to write their name on.
- Give out the pieces of paper. SS write their names, fold up the piece of paper, and give it back to you. Put the names in a container, e.g. a box or bag.
- Tell the class that a murder was committed at 8.00 p.m. yesterday (the previous day). Invent a victim, e.g. the director of the school / the mayor(ess) / a local celebrity. (The more dramatic you make it, the more the SS will get involved in the activity.)
- Tell the class that there are two suspects. Pick two SS' names out of the box. The 'suspects' then go out of the class.

Tip It's important that the two suspects are confident, able speakers. In a class of mixed abilities it is better to select the suspects yourself.

- Divide the rest of the class into two groups of 'detectives'. They prepare questions to ask the two suspects. Tell the detectives:
  - the suspects were together from 7.00 p.m. until 11.00 p.m.
  - they saw a film.
- Give SS some ideas for questions, e.g. *Where did you meet at 7.00? How did you get to the cinema? What were you wearing? What was your friend wearing?*
- Tell the two suspects that they were together from 7.00 p.m. until 11.00 p.m., and saw a film. Tell them to prepare their **alibi** for the previous night very carefully, agreeing on every detail. They will be interviewed separately and must tell exactly the same story. Help the suspects with their **alibi**, e.g. *Where did they meet? How did they get to the cinema? What were they wearing?* etc. Set a time limit, e.g. 15 minutes, for suspects and detectives.
- Bring the suspects back into the classroom. **SUSPECT A** is interviewed by one group of detectives and **SUSPECT B** by the other group. The detectives note the suspects' answers. After a set time limit, e.g. eight minutes, the suspects change places and the detectives ask the other suspect the same questions. The suspects mustn't talk to each other.
- After the time limit is up, give the two groups of detectives a minute to compare the suspects' alibis. Do they match? Are the suspects 'innocent' or 'guilty'? **If the suspects contradict each other's story more than twice in important details they are 'guilty' of the crime.**

Tip With a small class you could just have one group of detectives. When the first suspect is being interviewed the second must wait outside. This activity works best if the teacher moves between detectives and suspects, helping both groups with their questions and stories.

The describing game

Aim	To revise any vocabulary group and the language of definitions. To encourage SS to talk.
Example	Adjectives of personality

- SS in pairs, **A** and **B**. **A** needs a piece of paper.
- Student **A**s turn their chairs round so that they can't see the board. **B**s can see the board.
- Write six words on the board that you want SS to practise or revise, e.g. adjectives of personality *selfish, shy, friendly, talkative,* etc.
- **B** has to describe the first word from the board to **A** without using the word, and speaking only in English, e.g. *It's a negative adjective. It's a person who only thinks about himself. He never thinks about other people.* **A** listens and then writes down the word he / she thinks it is and shows it to **B.** If it's correct, **B** then defines the second word. If it's wrong then **B** must try to give a clearer definition or give a clue, e.g. *It begins with 's'.*
- Demonstrate yourself first. Write a word in large letters on a piece of paper but don't show it to the class. Then define the word to the class. When they guess it correctly show them the word on the paper. **Tell the SS to write their guesses down, not call them out, or the other SS will hear.**
- When all the pairs have finished, SS swap roles. Write six new words on the board and continue.

Tip This game works better if it is not competitive, i.e. if SS are co-operating in pairs to define / guess all the words.

You can use **The describing game** to revise:
- any group of words, e.g. jobs, activities, etc.
- phrases from the **Travel phrasebook SB** *p. 132.*
- random words or phrases.

Glug

Aim	To revise tenses

- Play *Glug* in groups of 4 or 5 or with the whole class. S1 chooses a verb, e.g. *have a shower,* and writes it on a piece of paper.
- The other SS have to guess the verb by asking questions in using the invented verb *glug*, which replaces the mystery verb S1 has chosen, e.g.

S2 *Have you ever glugged?*	**S1** *Yes, I have. Very often.*
S3 *Are you glugging now?*	**S1** *No, I'm not.*
S4 *Do you glug every day?*	**S1** *Yes, I do.*
S2 *Did you glug this morning?*	**S1** *No, I didn't.*
S3 *Can you glug in the kitchen?*	**S1** *No, you can't.*
S4 *Is it difficult to glug?*	**S1** *No, it's easy.*

- SS have to try to guess the verb within a limit of 15 guesses.
- The student who guesses the verb then has a turn to choose.

Verbs which work well: *sleep, kiss, ski, cook, sing.*

Tip Demonstrate the activity with the whole class first. Get SS to use as wide a variety of tenses as possible and to correct each other's incorrectly formed questions.

🎲 The long sentence game

Aim	To practise / revise any structure
Example	Daily routine verbs (present simple)

- The teacher starts by saying a daily routine sentence, e.g. *I get up.* and then names a student (*Jean*).
- Jean then repeats the sentence, adds a verb phrase, and names the next student, e.g. *I get up and I have a shower. Noel.*
- Noel repeats the sentence and adds another new verb phrase, e.g. *I get up, I have a shower, and make a coffee. Ana.* etc.
- A different student must be nominated each time. The game continues round the class. **The object of the game is for SS to remember and say the ever lengthening sentence.** When the sentence is long enough and SS are struggling to remember it, finish by getting the whole class to try to say the final sentence together.

  You can use **The long sentence game** for any structure, e.g.
  - **present perfect (experiences)** *I've been to Paris, I've seen the Eiffel Tower* (SS should use different verbs each time).
  - **have to** *I have to get up early, go to the bank.*
  - **to + infinitive** *I went to London to see Big Ben, to visit the Tower of London,* etc.

🎲 Noughts and crosses

Aim	To practise / revise structures, spelling, pronunciation, etc.
Example	*somebody* / *anybody*, etc.

- Draw on the board a *Noughts and crosses* grid with your target language in the squares:

somebody	anything	nowhere
nothing	anywhere	somewhere
anybody	something	nobody

- Divide the class into two teams. **TEAM A** plays with an *X* and **TEAM B** with an *O*.
- **TEAM A** chooses a square (e.g. *anything*) and makes a sentence using the word, e.g. *Did you do anything last night?* Write it on the board.
- If their sentence is correct, rub out *anything* from the square and write in an *X*. If the sentence is wrong and **TEAM B** can correct it with their first guess, they win the square and you write an *O* in the square.
- Then **TEAM B** have their turn, etc. **The first team to get a straight line of three *X*s or three *O*s in any direction wins the game.**

- If time, repeat the game with a new set of words.

  You can use *Noughts and crosses* to revise recently taught language points, e.g.
  - **quantifiers** *a lot (of), many* +, *much* +, *some, a little, a few, much* −, *many* −, *any*, etc.
  - **time expressions** *yet, already, just, ago, since, for, never, ever, usually*, etc.
  - **phrasal verbs** *turn on, look after, fill in, pick up, throw away, put on, take off, look up, get on*, etc.
  - **So (do) I. / Neither (do) I.** Have a list of sentences prepared for each square with a variety of tenses, e.g. *I don't smoke. I saw a good film last night. I've been to New York.* When SS choose a square you read the sentence and the team has to respond with *So / Neither* and the correct auxiliary.

  You can also use *Noughts and crosses* as an end-of-term quiz for general revision.

- Choose nine categories you want to revise, e.g.

1 Opposites	2 Spelling	3 Prepositions
4 Word order	5 Pronunciation	6 Travel phrasebook
7 Verbs	8 People	9 Things

- Prepare several questions for each category, e.g.
  1 What's the opposite of *clean*? (dirty)
  2 How do you spell *February*?
  3 Where did you go ____ the weekend? (at)
  4 just 've I lunch had (I've just had lunch).
  5 How do you pronounce …? (behind)
  6 You're lost. You want to find the station. What do you say? (Excuse me, can you tell me the way to the station, please?)
  7 Can you ___ me some money until tomorrow? (lend)
  8 He / she translates orally from one language to another. (interpreter)
  9 Something which you buy cheaply in a shop. (bargain)
- SS choose a square, you read out a question for them to answer, and mark an X or O in the square, as above.

🎲 The sound game

Aim	To practise pronunciation and spelling patterns

- **Odd-one-out**
  Put four words on the board (e.g. from the lesson or the **Sound bank** (*WB p. 81*) in the Workbook). Three should have the same vowel sound, and one should be different. SS have to find the different word, e.g. *door floor walk* <u>*work*</u>

- **What's the common sound?**
  Put four words on the board as above. SS have to find the common sound, e.g. *biscuits English since biggest* (= /iː/)

Telepathy

Aim	To practise first conditional sentences
Example	*If you go to bed late, you'll be tired tomorrow.*

Prepare a set of half sentences (first conditional) which SS have to use 'telepathy' to complete.

- Form teams of 4 to 6 SS.
- Write the first half sentence on the board and indicate if the second half is ⊟ or ⊞, e.g. *If you go to bed late you … ⊟, We'll go to the beach tomorrow, if …* ⊟ or ⊞.
- **SS have to try to finish the sentences in exactly the same way**, i.e. write the most obvious ending to the sentence that they think their team mates will also have put, e.g. *… won't wake up tomorrow.*
- SS read out their sentences.
  - For every correct sentence the team gets 1 point.
  - If two SS have written exactly the same sentence the team gets an extra point for each sentence.
  - If the whole team have written exactly the same sentence they get a bonus of 5 points.
- Now write another sentence half, keeping the score on the board.

Who are you?

Aim	To practise / revise verb *be*, nationalities, jobs, adjectives, all verb forms, etc.

- Write the names of famous living people on cards (or use magazines photos).
- Demonstrate the activity yourself first. Choose the identity of one of the famous people. SS have a maximum of fifteen guesses to find out who you are. You can only answer *Yes, (I am). / No, (I'm not).*
- Help SS by writing on the board the kinds of questions they could ask, e.g.

> Are you a man / woman?
> Are you an actor?
> Are you a film star?
> Are you going out with … at the moment?
> Have you got any children?

- You can play the game in pairs / groups / as a class. The student who guesses correctly is given the next famous name for the other SS to guess.

Tip This works much better if you give SS the names rather than ask them to think of their own.

You can also play *Who were you?* with famous dead people to practise the past simple.

 ## Word tennis

Aim	To practise / revise any vocabulary group

- Divide the class into **TEAM A** and **TEAM B**. Call out a word group, e.g. *vegetables*.
- **TEAM A** 'serves' by saying a word in that group, e.g. *potatoes.*

- **TEAM B** 'returns the serve' by saying another word, e.g. *carrots.* **TEAM A** says another word, etc. The game ends when one team (in five seconds) can't think of another word in that category.
- Then call out another word group (e.g. *the body*), and continue.

You can also use **Word tennis** to revise irregular past participles. **TEAM A** 'serves' the infinitive (e.g. *write*). **TEAM B** has to say the past participle, and then 'returns' another infinitive (e.g. *written, drive*).

Ten ideas to use in an emergency

These are quick five-minute revision activities to use as lesson warmers, fillers, or in an emergency (e.g. if you run out of material or don't want to start a new File).

1 Do an exercise from the next **Vocabulary file**.

2 Get SS to cover the words in **Wordbank** and test each other in pairs, e.g. **Food**:
A (points at a picture) *What are those?*
B *They're onions.*

3 Play a memory test. In pairs, SS look at any page of **Wordbank** for a minute. Then they close the books and try to remember / write all the words / phrases.

4 Get SS to test each other on the **Travel phrasebook**, e.g.
A *How do you say '…' in English?*
B *'…'*

5 Write jumbled sentences from the previous lesson on the board for SS to order correctly, e.g. *last go did night anywhere you?* (= Did you go anywhere last night?)

6 Use the **Sound bank WB** *p. 81* to practise vowels and consonants that are difficult for your SS. Choose a sound and ask SS to repeat after you. Then ask them to think of other words containing the sound. Write them on the board and SS can write them in their notebooks.

7 Give a quick dictation, e.g. dictate five sentences from the **Travel phrasebook** or the **Listening** tapescripts. Only use sentences SS have read / heard before.

8 Do a **Workbook** exercise in class in pairs / small groups.

9 Give SS a quick test on **Words to learn** from the previous lesson in the **Workbook**, e.g. anagrams or translation.

10 Play a game from the **Games bank**.

Tests

- There are four **Workbook Quicktests** after **File 2**, **4**, **6** and **8**
- There are three photocopiable **Teacher's Book** tests, after **Files 3** and **6**, and an End-of-book test after **Files 8** or **9**. These can be used as:
  - informal tests to provide you with feedback on how well SS have assimilated the language of the preceding three files, **OR**
  - formal tests to assess your SS' progress and to decide if they are ready to move on to the next level in your school.

■ Before the tests

To help SS revise, tell them that they will be tested on the **Grammar files**, the **Vocabulary files**, the **Word bank**, and the **Travel phrasebook**, pronunciation (word stress and English sounds), writing, (a short text), listening, and speaking (if you do the oral test).

■ How to give and mark the tests

- Copy and give out one test per student.
- Quickly go through each part of the test. Explain that SS will get one mark for each answer (listening and writing are marked differently).
- SS work individually and write their answers on the test paper. The writing exercise should be written on a separate sheet with their name.
- **Tests 1** and **2** should take **45** to **60** minutes. The **End-of-book** test should take **60** to **75** minutes so you may have to do the listening and / or writing in another class.
- Collect and correct the tests.
- All three tests have a total of **100 marks**. If you give an oral test you should give a separate mark out of **10**.

■ Writing

The writing task is marked out of 20. We suggest you allocate:
10 marks for grammar, vocabulary, and spelling.
10 marks for content, presentation, and layout.

■ Listening

The recordings for the tests are at the end of Class cassette 3. Tapescripts for the listening exercises:

Test 1

A Good evening, Do you have a single room?
B For how many nights?
A Just for tonight.
B Yes, we've got a single room with a shower.
A How much is it?
B $75 including breakfast. Would you like to see the room?
A No, that's OK. Can I pay by credit card?
B Yes, you can.
A Is there a TV in the room?
B No, there isn't but there's one in the dining-room.
A What time's breakfast?
B Seven thirty to nine thirty.
A And where's the dining-room?
B On the first floor.
A What time do I have to leave the room tomorrow?
B 12.00 midday. Here's your key. Room number 206.

Test 2

A Excuse me. Have you got these jeans in my size?
B What size are you?
A Forty.
B This is a forty.
A How much are they?
B 39.99
A Can I try them on?
B Of course. The changing room's over there.
B Are they OK?
A No, they're too big.
B Do you want to try a 38?
A No thanks. I'll leave it.
C Excuse me, I bought this shirt here last week. I'd like to change it please. It's too small for me.
B Have you got the receipt, please?
C No, I'm sorry I haven't. I've lost it. But what's the problem? I bought the shirt here.
B I'm sorry, we can't change anything without the receipt.
C Well that's ridiculous.
B I'm sorry but that's our policy.

End-of-book test

A

1 A Excuse me! Could you tell me the way to the Museum of Modern Art?
  B Yes. Go down this street. It's on the left, opposite the park.

2 A Can I help you?
  B Yes, Could I have a quarter of a kilo of that ham?
  A This one?
  B No, that one.
  A Anything else?
  B No thanks. How much is that?
  A That'll be £4.40.
  B 4.40?
  A Yes, that's right.

3 A Medical Centre. Can I help you?
  B Yes, I'd like to make an appointment to see the doctor this morning.
  A What's the problem?
  B I've got a stomach-ache. I've had it for two days.
  A Is 10.45 OK for you?
  B Yes, that's fine.

4 A Excuse me. What time's the next train to London?
  B The next one's at 14.25, platform five.

5 A Hello, can I speak to Gina please?
  B I'm afraid she isn't here – she's at work. Who's calling?
  A This is Jack. I'm a friend. Do you know what time she'll be back?
  B Well, she usually gets home about a quarter to seven.
  A OK. I'll call back then. Thank you.
  B Goodbye.
  A Bye.

211

End-of-book test *cont.*

B

A Where did you meet your wife, Bill?

B I met Paula at a party in Argentina about six years ago when I was out there on business. Paula was working as a nurse in a hospital in Buenos Aires. I was working for a British company there.

A And when did you get married?

B About six months later. We got married twice in fact, in Argentina and in Britain. The idea was that we would live and work in Britain and Paula got a job in one of the London hospitals. But what happened was that after two or three months she got very depressed, firstly because of the weather – it was a very cold, dark winter – and secondly because she wasn't very happy in her job. So we decided that the best thing to do was to go somewhere where it was a bit hotter and we finally decided on Italy, which is a country we both like and where we've both found jobs and we're very happy there.

■ Oral tests

If you want to encourage your SS to speak, you should give oral tests from time to time and include speaking in their evaluation. They are very motivating for SS, although time-consuming and sometimes difficult to arrange. Here are two simple options:

1 Continuous assessment

Give a mark from 1 to 5 for general willingness and ability to speak in class, and / or for a specific activity (e.g. the regular **Talk about** from the **Student's Book** or the P **Talk about …** games).

This works best if you tell SS that you're going to give them a mark each time. Mark SS. Position yourself in the middle of the class so you can hear and mark the maximum number of SS at once without intimidating.

2 Short oral interviews

Interview SS individually for three to five minutes. Meanwhile the rest of the class can revise together, do written exercises, or read an *Easy Reader*. You can choose questions to ask from P **23** or **60** *p. 165* and *p. 202*, make up your own, or see the suggestions below.

Give the whole class a list of general topics to prepare before you intend to test them (e.g. yourself, your family, your town.) Even though they won't know which topics you will choose, it should motivate SS to practise a bit more both in and out of class.

Suggested questions for oral tests

Below are suggested questions for oral tests to accompany the three **Teacher's Book** tests. It's a good idea to use a mixture of **direct questions** and **Tell me about …**

Test 1 | Files 1 to 3

Direct questions

1 What do you do?
2 Why are you learning English?
3 Where were you born?
4 How do you get to work / school?
5 How long does it take?
6 What are you doing (tonight)?
7 What are you going to do (at the weekend)?
8 What did you do last night?
9 What were you doing at (3.00 yesterday afternoon)?
10 Have you ever been to (Britain)?
11 How often do you (go to the theatre)?
12 What was the weather like yesterday?
13 What do you do in your free time?
14 What time do you usually (go to bed)?

Tell me about …

your job	your family
your last holiday	your lifestyle
your plans for (tomorrow)	your typical Saturday
the weather in your country in the summer and winter	

Test 2 | Files 4 to 6

Recycle questions from **Test 1** above, and add from the following:

Direct questions

1 Have you ever been to (name of city)?
2 How long have you lived here?
3 What problems are there in this town / city?
4 What jobs do you do in the house?
5 What does your (best friend) look like?
6 What's your (best friend) like?
7 Did you go anywhere last night?
8 What do you like doing in your free time?
9 What are you planning to do (at the weekend)?
10 Where would you like to go this summer?

Tell me about …

some of the differences between this town and (name of city)
your (brother)
your diet
your plans for (next weekend / summer)

End-of-book test

Recycle questions from **Tests 1** and **2** above and add from the following:

1 What should I do if I want to learn (Arabic) quickly?
2 What do you think the weather will be like tomorrow?
3 What are the first two things you turn on in the morning?
4 What kind of films do you like?
5 What things are made in your / this country?

Marking oral tests

Marking an oral test is always very subjective. We recommend giving **1 to 5** marks for fluency and vocabulary, and **1 to 5** marks for accuracy of grammar and pronunciation.

Name

© Oxford University Press photocopiable

1 Grammar

One mark for each correct answer.

A Put the verbs in the right tense.

Example: They *went* to Florida last year (go)

1 When I woke up yesterday it _____ _____. (rain)

2 She can't come. She _____ tonight. (study)

3 He always _____ swimming before breakfast. (go)

4 We _____ out last night. (not go)

5 Today's a holiday. We _____ work. (not have to)

6 She's a nurse but she _____ at night. (not work)

7 Last night my parents _____ home when I _____ on the phone to my girlfriend in Australia. (arrive, talk)

B Write the questions.

Example: *What do you* do? I'm a doctor.

1 What _____ the weather _____ yesterday? It was warm and sunny.

2 How _____ _____ it take to drive to London? About three hours.

3 _____ _____ that jacket? It's mine.

4 What _____ _____ doing tonight? Nothing special.

5 _____ you _____ to Japan? No, I haven't.

6 What _____ you _____ at 8.00 last night? I was working.

7 Where _____ you _____ on holiday last year? We went to Turkey.

8 Where _____ your brother _____ ? He lives in New York.

C Complete with one word.

Example: A post office is a place *where* you buy stamps.

1 Is that Maria's coat? Yes, it's _____ .

2 A camera is a thing _____ takes photos.

3 In Britain you _____ vote until you're 18.

4 A _____ you like to see a film ? B Yes, I'd love to.

5 A pilot is a person _____ flies a plane.

6 It _____ two hours to fly to Madrid from London.

7 She works as _____ interpreter.

8 _____ your sister worked in a shop before?

9 Have you _____ been to an opera?

10 Go _____ this road and then turn right at the end.

Grammar	25

2 Vocabulary

One mark for each correct answer.

A Complete with a preposition.

Example: She's waiting *for* the bus.

1 _____ the weekends I often go to the beach.

2 A Did you speak _____ Jane? B No, she was out.

3 They stayed _____ a week.

4 In Spain people often have a sleep _____ lunch.

5 In the afternoon he went _____ a walk.

6 They can't go to the party _____ Saturday.

7 Has your brother been _____ Italy?

8 When I'm at work a friend looks _____ my children.

9 Where are you going _____ holiday this year?

10 Look _____ those birds! They're beautiful.

B Complete the sentences with one word.

1 *It's very* _____ .

2 *They're* _____ .

3 *She's got* _____ *hair.*

4 *He's* _____ .

5 *He's going* _____ *the wall.*

213

C What's the missing word?

Example: one / once   two / *twice*

1 north / south   east / _____
2 Everest / a mountain Loch Ness / _____
3 play / tennis   _____ / photos
4 interesting / boring well-paid / _____
5 a CD box / square   a plate / _____
6 hear / ears   see / _____
7 table / wood   a knife and fork / _____
8 good / fantastic   bad / _____
9 one / first   ten / _____
10 trousers / a zip   a shirt / _____

| **Vocabulary** | **25** |

3 Travel with English

One mark for each correct answer.

A Write the questions.

Example: gate which it is? *Which gate is it?*

1 a could have I please seat window?

_____

2 arrived cases excuse hasn't me my of one.

_____

3 centre city next the the time's to train what?

_____

4 at could half me past seven up wake you?

_____

5 please can the take you to me station?

_____

B Complete with one word.

Example: Smoking or *non-smoking*?

1 Board at 12.50 at _____ number 11.
2 A A ticket to London please.
   B single or _____?
3 There's a train in ten minutes from _____ 7.
4 Would you like a single or a _____ room?
5 The TV in my room doesn't _____.

| **Travel with English** | **10** |

4 Pronunciation

One mark for each correct answer.

A Underline the stress.

Example: uni*ver*sity

1 temperature   4 qualifications
2 degree   5 interesting
3 incredible

B Circle the different sound.

Example: iː   three   speak   (friend)   see

1 əʊ   coat   hope   how   cold
2 ɔː   door   walk   clock   saw
3 ɑː   arm   glass   man   park
4 ɜː   first   four   shirt   work
5 eɪ   rain   wake   can't   stay

| **Pronunciation** | **10** |

5 Writing

Twenty marks

Write 100 words about your last holiday. Say :

- where / when / how you went, and who with
- how long you stayed
- what you did (morning, afternoon, evening)
- what the weather / food was like

| **Writing** | **20** |

6 Listening

Two marks for each correct answer.

▸ 1 ◂ **Listen to a conversation in a hotel. Answer the questions.**

1 How much is a single room?
2 What time does breakfast finish?
3 Is there a TV in the room?
4 Where's the dining-room?
5 What time do you have to leave the room?

| **Listening** | **10** |
| **Final Total** | **100** |

1 Grammar

One mark for each correct answer.

A Put the verbs in the right form.

Example: They *went* to Florida last year. (go)

1 If you _____ you _____ your exams. (not study, not pass)

2 She _____ in France since 1991. (work)

3 They're hoping _____ a new car. (buy)

4 _____ is one of the most popular forms of exercise. (jog)

5 He isn't very good at _____ . (iron)

6 A bus came immediately, so we _____ _____ wait. (not have to)

7 Would you like _____ for a walk? (go)

8 I love _____ . (cook)

B Write the questions.

Example: *What do you* do?   I'm a doctor.

1 _____ _____ *War and Peace*? Leon Tolstoy.

2 How _____ _____ _____ _____ married? They've been married for two years.

3 What _____ _____ like _____ do next year? I'd like to travel.

4 What _____ _____ like _____ in your free time? Reading and relaxing.

5 What _____ your sister _____ _____ ? She's short, with dark hair.

6 What's she _____ ? She's quite shy.

7 _____ _____ milk is _____ in the fridge? There's only half a litre.

C Complete with one word.

Example: A post office is a place *where* you buy stamps.

1 Where did you go last night? _____ . I stayed at home.

2 Rome isn't as noisy _____ Tokyo.

3 I drive more carefully _____ my mother.

4 The *Mona Lisa* is one of the _____ famous paintings in the world.

5 The shop was closed _____ I couldn't get any milk.

6 A How many cigarettes do you smoke a day?

   B Only a _____ . Two or three.

7 I couldn't buy the skirt because I didn't have _____ money.

8 I hate living in the city because there's _____ much traffic.

9 The River Nile is the _____ river in the world.

10 There's a _____ of traffic in the city centre.

Grammar	25

2 Vocabulary

One mark for each correct answer.

A Write the opposite adjective.

Example: tall   *short*

1 hard-working _____

2 dangerous   _____

3 generous   _____

4 clean   _____

5 exciting   _____

6 noisy   _____

7 narrow   _____

8 friendly   _____

B Choose the right verb.

Example: Look at / ~~watch~~ these photos.

1 I *met / knew* my boy-friend at a party.

2 Hurry up! We're going to *miss / lose* the bus.

3 Can I *lend / borrow* your dictionary?

4 Doctors *win / earn* a lot of money.

5 *Tell / Say* me what happened last night.

C Complete with a preposition.

Example: She's waiting *for* the bus.

1 She's been a teacher ____ twenty years.

2 It's the biggest country ____ the world.

3 I'm not very good ____ cooking.

4 He's afraid ____ flying.

5 We've worked here ____ 1989.

6 They fell ____ love at first sight.

D What's the missing word?

Example: one / once   two/ *twice*

1 chocolates / box   cigarettes / _____

2 four / fourth   three / _____

3 umbrella / carry   clothes / _____

4 8 years old / child   14 years old / _____

5 start work/ retire   be born / _____

6 polluted / pollution   unemployed / _____

Vocabulary	25

3 Travel with English

One mark for each correct answer.

A Order the sentences.

Example: gate which it is? *Which gate is it?*

1 back I'd money my like

_____

2 bill could have please the we?

_____

3 didn't excuse I me order this.

_____

4 first on right take the the turning.

_____

5 can cheese have I of please some that?

_____

B Complete with ONE word.

Example: Smoking or *non-smoking*?

1 Could you tell me the _____ to the station.

2 Have you got these jeans in my _____ ?

3 Go _____ on, past the hospital and turn left.

4 Can I try them _____ ?

5 I'll _____ the roast chicken.

Travel with English	10

4 Pronunciation

One mark for each correct answer.

A Underline the stress.

Example: uni*ver*sity

1 along   4 politician

2 different   5 pollution

3 dessert

B Circle the different sound.

Example: far   glasses   (have)   can't

1 [ʌ]   fun   some   home   nothing

2 [ɪ]   five   in   if   since

3 [iː]   team   speak   steak   seen

4 [eə]   hair   where   there   here

5 [ɪə]   hear   near   wear   beer

Pronunciation	10

5 Writing

Twenty marks

Write a paragraph about a good friend. Say :

• where you met.

• how long you've been friends.

• what he / she looks like.

• what he / she is like.

• something about his / her life and interests.

• how often you meet

Write about 100 words.

Writing	20

6 Listening

Two marks for each correct answer.

° 2 ° **Listen to a conversation in a clothes shop. Answer the questions.**

1 What size is the girl?

2 How much are the jeans?

3 Why doesn't the girl buy them?

4 What does the man want to do?

5 Why does the shop assistant say no?

Listening	10

Final Total	100

End-of-book test

1 Grammar

One mark for each correct answer.

A Put the verbs in the right form.

Example: They *went* to Florida last year. (go)

1 The plane _____ ! (just / land)

2 A lot of Ford cars _____ in Spain. (make)

3 I don't think there _____ another world war. (be)

4 She phoned me when I _____ the dinner. (cook)

5 I _____ an old friend last night for dinner. (meet)

6 We'll be late if they _____ soon. (not arrive)

7 I don't like _____ the kitchen. (clean)

8 I'd like _____ rich and famous. (be)

B Write the questions.

Example: *What do you* do?   I'm a doctor.

1 _____ _____ booked the tickets yet? Yes, I've already booked them.

2 When _____ the palace _____ ? It was built in 1876.

3 _____ _____ _____ you lived here? For two years.

4 _____ _____ ever _____ to China? Yes, I have. I went there in May.

5 _____ _____ the *Mona Lisa?* Leonardo da Vinci.

6 How _____ _____ you go out? It depends. Once or twice a week.

7 What _____ you _____ last night? I went to the theatre.

C Complete with one word.

Example: A post office is a place *where* you buy stamps.

1 He went to Brazil _____ see the carnival.

2 It's very cold. Put your coat _____ .

3 A I saw a great film last night.

   B _____ you? What film?

4 A I don't like ironing. B _____ do I.

5 We didn't do _____ special last night. We just stayed at home and watched TV.

6 My brother's much taller _____ me.

7 I spent a _____ of money.

8 He's 16. He isn't old _____ to drive.

9 She looks _____ her mother. They've got the same eyes.

10 We went to Mexico _____ a holiday.

Grammar	25

2 Vocabulary

One mark for each correct answer.

A Complete with the correct preposition.

Example: She's waiting *for* the bus.

1 I usually go on holiday _____ August.

2 She's very interested _____ modern art.

3 Wait _____ me! I want to go with you.

4 Let's go _____ car. It's cheaper.

5 Can I try _____ this T-shirt, please?

B Write the word.

Example: It's a very fast road m*otorway*

1 It's like a mountain but smaller. h_ _ _

2 The list of food in a restaurant. _ _ n _

3 Part of the body. You walk on them. l _ _ s

4 A fruit you can make wine with. g _ _ _ _ s

5 Look at monuments and buildings when you're in a new city. go s _ _ _ _ _ _ _ ing.

C Complete with a verb.

Example: I always *wear* a suit to work.

1 If you don't take a map, you'll get _____ .

2 When I speak English I often _____ mistakes.

3 You need to _____ exercise every day.

4 Could you _____ me some money until tomorrow? I didn't have time to go to the bank.

5 Film stars _____ a lot of money.

D Cross out the wrong word.

Example: She plays as / like Steffi.

1 But / Although he was late they waited.

2 Write soon / early.

3 Do you still / yet work for IBM?

4 I've near / nearly finished.

5 He's just / yet arrived.

Vocabulary	20

217

End-of-book test

Name

3 Travel with English

Two marks for each correct answer.

A Write the phrases.

Example: You're in a Bureau de Change.
You want to change 100 dollars.
What do you say?
Can I change 100 dollars please?

1 You're in a hotel. You need to get up tomorrow at 7.00. What do you say to the receptionist?

_____

_____

2 You want to know the price of some jeans. What do you say to the shop assistant?

_____

_____

3 You're in Oslo. You don't speak Norwegian. You want to find the station. What do you say?

_____

_____

4 You're in a restaurant with a friend in London. You want to pay. What do you say to the waiter?

_____

_____

5 You want to phone your parents. They're going to pay for the call. What do you say to the operator?

_____

_____

Travel with English	10

4 Pronunciation

One mark for each correct answer.

A Underline the stress.

Example: uni**ver**sity

1 dangerous   3 organization   5 intelligent
2 behind   4 interested

B Circle the different sound.

Example: /ɑː/ far glasses (have) can't

1 /ʌ/ one lot much love
2 /ɜː/ first work near learn
3 /aʊ/ now close our town
4 /dʒ/ job great jeans Germany
5 /θ/ those Thursday thousand think

Pronunciation	10

5 Writing

Write a letter to a pen-friend.

Write 120 words. Include information about yourself, your lifestyle, your town, your reasons for learning English and your future.

Writing	20

6 Listening

A ◦3◦ Listen and answer the questions.

One mark for each correct answer.

1 Where exactly is the museum?
2 How much does the woman's shopping cost?
3 What's the matter with the man?
4 What time's the next train to London?
5 What time will Gina be back?

B Listen to Bill and Paula's story and complete the blanks with one word.

One mark for each correct answer.

Bill met his wife, Paula at a ¹_____ in ²_____ . She was working as a ³_____ and he was on ⁴_____ .

They got married ⁵_____ months later and they planned to live in ⁶_____ . But after a few months Paula got very ⁷_____ because she didn't like the ⁸_____ or her ⁹_____ . So finally they decided to live in ¹⁰_____ .

Listening	15

Final Total	100

218

Tests key

Test 1 — Files 1 to 3

1 Grammar
A 1 was raining 2 is studying / is going to study
  3 goes 4 didn't go 5 don't have to
  6 doesn't work 7 arrived, was talking.
B 1 was, like 2 long does 3 Whose is 4 are you
  5 Have, been 6 were, doing 7 did, go
  8 does, live
C 1 hers / Maria's 2 which / that 3 can't
  4 Would 5 who / that 6 takes 7 an
  8 Has 9 ever 10 along / up / down

2 Vocabulary
A 1 At 2 to 3 for 4 after 5 for 6 on / next
  7 to 8 after 9 on 10 at
B 1 windy 2 mushrooms 3 curly 4 sunbathing
  5 over
C 1 west 2 a lake 3 take 4 badly-paid 5 round
  6 eyes 7 metal 8 awful / terrible / horrible
  9 tenth 10 (a) button(s)

3 Travel with English
A 1 Could I have a window seat, please?
  2 Excuse me. One of my cases hasn't arrived.
  3 What time's the next train to the city centre?
  4 Could you wake me up at half past seven?
  5 Can you take me to the station please?
B 1 gate 2 return 3 platform 4 double 5 work

4 Pronunciation
A 1 temperature 2 degree 3 incredible
  4 qualifications 5 interesting
B 1 how 2 clock 3 man 4 four 5 can't

5 Writing
See **Teacher's notes** p.211

6 Listening
1 $75 2 9.30 3 No, (there isn't).
4 (On the) first floor. 5 12.00 / midday

Test 2 — Files 4 to 6

1 Grammar
A 1 don't study, won't pass 2 has worked
  3 to buy 4 Jogging 5 ironing 6 didn't have to
  7 to go 8 cooking
B 1 Who wrote 2 long have they been
  3 would you, to 4 do you, doing
  5 does, look like 6 like 7 How much, there
C 1 Nowhere 2 as 3 than 4 most
  5 so / and 6 few 7 enough / any 8 too / so
  9 longest 10 lot

2 Vocabulary
A 1 lazy 2 safe 3 mean 4 dirty 5 boring
  6 quiet 7 wide 8 unfriendly
B 1 met 2 miss 3 borrow 4 earn 5 Tell
C 1 for 2 in 3 at 4 of 5 since 6 in
D 1 packet 2 third 3 wear 4 teenager
  5 die 6 unemployment

3 Travel with English
A 1 I'd like my money back.
  2 Could we have the bill please?
  3 Excuse me. I didn't order this.
  4 Take the first turning on the right.
  5 Can I have some of that cheese, please?
B 1 way 2 size 3 straight 4 on 5 have

4 Pronunciation
A 1 along 2 different 3 dessert
  4 politician 5 pollution
B 1 home 2 five 3 steak 4 here 5 wear

5 Writing
See **Teacher's notes** p.211

6 Listening
1 40 2 39.99 3 (They're) too big.
4 Change a shirt 5 He hasn't got the receipt

End-of-book test

1 Grammar
A 1 has just landed 2 are made 3 will be
  4 was cooking 5 met 6 don't arrive
  7 cleaning 8 to be
B 1 Have you 2 was, built 3 How long have
  4 Have you, been 5 Who painted 6 often do
  7 did, do
C 1 to 2 on 3 Did 4 Neither 5 anything
  6 than 7 a lot 8 enough 9 like 10 for

2 Vocabulary
A 1 in 2 in 3 for 4 by 5 on
B 1 hill 2 menu 3 legs 4 grapes 5 sightseeing
C 1 tired 2 make 3 do 4 lend
  5 earn / get / make
D 1 Although 2 soon 3 still 4 nearly 5 just

3 Travel with English
A (suggested answers)
  1 Could / can you call me / wake me up at 7.00
    tomorrow (morning) please?
  2 How much are these (jeans)?
  3 (Excuse me) Could / can you tell me the way to the
    bus station, please?
  4 Could / can we have the bill please?
  5 I'd like to make a reverse charge call, please.

4 Pronunciation
A 1 dangerous 2 behind 3 organization
  4 interested 5 intelligent
B 1 lot 2 near 3 close 4 great 5 those

5 Writing
See **Teacher's notes** p.211

6 Listening
A 1 on the left, opposite the park 2 £4.40
  3 He's got a stomach-ache. 4 14.25
  5 at about quarter to seven (6.45)
B 1 party 2 Argentina 3 nurse 4 business
  5 six 6 Britain 7 depressed 8 weather
  9 job 10 Italy

File-by-file list of active words

Key

⊙◄◄	Level 1 Grammar review
🏛	Travel with English
◄▷	Revision and extension
🔍	Focus on (skills)
V	Vocabulary file
G	Grammar file
🖊	Word Bank

This is a list of key words in the course, and how to pronounce them. It lists all the words students have to use actively in *English File 2*. It does not include days, months, numbers, countries, languages, nationalities, proper names, or words from the Photocopiable Masters. Adverbs are only listed when they appear before the corresponding adjective. Words from the **Word Bank** are listed under the **Word Bank** title, e.g. 🖊 **Activities A**, rather than individually.

Students are given a lesson-by-lesson list of key new words to learn in the Workbook. The lesson notes provide you with a list of the words which are new in key texts.

Introduction

abroad /ə'brɔːd/
(place of) birth /bɜːθ/
check (v) /tʃek/
🖊 **Classroom language A**
complete (v) /kəm'pliːt/
correct (v) /kə'rekt/
cover (v) /'kʌvə/
difficult /'dɪfɪkəlt/
finally /'faɪnəlɪ/
form (= paper) (n) /fɔːm/
interests /'ɪntrests/
interview /'ɪntəvjuː/
Introduction /ɪntrə'dʌkʃn/
mistake /mɪs'teɪk/
occupation /ɒkjuː'peɪʃn/
perhaps /pə'hæps/
previous /'priːvɪəs/
reason /'riːzn/
repeat /rɪ'piːt/
text /tekst/
underline /ʌndə'laɪn/

File 1

ache (v) /eɪk/ 1🔍
🖊 **Activities A** 1B
🖊 **Activities B** 1C
adult /'ædʌlt/ 1A
(be) afraid of /ə'freɪd əv/ 1C
aisle /aɪl/ 1🏛
answerphone /'ɑːnsəfəʊn/ 1B
anybody /'enɪbɒdɪ/ 1C
anyone /'enɪwʌn/ 1🏛
around /ə'raʊnd/ 1🔍
(be) asleep /ə'sliːp/ 1🔍
baggage (n) /'bægɪdʒ/ 1🏛
belong (to) /bɪ'lɒŋ/ 1🔍
beside /bɪ'saɪd/ 1**V**
bi-lingual /'baɪ'lɪŋgwəl/ 1◄▷
biography /baɪ'ɒgrəfɪ/ 1D
boarding pass /'bɔːdɪŋ pɑːs/ 1🏛
boiling (adj) /'bɔɪlɪŋ/ 1A
bond (n) /bɒnd/ 1🔍
bore (n) /bɔː/ 1D
bored /bɔːd/ 1🔍
both /bəʊθ/ 1B

breath /breθ/ 1🔍
business /'bɪznɪs/ 1🏛
centigrade /'sentɪgreɪd/ 1A
changeable /'tʃeɪndʒəbl/ 1A
check-in (n & v) /'tʃekɪn/ 1🏛
circle (v) /'sɜːkl/ 1A
cloudy /'klaʊdɪ/ 1A
concert /'kɒnsət/ 1🔍
contact (n) /'kɒntækt/ 1◄▷
contain /kən'teɪn/ 1🏛
contents /'kəntents/ 1🏛
cook (n) /kʊk/ 1B
cool (adj) /kuːl/ 1A
cost (v) /kɒst/ 1C
cross (out) (v) /krɒs/ 1🏛
cry /kraɪ/ 1C
decide /dɪ'saɪd/ 1C
degree(s) /dɪ'griː(z)/ 1A
delay /dɪ'leɪ/ 1🏛
delicious /dɪ'lɪʃəs/ 1C
destination /destɪ'neɪʃn/ 1🏛
detail(s) /'diːteɪl(z)/ 1🏛
dialogue /'daɪəlɒg/ 1🏛
(be) divorced /dɪ'vɔːst/ 1B
document /'dɒkjʊmənt/ 1🏛
dots (n) /dɒts/ 1🔍
dream (v) /driːm/ 1🔍
during /'djʊərɪŋ/ 1B
east /iːst/ 1A
electrical /ɪ'lektrɪkl/ 1🏛
embrace (n) /ɪm'breɪs/ 1🔍
engineer /endʒɪ'nɪə/ 1🔍
🖊 **English Sounds** 1🔍
especially /ɪ'speʃəlɪ/ 1B
even /'iːvn/ 1A
everybody /'evrɪbɒdɪ/ 1**V**
everywhere /'evrɪweə/ 1B
example /ɪg'zɑːmpl/ 1A
experience /ɪk'spɪərɪəns/ 1D
face (n) /feɪs/ 1🔍
(in) fact /fækt/ 1D
favourite /'feɪvərɪt/ 1A
final /'faɪnl/ 1C
flight /flaɪt/ 1🏛
foggy /'fɒgɪ/ 1A
freezing /'friːzɪŋ/ 1A
friendly /'frendlɪ/ 1🔍
fur (adj) /fɜː/ 1A
generally /'dʒenrəlɪ/ 1D

good at /gʊd ət/ 1B
grapefruit /'greɪpfruːt/ 1B
health /helθ/ 1B
heart /hɑːt/ 1🔍
heating /'hiːtɪŋ/ 1A
highlighter (pen) /'haɪlaɪtə/ 1B
highlight (v) /'haɪlaɪt/ 1A
homesick /'həʊmsɪk/ 1C
How long? /haʊ lɒŋ/ 1C
hurt /hɜːt/ 1🔍
if /ɪf/ 1B
incredible /ɪn'kredəbl/ 1C
interested /'ɪntrəstɪd/ 1B
intonation /ɪntə'neɪʃn/ 1🔍
🖊 **Irregular verbs A** 1D
island /'aɪlənd/ 1C
item /'aɪtəm/ 1🏛
keep (v) /kɪːp/ 1🔍
(at) least /lɪːst/ 1B
long for (v) /'lɒŋ fə/ 1🔍
luggage /'lʌgɪdʒ/ 1🏛
mark (v) /mɑːk/ 1B
marvellous /'mɑːvələs/ 1C
match (v) /mætʃ/ 1A
mind (v) /maɪnd/ 1C
minus /'maɪnəs/ 1A
move (v) /muːv/ 1B
(Me) neither. /'niːðə, naɪðə/ 1D
news /njuːz/ 1A
nobody /'nəʊbədɪ/ 1C
north /nɔːθ/ 1A
note (v) /nəʊt/ 1B
over /'əʊvə/ 1A
pair (n) /peə/ 1B
passenger /'pæsɪndʒə/ 1🏛
pen-friend /'pen frend/ 1◄▷
practice (n) /'præktɪs/ 1A
practise (v) /'prætɪs/ 1B
prefer /prɪ'fɜː/ 1B
🖊 **Prepositions A** 1**V**
public (adj) /'pʌblɪk/ 1B
put on (clothes) /pʊt 'ɒn/ 1B
replace /rɪ'pleɪs/ 1🔍
rest (v) /rest/ 1B
restless /'restləs/ 1B
ring-file /'rɪŋfaɪl/ 1◄▷
script /skrɪpt/ 1B
security /sɪ'kjʊərətɪ/ 1🏛
send /send/ 1B

separate (*v*) /'sepəreit/ **1B**
sign (*n*) /sain/ **1**🛄
since /sins/ **1**🔍
(non) smoking (*n*) /'sməʊkiŋ/ **1**🛄
snow (*n*) /snəʊ/ **1A**
soon /su:n/ **1**◁▷
south /saʊθ/ **1A**
souvenir /su:və'niə/ **1C**
spend (time) /spend/ **1B**
step (*n*) /step/ **1**🔍
sunny /'sʌni/ **1A**
swap /swɒp/ **1C**
symbol (weather) /'simbl/ **1A**
teenager /'ti:neidʒə/ **1C**
temperature /'temprətʃə/ **1A**
temporary /'temprəri/ **1**🛄
test /test/ **1A**
tick (*v*) /tik/ **1**🛄
trace (*n*) /treis/ **1**🔍
tracksuit /'træksu:t/ **1B**
transport /'trænspɔ:t/ **1B**
trolley /'trɒli/ **1**🛄
typical /'tipikl/ **1B**
unforgettable /ʌnfə'getəbl/ **1C**
unfriendly /ʌn'frendli/ **1**🔍
voice (*n*) /vɔis/ **1D**
warm /wɔ:m/ **1A**
west /west/ **1A**
windy /'windi/ **1A**
yourself /jɔ:'self/ **1**🛄
zero /'ziərəʊ/ **1B**

File 2

across /ə'krɒs/ **2D**
agent [KGB] /'eidʒənt/ **2A**
allowed /ə'laʊd/ **2C**
although /ɔ:l'ðəʊ/ **2A**
ankle /'æŋkl/ **2A**
audience /'ɔ:diəns/ **2A**
baseball /'beisbɔ:l/ **2C**
birth certificate /'bɜ:θ sətifikət/ **2A**
✎ **The body A** **2C**
✎ **The body B** **2V**
bone /bəʊn/ **2A**
bullfight /'bulfait/ **2**◁▷
bullfighter /'bulfaitə/ **2**◁▷
bus-driver /'bʌsdraivə/ **2B**
canary /kə'neəri/ **2**◁▷
captain (*n*) /'kæptin/ **2A**
certainly /'sɜ:tnli/ **2**🛄
chance (*n*) /tʃɑ:ns/ **2B**
chef /ʃef/ **2B**
cigar /si'gɑ:/ **2A**
civil servant /'sivl 'sɜ:vənt/ **2D**
climb /klaim/ **2A**
commit (suicide) /kə'mit ('su:isaid)/ **2**🔍
community /kə'mju:niti/ **2C**
concentrate /konsntreit/ **2B**
conduct (*v*) /kən'dʌkt/ **2A**
conductor /kən'dʌktə/ **2A**

connect /kə'nekt/ **2D**
crash /kraeʃ/ **2**🔍
crossword /'krɒswɜ:d/ **2D**
crutches /'krʌtʃiz/ **2A**
curl (*v*) /kɜ:l/ **2C**
cut /kʌt/ **2C**
definition /defi'niʃn/ **2D**
department store /di'pɑ:tmənt 'stɔ:/ **2**🔍
depressed /di'prest/ **2**🔍
dry (*adj*) /drai/ **2**🔍
earn /ɜ:n/ **2B**
education /edju'keiʃn/ **2C**
electricity /ilek'trisiti/ **2C**
equipment /i'kwipmənt/ **2B**
estate agent's /i'steit eidʒənts/ **2D**
everything /'evriθiŋ/ **2**🔍
exciting /ik'saitiŋ/ **2**◁▷
expect /ik'spekt/ **2**🔍
extract (*n*) /'ekstrækt/ **2A**
fail /feil/ **2A**
farm (*n*) /fɑ:m/ **2C**
ferry /'feri/ **2A**
fortune-teller /'fɔ:tʃu:n telə/ **2A**
full-time /ful'taim/ **2B**
fun /fʌn/ **2B**
gold (*adj*) /gəʊld/ **2C**
government /'gʌnənmənt/ **2D**
grow /grəʊ/ **2C**
guess (*v*) /ges/ **2B**
guest /gest/ **2B**
hard (= difficult) /hɑ:d/ **2**◁▷
have to /'hæf tə/ **2B**
helmet /'helmit/ **2C**
✎ **High numbers** **2**🛄
hitch-hike /'hitʃ'haik/ **2A**
hot dog /hɒt dɒg/ **2C**
housework /'haʊswɜ:k/ **2B**
international /intə'næʃnəl/ **2**🔍
interpreter /in'tɜ:pritə/ **2B**
✎ **Irregular verbs B** **2A**
jewellery /'dʒu:əlri/ **2C**
journey /'dʒɜ:ni/ **2**🛄
jump /dʒʌmp/ **2**🔍
kill /kil/ **2**🔍
light (*v*) /lait/ **2C**
look after /lʊk 'ɑ:ftə/ **2B**
lottery /'lɒtəri/ **2A**
(be) made of /'meid əv/ **2D**
make-up /'meikʌp/ **2**◁▷
manage /'mænidʒ/ **2B**
marry (*v*) /'mæri/ **2C**
material (*n*) /mə'tiəriəl/ **2D**
materialism /mə'tiəriəlizəm/ **2C**
metal (*n*) /'metl/ **2D**
military service /'militri sɜ:vis/ **2C**
mix (*v*) /miks/ **2A**
motorway (*n*) /'məʊtəwei/ **2C**
orchestra /'ɔ:kistrə/ **2A**
(on my) own /əʊn/ **2**◁▷
parking ticket /'pɑ:kiŋ 'tikit/ **2**🔍
pianist /'piənist/ **2A**
plastic (*n*) /'plæstik/ **2D**

platform /'plætfɔ:m/ **2**🛄
port /pɔ:t/ **2A**
prepare /pri'peə/ **2B**
prison /'prizn/ **2C**
prize /praiz/ **2A**
pub /pʌb/ **2**◁▷
qualification(s) /kwɒlifi'keiʃn(z)/ **2B**
reach /ri:tʃ/ **2**🔍
reader /'ri:də/ **2**🔍
rectangular /rek'tæŋgjələ/ **2D**
relative pronoun /'relətiv 'prəʊnaʊn/ **2D**
religious /ri'lidʒəs/ **2C**
required (*adj*) /ri'kwaiəd/ **2**🛄
reserve (*v*) /ri'zɜ:v/ **2**🛄
responsibility /ri,spɒnsə'biləti/ **2B**
(the) rest /rest/ **2**🔍
ridiculous /ri'dikjʊləs/ **2**◁▷
ring (*n*) /riŋ/ **2C**
route /ru:t/ **2B**
satellite /'sætəlait/ **2**🔍
satisfying /'sætisfaiŋ/ **2B**
(What) shape /ʃeip/ **2D**
silver (*adj*) /'silvə/ **2C**
somebody /'sʌmbədi/ **2A**
someone /'sʌmwʌn/ **2**🔍
somewhere /'sʌmweə/ **2**◁▷
square (*adj*) /skweə/ **2D**
steal (*v*) /sti:l/ **2D**
stressful /stresfʊl/ **2B**
strict /strikt/ **2C**
subtitle(s) /'sʌbtaitl(z)/ **2**🔍
team (*n*) /ti:m/ **2**◁▷
technology /tek'nɒlədʒi/ **2C**
thief (*pl* ves) /θi:f (θi:vz)/ **2D**
together /tə'geðə/ **2C**
tractor /'træktə/ **2C**
training (*n*) /'treiniŋ/ **2A**
travel agent's /'trævl eidʒənts/ **2D**
uniform /'ju:nifɔ:m/ **2B**
violin /vaiə'lin/ **2A**
vote (*v*) /vəʊt/ **2C**
weak forms /wi:k forms/ **2**🔍
well-paid /wel'peid/ **2B**
wood (*adj*) /wʊd/ **2D**
writer /'raitə/ **2D**

File 3

actually /'æktʃuli/ **3B**
adventure /əd'ventʃə/ **3C**
against /ə'genst/ **3C**
air-conditioning /'eəkən'diʃəniŋ/ **3**🛄
appointment /ə'pɔintmənt/ **3B**
arrangement /ə'reindʒmənt/ **3B**
auction (*n & v*) /'ɔ:kʃn/ **3A**
autobiography /ɔ:təbai'ɒgrəfi/ **3**🔍
ballet /'bælei/ **3B**
battle /'bætl/ **3C**
beer /biə/ **3**🛄
blanket /'blæŋkit/ **3**🛄

blow (v) /bləʊ/ **3C**
building /'bɪldɪŋ/ **3B**
✏ **Classroom language B**
coast (n) /kəʊst/ **3C**
condition /kən'dɪʃn/ **3◁▷**
conference /'kɒnfərəns/ **3B**
copy (v) /'kɒpɪ/ **3B**
corridor /'kɒrɪdɔ:/ **3🔍**
cover (of a book) /'kʌvə/ **3🔍**
darling /dɑ:lɪŋ/ **3A**
death /deθ/ **3🔍**
difficulty /'dɪfɪkəltɪ/ **3C**
doorbell /'dɔ:bel/ **3D**
earrings /'ɪərɪŋz/ **3A**
either /'i:ðə, aiðə/ **3◁▷**
emergency /ɪ'mɜ:dʒənsɪ/ **3C**
escape (v) /ɪ'skeɪp/ **3C**
(news) event /ɪ'vent/ **3◁▷**
everyone /'evrɪwʌn/ **3◁▷**
explore /ɪk'splɔ:(r)/ **3◁▷**
farmer /'fɑ:mə/ **3D**
few /fju:/ **3◁▷**
field /fi:ld/ **3C**
fight (v) /faɪt/ **3C**
fill (in) /fɪl/ **3B**
✏ **Food A 3🅥**
forest /'fɒrɪst/ **3C**
fulfil /fʊl'fɪl/ **3A**
giant (n) /'dʒaɪənt/ **3C**
ground (n) /graʊnd/ **3🔍**
handsome /'hænsəm/ **3🔍**
hers /hɜ:z/ **3A**
hill /hɪl/ **3C**
historical /hɪ'stɒrɪkl/ **3🔍**
history /'hɪstrɪ/ **3C**
hit (= crash into) /hɪt/ **3D**
How far? /haʊ 'fa:/ **3C**
(be in a) hurry /'hʌrɪ/ **3D**
immediately /ɪ'mi:dɪətlɪ/ **3🏠**
instructions /ɪn'strʌkʃns/ **3C**
invitation /ɪnvɪ'teɪʃn/ **3B**
kind (adj) /kaɪnd/ **3C**
lake /leɪk/ **3C**
land (n) /lænd/ **3C**
level (n) /'levl/ **3🔍**
look (= appear) /lʊk/ **3B**
look forward to /lʊk 'fɔ:wəd tə/ **3B**
(What's the) matter? /'mætə/ **3D**
May I ...? /meɪ aɪ/ **3🏠**
monster /'mɒnstə/ **3C**
most /məʊst/ **3A**
non-fiction /ˌnɒn'fɪkʃən/ **3🔍**
ours /'aʊəz/ **3A**
painting (n) /'peɪntɪŋ/ **3A**
part (v) /pɑ:t/ **3A**
past continuous /pɑ:st kən'tɪnjʊəs/ **3D**
path /pɑ:θ/ **3C**
✏ **Prepositions B 3C**
prisoner /'prɪznə/ **3C**
railway /'reɪlweɪ/ **3C**
rainforest /'reɪnfɒrɪst/ **3🔍**
recently /'ri:sntlɪ/ **3A**

repair /rɪ'peə/ **3🏠**
return (v) /rɪ'tɜ:n/ **3C**
Right away. /raɪt ə'weɪ/ **3🏠**
romantic /rəʊ'mæntɪk/ **3🔍**
sail (v) /seɪl/ **3C**
science fiction /'saɪəns 'fɪkʃn/ **3🔍**
scientist /'saɪəntɪst **3◁▷**
scream (v) /skri:m/ **3🔍**
shoot /ʃu:t/ **3D**
shotgun /'ʃɒtgʌn/ **3D**
shout (v) /ʃaʊt/ **3D**
speckled (adj) /'spekld/ **3🔍**
squash (sport) /skwɒʃ/ **3B**
stepfather /'stepfɑ:ðə/ **3🔍**
storm (n) /stɔ:m/ **3C**
striped /straɪpt/ **3A**
stylish /'staɪlɪʃ/ **3A**
tender /'tendə/ **3A**
terrified /'terɪfaɪd/ **3D**
theirs /ðeəz/ **3A**
thriller /'θrɪlə/ **3🔍**
through /θru:/ **3A**
till = until /tɪl/ **3A**
title(s) /'taɪtl(z)/ **3◁▷**
toilet paper /'tɔɪlɪt 'peɪpə/ **3🏠**
tour (v) /tʊə(r), tɔ:(r)/ **3◁▷**
towel /'taʊəl/ **3🏠**
unhappy /ʌn'hæpɪ/ **3🔍**
valley /'vælɪ/ **3C**
van /væn/ **3D**
war /wɔ:/ **3C**
while /waɪl/ **3◁▷**
whistle (v) /'wɪsl/ **3🔍**
Whose? /hu:z/ **3A**
yet /jet/ **3A**
Youth hostel /'ju:θ hɒstl/ **3C**

File 4

addictive /ə'dɪktɪv/ **4◁▷**
✏ **Adjectives A 4A**
aggressive /ə'gresɪv/ **4A**
alarm (n) /ə'lɑ:m/ **4C**
anywhere /'enɪweə/ **4C**
apart from /ə'pɑ:t frəm/ **4A**
architecture /'ɑ:kɪtektʃə/ **4A**
(car park) attendant /ə'tendənt/ **4C**
bay /beɪ/ **4A**
blister (n) /'blɪstə/ **4◁▷**
break down /breɪk 'daʊn/ **4B**
cable-car /'keɪblkɑ:/ **4A**
camping /'kæmpɪŋ/ **4A**
cheesecake /'tʃi:zkeɪk/ **4🏠**
chimpanzee /tʃɪmpən'zi:/ **4D**
choice /tʃɔɪs/ **4A**
cold (n) /kəʊld/ **4C**
company /'kʌmpəni/ **4B**
confusing /kən'fju:zɪŋ/ **4B**
continent /'kɒntɪnənt/ **4◁▷**
cosmopolitan /kɒzmə'pɒlɪtən/ **4D**
cost (of living) /kɒst/ **4A**
cream /kri:m/ **4🏠**

create /kri:'eɪt/ **4◁▷**
culture /'kʌltʃə/ **4A**
customer /'kʌstəmə/ **4🏠**
deliver (v) /dɪ'lɪvə/ **4B**
diet (foods) /'daɪət 'fʊdz/ **4A**
disappointed /dɪsə'pɔɪntɪd/ **4A**
dish /dɪʃ/ **4🏠**
dress (v) /dres/ **4A**
election /ɪ'lekʃn/ **4◁▷**
(arts) festival /'ɑ:ts festəvl/ **4D**
(cigarette) filter /'fɪltə/ **4D**
first conditional /fɜ:st kən'dɪʃənl/ **4B**
fit (in) /fɪt/ **4◁▷**
flu (n) /flu:/ **4C**
✏ **Food B 4🏠**
fountain /fauntɪn/ **4A**
freedom /'fri:dəm/ **4A**
gateau /'gætəʊ/ **4🏠**
generous /'dʒenərəs/ **4D**
get injured /get 'ɪndʒəd/ **4D**
golf /gɒlf/ **4◁▷**
handbag /'hændbæg/ **4C**
homeless /'həʊmləs/ **4◁▷**
Hurry up! /'hʌrɪ ʌp/ **4B**
impressive /ɪm'presɪv/ **4D**
insurance (adj) /ɪn'ʃɔ:rəns/ **4B**
king-size /kɪŋ saɪz/ **4D**
lager /la:gə/ **4◁▷**
lasagne /lə'zænjə/ **4🏠**
lazy /'leɪzɪ/ **4D**
line (face) /laɪn/ **4◁▷**
logically /'lɒdʒɪklɪ/ **4A**
(football) match /mætʃ/ **4B**
medium /'mɪ:dɪəm/ **4🏠**
monument /'mɒnjumənt/ **4A**
mustard /'mʌstəd/ **4🏠**
nightclub /'naɪtklʌb/ **4A**
nightlife /'naɪtlaɪf/ **4D**
nowhere /'nəʊweə/ **4C**
paradise /'pærədaɪs/ **4A**
pass (exam) /pɑ:s/ **4B**
pension /'penʃn/ **4◁▷**
polluted /pə'lu:tɪd/ **4A**
popular /'pɒpjʊlə/ **4D**
pretend /prɪ'tend/ **4◁▷**
product /'prɒdʌkt/ **4D**
promise (n) /'prɒmɪs/ **4◁▷**
quality /'kwɒlɪtɪ/ **4A**
rare /reə/ **4🏠**
recommend /rekə'mend/ **4🏠**
refund (v) /ri:'fʌnd/ **4B**
rugby /'rʌgbɪ/ **4D**
sauce /sɔ:s/ **4🏠**
serve /sɜ:v/ **4A**
slogan /'sləʊgən/ **4D**
smoked (adj) /sməʊkt/ **4🏠**
sole /səʊl/ **4◁▷**
spectator-sport /spek'teɪtə 'spɔ:t/ **4D**
standard (of living) /'stændəd/ **4A**
stimulating /'stɪmjuleɪtɪŋ/ **4A**
superlative /su:'pɜ:lətɪv/ **4D**

tobacco /tə'bækəʊ/ 4◁▷
trapped (adj) /træpt/ 4C
vegetarian /veʤɪ'teərɪən/ 4🗔
📓 **Verbs A 4B**
violent /'vaɪələnt/ 4A
vitamins /'vɪtəmɪnz/ 4A
well-done /wel'dʌn/ 4🗔
whisky /'wɪskɪ/ 4D
will/won't /wɪl, wəʊnt/ 4B
worker(s) /'wɜːkə(z)/ 4C
worst /wɜːst/ 4D

File 5

(for) ages /'eɪʤɪz/ 5A
amnesia /æm'niːzɪə/ 5◁▷
appear /ə'pɪə/ 5C
archaeologist /ɑːkɪ'ɒləʤɪst/ 5◁▷
athlete /'æθliːt/ 5D
attitude /'ætɪtjuːd/ 5B
avenue /'ævənjuː/ 5🗔
(be) awake /ə'weɪk/ 5A
balcony /'bælkənɪ/ 5C
bracelet /'breɪslɪt/ 5A
bronze /brɒnz/ 5A
championship /'tʃæmpɪənʃɪp/ 5A
character (n) /'kærəktə/ 5◁▷
cholesterol /kə'lestərɒl/ 5B
crime /'kraɪm/ 5◁▷
desperate /'desprət/ 5C
direct (v) /daɪ'rekt/ 5D
direction(s) /daɪ'rekʃnz/ 5🗔
drug /drʌg/ 5C
enemy /'enəmɪ/ 5C
fight (n) /faɪt/ 5C
former /'fɔːmə/ 5A
get engaged /get ɪn'geɪʤd/ 5◁▷
hairstyle /'heəstaɪl/ 5A
handball /'hændbɔːl/ 5A
herself /hɜː'self/ 5C
himself /hɪm'self/ 5C
iceberg /'aɪsbɜːg/ 5D
lifeline /'laɪflaɪn/ 5◁▷
marriage /'mærɪʤ/ 5C
medal /'medl/ 5A
member /'membə/ 5A
messenger /'mesɪnʤə/ 5C
middle-aged /mɪdl'eɪʤd/ 5B
novel (n) /'nɒvl/ 5◁▷
(make) peace /piːs/ 5C
period /'pɪərɪəd/ 5A
poison (n) /'pɔɪzən/ 5◁▷
present (= gift) /'prezənt/ 5A
republic /rɪ'pʌblɪk/ 5A
resign /rɪ'zaɪn/ 5D
responsible /rɪ'spɒnsəbl/ 5B
result /rɪ'zʌlt/ 5C
score /skɔː/ 5B
several /'sevrəl/ 5🗔
ship /ʃɪp/ 5D
success /sək'ses/ 5◁▷
suffer from /'sʌfə frɒm/ 5◁▷

tomb /tuːm/ 5C
torch /tɔːtʃ/ 5A
trophy /'trəʊfɪ/ 5A
tunnel /'tʌnl/ 5D
turning (n) /'tɜːnɪŋ/ 5🗔

File 6

📓 **Activities C 6A**
📓 **Adjectives B 6B**
air /eə(r)/ 6D
almost /'ɔːlməʊst/ 6D
as for /æz fə/ 6C
bacon /'beɪkən/ 6C
ball /bɔːl/ 6◁▷
bargain (n) /'bɑːgɪn/ 6A
bat /bæt/ 6◁▷
breathe /briːð/ 6D
catalogue /'kætəlɒg/ 6A
(be) caused by /kɔːzd baɪ/ 6D
channel (TV) /'tʃænl/ 6A
control (v) /kən'trəʊl/ 6D
(be) covered by /'kʌvəd baɪ/ 6D
croissant /'krwʌsɒŋ/ 6🗔
darts /dɑːts/ 6◁▷
delicatessen /delɪkə'tesn/ 6🗔
📓 **Do, Make, Get A 6Ⓥ**
eat out /iːt 'aʊt/ 6B
endless /'endləs/ 6D
enormous /ɪ'nɔːməs/ 6D
environment /ɪn'vaɪrənmənt/ 6C
except (for) /ɪk'sept/ 6C
📓 **Food C 6C**
frozen /'frəʊzn/ 6C
gerund /'ʤerənd/ 6A
get on with /get ɒn wɪð/ 6B
ginger beer /'ʤɪnʤə 'bɪə/ 6C
gymnastics /ʤɪm'næstɪks/ 6◁▷
happiness /'hæpɪnəs/ 6A
How tall? /haʊ tɔːl/ 6B
ideal /aɪ'dɪəl/ 6B
impression /ɪm'preʃn/ 6B
instead of /ɪn'sted əv/ 6C
(do) karate /kə'rɑːtɪ/ 6◁▷
(the) least /liːst/ 6C
live (adj) /laɪv/ 6◁▷
martial arts /'mɑːʃl 'ɑːts/ 6◁▷
nature /'neɪtʃə/ 6D
nightmare /'naɪtmeə/ 6A
obviously /'ɒbvɪəslɪ/ 6C
occasionally /ə'keɪʃənlɪ/ 6C
organization /ɔːgənaɪ'zeɪʃn/ 6D
over-populated /əʊvə'pɒpjʊleɪtɪd/ 6D
packaging /'pækɪʤɪŋ/ 6C
pain /peɪn/ 6A
perfectionist /pə'fekʃənɪst/ 6A
pleasure /'pleʒə(r)/ 6A
pollution /pə'luːʃn/ 6D
population /pɒpjʊ'leɪʃn/ 6D
(by) post /pəʊst/ 6A
pretty /'prɪtɪ/ 6B

quantifier /'kwɒntɪfaɪə/ 6C
racket /'rækɪt/ 6◁▷
re-use (v) /riː'juːz/ 6C
recycled /riː'saɪkld/ 6C
rubbish /'rʌbɪʃ/ 6C
sales (n) /seɪlz/ 6A
scuba-diving /'skuːbə daɪvɪŋ/ 6◁▷
shopping centre /ʃɒpɪŋ 'sentə/ 6D
(be) situated /'sɪtjueɪtɪd/ 6D
sky /skaɪ/ 6D
smog /smɒg/ 6D
smoke (n) /sməʊk/ 6D
snooker /'snuːkə/ 6◁▷
snow-capped /'snəʊkæpt/ 6D
society /sə'saɪətɪ/ 6C
specialist /'speʃəlɪst/ 6B
(sports) facilities /fə'sɪlətɪz/ 6D
sportsperson /spɔːts'pɜːsn/ 6◁▷
surprise (v) /sə'praɪz/ 6◁▷
surrounded (by) /sə'raʊndɪd/ 6D
survey (n) /'sɜːveɪ/ 6A
table-tennis /'teɪbl tenɪs/ 6◁▷
talkative /tɔːkətɪv/ 6B
throw away /'θrəʊ ə'weɪ/ 6C
tonne(s) /tʌn(z)/ 6C
traffic jam /'træfɪk ʤæm/ 6D
unemployment /ʌnɪm'plɔɪmənt/ 6D
violinist /vaɪə'lɪnɪst/ 6B
volcano(es) /vɒl'keɪnəʊ(z)/ 6D
volume control /'vɒljuːm kən'trəʊl/ 6🗔
wardrobe /'wɔːdrəʊb/ 6A
wash-up /wɒʃ 'ʌp/ 6A
Which one(s)? /wɪtʃ wʌn(z)/ 6🗔
wrapper /'ræpə/ 6C

File 7

advice /əd'vaɪs/ 7C
aid (n & adj) /eɪd/ 7B
already /ɔːl'redɪ/ 7A
annoyed /ə'nɔɪd/ 7C
attic /'ætɪk/ 7◁▷
award /ə'wɔːd/ 7B
beep /biːp/ 7🗔
border /'bɔːdə/ 7B
boxing /'bɒksɪŋ/ 7◁▷
builder /'bɪldə/ 7B
businessman /'bɪznɪsmən/ 7D
cage (n) /keɪʤ/ 7D
cancel /'kænsl/ 7A
civilian /sɪ'vɪlɪən/ 7B
collect (v) /kə'lekt/ 7B
confirm /kən'fɜːm/ 7A
(the Red) Cross/Crescent /krɒs, 'kresnt/ 7B
danger /'deɪnʤə/ 7B
dial (v) /'daɪəl/ 7🗔
disaster /dɪ'zɑːstə/ 7B
📓 **Do, Make, Get B 7Ⓥ**
dressing-gown /'dresɪŋ gaʊn/ 7D
elderly /'eldəlɪ/ 7D

(get) fit /fɪt/ **7C**
forgetful /fə'getfl/ **7C**
frightened /'fraɪtnd/ **7C**
gas fire /'gæs faɪə/ **7D**
gasman /'gæsmæn/ **7D**
go ahead /gəʊ a'hed/ **7**⌂
grass /grɑ:s/ **7A**
illegal /ɪ'li:gl/ **7**◁▷
🖉 **Irregular Verbs C 7A**
lift (v) /lɪft/ **7D**
lonely /'ləʊnlɪ/ **7C**
loud /laʊd/ **7D**
mayor /meə(r)/ **7B**
medical /'medɪkl/ **7B**
memorize /'meməraɪz/ **7C**
nought(s) /nɔ:t(s)/ **7**◁▷
nuclear (testing) /nju:klɪə 'testɪŋ/ **7B**
obsessed /əb'sest/ **7C**
orphanage /'ɔ:fənɪdʒ/ **7B**
owner /'əʊnə/ **7C**
particle /'pɑ:tɪkl/ **7D**
patient (hospital) /'peɪʃnt/ **7D**
perch /pɜ:tʃ/ **7D**
phrasal verb /'freɪzl vɜ:b/ **7D**
pick up (collect) /pɪk 'ʌp/ **7A**
profession /prə'feʃn/ **7B**
protect /prə'tekt/ **7B**
provide /prə'vaɪd/ **7B**
put through /pʊt 'θru:/ **7**⌂
receive /rɪ'si:v/ **7**◁▷
reply (v) /rɪ'plaɪ/ **7D**
reverse charge /rɪ'vɜ:s tʃɑ:dʒ/ **7**⌂
sense (of direction) /sens/ **7**◁▷
share (v) /ʃeə/ **7C**
should/shouldn't /ʃʊd/ʃʊdnt/ **7C**
soldier /səʊldʒə(r) **7B**
tiger /'taɪgə/ **7B**
trip (n) /trɪp/ **7A**
🖉 **Verbs B 7D**
victim /'vɪktɪm/ **7B**
visa /'vi:zə/ **7B**
water (v) /'wɔ:tə/ **7A**
wounded (adj) /ˌwu:ndɪd/ **7B**

File 8

(be) able to /'eɪbl tə/ **8B**
addict /'ædɪkt/ **8C**
alcoholic /ælkə'holik/ **8C**
(be) arrested /ə'restɪd/ **8D**
assassin /ə'sæsɪn/ **8**◁▷
assassinate /ə'sæsɪneɪt/ **8**◁▷
bar (of) /bɑ:(r)/ **8C**
beauty (product) /'bju:tɪ/ **8C**
bloody /'blʌdɪ/ **8D**
brain /breɪn/ **8C**
calories /'kæləri:z/ **8C**
cartoon /kɑ:'tu:n/ **8A**
chemical /'kemɪkl/ **8C**
chocoholic /tʃɒkə'hɒlɪk/ **8C**
cocoa (adj) /'kəʊkəʊ/ **8C**
coincidence /kəʊ'ɪnsɪdəns/ **8**◁▷
come true /'kʌm tru:/ **8**◁▷
comedy /'kɒmədɪ/ **8A**
(in) common /'kɒmən/ **8**◁▷
conqueror /'kɒŋkərə/ **8D**
cough /kɒf/ **8**⌂
court (royal) /kɔ:t/ **8C**
definitely /'defɪnətlɪ/ **8B**
diamond (n) /'daɪəmənd/ **8C**
drama /'drɑ:mə/ **8A**
dry (v) /draɪ/ **8C**
echo question /'ekəʊ 'kwestʃən/ **8A**
elect /ɪ'lekt/ **8**◁▷
execute /'eksɪkju:t/ **8D**
fatal /'feɪtl/ **8C**
fluently /'flu:əntlɪ/ **8B**
ghost /gəʊst/ **8D**
guard /gɑ:d/ **8D**
headache /'hedeɪk/ **8**⌂
horror /'hɒrə(r)/ **8A**
innocent /'ɪnəsnt/ **8D**
invention /ɪn'venʃn/ **8D**
lie down /laɪ daʊn/ **8**⌂
liqueur /lɪ'kjʊə(r)/ **8C**
medicine /'medsn/ **8**⌂
mine (v) /maɪn/ **8C**

passion /'pæʃn/ **8C**
passive /'pæsɪv/ **8C**
pay back /peɪ 'bæk/ **8B**
per (person) /pɜ:/ **8C**
pint /paɪnt/ **8**◁▷
pod /pɒd/ **8C**
powder /'paʊdə/ **8C**
prince /prɪns/ **8D**
princess /prɪn'ses/ **8D**
produce (v) /prə'dju:s/ **8C**
pyramid /'pɪrəmɪd/ **8D**
raven /'reɪvn/ **8D**
recipe /'resəpɪ/ **8C**
shall /ʃəl, ʃæl/ **8B**
shopaholic /ʃɒpə'hɒlɪk/ **8C**
sights (places) /saɪts/ **8D**
So (do you.) /səʊ/ **8A**
sore /sɔ:/ **8**⌂
spice /spaɪs/ **8C**
stomach-ache /stʌməkeɪk/ **8**⌂
tablet /'tæblɪt/ **8**⌂
throat /θrəʊt/ **8**⌂
tower /'taʊə/ **8D**
uranium /ju'reɪnɪəm/ **8C**
virus /'vaɪərəs/ **8**⌂
warehouse /'weəhaʊs/ **8**◁▷
western /'westən/ **8A**
workaholic /wɜ:kə'hɒlɪk/ **8C**
zoo /zu:/ **8**◁▷

File 9

citizen /'sɪtɪzn/ **9C**
consul /'kɒnsl/ **9A**
entrance /entrəns/ **9C**
foreigner /'fɒrənə/ **9A**
granny /'grænɪ/ **9B**
influence /'ɪnflʊəns/ **9B**
luxury /'lʌkʃərɪ/ **9C**
servant /'sɜ:vənt/ **9A**
telegram /'telɪgræm/ **9A**
(tell the) truth /tru:θ/ **9C**